ADDITIONAL PRAISE FOR *THE ILLUSION*

"Have you ever wondered how the majority of humans are religious, but their religions teach them entirely different things about the world we live in, the nature of divinity, and the human condition? This polemical book discusses these issues, and many more, in detail. The author's thesis is that since everyone would agree that not all religions (thousands of them) are correct, it must be the case that none of them are correct. Yet this obvious contradiction is generally ignored. Religion is not subject to rational or empirical tests, and when it wanders into the realm of science or historical fact (as in the heliocentric theory or the age of the earth) it does very poorly. The book demolishes the idea that religion teaches universal moral truths, quoting as an example the instruction from 'God' to the Israeli invaders of Canaan to kill every man, woman, and child, and the command that a parent kill any son who drifts into alternative religions. Its fact-filled pages also include a devastating critique of Creationism (informed by the author's experience teaching science to college students in Louisiana). Unfortunately, this fine book is unlikely to be read by those who need it most, but skeptics will want to have it on their bookshelves."
—David Morrison, Committee for Skeptical Inquiry Fellow

"Biblical literalists will have more than they can handle in this engagingly wicked book. Combining relativism, rationalism, and a liberal dose of snark, Houk takes careful aim at the ostentatiously and ignorantly pious. The result is a withering attack on religious fundamentalism and creationism, and some important schooling about the Bible!"
—Jonathan Marks, anthropologist and
author of *Tales of the Ex-Apes*

"This very powerful and informative book exposes the illusion of certainty borne of religious fundamentalism for what it really is, unsubstantiated ignorant beliefs that masquerade as certainty. Using several key examples, Houk illustrates that 'virtually anything and everything, no matter how absurd, inane, or ridiculous, has been believed or claimed to be true at one time or another by somebody, somewhere in the name of faith.' He proves that to adopt faith-based claims with blind certainty has caused untold misery and death and must be jettisoned from modern life if we want a good society. Excellent and highly recommended!"

—John W. Loftus, author of *Why I Became an Atheist,*
The Outsider Test for Faith, and
Unapologetic: Why Philosophy of Religion Must End

"Houk clearly demonstrates the importance of epistemology and evidence in his critique of religious fundamentalism. His analysis of the errors rooted in fundamentalism's 'faith-based epistemology' is convincingly argued and based on solid research."

—Barbara Forrest, coauthor with Paul R. Gross of
Creationism's Trojan Horse: The Wedge of Intelligent Design
and expert witness for the plaintiffs in
Kitzmiller et al. v. Dover Area School District

THE ILLUSION OF CERTAINTY

THE ILLUSION OF CERTAINTY

HOW THE FLAWED BELIEFS

OF RELIGION

HARM OUR CULTURE

JAMES T. HOUK

Prometheus Books

59 John Glenn Drive
Amherst, New York 14228

Published 2017 by Prometheus Books

Cover design by Liz Mills
Cover design © Prometheus Books

Trademarked names appear throughout this book. Prometheus Books recognizes all registered trademarks, trademarks, and service marks mentioned in the text.

The Internet addresses listed in the text were accurate at the time of publication. The inclusion of a website does not indicate an endorsement by the author(s) or by Prometheus Books, and Prometheus Books does not guarantee the accuracy of the information presented at these sites.

Scripture quotations are from the New Revised Standard Version Bible, copyright © 1989, the Division of Christian Education of the National Council of the Churches of Christ in the United States of America. Used by permission. All rights reserved.

Inquiries should be addressed to
Prometheus Books
59 John Glenn Drive
Amherst, New York 14228
VOICE: 716–691–0133
FAX: 716–691–0137
WWW.PROMETHEUSBOOKS.COM

21 20 19 18 17   5 4 3 2 1

Library of Congress Cataloging-in-Publication Data

Names: Houk, James T. (James Titus), 1955- author.
Title: The illusion of certainty : how the flawed beliefs of religion harm our culture / by James T. Houk.
Description: Amherst : Prometheus Books, 2018. | Includes bibliographical references and index.
Identifiers: LCCN 2017017359 (print) | LCCN 2017042647 (ebook) | ISBN 9781633883246 (ebook) | ISBN 9781633883239 (pbk.)
Subjects: LCSH: Religion—Controversial literature. | Atheism. | Fundamentalism—Controversial literature.
Classification: LCC BL2775.3 (ebook) | LCC BL2775.3 .H68 2018 (print) | DDC 200—dc23
LC record available at https://lccn.loc.gov/2017017359

Printed in the United States of America

CONTENTS

PART THREE: FOUR IMPORTANT (AND POTENTIALLY FLAWED)
        SOURCES OF RELIGIOUS KNOWLEDGE

PART FOUR: HOLY SCRIPTURES ARE MUNDANE,
        FLAWED, AND UNRELIABLE

PREFACE

While I am a fan of Christopher Hitchens and would certainly argue that his life's work served to correct much of what passes for rational discourse—especially that which emanates from talk radio and from behind pulpits every Sunday—I can understand why some have a problem with his notion that "religion poisons everything," as he states in the subtitle of his work *god Is Not Great.*[1] For example, I teach at a Catholic college where the Franciscan values of humility, justice, service, joyfulness of spirit, and a reverence and love for all life serve as a foundation for instruction. Hard to argue with that. Also, one might argue that religion has been a catalyst for some of the greatest works of art in existence. One might also argue that religion has motivated tens of thousands of good souls to do wonderful work serving the poor, the indigent, and the marginalized. Even if the believer concedes the point that agnostics and nonbelievers of all stripes have also produced great works of art and served humanity in a charitable fashion, she might continue a defense of her position by noting that, in regard to those folks who were motivated by religious reasons to paint, sculpt, and serve, who knows if they would have not done otherwise had they not been so influenced.

I am more sympathetic, however, to those irreligionists who say, "Yes, yes, of course, religiously motivated folks have engaged in charitable work, been active in the cause of social justice, and produced great works of art, but at what costs?" The implication here is that the "good" that has been motivated by religion has been more than countered by the "bad"—for example, religious wars, killing in the name of this or that god, the marginalization (and worse) of women and girls, and the tendency of religions to push humans in directions that are unnatural (such as the negative obsession with human sexuality and the denial of human sexualities that do not fit neatly within the confines of a strict, patriarchal-based, heteronormativity). In my mind, the sum total of the positive, life-enhancing, religion-based contributions to humanity do not outweigh or even counterbalance the harm done by the irrational faith-based epistemology or the horrible suffering that has occurred in the name of this or that religion.

The believer (of whatever faith) might point to the fact that religion inspires us to contemplate the possibility of the transcendent or, put another way, the possibility of there being something more than simply the materialistic, physical, tangible universe in which we live. While I may be a bit partial to materialism of this sort for empirical reasons (much discussion of this topic to follow in the book), I cannot deny that a strictly materialistic philosophy is not exactly satisfying or comforting for some, to say the least. Nevertheless, it is not nature's place to make us feel good about ourselves; the world may simply be a relatively unpleasant, materialistic abode of which we are aware during that eighty or so years of consciousness that punctuates eons of oblivion both before and after. I will grant that religion is the only human institution that does not throw in the towel, so to speak, when faced with the admittedly strong empirical challenge to transcendentalism, and is, thus, the only means we have to pursue questions of meaning and purpose vis-à-vis a realm of existence that may lie beyond this one. But, again, at what costs?

Religion could, I suppose, be viewed as a source of hope (not certainty) for what may potentially be a rich understanding of the human condition. Intellectually mature religionists (not fundamentalists) grasp this point, and grasp it in a heartfelt yet forlorn fashion. Why "forlorn," you may ask? Because mature thinkers embrace the mystery that is human existence and realize that no dogmas, human created as they are, can ever bring us certainty. There may be trust, there may even be faith, albeit a tentative, constructed, and negotiable one, but there is always mystery for the intellectually mature thinker, the intellectually mature religionist. Most of what I write in this book is not directed at such "believers." Rather, as the title says, this work addresses the "illusion of certainty" and all of its nasty byproducts.

Consider, for example, the following quotes from individuals in positions of great influence and authority:

"God's word is true. I've come to understand that. All that stuff I was taught about evolution and embryology and the big bang theory, all that is lies straight from the pit of Hell."[2] (Paul Broun, Republican congressman)

"I would point out that if you're a believer in the Bible, one would have to say the Great Flood is an example of climate change and that certainly wasn't because mankind had over-developed hydrocarbon energy."[3] (Joe Barton, Republican congressman)

"After the Christian majority takes control, pluralism will be seen as immoral and evil and the state will not permit anybody the right to practice evil."[4] (Gary Potter, president of Catholics for Christian Political Action)

"The only way we can determine the true age of the earth is for God to tell us what it is. And since He has told us, very plainly, in the Holy Scriptures that it is several thousand years in age, and no more, that ought to settle all basic questions of terrestrial chronology."[5] (Henry Morris, president of Institute for Creation Research)

". . . this monkey mythology of Darwin is the cause of permissiveness, promiscuity, prophylactics, perversions, pregnancies, abortions, pornotherapy, pollution, poisoning and proliferation of crimes of all types."[6] (Judge Braswell Deen Jr., Chief Judge of the Georgia Court of Appeals)

"AIDS is the wrath of a just God against homosexuals. To oppose it would be like an Israelite jumping in the Red Sea to save one of Pharaoh's charioteers. AIDS is not just God's punishment for homosexuals. It is God's punishment for the society that tolerates homosexuals."[7] (Jerry Falwell, minister and televangelist)

These quotes show a distinct lack of knowledge, compassion, and tolerance and would be unexceptional if they were stated by individuals in France in the late Middle Ages, but these are folks who live in our time, individuals who have access to a wealth of data that manifestly disconfirms virtually everything they are saying. What would make someone look to the musings of a Bronze Aged people to understand nature rather than simply accessing the mountain of reliable data we've collected over the last couple of centuries? What would make an individual believe that a virus that causes an immune deficiency syndrome mysteriously searches out only individuals of a particular sexual orientation and leaves others unscathed? What would make an individual feel that everyone else's religion is evil and worthy of condemnation? The answer, of course, is the illusion of certainty that is borne of religiosity of the worst sort, namely, religious fundamentalism. To the fundamentalist, everything is black and white, the truth is absolutely known (to them) and absolutely nonnegotiable. Thus, no amount of data collection, even if that includes data that manifestly disconfirms their absolutist position, will ever sway them from their assumed truths. To make matters worse, "faith" (of the most brazen, "blind" sort) gives them an excuse to revel in their ignorance.

This is not a trivial issue. According to the Pew Research Center, 25.4 percent of Americans are "evangelical Protestants,"[8] a category that includes biblical literalists and Christian absolutists. I would consider this to be a very conservative estimate of fundamentalists, however, as there are some conservative Catholics with similar beliefs. There are thousands of Christian private schools in the United States that don't spend one minute on anything science knows today about the age of the earth, the age of the universe, the evolution of life, human fossil evolution, the genetics of sexual orientation, or many more aspects of science (or even the social sciences) that are too numerous to mention here. Not an insignificant number of Americans believe that humans and dinosaurs coexisted, the Bible was "handed down to us" as a complete book, evil spirits can possess individuals and be subsequently exorcised, and praying is sufficient to heal sickness.

So, at this point, with apologies to Hitchens, let me state that religious fundamentalism poisons everything. While I have written this book with the intent of illustrating just how "slippery" and potentially fallacious religion is, and while it may seem to the reader that I am, at times, overly harsh with my critique, my point is to expose fundamentalist absolutism for what it is: hope in beliefs, claims, and dogmas that are unsubstantiated and unsubstantiable yet masquerade as certainty.

It is the certainty that is often part and parcel of religion that harms our culture. In this book, then, my primary concern is exposing the illusion that is religious certainty. If we ponder some of the worst episodes and aspects of human history (e.g., the tens of thousands burned at the stake for the fictional crime of witchcraft; the horrible treatment of women; the subjugation and, in some cases, the extermination of whole cultures in the name of Christianity; bloody religious conflicts; suicide bombings; and "honor" killings; just to mention a few), it is frustratingly obvious that it is doubt, not certainty, that should be celebrated and embraced. Given the subject matter under consideration here, namely a putative transcendental realm replete with celestial creatures of all sorts and their supposed concern with the activities of humans in this world, doubt, not faith, is the only rationally defensible response.

I will begin my defense of doubt and, consequently, my argument against the illusion of certainty in part one, with a discussion of the "faith-based epistemology" that has generated fantasies, fallacies, falsehoods, and misinformation in our cultural ideology regarding not only religion but sexual orientation, race and racism, and bigotry in the form of anti-Semitism. In part two, I will deconstruct what is, perhaps, exhibit A for irrational, faith-based thinking, an idea that is so antithetically empirical that only the inertia, power, and influence of religion could possibly persuade ostensibly sane and reasonable folks to embrace it—namely young-earth creationism. In part three, continuing with the general theme, the sources of religious knowledge are critiqued, and they are found wanting at best and totally unreliable at worst. Holy scriptures and the many unfounded and false assumptions made regarding these ancient writings are the subject of part four. The illusion of certainty is on full display here as believers make assumptions regarding, for example, the inerrancy and divine literality of the Bible that are clearly unwarranted. Finally, in part five, even the best objective arguments for the existence of God made by brilliant thinkers throughout the centuries are examined and found to be unconvincing. We will also look at the problem of evil that, according to many, constitutes perhaps the best argument for atheism, or at least the best argument against the existence of a personal God in the Judeo-Christo-Islamic mold.

A close and thorough examination of the products of the faith-based epistemology that, unfortunately, serves as the foundation for not only religion but popular thinking regarding many aspects of the human condition, will show unequivocally that it is horribly flawed. If humanity is to finally shake off this cultural absolutist, nonempirical, faith-based mode of thinking birthed during a time when individuals did not know where the sun went at night, it will have to become intellectually mature enough to embrace nature, pure and unadulterated, warts and all, stripped of the fantasies, fallacies, and falsehoods of religious fundamentalism.

CHAPTER ONE

INTRODUCTION

There are over 10,000 religions practiced somewhere in the world today (and this is not counting the thousands of sects and denominations of those religions). (Perhaps the most definitive and authoritative count of extant religions in the world is found in the *World Christian Encyclopedia: A Comparative Survey of Churches and Religions in the Modern World.* According to David Barrett, George Kurian, and Todd Johnson, the editors of this two-volume work, there are approximately 10,500 distinct religions in the world today.) This is a sociological fact that should trouble even the most confident believer. There is, of course, the obvious problem that most of these religions embrace dogmas and principles that are mutually contradictory, yet the respective believers are all equally confident that they are right and the others are wrong. This, in itself, leads logically to another (potentially) troubling issue for the true believers, namely, that the existence of a variegated multiplicity of religions—a number, by the way, that is steadily increasing with time—empirically validates the fact that no one religion is viewed as inherently or intuitively correct by the world's peoples; in fact, no religion even comes close to attaining such a status since even the largest (Christianity) is rejected by almost 70 percent of the world's population. In fact, even roughly one-half of all Christians reject many of the important dogmas and teachings of the largest Christian sect, Roman Catholicism.

As problematic as those issues are, however, there is another matter that (potentially) should be even more vexing to the true believer: the thousands of wildly disparate and contradictory belief systems embraced today are all generated by the same basic, faith-based epistemology. At least in regard to the eleven "great" or "world" religions (whose adherents comprise over 70 percent of the world's population), religious doctrine and belief is engendered primarily by a handful of "mechanisms," the most significant being faith, revelation, and (presumed) holy scriptures.

Of the three, it would appear that faith is the most problematic, for virtually anything and everything, no matter how absurd, inane, or ridiculous, has been believed or claimed to be true at one time or another by somebody, somewhere, in the name of faith. That is simply because faith requires nothing but hope; data, reason, logic, and even common sense are all irrelevant. Faith is essentially unabashed optimism in the absence of evidential substantiation. That is precisely why one hundred different people, all using the same faith-based epistemology, can come to one hundred different conclusions about the nature of God or gods, the human soul, heaven, hell, etc. The news doesn't get much better regarding revelation or holy scriptures, either; these "mechanisms" have produced the same dizzying array of conflicting and mutually contradictory beliefs, claims, and dogmas as faith.

What this means, of course, is that religions require a considerable amount of cultural myopia, intellectual indolence, or simple delusion to sustain them. Why? Quite simply because thousands of groups (and hundreds of millions of individuals) employing the same methods are all arriving at very different and often mutually contradictory conclusions, but these hundreds of millions of individuals either don't know this or do know and simply aren't concerned about what should be the troubling implications of this fact. If there were, for example, anything valid about faith at all, then it would at least pass the simple test of consistency that we require of other theories, laws, methods, algorithms, and so on, that are used to generate actual empirical knowledge of our world.

In the real world, where events and circumstances can literally be a matter of life and death, very few individuals, believers or otherwise, put up with such foolishness. When we board a plane, we want the flight crew to be competent, the aircraft to be mechanically sound, and the cockpit to contain all the latest aeronautical technology; virtually no one could care one whit whether or not the pilot or the navigator is a Christian (or Muslim or Hindu, depending, I guess, on the geography of the air space) or whether or not the right prayers have been said and so on. The same thing can be said of a visit to the hospital for heart surgery. When it comes to picking a surgeon, good common sense and an overwhelming amount of anecdotal evidence tells us that very few individuals would choose the pious Christian (or Muslim or Hindu) who was a mediocre student at a second-tier medical school over an agnostic who graduated at the top of her class at Johns Hopkins. Living in the real, tangible, empirical world, then, requires us to make our way carefully and judiciously, for actions have consequences. Thus, in the real world, where mistakes can be lethal, where our actions really matter, virtually all individuals employ logic, reason, and empiricism.

What, then, of the other mode of thinking spoken of earlier, the flawed faith-based epistemology that gives us thousands of different "solutions" to the same problem? Well, we must remember that no sane individual will apply this epistemology to the problems and challenges of this world or they probably won't be around very long, or, if they do manage to survive for any length of time, they will almost certainly endure a tremendous amount of needless suffering. When, however, it comes to questions of a decidedly transcendental nature—for example, why are we here, is there a purpose to our life and if so what is it, does God exist and if so does God care, and what happens after we die—all the answers are necessarily nonfalsifiable and, thus, remain "in play" for eternity. So why do thousands of different religions and religious ideologies exist in the world today? Because they can. The success or failure of a religion does not now, has not in the past, and never will have anything to do with its truth content. In fact, of the various factors that will determine whether or not a particular religion will be successful or not—for example, the charisma of its founder, the eloquence of its champions and apologists, the extent of the military and political might behind it, historical accident, etc.—whether or not its teachings are actually correct is virtually irrelevant. In fact, it is the nonfalsifiability of religious doctrine that ensures that the important principles and dogmas of a religion will live on in perpetuity, even though they generally run counter to common sense, logic, and reason. In brutally simple terms, religions stand the test of time for one reason and one reason only: their foundational principles, beliefs, tenets, and dogmas are nonfalsifiable and, thus, immune to critique.

This basic fact becomes immediately apparent when one considers an epistemology that takes the issue of falsifiability seriously, namely the epistemology employed by science. Scientific theories do not "stand the test of time" (except in a transitory sense), never have and probably never will. Lest the reader misunderstand the basic point that is being made here, it should be noted that science, of course, gives us fairly reliable descriptions, laws, and theories of our world, but no sane scientist would ever make absolutist claims regarding these descriptions, laws, and theories. If a general notion (comprised of a set of coherent hypotheses) stands the test of time (for the time being), and if its claims are testable and publicly verifiable, then scientists slap the label "theory" on the paradigm in question and it will reign until something better comes along. Thus, in regard to both science and religion, it's sort of a good news/ bad news situation. In regard to science, the good news is that its methods and epistemology generate useful models that go a long way toward helping us understand the complex world we live in; the bad news is that scientific "truth" is contingent, tentative, and provisional. In regard to religion, the good news is that its methods and epistemology produce (putative) absolute truths, but the bad news is that we have no way of knowing whether these supposed truths are spurious or genuine. Science, then, at least gives us a small amount of something, whereas religion quite possibly gives us a large amount of nothing.

These important issues will be explored further later in the book, but this brief discussion does point us toward a question that is practically begging to be addressed at this point: why then, given the woefully problematic issues of religion, religious dogma, faith, revelation, the multiplicity of religions, and so on, do so many individuals practice or embrace some form of religion? Why are approximately 85 percent of the world's peoples religious to some extent?

Before answering this question, I feel it is important to address a very common misunderstanding about religion and what is ostensibly the overwhelming popularity of religion. During one of my lectures in a world religions class that I teach, a student raised her hand

and asked why, if religion is so problematic and so nonsensical on so many levels, is the overwhelming majority of the world's population religious? A good question and, in fact, many individuals use this fact to argue for the general reasonableness of religiosity. C. S. Lewis, for example, argued that given the sheer weight of the many great minds that have embraced Christianity it follows that it is at least plausible.[1] Upon further reflection, however, this argument turns out to be fallacious for two primary reasons.

First, there is the multiplicity of religions issue discussed above; if there was anything reasonable or intuitively correct about religion, we would not have 10,500 different and often contradictory versions. I seriously doubt that anyone who is making such an argument is simply supporting the notion that it is reasonable to be religious (in a generic sense) even though all or virtually all of them are manifestly false (given their mutually contradictory nature taken as a whole). In other words, the individual making such an argument is attempting to justify why it is that they are religious, or, put another way, why practicing their particular religion is a reasonable thing to do; drawing attention to the 10,500 or so different versions that exist today will obviously not advance their cause.

The second reason why this line of argument is fallacious, however, is even more damning than the first, and it has to do with the nature of the research design that is being employed here. If we are to assume that the datum in question, namely, the 85 percent of the world's population that is religious to some extent, actually means something, then one might rightly question the accuracy and validity of that datum. Well, let us examine this information more closely.

If we were to couch the description of this datum in terms of an experiment, then it would be described as follows: "After subjecting a great majority of one group of individuals from birth to late adolescence to intense religious instruction and indoctrination, employing, in many cases, fear, punishment, and the threat of eternal damnation to enhance learning, it was discovered that a large portion (about 85 percent), upon reaching adulthood, were religious to some extent." Doesn't look so impressive now does it? I should hope the problem with this research design is by now apparent to the reader: there is no control group! If this datum is ever to have any real value at all, then a large group of people will have to be raised from birth to late adolescence in a social and cultural context that is largely bereft of religiosity, and then the religious attitudes (or not) of the adults will have to be surveyed. Such an experiment, at least on the scale of what is being discussed here, is, of course, probably not feasible, but we can certainly do a thought experiment along these lines and conclude that the religiosity of the experimental group is being strongly influenced by a long period of intense religious enculturation. While such an experiment is, perhaps, not realistic or practical, research shows that children that do not undergo twenty years of intense religious instruction or, better yet, children who receive little or no religious instruction, will generally not be religious as adults.[2] I should also add here that Europe has grown increasingly secular over the last three or four generations, representing, perhaps, a confirmation of sorts of my general argument. In the general absence of religious instruction and indoctrination, the result in Europe has been a population that is trending strongly toward an irreligious mindset. (By the way, in regard to raising children in secular households, one study showed that children reared in religious homes who were taught the religion of their parents were less kind and altruistic than their secular counterparts.[3])

What, then, of the question posed by my student earlier? Why, precisely, are so many individuals religious at least to some extent when there seem to be many good reasons for them not to be? Of all the specific factors that one might invoke at this point, in my mind, the most significant has to be simply the accident of one's birth.

Human nature is such a vast and complex subject that volumes have been written on the topic by some of the greatest minds, and it is not my intention here to add to that literature. I would like to note, however, that I feel confident that we do possess what I would refer to as an incontrovertible fact of human nature: the greatest predictor of religious affiliation is geography. In that one statement is contained virtually every argument for cultural relativism, religious pluralism, agnosticism, and, I suppose, atheism, if one wishes to take it that far. For those who may want to question the validity of this fact, consider that approximately 81 percent of the total population of India is Hindu, a number that has held steady for generations if not centuries; then consider that virtually 100 percent of those individuals were born into a Hindu family. Consider Thailand. If the reader had been born in Bangkok some twenty to eighty years ago, today he would almost certainly be a practitioner of Theravada Buddhism, and he would be at least moderately contented if not absolutely contented with his religion. I can say that with a great degree of conviction because approximately 95 percent of the population of Thailand is Buddhist.

If an individual insists on arguing the contrary, he should consider two points. First, there is his own affiliation with Christianity (for residents of the United States, approximately an 80 percent probability; for residents of Canada, approximately a 70 percent probability) or Islam (for residents of Turkey, approximately a 99 percent probability; for residents of Iran, approximately a 98 percent probability) or some other religion that is probably the most statistically prevalent faith in the area of their birth. Here is an even more striking way to view these numbers: all things being equal, the probability that, say, 99 percent of all people born in Turkey generation after generation will just happen to choose Islam, or that 80 percent of all people born in the United States generation after generation will just happen to choose Christianity is practically zero. Even if one is born in a country where religious affiliation is divided among a number of faiths (for example, Sri Lanka—Buddhist, Muslim, Hindu, and Christian; Nigeria—Muslim, Christian, and tribal/indigenous; Trinidad and Tobago—Christian, Hindu, and Muslim), he is almost certainly an adherent of the faith that his family has embraced for generations. (This fact also illustrates the "law of geography," only on a more acute level.) In the three colleges and universities where I teach and have taught in Louisiana, I often make this point by simply asking for a show of hands from those who affiliate with Christianity. After virtually every hand goes up, I conclude my discussion by simply saying thank you.

Second, if an individual continues to argue against this "law of geography," I would then ask him to explain why he is so special. Are we to believe that he would engage in a heartfelt search for the "right" religion by reading the various holy books of the world's religions, traveling to the various areas where these religions are practiced, and so on? And that only after a long period of searching would he settle on the "right" religion? And that this "right" religion would just so happen to be the very one he embraces today? In reality, only a tiny percentage of individuals actually do this sort of thing. Nevertheless, in those few and relatively rare cases, I am willing to concede the point. Or one might argue that they rejected the faith of their family and, thus, could certainly have done the same thing had they been born in, say, Thailand. Again, while that may be true, we are once again dealing with a statistically insignificant number of individuals. Besides, many of these individuals would be agnostics or atheists and, thus, would have no religious affiliation at all and would not be part of the religiously inclined 85 percent.

Now, assuming the general validity of the "law of geography," we are but a tiny conceptual step away from another generalization about religion. This observation goes a long way toward explaining the existence of thousands of religions and religious groups in the world, and it goes something like this: Individuals tend to relate to the uncertainty of being, existence, and purpose in ways that are reasonable, sensible, and familiar to them (i.e., in ways that are distinctly cultural). There is nothing really earth shattering about this observation since it is, no doubt, well-known to social scientists and the generally informed, but, while this notion is reasonable and commonsensical, many who accept its validity fail to apply it to their own religiosity. This is a reflection of the fact that critical thinking is not generally present in the conceptual repertoire of religious fundamentalists. Otherwise, one would think they would not be inclined to accept as factual truth talking snakes, magically parting seas, virgin births, angels, purgatory, demon possession, faith healing, and the like. Let us assume, however, that one does accept the basic gist of this observation and that she objectively applies it to all religions including her own. She is then ready and willing to acknowledge religious or, more generally, cultural pluralism and, further, will agree that no one religion (or culture) should serve as a standard by which others should be judged.

It is at this point that "postculturalism" becomes relevant. A global movement in the direction of the cultural relativism and religious pluralism of postculturalism would go a long way toward solving many of the problems that have distressed and haunted humanity for ages. Postculturalism points us toward a future bereft of religiously motivated misogyny yet replete with true gender equality; toward a future bereft of religiously motivated homophobia yet replete with individuals who reserve the right to be (not choose to be) gay or lesbian; toward a future bereft of the "shame" of sexual pleasure yet replete with a totally natural appreciation of the human body; toward a future bereft of intellectual compromise yet replete with a new spirit of intellectual freedom where individuals can think and act without being encumbered with the guilt of not thinking and acting in a "proper" (read religiously mandated) fashion; and toward a future bereft of religiously inspired hate and xenophobia yet replete with respect and compassion for all peoples and a complete abrogation of the alterity of the "other."

Sometime in the future, perhaps, we will look back on this time as a sort of transitional period linking a long period of culturally myopic transcendentalism characterized by a faith-based epistemology and an adherence to the dictates of dogma, tradition, and authority, with a new age characterized by reason, cultural relativism, religious pluralism, and objective rationalism. Michel Onfray, the prominent French philosopher, in fact, claims that we are in such a transitional period, one he refers to as "post-Christian":

> We are now living in a new transitional phase, heading toward a third era, the *post-Christian era.* In some ways, our current period is similar to the transitional stage between the pagan and Christian eras. Thus, the end of the pre-Christian and the beginning of the post-Christian both exhibit the same nihilism, the same anxieties, the same dynamic interplay between progressive and reactionary trends. Today we have conservatism, reaction, yearning for the past, and rigid religion vying with liberalism, progressivism, social reform and movements dedicated to building a better future.[4]

Onfray's perspective is a bit more focused than my own as he is referring primarily to the lands of Western monotheism, while my comments thus far have been directed toward religion as a pan-human or global phenomenon, but we are both referring to the same "movement"—namely a conceptual and emotional shift away from the fog of assumed cultural absolutism to the clarity of sound reasoning and empirical objectivity.

❧❧

Now that we are at least pointed in the right direction, I feel it would be a good idea at this point to examine the concept of postculturalism more closely, since it is a postcultural mindset that will serve as the foundation of my extended commentary and critique of religion in general and Christian fundamentalism in particular.

Quite simply, "culturalism" is a form of cultural myopia that one naturally (i.e., unwittingly) embraces, although "embraces," even with the quotation marks, is probably too strong a term here; for most, it will eventually come to that but only after the local cultural ideology is sufficiently internalized and the individual is ready to defend, justify, and rationalize it. Before that point, however, we have what anthropologists refer to as "enculturation," the process whereby a new member of society learns his or her culture. Given the relative lack of intellectual sophistication and psychological maturity of toddlers, children, and adolescents, these social "newcomers" are much like sponges that soak up any and all customs, beliefs, mores, dogmas, prejudices, etc., that are part and parcel of whatever cultural group into which they happen to be born.

Enculturation is such a powerful force that it can overcome even biology. It is now common knowledge in social science circles that culture is learned and that the racial paradigm that assigned behavior to phenotype is nonsense. Any individual has the potential to learn and function within the confines of any culture and, put another way, no individual is born preadapted to speak a certain language, crave a certain diet, etc. A quick glance at the various cultures and peoples in the world today confirms this fact beyond a shadow of a doubt. So, for example, two adult males, one Nigerian and the other Jamaican, may be very similar phenotypically yet differ greatly culturally (behaviorally).

Enculturation can also (unfortunately) overcome empirical data. Once one "constructs" (this process is, in large part, passive) or internalizes his or her cultural ideology, it stands like a bulwark that fends off the challenge of contrary information. Cultural "truths" can become virtually impervious to criticism, even criticism of an objective, empirical sort. Very few racists pay much attention to the biologists, geneticists, and anthropologists who argue that distinct biological races actually do not exist. A Christian or Islamic fundamentalist homophobe could not care less about twin and sibling studies that show that genetic/biological factors influence sexual orientation or the fact that their myopic reading of the story of Sodom is mistaken. Of course, not all individuals allow themselves to be ruled by cultural orthodoxy. The more existentially inclined among us, for example, play a very active role in the shaping of our worldview. Nevertheless, such individuals are in the minority; as was noted earlier, for every individual who, say, abandons the faith of their parents for another one or who simply drops religion all together, there are thousands who do not.

Early on in this process, the social neophyte equates her local culture with the world at large. In fact, the concept of "local culture" is nonsensical at this point since she does not yet possess any standard of comparison. So, for example, one's religion seems awfully impressive until one learns that there are literally thousands of other religions and religious groups in the world, each with their own notions of God or gods, humankind's relationship with God or the gods, the afterlife, what constitutes pious behavior, and so on. Initially, one can simply ignore this implicit challenge to their assumptions regarding their own religion but such a reaction is not rational in the strict sense of the term, although one could say the same thing about faith, which, after all, got them into this mess to begin with. Good "Christian soldiers" (and Hindu "soldiers," Islamic "soldiers," etc.) fight off this challenge by hunkering down and digging themselves in even further, a common response to any data that conflict with their presumed worldview. This mindset—one I refer to as "obsessive deductivism"—is (regrettably) ubiquitous in all cultures around the world.

Actually, as was noted earlier, the mindset is somewhat understand-able given the manifestly nonempirical nature of religious claims, virtually all of which are nonfalsifiable and, thus, can weather the storms of logic, reason, empiricism, and, in some cases, common sense. In effect then, virtually all religious claims are equally "true," which, *prima facie*, makes them all equally false. This statement would be patently nonsensical, contradictory, and illogical if the subject in question were the things of the natural world but, in fact, the things in question here, if such things exist at all, are transcendent in nature and, thus, not accessible to us in an empirical sense.

Culturalism, then, particularly as it manifests itself in the practice of religion, is the belief or conviction that one's cultural ideology offers a correct interpretation of the world we live in and the rela-tionship that obtains between humans and (putative) transcendental entities. It follows that all other cultural ideologies are incorrect at least in part, if not entirely. Once one internalizes a specific cultural identity, individuals who adopt other cultural identities become the "other," a designation that has been used to justify all manners of abuse, from segregation to outright ethnic cleansing and genocide. This points to what is, perhaps, the most insidious characteristic of culturalism: it drives ideological wedges between groups, creating enemies where none inherently exist. Religion is arguably the cul-tural institution that is most guilty in this regard since for ages it has acted as a force of intercultural divisiveness rather than unity.

Culturalism is deceptively pernicious, ethnocentric in form, and intellectually stultifying. While one might argue that an indi-vidual not grounded in the bosom of mother culture simply cannot handle the challenges of existential angst, finitude, and annihilation, I would respond by pointing out that, while it may be true that indi-viduals need some sort of ideology, some sort of psychological resting place, if you will, when they are overwhelmed by the challenges of the human condition, the form and content of this ideology need not necessarily be ethnic, sectarian, or culture-specific. In other words, while some sort of ideological foundation is perhaps necessary, this foundation does not have to resemble the hyperlocalized and xeno-phobic versions that currently exist. What I am suggesting here is a rejection of culturalism and a movement toward "postculturalism."

This, then, is what postculturalism is "post" to. Moving beyond the admittedly comfortable and accommodating mindset of culturalism will be no easy task, especially since what I am championing here is not the "conversion" of this or that individual but, rather, millions of conversions, a global transformation, if you will, from a world characterized by islands of cultural specificity to a world characterized by a shared, panhuman, *post*cultural consciousness.

Sadly, such a transformation is, perhaps, unlikely, and expecting or even hoping for such a change in the near future is probably unrealistic. Nevertheless, it should be manifestly obvious to anyone who cares to think about such things that the old paradigm ("islands of cultural specificity") has failed us. We still continue to fight and kill one another for reasons of religion and ethnicity. In the roughly 200,000 years or so that groups of modern *Homo sapiens* have been fighting one another, the only real change that has occurred—other than the sophistication of our material culture—is our ability to kill more fellow humans while expending correspondingly less effort.

Perhaps this is a bit harsh. There is, after all, one region of the world where individuals hailing from a variety of ethnic and cultural backgrounds enjoy a relatively violence- and conflict-free existence and a high quality of life for the majority of its citizens: Western Europe. It just so happens that this region is arguably the most (voluntarily) secular in the world. Is there a connection? Well, I don't think it's a coincidence. A world filtered through religion-tinted glasses looks hostile and threatening; take the glasses off and one tends to see people rather than Muslims or Hindus or Christians or infidels or heathens. (Unfortunately, the citizens of Europe have recently been subjected to Islamic terrorism-inspired violence, but that just validates the general point I am making here regarding religion and violence.)

Sadly, this example, which should be emulated by other regions and cultures, was, instead, criticized by Cardinal Ratzinger (later Pope Benedict XVI), who bemoaned a secularized Europe.[5] In my mind, he had no good reason as a ranking member of the Catholic clergy to even implicitly suggest that a religious Europe was desirable over a secularized Europe. Using history as our guide, we might argue that, granted, a secular Europe does not burn heretics at the stake, place scientists under house arrest, or, worse, ethnically cleanse Jews or force women to accept a subservient status, but, other than that, I'll think it will be just fine. Perhaps it is a bit unfair to reach back into history for ammunition to attack the church, but it can't be denied that when the church had the chance to rule over or at least oversee Europe, it failed miserably. Give secularism a chance; it could hardly do worse. Thus far, at least, it has done much better.

Unfortunately, as was noted parenthetically above, this secularized Europe that currently serves as a global standard to be emulated, is being threatened by fundamentalist Islam . . . *fundamentalist* Islam, not necessarily Islam *per se*. Ironically, the nations of Western Europe could possibly have sown the seeds of their ultimate destruction when they embraced a policy of openness and tolerance (the secular thing again). It remains to be seen whether the recent influx of Muslims into Western Europe will threaten and perhaps destroy Western Europe's generally postcultural societies. It is my hope that moderate Muslims will be able to control the fundamentalists in their midst, but I can't honestly say that I am confident that will happen. The world will have definitely taken a major step backward if the misogyny, homophobia, and general intellectual and social totalitarianism that we see in so much of the traditional Islamic world are imported to secular, democratic, and free-thinking Europe.

The foregoing somewhat pessimistic comments regarding religion and cultural myopia notwithstanding, there is some reason for optimism. There is, after all, the secularized Europe that was noted earlier. Additionally, I should point out that this trend toward secularization, or at least an increase in the number of "unchurched" individuals, is evident to some extent even here in the traditionally richly religious United States. For example, the *American Religious Identification Survey* published by Trinity College reports that those individuals who choose not to affiliate with any religion increased from 8.2 percent in 1990 to 15.0 percent in 2008.[6] A 2015 Pew Research Center report notes that almost one in four Americans do not claim affiliation with any religion.[7] One indication of this is the growing popularity of the term "spiritual," which connotes a more personal or existential religiosity as opposed to "religious." Thus, for whatever reason, a steadily increasing number of individuals have abandoned institutionalized religion. Perhaps standing, kneeling, and praying on cue insults their individual integrity; if it doesn't, it should. Perhaps having to play second fiddle (intellectually) to a preacher or minister they suspect is far less educated and informed than they are is demeaning; if they don't feel that way, they should. Perhaps having to swallow whole the various dogmas of their faith, no matter how nonsensical or ridiculous, makes them choke or at least gag; if they don't, they should. Finally, in the most general sense, perhaps they resent being forced to exchange the freethinking spirit of ingenuous and unfettered inductive reasoning for the a priori pathology of an obsessively deductive, faith-based epistemology.

Nevertheless, while they have abandoned the institutionalized forms of religion, they are still animated by the basic motivation that makes humankind religious in the first place: an awareness, sometimes acute, sometimes subconscious, of finitude and certain mortality. Some can, without too much difficulty, abandon the standard response (religion) to the problem of annihilation, but many individuals are not willing to scrap it entirely. The literally heroic actions of Camus's Meursault, Nietzsche's *Übermensch*, or the true Sartrean existentialist are certainly admirable but difficult to emulate; there are, of course, a few true "heroes" that walk among us, individuals who find meaning and purpose in individualism and personal dignity rather than a cultural ideology that is foisted upon them, but most of us mere mortals are not quite ready to take that existential leap just yet. Even Theravada Buddhists, who are encouraged to reject the idea of a God or gods that should be worshiped, nevertheless have a standard of right comportment to guide their actions, Siddhārtha Gautama (the Buddha), and a transcendental goal to aspire to, *Nibbana* (Nirvana).

What, then, is the frustrated individual to do if she is not quite ready to assume total responsibility for exercising true individual freedom and forging her own path? Probably the most popular strategy is one that involves a compromise of some sort between the desire for a permanent, institutionalized religion and more fluid individual needs and sentiments. Ironically, it is just this sort of dynamic that characterizes the early formative period of all religions. Before a religion becomes monolithic, or at least relatively so, there is a dialectic give and take that characterizes its development: on the one hand, there is the collective need for a structure that provides a solid foundation for the standardization of behavior, ideology, ethics, and morality (i.e., religion understood in the Durkheimian sense that functions as a "social glue" that steadfastly serves to undergird a common ideology shared by all members of a society) and, on the other hand, there is the individual need for a degree of flexibility and freedom that will accommodate existential and subjective needs and desires. Those that are partial to the former could be described as, say, church-going defenders of traditional, fundamentalist Christianity, and those that are partial to the latter, largely "unchurched" theists in the broad sense of the term, could be described as "spiritual."

According to the Barna Group, which tracks religious behavior in the United States, approximately 100 million Americans (about one-third of the total population) do not attend church.[8] (Not surprisingly, the Barna Group also reports that almost half of political liberals are unchurched compared to only about one-fifth of political conservatives.) The unchurched of Europe make up an even greater proportion of the total population.[9] Some of those included in this number, would, of course, be atheists or agnostics, but all these unchurched individuals have, for whatever reason, rejected institutionalized religiosity; some of these individuals, in fact, continue to embrace notions of divinity, humanity, and morality that are at least vaguely similar to those of the faith of their birth, but even this illustrates a shift away from the "conventional" Judeo-Christian tradition that held sway for centuries.

From this point, we are but one small conceptual step away from a postcultural spiritualism that, while still manifesting at least the trappings of religion (understood in the traditional sense), at least moves us one step closer to a world that is characterized by, to use the phasing employed above, "the clarity of sound reasoning and empirical objectivity." While such a mindset (postcultural spiritualism) is characterized by a vestigial belief that there is, perhaps, some force, entity, or mode of being that transcends the purely material world in which we live and a (again) vestigial longing for the trappings of the culture with which one is most familiar, there is also the realization that religions and cultures, and, in some cases, irreligious ideologies, play the same roles for all peoples. In other words, postcultural spiritualism rejects the notion of one, true religion and instead embraces a strict religious and ideological pluralism. In the world of postcultural spiritualism, Hinduism, Shinto, Daoism, Christianity, Wicca, Islam, Mormonism, Vodoun, tribal/indigenous religions, atheism, agnosticism, and humanism are all functionally equivalent; in actuality, this has always been the case, but in this new world individuals are growing increasingly aware of this fact. This religion, that religion, no religion; all are welcome in this new world of postcultural spiritualism. A postcultural historical "moment," should it come to pass, will serve as the final stage in a global movement toward a world where religion is virtually nonexistent or the role of religion is minimal at best, and religious fundamentalism is a historical relic finally relegated to the dustbin of tragic human mistakes.

In the most general terms, postculturalism is a reasonable and logical extension of postmodernism, a sort of post-postmodernism if you will. As this point is crucial to a full understanding of postculturalism, let us briefly examine postmodernism and the link to postculturalism.

Postmodernism is a concept that can be addressed in any number of ways, as a purely philosophical notion or through a discussion of architecture, art, film, literature, or even science. In my classes, some of which are introductory college-level courses, I try to keep the discussion as "real world" as possible, as my students are not generally aware of theoretical notions such as "deconstruction," "reflexivity," etc. I will employ this strategy here.

Let us first consider what is arguably the last traditional, apple-pie, mom-in-the-kitchen/dad-at-work decade in the United States, the quintessentially "modern" 1950s. This decade was characterized by the following: a high degree of trust in authority figures, a distinctly essentialist (i.e., traditional, conservative) mindset regarding gender (only two, male and female, corresponding to 46 XY and 46 XX karyotypes respectively) and gender relations, the belief that marriage and family structure should adhere only to socially acceptable models, an acceptance of a simplistic racial paradigm, and the presumption that salvation can only be attained through the one true religion, Christianity. In short, it was a decade defined by an implicitly and explicitly enforced sociocultural homogeneity.

Now, if we fast forward to the second decade of the third millennium CE, we see that the sociocultural landscape has been drastically altered. Pronouncements of authority figures are met with skepticism or rejected outright, transgendered individuals (a vast group ranging from gays and lesbians to the intersexed to the gender atypical) are recognized and accommodated, the equality of the sexes is championed, a variety of family types from blended families to gay families with children are prevalent, "race" is no longer as meaningful or culturally relevant as it once was, and religious pluralism is growing in popularity. In short, sociocultural heterogeneity is the order of the day. Postmodernism, then, can be defined as the encroachment of the "other" (defined in the broadest terms possible) into what was once considered to be privileged space.

The first major challenge to the "privileged" status quo was, of course, the Civil Rights Movement, which officially began with the *Brown v. Board of Education* case (1954) that ruled that segregation in public schools was unconstitutional and continued through the Women's Liberation Movement and, later, the Gay Rights Movement. We have, then, been living in a postmodern world for a few decades now, and we are, thus, in the process of a transformation that is moving us toward a postcultural world. This is a sociological fact that cannot be denied. That does not mean, however, that everyone is happy about it; quite far from it, in fact. Traditional, "God-fearing," "patriotic" Americans that look back on pre-1960s America as some sort of golden age are still among us. The majority of these folks are older or elderly, so it appears as though this nostalgia will not be with us for long.

I, for one, will not mourn the demise of this presumed golden age. I find it ironic that some folks bemoan today's more tolerant, secular, and pluralistic society and, instead, long for the "good old days" of traditional America, when, in reality, traditional, pre-1960s America was a horrible place for anyone who wasn't white, male, and relatively affluent. Misogyny was rampant and tolerated, as indicated by shameful rates of spousal abuse, and women were routinely blamed and publicly shamed for being raped. Gays and lesbians dared not come out of the closet unless they were prepared to lose their professions, their families, their churches, their children, or their lives. The dominant white majority publicly flaunted their hate and disdain for African Americans and sought to deny them even the most basic civil rights, like education, employment, and suffrage. The "good old days" or the "golden age" of pre-1960s America is, in fact, a mirage or an illusion in the minds of those who are either ignorant of, choose to ignore, or are simply not bothered by the fact that women and people of color endured horrible suffering at the expense of white, male hegemony.

It is true, of course, that many suffer from the general anomie and anxiety brought on by the rapid social change that has occurred over the last few decades, and it is also true that tolerance, secularism, and pluralism bring with them new challenges and unforeseen consequences. Nevertheless, as a humanist, I celebrate and applaud the general movement away from a privileged, essentialist, conservative society to one where everyone matters, especially since that also entails the social, cultural, and political vitiation of the (heretofore) one dominant and powerful religious group in America, Christian fundamentalists. It is my hope that this book will continue to move us in that general direction.

PART ONE

CULTURE IS FICTIONAL AND ILLUSORY

CHAPTER TWO
THE ETIOLOGY OF THIS PATHOLOGY

Émile Durkheim, the French sociologist and champion of functionalism, wrote that there are no false religions.[1] Clearly, he is not implying (conversely) that all religions are true, for that is simply illogical given the fact that the dogmas, beliefs, and assorted claims of the various religions are contradictory when taken as a whole. For example, those individuals who affiliate with the three Western monotheistic religions, Christianity, Islam, and Judaism (approximately one-half of the world's peoples) believe that an individual lives one life on this earth and is judged by God sometime after death; on the other hand, those individuals who affiliate with the Eastern religions Hinduism, Buddhism, and Jainism (approximately one-fifth of the world's peoples) believe that an individual has many lives and, consequently, a very long time if necessary in order to elevate themselves sufficiently to become reunited with the *Brahman* (Hinduism) or to attain *Nibbana* (Buddhism) or to reach *Siddha-sila*, the abode of perfected souls in Jainism. So, in regard to this very significant component of some of the world's great religions, there is no compromise to be made as the affirmation of one is equivalent to the negation of the other.

A common sentiment is that "all religions are basically the same." Well, yes and no. Yes, in the most general sense, all religions provide a link between the natural world of humankind and the (presumed) transcendental world of gods, entities, or forces from which they seek ultimate approval or modes of blissful and eternal being that they hope to eventually attain. Thus, all religions, in the most general sense, provide humans with a transcendental focal point that guides their actions and shapes their ideologies. But, on the other hand, no. Basic beliefs concerning the nature of God or gods (some, in fact, like Theravada Buddhists, Jains, and Daoists, for example, don't pay much attention to gods at all), the precise manner in which humans should interact with God or the gods, and the general dos and don'ts of "proper" (religious) human comportment vary considerably from one religion to the next. As far as I am concerned, the noes far outweigh the yeses; all religions are not basically alike except in regard to characteristics that are so general as not to mean much of anything noteworthy.

If, then, we consider the totality of the world's religions, we are left with four basic choices: 1) one religion is completely right and all the others are either totally or partially wrong; 2) all religions are either wrong or partially right; 3) all religions are wrong; and 4) all religions are right.

Option one is held by the true believers, a group that comprises approximately 85 percent or so of the world's population. Given the basic irrationality of religious belief, based largely as it is on a strict faith-based epistemology and the fact that religious claims are non-falsifiable, it follows that the validity of option one is indeterminable—thus, it could be right or wrong but we cannot know which. The defender of religion X is incapable of putting forth any arguments that would convince a cross section of the world's peoples.

Option two, again, given the nature of religion and religious belief and the manifestly culture-relativistic nature of religion, seems reasonable. It is certainly possible that all religions are wrong. Nevertheless, if, in fact, there is some force, entity, or mode of being that transcends the quotidian sphere of human existence (by the way, a hypothesis that can neither be confirmed nor disconfirmed), then it is possible that many different religions have gotten it partially right, but, again, we cannot know if that is the case.

Option three is appealing from a strict materialist point of view, and there is no doubt that the strongest arguments can be made in support of this option, but, again, the claim is not falsifiable and, thus, meaningless in a conceptual sense. While I, like many others, feel that the burden of proof, in fact, lies with those who assert the existence of spirits, gods, angels, divine entities, and alternate modes of being on a preternatural plane, that general hypothesis is not testable, meaning the "dispute" cannot be resolved with any degree of certainty. The belief that all religions are wrong, like the belief that one particular religion is correct, while easily the most compelling position, admittedly simply hangs out there in conceptual space, floating in a cloud of ambiguity, never alighting on the ground of certainty. One may resort to faith to "ground" belief in a religion, but such an exercise is necessarily subjective (i.e., meaningful on an individual basis and meaningless from an objective, universal perspective). For many, however (about 85 percent of all people around the world), this is good enough. After all, the only other option is to persist in objectivity, which, as Kierkegaard never tired of telling us, is ultimately futile, or to give up on the project entirely, which leads one to agnosticism.

We now reach option four. As was noted earlier, in a strict logical sense option four cannot be true anymore than A can be A and not A at the same time. Nevertheless, I don't wish to abandon this option just yet. While there is no doubt that the hypothesis is false in a strict, logical, truth-claim sense, there is one sense in which it is valid. And that brings us back to Durkheim. Clearly, when Durkheim wrote that no religions are false, he was not assessing the truth content of religious claims; he was, after all, an atheist. Durkheim, an astute observer of cultural practices, noticed that religions are, regardless of time or place, functional in the sociological sense of the term. In simple terms, they "work"—i.e., they provide for all groups an ethical foundation for social behavior and, in general terms, give individuals a meaning and purpose for their lives. Unlike those atheists who have little good to say about religion (see, for example, Nietzsche,[2] Freud,[3] Marx,[4] Dawkins,[5] and Hitchens,[6] among many others), Durkheim argued that, while religions are invalid in an objective sense, they nevertheless contribute greatly to the maintenance and preservation of society, and in this way endure generation after generation. This ingenious and prescient observation predated by decades the foundational paradigm upon which modern anthropology is based, namely cultural relativism, a topic to which we now turn.

Finitude. Mortality. Speaking in mathematical terms, we might say that culture is a function of these two variables. Put another way, the nature and form of cultural behavior and ideology is a response to finitude and mortality or, in simple terms, annihilation awareness. As Ernest Becker so brilliantly points out, humans are cursed (or blessed, I guess, depending on one's perspective) with a bipartite nature, one part symbolic, spiritual, cultural, the other part biological, animalistic, organic.[7] We are in the world like all animals are, but, unlike other animals, we know we are in the world—i.e., we have a conscious awareness of our independence from our environment. Put another way, like animals we too will eventually become, as Becker liked to say, food for worms, but, unlike the animals, we are aware of that fact. Thus, our awareness of annihilation (finitude and mortality) is acute. We do not, however, give nature the last word. Instead, we immerse ourselves in the warm, clear waters of a culture of our own making, and it is from the perspective of this relatively safe and comforting pool that we gaze out at the terrifying natural world that surrounds us. Culture, then, represents the human attempt to maintain sanity in a hostile world that constantly and obstinately seeks our destruction.

Before proceeding further, I feel I need to clarify my earlier comment that humans are cursed (or blessed) by their predicament. According to Judeo-Christian orthodoxy, the curse of humankind can be traced back to the fall of Eve and Adam in the Garden of Eden. The standard teachings of this tradition hold that Eve and Adam were perfect creatures living in a perfect world until first Eve and then Adam ate of the tree of knowledge of good and evil. (The ancient writer of this biblical passage effectively makes his own very special contribution to centuries of mistreatment of women that would be justified by this and other writings in the Bible, a book conceived of and penned by males, all writing from the manifestly misogynistic, hyper-patriarchal perspective of the Bronze Age.) After the dirty deed, it is written that Eve and Adam became aware of their nudity. (By the way, claims of the supposed universal relevance of the Bible are vitiated by the fact that many tribal/indigenous peoples living in tropical areas around the world cover themselves only minimally or not at all. They express no shame à la Eve and Adam but do, however, show a good deal of common sense living as they do in very hot and humid environments. I'll conclude this tangential aside with one more point: According to the third chapter of Genesis, because of Eve's disobedience God punished all women—for all time—with the pain of childbirth. But what can be said, then, of the omnipotence and omniscience of a God whose punitive actions can be mitigated with simple anesthesia?) Thus, by virtue of eating from the forbidden tree, the first humans gained an awareness that they did not possess before but, as a consequence, humans were now corruptible, mortal, and inherently sinful, at least according to the Christian doctrine of original sin.

One might ask, however, absent the curse of this presumed (and clearly mythological) original sin, exactly what sort of existence would humans have? The Bible doesn't help us much here, but, as was noted above, we are told that after Eve and Adam ate from the tree they were aware of their nudity. Thus begins the long sordid history of the Judeo-Christian (actually, much more Christian than Judeo-) obsession with the human body and human sexuality as agents of shame and sin. But, if we assess this situation reasonably and rationally, we might take it in another direction. We might conclude, for example, that accompanying Eve's and Adam's "pre-fall" unawareness of nudity, was a lack of appreciation for the sexual beauty of the opposite sex, a consequent lack of lust and libidinal impulses, and, perhaps, even an inability to experience orgasms, which, after all, seems very likely in the absence of everything else. Supposedly the original couple was happy before their egregious transgression, but what kind of happiness are we talking about here? Young children (for the most part) are "happy"; fish are "happy"; dogs are "happy"; and religious fundamentalists are "happy." But "happiness" of this sort is intrinsically linked to ignorance; it's a package deal, so to speak. Christian or Muslim fundamentalists who dutifully absorb everything they are told and taught and are never challenged to think otherwise, who, as far as they are concerned, already have their tickets punched for entry into heaven, are happy, but, as I noted earlier, such "happiness" comes at a cost—a cost that some, at least when given the opportunity, are not willing to pay. And, make no mistake, the costs are great—doubt is forced to yield to dogma;

data-based knowledge is forced to yield to faith-based assumptions; criticism is forced to yield to authority; curiosity is forced to yield to "truth" (a priori, cultural, deductive); and freethinking is forced to yield to intellectual obsequiousness. So, yes, I suppose it is true that ignorance is bliss . . . until, of course, one discovers that they are ignorant. Was, then, the primal serpent, being the source of doubt, criticism, curiosity, and freethinking, a friend of humankind rather than an enemy? Or, put another way, was the serpent the "good guy"?

If we begin with the ignorance of religious fundamentalism, we need only a small conceptual step to reach ignorance on a broader and more general scale. I am referring here to culture. (I am using the term "culture" to denote the ideological foundation of a localized adaptational response to a particular environment.) The ignorance of culture arises from the human need to obviate the challenge of materialism. Nature says that we are simply another member of the kingdom Animalia and the class Mammalia, culture says we are made in the image of God; nature says that we possess a spark of consciousness that punctuates very long periods of oblivion and nonexistence both before and after, but culture says that we live on after death; in simple terms, nature says we don't matter but culture says we do. Very few individuals, however, allow nature to have the last say. To do so would be to admit defeat in the face of certain annihilation, to accept the notion that at some fundamental level life itself is utterly devoid of an inherent meaning and purpose. Very few individuals are willing to face existence on those terms as witnessed by the thousands of religions and cultures around the world that respond to this existential challenge with a defiant "No!" *Homo religiosus* indeed!

Now, precisely how does humankind tame a natural world that seeks only to destroy it? Well, if we approach this problem analytically, it becomes clear that any number of stratagems are available that might be used to "humanize" the natural world or, put another way, to trick ourselves into believing that the world really is how we conceptualize it. In a more general sense, what all these stratagems have in common is what I refer to as "culturization." What I mean by this is that humans have a tendency, nay, a need and a desire, to "culturize" their natural world by cutting it down to a size they can deal with. The world, in its natural state, is much too overwhelming, much too complicated, and much too mysterious for mere humans to tame. The sensible response, then, is to remake the world in our own image, thus at least giving us the impression that we can overcome our biology and that we can prevail in our struggle against annihilation. While there are, no doubt, many ways in which this human response to annihilation can be demonstrated, I will consider two—one involving a distinctly self-serving interpretation of natural phenomena, the other involving a conceptual paring down of the incredibly complex and overwhelming world in which we live.

In regard to a "self-serving interpretation of natural phenomena," I should begin by stating the obvious. Going back in time as far as sound archaeological data can take us, we can see a universal tendency among humans to anthropomorphize their world. (See, for example, Stewart Guthrie's *Faces in the Clouds* for a thorough exploration of this topic.[8]) Thus, God, or the gods, are made in our image as gender, human behavior, and even human physical attributes are projected outward into some parallel or transcendental world. Vestiges of this tendency have persisted into recent times. So, for example, the God of the Tanakh (the Christian Old Testament—"Old Testament" is an a posteriori designation that Christians coined to emphasize the fact that the Hebrew scriptures simply serve as a "backdrop" for *their* story), wrestles with men, makes contracts, is wrathful, belligerent, loving, merciful, etc.; the Greek gods quarrel among themselves, lust for one another, even steal from one another; Hindu gods (who, by the way, are ultimately all manifestations of Brahman, the one supreme spiritual reality) are distinctly "genderized," have consorts of the opposite sex, and exhibit the full range of human emotions; and the *orisha* and *lwa* (gods and spirits) of sub-Saharan West African and New World African-derived religions carry on much like humans: fighting, quarreling, lusting after one another, and so on. In fact, the *orisha* and *lwa* have been so anthropomorphized that the possession of worshipers (a common and expected occurrence during religious rites and ceremonies) is virtually a seamless process, with the worshiper easily taking on and exhibiting the various behavioral attributes of the *orisha* or the *lwa*.

In addition to the gods recognized by groups all over the world, natural phenomena have been widely interpreted as having some relevance to the human world. Thus, eclipses, especially solar, and comets were commonly perceived as harbingers of doom; thunder and lightning have long been interpreted as vindictive divine commentary on human behavior; and, of course, how could we forget astrology, an ancient and widespread "science" that claims that patterns in the arrangement of the sun, moon, and stars at one's birth determine, or at least correspond to, particular behavioral attributes of that individual. (I wonder how many of the 29 percent[!] of Americans who believe that astrology is valid[9] are aware that the constellations of the zodiac are optical illusions visible only from Earth, since the stars of which they are comprised are often thousands of light years apart and are located at vastly different distances from Earth?)

The human tendency to anthropomorphize natural events also extends to other phenomena as well. Consider, for example, the popular demonic "possession" diagnosis for various dissociative and psychotic episodes and the "cure," exorcism. Exorcism is arguably the most popular form of healing cross-culturally, and everything from the singing of songs, the recitation of liturgies, beatings, sweat baths, trephining, and tempting the offending entity with food is used around the world to exorcize unwanted spirits.[10] In northern India, malevolent spirits are forced out of the victims into a piece of cloth that is then nailed to a tree;[11] the Polynesian Maori of New Zealand conduct a ceremony during which water is forced down the possessed individual's throat and his eyes are flushed out and scratched in an attempt to exorcize the invading spirit[12]; Christian fundamentalist "deliverance ministries" in the United States commonly exorcize demons of lust, greed, divorce, homosexuality, etc.; and demonic "possession" and exorcism is recognized and practiced in Judaism, Islam, and Hinduism, as well as in many tribal/indigenous religions around the world.

Generally speaking, (putative) supernatural phenomena are very "slippery" in a conceptual or empirical sense, but in this case we have data aplenty that allow us to interpret and explain exorcism with a relatively high degree of certainty. We can begin by stating two facts: 1) exorcism is practiced by hundreds, perhaps thousands of religious and cultural groups, and 2) in all of these various and sundry groups around the world, exorcism "works." I've enclosed works in quotation marks to signify that exorcism cannot be real in an objective sense, since the "possessing" agents and, in fact, entire religious systems differ from group to group, sometimes dramatically. Clearly, individuals worldwide are mistaken, in an empirical sense, regarding the etiology, diagnosis, and cure of demon "possession." As I stated earlier, we could, I guess, admit the possibility that perhaps one of these religious traditions has actually gotten it right, but, again, given the distinctly nonempirical nature of "possession" and the spirits said to be the acting agents, that notion will never be more than an interesting, albeit nonfalsifiable hypothesis.

There is no reason, however, for us to pursue that strategy here, for there is a much more logical and reasonable explanation. If we keep in mind that exorcism is virtually always efficacious regardless of where it is practiced, we need to put aside the notion of therapeutic healing and look to subjective factors, since, after all, the formerly "possessed" individuals certainly believe they have been healed or delivered from "possession" by a malevolent entity. Thus, what we have here is psychotherapeutic healing, a very real form of healing from a subjective point of view. As is the case with the "placebo effect," an expectation of a positive outcome results in the same. We can surmise that these individuals have sufficiently internalized their local cultural ideology, at least to the extent that claims regarding spirits, good and evil, possession, etc., are accepted as being objectively true. That psychotherapeutic healing occurs is not really difficult to understand given the elaborate production that is made during the exorcism and the personal attention the "possessed" receives from individuals in positions of authority; it should also be noted that everything that takes place during the entire course of the "possession" can be readily interpreted and "explained" within the context of that particular religious system. It's a pretty damned impressive show, after all!

Essentially, what these examples show us is that individuals have a much greater tendency to fit natural phenomena to cultural ideology than cultural ideology to natural phenomena; consider, for example, the young-earth creationist who refuses to yield to mountains of empirical data to the contrary. So, to return briefly to "possession," take a look at the various phenomena that have been attributed to possession by evil spirits: epilepsy, Tourette's syndrome, dissociative identity disorder, schizophrenia, and other forms of psychosis. From ancient times up through the Middle Ages, all of these maladies were mistaken for demonic possession, but, at least from an objective, empirical, "scientific" point of view, they are now all thought to be attributable to natural rather than supernatural causes. Nevertheless, the demonic possession explanation is still wildly popular, even in the United States. This is not really that surprising, however, considering the fact that the theory of evolution, the standard, mainstream explanation of human origins virtually unanimously accepted by scientists around the globe, is rejected by over 40 percent of individuals in the United States, a technologically sophisticated, Western, industrialized nation (42 percent of those polled by Gallup in 2014 agreed that "God created humans in [their] present form."[13]).

Just a thought here: Jesus seemed to be just as confused as everyone else if we take the Gospel narratives at face value. On at least five specific instances, in addition to the more general references made regarding Jesus releasing individuals from unclean spirits, Jesus confronts individuals that exhibit signs of some form of mental disorder, immediately concludes that they are possessed by demons, and commences to exorcize them of their spiritual burdens. Can one imagine how different Christianity and, indeed, the world would be today if on one single occasion Jesus had proclaimed that an individual was suffering from a psychological disorder and advised his family how to care for him? What a real difference Jesus could have made if, in fact, he had shown at least a minimal knowledge of the workings of the human mind possessed by psychologists and psychiatrists today. It seems very unlikely that of all the individuals Jesus diagnosed as demon possessed, not a single one was suffering from epilepsy, schizophrenia, Tourette's, or any number of psychoses, since today we know that these disorders account for a large majority of dissociative episodes. After all, Jesus would know this if he were God, wouldn't he? Instead, he behaved just like everyone else and displayed the same ignorance of the natural world that others of his time period exhibited. In my mind, this is simply one reason among many others why we should not confer a "special" or divine status on a book obviously written by humans.

It seems clear to me that this human tendency to anthropomorphize, this need to "humanize" natural phenomena, is closely linked to a basic human need to control the world in which we live. After all, the empirically incorrect geocentric "theory" of the cosmos lived on in the Western world some 1,600 years after the time of Christ. Roman Catholic prelates (who for centuries closely guarded and protected [the assumed truth of] religious dogma) simply refused to accept the fact that humanity was not located at the center of God's creation. (As late as 1616, Galileo was ordered by Cardinal Robert Bellarmine, at the request of Pope Paul V, to "abandon completely . . . the opinion that the sun stands still at the center of the world and the earth moves, and henceforth not to hold, teach, or defend it in any way whatever, either orally or in writing."[14]) To repeat what I stated earlier, humans will not let nature have the last word on the workings of the world in which we live or, if they do, they basically have to be dragged into it kicking and screaming, in an intellectual sense. Culture is, then, in large part, an audacious and defiant response to materialism and the cold hard facts of finitude and mortality.

Now, let us move on to the second "culturization" strategy utilized by humankind, namely the one that involves conceptually paring down the incredibly complex and overwhelming world in which we live. This is especially evident in regard to two aspects of culture, diet and sexuality.

It is well known in the circles of cultural anthropology that no cultural group anywhere in the world consumes everything in its local environment that is palatable, digestible, and at least somewhat nutritious. So, for example, Americans do not eat horses, even though horse meat is tender, lean, and, like many meats, high in protein; horse meat is commonly consumed in parts of Europe and Asia. Americans also do not eat dogs, even though, as many Koreans will attest, they are quite tasty and, of course, nutritious. I am from Louisiana, and my Trinidadian friends and contacts were shocked to learn that, at least in this part of the United States, frog legs are quite popular and somewhat of a staple on seafood platters at restaurants. Of course, I can't discuss this issue without at least mentioning the prohibitions against eating pork for Jews and Muslims and against eating beef for Hindus. Many more examples could be provided, but I think these will suffice to make the general point that people around the world quite commonly avoid foods that are readily available, nutritious, digestible, and at least minimally palatable if not downright tasty.

What is going on here? Well, let me begin by bracketing the origins of many popular food taboos—for example, those regarding pork and beef. At one time, these food prohibitions were actually conducive to survival, given the ecological context of the time and place in which they originated. Without getting too off topic here, the pork taboo, for example, discouraged an unsound subsistence practice in a part of the world (the ancient Middle East) where great effort had to be expended to raise pigs. Eventually, however, we reach a time when the context that generated the taboo in the first place no longer exists, the present day, for example. Today, however, Jews and Muslims avoid consuming pork for strictly religious or, in other words, cultural reasons. Thus, the "logic" being employed today regarding these food taboos is not strictly rational or objective but, rather, subjective and cultural. In other words, dietary prohibitions and taboos are prescribed by the dictates of culture (for both religious and social reasons) not nature. The literature on the anthropology of food is voluminous, and it is not my intention to discuss this issue at length. What is important for us, however, is how diet illustrates the human tendency to culturize the natural world but cutting it down to (a humanly acceptable) size. Remember, the intent here is to reduce the vast, overwhelming, and thus intimidating world to something that we can relate to. Only gods can relate to the world as it is; humans, however, are not equipped to handle this task.

Let us turn now to sexuality, probably the one aspect of human behavior that best illustrates the human tendency to culturize the world. Again, as was the case with diet, if one resorts only to reason, empirical data, and objectivity in an attempt to understand the sexual behavior of *Homo sapiens*, he will grow increasingly discouraged and will eventually give up. There are, of course, dos and don'ts, rules and exceptions to rules, and social sanctions for transgressing those rules, but because these strictures are manifestly cultural (i.e., generally having little or nothing to do with biology), they vary greatly from one group to the next. With a few exceptions (nuclear family incest for example), what is considered to be "proper" or "improper" sexual behavior differs greatly cross-culturally. Nevertheless, one important generalization can be made: no culture simply accepts the very large range of all possible human sexual activities as being "proper"; rather, the theoretically possible is pared down to the culturally permissible.

Once again, if strictly biological or natural concerns were at work here, we would see some consistency in human sexual behavior cross-culturally. But, in fact, virtually all of the anthropological data point to the fact that there is little or no consistency in sexual norms and mores from one group to the next. The American anthropologist George Murdock, in a comprehensive analysis of the world's tribal cultures, notes that 70 percent permit premarital coitus (thus 30 percent do not) and approximately 20 percent approve of extramarital coitus (thus 80 percent do not).[15] In some societies (especially Muslim) virginity in young women is mandated sometimes on punishment of death or exile or social ostracization and in others—for example, the tribal societies of the Solomon Islands, the circumpolar peoples of Alaska and Canada, and some Siberian groups—virginity in young women is inconsequential. In regard to homosexuality, there is no consistency whatsoever. Much of the Western world could be described as relatively permissive. For example, twenty-three countries allow same-sex partners to marry, but only one of those (South Africa) is not a Western nation. Contrast that with all of Asia and virtually all of Africa where it remains illegal, including the ten countries (all predominately Islamic) where homosexuality is punishable by death.[16] Many more examples could be cited to demonstrate the inconsistency of sexual norms, but these should suffice to demonstrate my point.

There is a clear need, an obvious tendency to control nature, that is at work here. To simply allow the theoretically possible—which, once again, no culture does—would be tantamount to surrendering our spiritual, symbolic, god-aspiring selves to the purposeless dictates of the strictly organic world. We stubbornly hold onto the belief that we are not mere biological creatures but, rather, (demi-)gods made in the image of God "Himself." This myth must be grounded upon the belief that we control nature rather than the other way around.

Again, humankind says no to materialism, no to mortality—in a word, no to annihilation.

Cultural relativism, then, is not simply an abstract conceptual construct that exists only in the rarified air of postmodern anthropology; it is a cold hard fact of the world in which we live. There truly exists no one culture that serves as the standard whereby all other cultures can be judged. The dizzying array of social and cultural customs and ideologies that exist cross-culturally is an empirical testament to that fact. And don't forget Durkheim: the social and psychological functionality of cultures around the globe cannot be denied—they are all (functionally) true and they are all (functionally) valid. It is perhaps in the religious sphere of human existence where we find the most compelling illustration of these observations, a subject to which we now turn.

CHAPTER THREE

RELIGION

I t has been said that religious fundamentalists are some of the most critical people in the world. On the face of it, of course, that notion seems preposterous; after all, in the world of fundamentalism we find literal belief in teleportation (Islam); insects with souls (Jainism); baptism of the dead (Mormonism); the transmigration of souls (Hinduism, Buddhism, Jainism); natural forces that affect us yet are undetectable (Daoism); miraculously parting seas and rivers (Judaism); young-earth creationism, faith healing, and demon possession (Christianity); virgin births (any number of religions); and so on. Trust me, I have barely scratched the surface here, but I'm sure the reader gets the point. How, then, can it be said that individuals who are willing to accept these dubious and problematic notions are "critical"? They are critical, in fact very critical, when it comes to the religious beliefs of *others*. By some inexplicable logic, such individuals have no problem accepting the incredible, miraculous claims of their own religion, claims that should tax the patience of even the most gullible folks, while at the same time rejecting outright the incredible, miraculous claims of other religions. There is no substantive difference between the miracles of one religion vis-à-vis the miracles of another religion other than the fact that one set of miracles is culturally relevant to certain individuals and the other set of miracles is not. So a Catholic, armed with his immaculate conceptions, apostolic successions, and trinitarian Gods might face off with a Mormon, with his belief in golden tablets, angelic translators, posthumous baptisms, and sacred undergarments, but no one is backing down. An impartial observer who has agreed to serve as the referee in this strange face-off between competing metaphysics would eventually throw up his hands in frustration, declare the contest a tie, and send both participants home.

What is it, then, about religion that makes so many ostensibly reasonable individuals so unreasonable? Why do individuals generally make certain empirical demands of scientific claims yet give religious claims a pass? Why do beliefs, dogmas, and "truths" vary so greatly from one religion to the next? Why do literally thousands of religions and religious groups exist—a number that increases through time rather than decreases? And, why do miraculous claims persist generation after generation, hanging out there in the conceptual ether of uncertainty, never attaining anything like universal or global acceptance? The short answer to the last two questions: Because (once again) they can; by their very nature, I should add, they can. There is no claim that is so preposterous and absurd that it could not potentially become an acceptable religious belief to someone. Unlike scientific claims, religious claims are privileged; they are not subjected to objective scrutiny and empirical testing. In fact, religious claims are so meaningless in the strict logical sense of the term that they are not even falsifiable, and if a claim is not falsifiable it stays "in play" forever.

This, then, brings us to the first "law" of religion: *the significant claims, principles, and dogmas of the world's religions cannot be empirically substantiated.* Such claims, principles, and dogmas are nonempirical and, thus, have to be accepted, if they are accepted at all, on faith. Nevertheless, the impartial observer simply shakes her head at this point since, to her, reincarnation, virgin births, resurrections, and other such phenomena are all equally meaningless. After all, if we cannot know whether a claim, principle, or dogma is true or false, precisely what value does it have? Some may fault our impartial observer, I suppose, for the literal application of the positivist rule of falsifiability, the notion that statements that are not at least potentially falsifiable are meaningless, but how can she be faulted for seeking a rational substantiation of a miraculous claim while her religious counterpart's reasons for accepting such claims relies on nine parts hope and (at best) one part reality? As the folk saying puts it, "Wish in one hand and shit in the other, see which one fills up first." Indeed.

Now, before we get too excited about the "objective process," as some might call it, it should be noted that objectivity will never get us to absolute truths. After all, our understanding of kinetics has moved through Aristotelian, Newtonian, Einsteinian, and modern cosmological models, but we are not "there" yet and, presumably, never will be. Science, in other words, does an admirable job of generating models, theories, and laws that are better and better facsimiles of the truth but are not truth itself. Søren Kierkegaard, the brilliant Danish theologian, described this objective movement from one tentative truth to the next as an "approximation process."[1] It was, he would tell us, a frustrating fact of life that the Absolute lies just beyond our empirical grasp. Nevertheless, all he could offer us in its place is the now-legendary "leap of faith" toward subjective "truth." It should be noted that, according to Kierkegaard, this "leap" came with no guarantees; thus, in a true expression of individual freedom, one might make this "jump," but it is possible that he may not land on anything. And this, dear reader, is precisely the problem. What if I exchange the "objective process" for this momentous leap of faith, only to learn that I am just as lost as I was before only now, instead of standing on something, I am freefalling through a void of nothingness? After all, with objectivity, I at least know what I have: a small amount of something. And, as I stated earlier, perhaps I am not willing to exchange this for what could quite possibly be a large amount of nothing.

C. S. Lewis, another celebrated Christian theologian, has a different take on the issue. As a Christian apologist, Lewis simply has no choice but to defend faith, and I suppose he does about as good a job as can be expected given the inherent difficulty of his task. Nevertheless, even this able defender of the faith smells a rat. According to Lewis, faith/belief, on the one hand, involves the absolute repudiation of doubt on a psychological or emotional level but, on the other hand, the at-least-grudging admission that logical dispute cannot be abrogated.[2] To put it another way, the world of empirical data is potentially a faith wrecker. I have always thought that this conception of faith, combining equal parts hope and realism, is one of the most ingenuous, especially given the fact that it was conceived by a notable Christian apologist.

Augustine of Hippo (d. 430 CE) gave us yet another take on the notion of faith. According to this "Father of the Church," "Understanding is the reward of faith. Therefore seek not to understand that thou mayest believe, but believe that thou mayest understand. . . . We believed that we might know. . . ."[3] Now, on the face of it, this statement is not very convincing to say the least. A more careful reading, however, reveals that Augustine was not referring to faith in the blind sense associated with fundamentalism today but more as trust, trust in God, trust in authority, and trust in revelation. Faith, in this sense, is (hopefully) a first step toward enlightenment and represents a willingness to pursue something one deems worthy and important even if one does not yet know precisely where it will take them.

Today's religious fundamentalists, however, would take Augustine's sentiments literally. They not only start with faith but end with faith as well (i.e., they believe for reasons that have nothing to do with empiricism, rationality, experimentation, observation, etc., but rather because the inertia of an uncritical tradition has convinced them they are right), and there is no "movement" toward a greater understanding of anything. So, if one starts with faith, where does she start? Which version or manifestation of faith does one start with? Given this approach, is there any claim or idea that is so patently absurd that it would be rejected outright? Apparently not. In my mind, this notion goes far beyond being merely irrational; it is downright dangerous. Given the manifest lack of critique and discernment encouraged by the fundamentalist version of faith, the end result would be precisely what we have: a world replete with believers all believing different things absolutely, a potential recipe for disaster since some feel that their set of beliefs and their holy books are divinely inspired and are ready to discriminate, subjugate, fight, die, and kill for those beliefs. In fact, it is precisely this mindset that has characterized our world for far too long and, as was noted in chapter one, belongs in the dustbin of history along with its unfortunate by-products, misogyny, xenophobia, homophobia, ethnocentrism, and cultural absolutism.

What the fundamentalists are embracing here is "obsessive deductivism," a mindset characterized by the acceptance of some general principle or idea (the "truth") that is grounded solely upon presumption and assumption that is always and in all circumstances considered to be immutable and invulnerable to disconfirmation. Actually, this mindset is, unfortunately, quite common. All it takes for an assumption to become a "truth" is a good dose of enculturation and, of course, the inertia of tradition and the sanction of authority to help it along. History is replete with examples. Consider, again, how long the (church-supported) geocentric theory held out against its more accurate rival. The claim of Mosaic authorship for the Torah was (and still is for some folks) "common knowledge," until Bible scholars finally put the claim to the test and found it to be false. Christians simply assumed that Eusebius's fourth century CE work on early church history[4] was valid for about sixteen centuries, until historians actually decided to critique his version; it turns out that he was an able spokesperson for what it is now referred to as "proto-Orthodox Christianity"[5] but not very forthcoming regarding the many competing Christian groups who eventually succumbed to the political hegemony of the dominant group.

In today's world it is common for individuals to embrace claims and notions with an absolute degree of certainty even though most of these individuals are generally oblivious to whatever data and research might be available on the subject and are often woefully uninformed regarding the various issues that have some bearing on the subject. For example, while over 40 percent of Americans embrace biblical creationism over evolutionary theory,[6] few Americans have even a minimal grasp of the concept of natural selection or can define the term "evolution." Numbers are difficult to come by regarding the general public's grasp of evolutionary theory, but, after twenty-five-plus years teaching in the college classroom, I can say with a high degree of certainty that evolutionary theory is generally not being taught in our high schools or, if it is, it is being taught in a cursory fashion at best. Nevertheless, this does not stop those with strong convictions (unfortunately for faith not data) from rejecting a theory they know nothing about. Once every two years or so, I teach a college-level biological anthropology course and my students, practically all of whom are totally unaware of the basic principles of evolutionary theory and the empirical evidence in support of the theory when the course begins, are quite impressed with the hominin fossils, mitochondrial DNA studies, homologies in the animal kingdom showing descent from a common ancestor, real-world examples of natural selection, etc., that are discussed in class.

Virtually none of my students are familiar with any of this material before taking this course.

Other examples of obsessive deductivism in today's world include the following (mistaken) assumptions and beliefs: human ethics and morals can only have their source in a god or religion of some sort; phenotype influences cultural behavior; African Americans abuse drugs at rates higher than other groups; and gays and lesbians choose their sexual orientation. These assumptions are embraced as gospel truth by many, even though one afternoon in a good library would serve to dispel them all. We can, perhaps, overlook strong beliefs in religious claims since they cannot be tested, but one cannot say the same about claims such as these. What is disturbing here is that individuals seem to be conflating these two very different types of claims; faith becomes so natural to them that they begin to apply the same mindset to claims that are matters of knowledge and data rather than faith. The end result is a gullible public that can and will swallow almost anything that is fed to them, especially when it is in the name of religion.

The first "law" of religion, namely that the significant claims, principles, and dogmas of the world's religions cannot be empirically substantiated, leads us naturally to a second "law": *religions generally do not spread outside their area of origin.* After all, we are speaking of ideologies built upon nonfalsifiable claims that are, thus, as was noted earlier, meaningless to those that are not a part of the culture that birthed them; the culturally "other" will be a hard sell at best, and understandably so. There is a reason why through time we get more and more religions rather than fewer. If there were anything close to a general consensus on things religious, we would have something like a world religion, or at least only a handful of relatively similar competing religious ideologies. Instead we have eleven "great" or "world" religions, thousands of sects, denominations, and subdenominations of those religions, and thousands of tribal/indigenous and "alternative" or "modern" religions (those that do not fit neatly under the rubrics of "great religions" or "tribal/indigenous religions"). Clearly, a striking lack of consensus in this case is a reflection of the culture-bound, nonsubstantive claims, principles, and dogmas that are associated with these many religions and religious groups.

If the claims, principles, and dogmas being discussed here were intuitively evident to a majority of people, the natural process of cultural diffusion would be enough to establish a particular religion as a universal standard of sorts. But, of course, no such religion exists. In fact, in regard to the global landscape of religions, it is chaos rather than order that reigns. It is the nature of religious belief that makes it so. Given the lack of logic, data, and empirical substantiation of any sort, a religious dogma, for example, must look elsewhere for validation. Such validation is relatively easy to find within the historico-socio-cultural context in which the dogma originated and currently resides. The Immaculate Conception (the notion that Mary, mother of Jesus, was born without the taint of original sin), for example, recognized as dogmatic by the Catholic Church in 1854, flows quite naturally from the assumed notions regarding original sin, virgin birth, and the divine nature of Christ. Stripped of this context, however, the dogma of the Immaculate Conception is nonsensical. In the Orisha religion in Trinidad, the head washing and incising ritual of initiation is nonsensical in the absence of notions regarding the nature of the *orisha* (gods), humans' relationship to them, and spirit possession. Neither of these notions (the Immaculate Conception and Orisha initiation) has moved nor will ever move beyond the conceptual boundaries of the contexts that birthed them. Put another way, they have no universal validity.

Such is not the case, for example, with Kepler's planetary laws, Newton's laws of motion, or Boyle's law of pressure and volume, just to mention a few; these laws can be demonstrated quite simply and are valid regardless of time or place. Thus, no individual has any difficulty seeing, for example, the validity of the equation $x + -x = 0$ since it appeals to our inherent sense of logic and reason. True, we are using symbols here, and symbols are arbitrary, but that is a trivial point in my mind; once an individual understands what the symbols represent, the cogency of the statement is immediately grasped. On the other hand, the equation $x + y = z$ would represent a religious belief or claim, and to understand it one needs much more than an explanation of the symbols. If there is a "logic" at work here, it will be a distinctly cultural "logic" not an intuitively understood universal logic. Again, stripped of the historico-socio-cultural context from which the notion is drawn, this equation is meaningless.

Now, we all are aware of the fact that, while it is generally true that religions remain in or around their area of origin there are, nevertheless, a few exceptions to this "law," most notably, at least, in regard to the larger religions, Christianity, Islam, and Buddhism. How are we to understand this? As was noted above, a specific religious belief or claim has some degree of validity within the confines of the culture that embraces it. Thus, if religious dogmas or whole religions are found in areas where they are not autochthonous, and if dogmas and religions are nonsensical outside the historico-socio-cultural contexts in which they were established, then these contexts must also be present outside of their area of origin and, in some cases, they are. This is most easily accomplished by mass movements of people and, concomitantly, their cultures and religions.

The most significant factor that led to the establishment of Christianity on a global scale was European colonialism, a formidable movement of ships, guns, steel, and disease driven by the fiction that Almighty God was on their side. Who could fault them for assuming this? After all, according to the Bible, let us not forget, to many the literal and inerrant word of God, Joshua, with Yahweh's blessing, slaughtered every man, woman, child, and beast in city after city, after invading the land west of the Jordan river (see Joshua 10:28–41). Thus, genocide and political hegemony in Christendom has an ancient pedigree. As was the case with the inhabitants of Makkedah, Libnah, Lachish, Eglon, etc., etc. exterminated by Joshua, the native peoples of five continents stood little or no chance against the military might and stark brutality of the conquering Europeans. (The Europeans subjugated, slaughtered, infected with fatal pathogens, or worked to death the indigenous inhabitants of every continent but their own, with one exception. Which raises the question: What if there actually were indigenous peoples in Antarctica?) Within two generations or so after the arrival of Europeans in the Caribbean, for example, disease, abuse, and the sword and gun had wiped out virtually the entire indigenous population of that area. Native Americans in North and South America met similar fates over much longer time periods. After killing off a sizeable fraction of the indigenous peoples of the New World, the Europeans looked eastward toward Africa for another source of cheap labor. As a consequence, the indigenous peoples of yet another continent would suffer grievously at the hands of these Christians doing the Lord's work. In Australia, within about one hundred years after the arrival of Europeans in 1788, a significant portion of the Aboriginal population had been decimated due to overworking, disease, and murder. Fertile lands were stolen from them and they were treated worse than animals until just recently. This same story was repeated over and over, but the pattern was always the same. The advent of Christianity for the indigenous peoples of the world brought little more than misery, bloodshed, death, and, in some cases, the extinction of whole cultures. While some Christians may take pride in the fact that it is the largest religion in the world, without the military might, brutality, bloodlust, pathogens, and technology of the colonizing Europeans, the power, influence, and presence of Christianity in today's world would be minimal at best.

Islam's history in this regard is similarly ignoble, as this religion spread quickly from its point of origin in the Arabian Peninsula primarily in the form of military conquests and forced conversions. Within about one hundred years after the death of Muhammad, Islam covered a territory that spread from the Iberian Peninsula in the west to Pakistan in the east. Nevertheless, the Islamic conquest was far less violent in general than the global Christian conquest, as many of the conquered peoples were encouraged to convert (and many did) or, if not, to pay the *jizya* (a special tax levied on the *dhimmi* or non-Muslims). Some peoples, those in Egypt for example, were happy to exchange their Byzantine masters for Islamic ones.

It is probably not fair, however, to compare Christianity and Islam along these lines, given that the European propensity for global exploration brought them into contact with peoples that were so dissimilar to themselves that they thought, in some cases, that they were not fully human. In the case of Islam, on the other hand, the peoples they came into contact with were not that different from themselves, certainly not phenotypically at least. Thus, in each case, the racial/ ethnic dynamic of the contact situation was quite different. Nevertheless, Christianity and Islam became global forces only through the mass movements of highly organized and militarily dominant peoples. In fact, given the military power and demographic inertia that drove the spread of both religions, the content of the "message" and the "teachings" was irrelevant; virtually any metaphysical claim, no matter how outrageous, asinine, sublime, or reasonable, could have piggy-backed on either one of these two runaway trains of conquest.

This brings us to the third and most interesting of the three major exceptions to the "law" regarding the tendency of religions to stay put in their area of origin: Buddhism. Buddhism dates back to its great teacher Siddhārtha Gautama, otherwise known by the honorific "Buddha," who lived during the period 563 BCE–483 BCE. The religion proper began when the Buddha gave his first teaching on the four noble truths to five disciples in Sarnath, India (just north of the sacred Hindu city of Varanasi), around the year 528 BCE. The *sangha* (community of Buddhist monks and nuns) flourished in India and later spread to Sri Lanka sometime during the second century BCE. From there, missionaries and travelers brought Buddhism to southeast Asia, where today Cambodia, Myanmar, Laos, and Thailand, like Sri Lanka, all practice Theravada Buddhism, arguably the oldest form of Buddhism, and certainly the oldest remaining sect. With the development of Mahayana Buddhism, according to some, a more user-friendly form of Buddhism compared to the austere, ascetic, and nontheistic Theravada tradition, the religion spread to China in the second century CE and later from there to Mongolia, Korea, Japan, and Vietnam. Finally, Buddhism was brought to Tibet in the seventh century CE by the Chinese wife of King Songtsen Gampo. This third basic form of Buddhism, Vajrayana, spread from Tibet to Nepal, Bhutan, and parts of Mongolia. In many cases, the spread of Buddhism was a two-way street, with native peoples leaving their home countries in search of Buddhist teachings and later returning, and missionaries, without a conquering army behind them, spreading Buddhism to neighboring nations.

As we've seen, given the localized and culture-relative nature of religion, a religion will either not spread out of its area of origin (as is the case with more than 99 percent of all religions) or it will but only if nations of "others" are overwhelmed by mass movements of conquering peoples and armies. With Buddhism, however, we have something unique: a great or world religion (the fourth largest in the world) that spread almost solely on the strength of its ideas and teachings. In other words, what we have here is a bona fide example of a religion that, for whatever reason, was more or less freely embraced by individuals that were not native to its area of origin. Now, it is true that Buddhism was shaped and molded to fit localized sentiments, but the result was still unmistakably Buddhist. While it is generally true that it is virtually impossible to compare the relative validity of religions since so many claims, principles, and dogmas are assumptive, culture-specific, and nonfalsifiable, one might rightly claim some sort of superiority for Buddhism given the patently non-violent and unforced manner in which it spread throughout Asia.

The first and second "laws" of religion lead us naturally to a third: *religions are culture-bound or, put another way, religions are highly culturized ideologies that (presumably) guide their adherents down the path to salvation or liberation.* This culture-boundedness, of course, is to be expected given the manifestly particularistic character of religion that is the by-product of generations of development in one specific area. And, since a religion is one interdependent component among many in a sociocultural system, it must be at least somewhat consistent with the other components of that system. Thus, one will generally not find religious teachings and dogmas that contradict norms and mores associated with dietary preferences, gender relations, sexual behavior, national identity, history, ethnic heritage, and so on. Consider, for example, the influence of the Bible and Christian teachings on common American beliefs regarding the status of men vis-à-vis women, sexual orientation, and the origin of life. For an even better example, consider Muslim nations ruled by Shariah.

One of my favorite examples in this regard involves the Yanomamo, the indigenous peoples of northern Brazil and southern Venezuela. According to one version of the Yanomamo creation myth, one of the "first beings," the Spirit of the Moon, was injured by an arrow and when a drop of his blood fell onto and mixed with the earth, man (read "males") was created.[7] One of these first men (these are brave, warlike men being the direct progeny of this great spirit) became pregnant in his right and left legs. (When I am telling this story in my anthropology classes, I remind those students who are snickering that those who accept biblical tales of talking serpents, giants, nine-hundred-year lifespans, humans living in the bellies of fish, etc., etc., thereby lose any right to question or belittle the fantastic content of the Yanomamo creation story.) Out of his left leg came women—the "mysterious" female is always associated with the left cross-cul-turally—and out of his right leg came docile, cowardly, effeminate males. One of the morals of the story is that some Yanomamo men, those who don't want to fight, those who are gay, and those who are gender atypical, are like women because they were created in essentially the same way. On the other hand, the only true fierce and masculine Yanomamo are those who are descended directly from the great spirit. Thus, we see here an intimate link between Yanomamo cosmogony, which in this case doubles as religious mythology (much like the Genesis creation myth for Christian fundamentalists), and cultural ideologies that undergird gender relations and, secondarily, human sexuality, family structure, and kinship.

Now, while it is true that religions are culture-bound, one should not assume, then, that there is a certain inevitability regarding the specific form and content of this or that religion. Given the fact that religions are manifestly nonempirical, they are created, generated, and developed in an intellectual space that is largely bereft of induc-tive logic, empirical data, and objectivity. If a religion is a good fit for this or that group, it is because it has been "shaped" and "crafted" by this or that group. Karl Marx cleverly demystified this entire process when he wrote, "The mode of production of material life conditions the social, political and intellectual life process in general. It is not the consciousness of men that determines their being, but, on the contrary, their social being that determines their consciousness."[8] Thus, ideology ("consciousness") is driven by the real-world con-tingencies that impact day-to-day survival. In short, as Feuerbach,[9] Freud,[10] Adler,[11] and many others have noted, humankind makes God in its own image rather than the converse; in fact, when one ponders not only the gods but also the many religions of the world, it is clear that they are human creations. There is, then, a wide range of acceptable types or forms of religion that will be compatible with the sociocultural patterns of behavior that are conducive to biological survival. As Marvin Harris writes, "Nature is indifferent to whether God is a loving father or a bloodthirsty cannibal. But nature is not indifferent to whether the fallow period in a swidden field is one year or ten."[12] In simple terms, biological survival needs must be met in certain ways given the exigencies of the local ecology, but whether or not these needs are being met by atheists or polytheists is immaterial.

In regard to the Marxian influence of material factors on religious ideology, consider the African-derived religions of Haiti and Trinidad. While the politico-historical contexts of both islands are dissimilar, in both cases we had "directed contact" situations where large populations of West Africans were enslaved by Europeans, and, in both cases, the Africans attempted to preserve and perpetuate their native religions. Even the resulting religions, Vodoun in Haiti and Orisha in Trinidad, were (and are) similar, being, in large part, syncretisms of Catholicism and two geographically contiguous West African religions. Nevertheless, in Haiti two basic forms of Vodoun, the *Rada* or "cool" side and the *Petro* or "hot" side, gradually developed. The period of slavery was particularly brutal in Haiti and *maroon* (escaped slave) settlements were established very early. This provided "bases of operations" of sorts for rebellion against their French masters and provided the context for the creation of a powerful and vengeful form of Vodoun that could be used to strike back at the French, which they did successfully, gaining their independence in 1804. In Trinidad, on the other hand, the period of slavery was short-lived and (relatively speaking) less harsh. The African-derived religion of Trinidad, Orisha, did develop along similar lines but, in this case, a "hot" or "negative" or vengeful component never appeared. One might quibble a bit with the cause and effect relationship being assumed here, but this comparison clearly illustrates the influence of material factors on the nature and form of religion.

Buddhism provides another interesting illustration of the manipulation of religious ideology to suit material (immanent) needs rather than spiritual (transcendental) ones. The oldest sect of Buddhism, or at least the oldest surviving sect of Buddhism, Theravada, recognized the Buddha as a saint (rather than a savior) and placed an emphasis on the ascetic monk seeking his liberation from *samsara*. A no-nonsense version of Buddhism if you will. As was noted earlier, this form of Buddhism spread to southeast Asia but was not able to penetrate China and other areas north and northeast of India. When Buddhism did finally spread to these areas it did so in the form of Mahayana Buddhism, which considered the Buddha to be a savior (thus, godlike) and placed less emphasis on the ascetic monk or nun pursuing his or her own liberation. Mahayanists also recognize *bodhisattvas* (enlightened beings who postpone their own ascension into *Nibbana* [Nirvana] in order to lead others to enlightenment), which quite naturally gave way to the notion of "celestial Buddhas" that can be worshiped and prayed to. If we were to stay with the general paradigm being discussed here, we would say that Buddhism was clearly manipulated in such a way so as to make it more accessible to regions where the highly theistic Mahayana ideology was a better fit to local religious sensibilities than the starkly nontheistic Theravada ideology. Other forms of Buddhism appeared as it continued to spread throughout eastern Asia, including Ch'an Buddhism of China, which later appeared as Zen in Japan, and Tibetan Buddhism (Vajrayana), an acutely localized version of Buddhism heavily influenced by Bon, the indigenous religion of Tibet.

Finally, consider once again the case of the Orisha religion in Trinidad. This dynamic, eclectic, and syncretic religion is a curious amalgam of West African, Catholic, Protestant, and Hindu beliefs and practices; in addition, a localized version of the Kabbalah (highly thaumaturgical in form) is also practiced.[13] Thus, for Orisha worshipers, God has many faces but it is obvious that the precise nature of this divine physiognomy is a by-product of a specific matrix of historical, political, and cultural factors. So, for example, if the colonizing British had not tempted Indian Hindus with land in exchange for labor in the sugar cane fields of Trinidad, today the annual rites held at many Orisha compounds would not include the Hindu "sit down prayers" that occur one week before the *ebo* ("feast") commences. Also, the small Hindu shrines that are found at many Orisha yards would not exist. Furthermore, had the original colonizers

(Spanish and French) of the island not been Catholic but instead, for example, Protestant, the African-derived religion practiced today in Trinidad (assuming there would even be one) would be virtually unrecognizable compared to the present day Orisha religion. Nevertheless, Orisha worshipers, much like the adherents of all faiths, view their religion as being absolutely valid or "True" in its present form.

The absolutist claims of religious fundamentalists around the world notwithstanding, it is obvious, at least to the impartial observer, that historical "accidents" are just as responsible for shaping and influencing religious beliefs and practices as any other factor. In fact, it could be argued that such "accidents" are the most important factor in this regard. So, if Muhammad had been better received by the Jews in Yathrib (later renamed "Medina" or "the City" of the Prophet) during that very important formative period of Islam, might Islam today be a sect of Judaism instead of an independent faith somewhat hostile to Judaism? If the Moors had prevailed at the Battle of Tours in 732 CE against Charles Martel and his Christian army, would Europe today be predominately Islamic? If the Babylonians had not conquered Judah in 587 BCE and destroyed the first Jewish temple in Jerusalem or the Romans the second temple in 70 CE, would rabbinic Judaism, the form of Judaism we are familiar with today, have developed? After all, the many independent foci of Jewish worship scattered around the ancient world would have been unnecessary if the original focal point of Judaism, the temple in Jerusalem, had not been destroyed.

Christianity provides us with a particularly interesting case here. What if James and the "Jesus movement,"[14] with their emphases on the Torah and Jewish religious customs, had prevailed over Paul and the "Christ movement," who desired to extirpate the Jesus cult from its Jewish roots? What if the Gnostic Christians had had the political clout to have their Gospels disseminated and recognized as canonical rather than the Gospels favored by the "proto-Orthodox" Christians? What if Constantine had lost the Battle of the Milvian Bridge to the Roman Emperor Maxentius? There are, of course, hundreds of similar "what ifs," but it is clear that if any one of these events had turned out differently (a very reasonable possibility), Christianity today would be virtually unrecognizable compared to its present form. It also seems clear that, whatever the nature and form of the present-day permutation of Christianity, its fundamentalist adherents would claim absolutism for that version. It seems to me that the only way out of this prickly issue for believers is to claim that the hand of God was at work at every step along the way and, *ipso facto*, the current version of Christianity is, thus, the True religion. Unfortunately for them, however, such a claim is fallacious for two reasons: 1) it is nonfalsifiable so the status of the claim will never rise above conjecture and 2) the same explanation could be used to defend any version of Christianity regardless of which form "won out" in the end.

One might assume after this very brief review of the origins and historical development of a handful of religions that the believers among us, be they Jewish, Hindu, Christian, Wiccan, or whatever, would benefit greatly from a study of the world's religions. That is assuming, of course, that such a study is undertaken with an open mind, but, unfortunately, few religious fundamentalists are willing to critique their own faiths. In the meantime, religious absolutism continues to tear the global community apart and will probably continue to do so for some time. If there is even a small chance that the fundamentalists of whatever faith may actually grasp the fact that religions, all religions, are accidental by-products of decidedly quotidian factors and influences, then we should encourage and support such study. Intellectual maturity of this sort would be a boon to inter-ethnic and intercultural relations everywhere.

Let us now combine the three "laws" of religion into one coherent statement: Since 1) *the significant claims and dogmas of the world's religions cannot be empirically substantiated,* they are meaningful only to those who conceived them; thus, it follows that 2) *religions do not spread outside their area of origin* given that they are manifestly 3) *culture-bound* belief systems. This observation follows from an investigation of religions as opposed to a religion (i.e., a research perspective that is anthropological and culture-relative rather than ethnocentric and absolutist). The fundamentalists of the world fail to see the validity of the statement since their focus is, by definition, myopic. If, however, the true believers should one day get up the gumption to peek behind the curtain that separates them conceptually, intellectually, and culturally from the rest of the world they will either cringe and slink back to their comfortable spot in the corner of the closet or they will be liberated from the straitjacket of authority, tradition, and dogma that has held them captive for so long.

When viewing religion in this way—that is, from a global, objective, "academic," in short, anthropological perspective—one cannot help but grasp the fact that concepts such as faith, miracles, souls, demons, angels, spirit possession, virgin birth, and so on can be rescued from doubt only by a will to believe that borders on the obsessive. I feel I am justified in making such a statement when one considers the incredible and fantastic things the practitioners of the world's religions believe: the pope (a human being) is infallible when speaking *ex cathedra*; the *Vedas*, the most ancient scriptures of Hinduism, contain the words and knowledge of the Absolute (God, if you will) as they were revealed to *rishis*; the hidden *imam* has been hiding since 868 CE and will later be revealed by God as the savior of humankind; an individual's spirit can be caught and trapped in a bottle; the only spiritually proper way of disposing of a body is to allow vultures to consume it; as an embryo, Mahavira (the twenty-fourth *Tirthankara* of Jainism) was transported from the womb of his mother to another woman; there are (undetectable) natural forces around us whose flow must not be impeded lest problems result; shamans have the ability to visit the world of the spirits; the world is six thousand years old; and on and on. If an ancient prankster had invented the story of a celestial race of beings that mated with primordial terrestrial beings resulting in the first humans, and then this prankster subsequently hijacked the power and authority of the state and used this influence to coerce or convince others of the veracity of his claims, it is likely that somewhere today some group would be worshiping and singing praises to this celestial race of beings. And everything we know about the course of human history suggests that they would fight and die in the name of these celestial beings. What is disturbing here is that this absurd notion would be no more or less falsifiable than any other religious claim or dogma.

Many of the general points being made here are illustrated nicely in the Roman Catholic notion of transubstantiation. According to this official dogma of the church, the communion wafer and wine that are offered up during the Mass actually become, *in substance*, the body and blood of Christ, hence the term "transubstantiation." The "accidents," the physical and tangible nature of bread and wine, remain but they are (putatively, of course) actually the body and blood of Christ, *in substance*. For the non-Catholics out there, let me point out that nothing at all actually happens to the bread and wine; they look, taste, feel, and smell exactly the same both before and after the priest performs the Eucharistic ritual. And, of course, that brings us to the crux of the issue: if nothing at all happens to the bread and wine, how is this dogma justified to reasonable folks with at least a general propensity for logic, reason, and empirical substantiation? Put another way, in the complete and utter absence of any empirical data whatsoever, how does the church explain or justify this dogma? Well, there are verses from the Bible, in John's Gospel, for example, that are cited and admittedly impressive theological writings on the ontological status of being and substance that defend the dogma. In the end, however (remember there is still the prickly issue of the absolute lack of empirical data), it comes down to . . . faith. Here is how the issue is dealt with on a popular Catholic website:

> The dogma of transubstantiation teaches that the whole substance of bread is changed into that of Christ's body, and the whole substance of wine into that of his blood, leaving the accidents of bread and wine unaffected. Reason, of course, can't prove that this happens. But it is not evidently against reason either; it is above reason. Our senses, being confined to phenomena, cannot detect the change; we know it only by faith in God's word.[15]

Where does one even begin here? So one is to accept the truth of this doctrine because it is "not evidently against reason"? By logical extension, doesn't this statement essentially infer that virtually any and every claim, no matter how outlandish or patently absurd, is in play? Of course it does, but, after all, this basic point was made earlier in regard to religious beliefs and dogmas in general. The writer of the statement then finally comes clean in the last sentence when he states that while it is true that we cannot detect the change through sense perception, we will, nevertheless, come to know it through faith. Once again, faith rescues yet another egregiously dubious claim from the potentially fatal challenge of reason, empirical data, and common sense.

Imagine that a scientist proposes a new theory of whatever (better yet, a Catholic scientist!) at an international gathering of physicists, and the "proof" he provides to substantiate his claim is precisely that noted above in support of the dogma of transubstantiation. This individual would be publicly excoriated on the spot and his career as a scientist, at least one that is taken seriously, would probably be over; for this reason, and, no doubt, others involving the application of basic principles of objectivity and sound empirical reasoning, this scientist would never propose such a thing. Nevertheless, it should be disturbing to most true believers that the very same theory, if considered dogma in a religious context, would be magically transformed into absolute truth. Religious claims have the "luxury" of claiming a nonempirical status that (conveniently) places them beyond the grasp of reason, logic, and data, whereas scientific claims do not. How ironic it is that a young-earth creationist scoffs at the mountain of empirical data offered in support of modern cosmology and evolutionary theory, yet at the same time readily accepts claims of talking snakes and virgin births without twitching even a little.

All the world's religions make vastly different claims and embrace a wide range of dogmas and doctrines, so, at least in regard to content, they appear to be very different. But, on a more significant, substantive, epistemological level, they are all the same: they are all built on a foundation of fantasies, fallacies, and falsehoods, all of which are stubbornly sustained by hope, optimism, and faith. This is precisely the reason why any group that seeks to establish its version of religion on a global scale (e.g., fundamentalist Muslims and Christians) will never be successful. Given the radically nonempirical and illogical nature of religious claims, beliefs, dogmas, and doctrines, they cannot survive in the absence of "buttressing" foundational contrivances—e.g., (presumed) sacred writings, a special history replete with miraculous figures and events, a hierarchy recognized as authoritative, etc. By the way, we can attribute the fact that only a tiny percentage of human beings actually abandon the faith they were born into for another to these foundational contrivances, aided by the inertia of a tradition that is never critiqued.

This line of discussion can lead us to ponder the issue of revelation and history. Virtually all of the important (putative) revelations from God or a god—Vyasa writing down the Vedas, Moses receiving the Torah, Allah speaking (through Gabriel) to Muhammad, Saul's Damascene epiphany, and many others—occurred well over a thousand years ago, or literally centuries before anything like scientific rationalism and objective, empirical research was recognized. One has to wonder whether such claims would be taken seriously if they were made today for the first time. For example, it is said that Muhammad would often go into a trance, shaking, sweating profusely, sometimes fainting, after which, of course, he would impart wisdom obtained straight from the Abrahamic God to his followers. Today, would we not simply declare him schizophrenic and be done with it? Or, wouldn't we, at least minimally, assume that he is suffering from some sort of psychosis and seek treatment for him? And what of claims of virgin births, demonic influences, angels, *jinn*, angry gods, and the like? It is only because such claims are driven by authority and tradition and clouded in the thick mist of eons that we bother with them at all. Here's how Christopher Hitchens sees it:

> Religion comes from the period of human prehistory where nobody—not even the mighty Democritus who concluded that all matter was made from atoms—had the smallest idea what was going on. It comes from the bawling and fearful infancy of our species, and is a babyish attempt to meet our inescapable demand for knowledge (as well as for comfort, reassurance, and other infantile needs). Today the least educated of my children knows much more about the natural order than any of the founders of religion.[16]

When religion is pared down to the bare essentials, when religion is stripped of the intimidating weight of tradition, authority, custom, and social sanction, there is virtually nothing left but an ideology that was created by ancient peoples who mistook epilepsy for demon possession.

I cannot leave this discussion of religion without addressing a reason-able question that has probably occurred to the reader at this juncture: Why, then, religion? Why haven't arguments such as those reviewed here had more of an impact on the religious landscape of our world, on the general propensity to be religious? As I stated earlier, intense indoctrination from an early age is, no doubt, mostly responsible for humankind's religious tendencies. The large majority of individuals, quite naturally and without much thought, simply assimilate the reli-gious ideology they are taught, as evidenced by the fact that the per-centages of individuals in a particular area affiliating with a specific religion remain virtually unchanged through time, and the fact that few individuals either give up the religion of their birth or convert to a different one; once an individual is christened/baptized/initi-ated into a particular religion they are, effectively, lifers. Remember, about the most reasonable thing that can be said regarding a specific religious ideology is that it is not falsifiable. For example, the believer will tell us that God watched over her today as she drove home and arrived at her destination safely. Or, if on her way home today the believer had gotten into an accident, she would attribute it to God's will. God's mercy (if good things happen) and God's justice (if bad things happen) can be used to explain any outcome of any event; which of these (if either) is at work at any point in time is anyone's guess. In the realm of nonfalsifiability where religion resides, every claim, no matter how absurd, can establish a permanent residence.

CHAPTER FOUR

SEXUAL ORIENTATION

The fallacies of religion and the faith-based epistemology having been addressed at some length, I will now turn to another aspect of sociocultural behavior that is also rife with myths, half-truths, assumptions, and irrationality—namely, sexual orientation. Again, the world in its natural state is much too complicated, intimidating, and overwhelming, so we respond to the challenge of materialism by carving out for ourselves a version of the world that we can deal with. Homosexuality is one of those natural aspects of our world that many individuals simply cannot accept. For example, 45 percent of Americans believe homosexuality is a sin, a number that jumps to 78 percent among white, evangelical Protestants.[1] By the way, religion is, not surprisingly, the most reliable predictor of homophobia.[2] Given the fictional, culture-bound, and contrived nature of religion, it should be clear, then, that homophobia, at least to the extent that it is generated by religiosity, cannot be justified or rationalized any more than religion can.

Perhaps the greatest American myth regarding homosexuality is the belief that one chooses to be gay or lesbian. Until just recently, this was the standard, mainstream belief in the United States. Of course, if one is working under the assumption that God has condemned homosexuality (which is, in turn, based on the assumption that the Bible is God's word, which is, in turn, based on . . . well, far too many other assumptions to pursue here), then the notion that one is "born that way" becomes untenable, since, surely, God "Himself" would be aware of that fact and would not relegate to perdition gays and lesbians who have no control over or responsibility for their sexual orientation. This is just the sort of reasoning that generated the fantasy of young-earth creationism; once one begins with a notion that is assumed to be absolutely true, inconvenient empirical facts have to be either ignored, reinterpreted, or derogated in some general way, but they cannot be accepted for what they actually are. Thus, while creationists go on and on about a Prime Mover, intelligent design, irreducible complexity, and other such things, the hominin fossil record, comprised of the remains of thousands of individuals dating back to around four and a half million years ago, all bipedal, showing a continuous development in cranial capacity, skeletal morphology, and culture, simply sits there implicitly and passively mocking attempts by faith-based fundamentalists to explain it away. I'll cut to the chase here: What the young-earth creationists are asking the rest of us to believe is this: thousands of experienced and highly trained and credentialed paleontologists are *completely* wrong about *everything*. It is a strong faith indeed that would lead a sane individual to embrace such nonsense.

It is just this sort of reasoning that engenders homophobia in otherwise ostensibly sane and reasonable folks. As is the case with young-earth creationism, there is a veritable ton of empirical data, not to mention simply good ol' common sense reasoning, that will make short shrift of, say, the notion that homosexuals choose their sexual orientation, one of the primary components of the homophobic mentality and a subject to which we will now turn.

First things first: The idea that one either learns/grows into/ chooses their sexual orientation or is born with such an orientation already present is a gross misstatement of the issue and reflects a basic misunderstanding of human nature. All of the data we have (much of it discussed below) point to the fact that, like many other human traits, this one is neither exclusively attributable to nature nor nurture although, in this case, it appears as though the former is the most influential. While some traits are Mendelian and, thus, manifest themselves directly in only a few forms based on genotype, many other traits, for example height and intelligence, are polygenic (produced by the alleles at many different chromosomal loci) and, thus, manifest themselves in many different forms. Not only that, but traits such as height and intelligence are greatly affected by environmental factors like nutrition and life experiences. Everything we currently know about sexual orientation points to the fact that we are dealing with a very complex trait that is almost certainly polygenic and is affected by environmental influences. In other words, it is a matter of both nature and nurture, again, with the former probably being the most significant.

A number of studies that have uncovered a genetic component to sexual orientation have been published, including Kendler et al.,[3] Långström et al.,[4] Witelson et al.,[5] Mustanski et al.,[6] and others. One of the most significant scientific studies published on this issue, however, was Richard Pillard and J. Michael Bailey's article in the journal *Human Biology*.[7] Their paper was essentially a summary of many other studies that had been done on the genetic component of sexual orientation. The data show that there is a marked and manifest tendency for a relatively high degree of concordance for the sexual orientation trait. Thus, for example, three different twin studies of males cited in the paper show that in dizygotic pairs 15 percent, 14 percent, and 22 percent respectively of gay males also had a gay twin. (By the way the "norm" or "baseline value" would be around 4–7 percent, the estimated range of the statistical prevalence of same-sex sexual orientation in our species. The genetic influence is, then, apparent from these figures.) In the same three studies of male twins, monozygotic pairs were also analyzed, and the values jumped to 100 percent, 60 percent, and 52 percent respectively. These numbers are just what one would expect, since monozygotic twins are genetically identical whereas dizygotic twins are no more genetically similar, on the average, than siblings. Other studies reviewed by Pillard and Bailey involving male (non-twin) siblings showed results similar to that of the dizygotic twins, precisely as one would predict if there were, in fact, some sort of genetic component at work. Pillard and Bailey's review of studies done on females, both twins and non-twin siblings, show similar results. Their estimate of the heritability of this trait for males is 0.31–0.74 and for females approximately 0.50. What this means is that, for example, in males, genetics is somewhere between 31 percent and 74 percent "responsible" for sexual orientation; the corresponding percentage range for environmental factors is, consequently, 26 percent to 69 percent.

Evolutionary theory tells us that those individuals who are siring more offspring than their species mates have a disproportionately higher probability of passing their DNA on to the next generation. In this way, some traits are "naturally selected" for and some "naturally selected" against. In fact, it is this process that gives us the simple and elegant definition of evolution as a change in allele (or gene) frequency through time. Now, we are all aware that homosexual individuals are not procreating at near the frequency of heterosexuals. (This does not mean, however, that gays and lesbians have no offspring. Pillard and Bailey note that homosexuals have about one-fifth as many offspring as heterosexuals.) So there is a problem here that needs to be addressed—namely, if this trait (same-sex sexual orientation) is clearly not conducive to biological reproduction, why then does it "hang around" in the gene pool? Why isn't it simply naturally selected out of existence?

There have been a few "solutions" to this problem that have been suggested (Pillard and Bailey discuss three in their paper), but I will discuss the one that I feel is probably the most robust and elegant, and it has to do with so-called resistance genes. In sub-Saharan West Africa, the advent of agriculture brought with it breeding areas for anopheline mosquitoes that were disease vectors for malaria, a condition that can be fatal, especially in underdeveloped areas. From time to time, a point mutation occurs in humans that causes the deleterious condition known as sickle-cell, a disease that negatively impacts both longevity and fecundity. Thus, like homosexuality and the putative homosexual gene(s) that influence its manifestation, here is another trait that should be gradually selected out of existence but, curiously, in sub-Saharan West Africa it was not. It has been determined that the healthiest individuals in malaria-infested areas of sub-Saharan West Africa are those individuals who are carriers (i.e., are genotypically heterozygous) of the sickle-cell condition. Individuals who are homozygous dominant (i.e., those who are not affected and are not carriers) are susceptible to malaria. Individuals who are homozygous recessive are affected, and, thus, susceptible to the complications of sickle-cell anemia. But the individual who only carries the trait (has one normal allele and one affected allele) actually possesses a built-in immunity to malaria. Over time, then, the individual that is most reproductively successful is the carrier, and the heterozygous genotype will eventually become the most prevalent, thus ensuring the continued presence of the affected allele. (This particular genotypic configuration is referred to as a "balanced polymorphism.")

What we have here, then, is an ostensibly deleterious trait (understood here as meaning not conducive to biological reproduction) that does, in fact, survive and flourish generation after generation. It has been suggested that, perhaps, other deleterious traits, like homosexuality, might "hang around" in the gene pool for similar reasons. Although we have no idea precisely what the advantage of carrying a homosexual gene (or genes) might be, we do know it is at least theoretically possible that, like the deleterious sickle-cell trait, it may confer upon its carrier some advantage over his or her species mates.

We have, then, the first reason why homosexuality is not a matter of choice, namely scientific studies of sexual orientation concordance rates that strongly suggest the presence of a genetic component. Let us now move on to another reason, in this case a biological factor referred to as gender atypicality. Gender atypicality is a condition that is characterized by the presence of female gender behavior in the male sex (such individuals are sometimes derisively referred to as "sissies") and masculine gender behavior in the female sex (often referred to as "tomboys"). (It is curious that the term "sissy" is wholly negative whereas "tomboy" is not and, in fact, can be a compliment given the context. Perhaps we see here yet another instance of the influence of patriarchy. There is something pristine and inviolate about the category "male" that cannot be manipulated: a man is a man period. The category of "female," on the other hand, is perceived as strictly utilitarian and can be "adjusted" or "manipulated" to suit cultural—read patriarchal—sensibilities.) Gender atypicality is noticeable in a child as young as two years old, and certainly by the time the child is around five or six years of age gender atypicality is overt and obvious. The data show that "a larger than expected percentage [of gender atypical individuals] will become gay and lesbian adults."[8] In other words, there is a relatively high positive correlation between the two variables gender atypicality and same-sex sexual orientation. It is not, mind you, a perfect positive correlation—i.e., there are gender atypical adults who are not gay or lesbian. Nevertheless, the tendency in this regard is significant and evident. Now, if gender atypical individuals have a higher tendency than the norm to be gay or lesbian and this condition is present in two- to five-year olds, then if one insists on the "homosexual by choice" hypothesis, one is required, by simple laws of logic and reason, to explain just how a three-year-old chooses to be gender atypical. This, of course, is nonsense, especially since youngsters do not even become aware of their own gender until they are well into their childhood years.[9]

Then there is the matter of universality. The historical and ethnographic data we have indicate that same-sex relations are ubiquitous in virtually all societies at virtually all times of recorded history. We could, I think, safely assume that this behavior was prevalent in prehistoric *Homo sapiens* and even earlier hominins as well, since it is found in primates, especially our closest genetic relative the bonobo chimpanzee. The ethnographic literature shows that many terms exist for third and fourth genders around the world, an accommodation often made to include homosexual as well as gender atypical individuals. The population ratio (calculated as a percentage) of homosexual/heterosexual in all the world's societies is somewhere in the range of 4–7 percent. The data we have for the United States show that this value has remained essentially unchanged since the earliest part of the twentieth century.[10]

Clearly the universality of this trait and the consistent rate at which it appears suggest that it is biologically inherent to our species. Let us, then, dispense with the unfounded and malicious notion that homosexuality is "unnatural." It is no more unnatural than red hair, a trait that occurs in approximately 1–2 percent of human beings. It is certainly not statistically prevalent, but that is hardly a good reason to infer the moral status of anything, much less a biological trait. It should also be noted that the frequency of homosexuality is much too high to be accounted for by mutation—it truly is a natural component of the human condition.

The universality of this trait also leads us to another interesting fact that can be used to refute the "homosexual by choice" hypothesis. One would think that a supposed optional behavior that is prohibited by penalty of death would not be very popular where so prohibited, but consider the fact that although, as was noted earlier, homosexuality is punishable by death in ten countries (all fundamentalist Islamic nations—this is not a coincidence), same-sex sexuality appears to be no more or no less prevalent in these nations than it is elsewhere. And, yes, individuals are executed in these countries for their homosexuality. Human rights activists claim that in Iran, for example, since 1979 more than four thousand people have been executed for crimes involving same-sex sexual behavior.[11] Certainly the reader can see where I am going with this. No sane individual would ever choose such a fate for themselves. For that matter, consider the United States in the 1930s and 1940s, where being gay or lesbian was widely reviled, condemned, and despised, and one could lose everything—family, church, career, etc.—if he or she were discovered to be homosexual. Nevertheless, as was noted above, the rate of homosexuality was roughly the same then as it is now.

In the face of such data and information, readily available to anyone, one wonders how any reasonable individual could actually believe that homosexuality is a matter of choice. But we should not overlook the power and intimidation of religion, for without religion as a backdrop this issue would be damned near inconsequential to virtually everyone. In fact, in the absence of religion, especially the big three Abrahamic faiths (Judaism, Christianity, and Islam), I would guess that we wouldn't much bother with homosexuality at all as a social issue.

If one examines this particular case of religious bigotry, it turns out that contrivance far outweighs substance. Consider, for example, the story of Sodom (Genesis 19), the one biblical myth that is probably more responsible for the enmity, mistreatment, and misunderstanding of gays and lesbians than any other. The authenticity and historicity of the story is dubious at best, given that it was written by an anonymous author approximately 1,400 years after the (alleged) event supposedly took place; we, of course, know nothing of the author's motivations, aspirations, biases, age, ethnicity, etc. Curiously, virtually the same story appears again in the book of Judges (chapter 19) with a few of the specific details changed, like the location and individuals' names, not an uncommon occurrence in the Bible; it is clear that one of these stories serves as a template for the other. This does not, to say the least, lend credence to the claim that the story is historical.

In addition to the very serious problems regarding the historicity of the story of the destruction of Sodom, there is the question of meaning and interpretation. Christians typically assume that the story shows God's displeasure with the "sin" of homosexuality. In my mind, that interpretation is facile at best and almost certainly incorrect. The citizens of Sodom gather at Lot's front door and demand that Lot send out his two male visitors so that they may "know them." The unruly crowd clearly seeks to violently gang rape the two men. A couple of points here. First, gay males are always far outnumbered by their straight counterparts. What kind of strange city is this where virtually all the male inhabitants are gay? Second, gang rape has long been used to humiliate one's foes and would not be something that gay males would ordinarily be party to; it certainly has nothing to do with two consenting adults willfully engaging one another sexually. Third, nowhere in the biblical account does God actually say anything at all about homosexuality and Sodom, and that goes for the human author as well. And, finally, for those who are still hanging onto the fundamentalist interpretation of the story of Sodom, especially those fundamentalists who believe that the Bible is the inerrant, literal word of God, here is what Ezekiel 16:49 says: "This was the guilt of your sister Sodom: she and her daughters had pride, excess of food, and prosperous ease, but did not aid the poor and needy." By the way, many Bible scholars (like Ezekiel) do not accept the homosexual interpretation of the story either. I think we can now dispense with this baseless and clearly mistaken fundamentalist interpretation of the story of Sodom. I guess I should also point out that Jesus, at least to the extent that the Gospels are actually a record of what he said, never addressed the issue of homosexuality. And homosexuality did not even make God's top-ten list.

There is another important aspect of the issue that I should address here and that is the question of whether or not the Bible says anything at all regarding same-sex sexuality involving women. There are actually only a handful of passages in the Bible that address the issue of same-sex sexuality: the Sodom account discussed above, virtually the same story told again set in a different time and place in Judges 19, and also in Leviticus 18:22 and 20:13, 1 Corinthians 6:9–10, and Romans 1:26–27. Of these, it is only in the latter passage where we find any sort of reference whatsoever to women in a context that one might argue pertains to homosexuality: "Their women exchanged natural intercourse for unnatural, and in the same way also the men, giving up natural intercourse with women, were consumed with passion for one another." I do not believe that this lone passage is a condemnation of lesbianism for the following reasons: 1) if it was specific women-with-women sexual behavior that was meant here, the writer could have quite simply said it outright since, after all, sexual behavior regarding men with men is explicitly mentioned in this very passage; 2) since the foundation of Christianity is Judaism and the Tanakh and lesbianism is mentioned nowhere in the Tanakh, and Jesus uttered not a single word on the topic, the sudden intrusion of homophobia directed at same-sex sexual behavior involving women seems incongruous (the point being, of course, that that is not what is meant here); 3) Augustine of Hippo, in his treatise *Marriage and Desire*, writes the following: "But if one has relations even with one's wife in a part of the body which was not made for begetting children, such relations are against nature and indecent. In fact, the same apostle earlier said the same thing about women, 'For their women exchanged natural relations for those which are against nature'";[12] one of the preeminent "Doctors of the Church," then, does not read this passage as referring to lesbianism; and 4) the passage in question goes on to refer to individuals engaging in such acts as "slanderers," "God-haters," "gossips," and "inventors of evil"; Paul hardly seems to be describing individuals in the twenty-first century engaged in loving, consensual, same-sex relationships, and, thus, certainly not women so engaged. For these reasons, I feel that the statement "the Bible says homosexuality is a sin" is patently disingenuous hyperbole since lesbianism is, in fact, not mentioned in the Bible. So, in a strict literal sense, the Bible says no such thing.

One of the strongest condemnations of male homosexuality is found in Leviticus 20:13: "If a man lies with a male as with a woman, both of them have committed an abomination; they shall be put to death; their blood is upon them." But we also find the following bits of "divine wisdom" in the Hebrew scriptures as well: 1) if a man rapes a young woman, he can keep her if he pays her father fifty pieces of silver (Deuteronomy 22:28–29); 2) slavery is explicitly condoned as witnessed by the many verses that instruct slavers on the fine points of human bondage (see Leviticus 25:44–46, Exodus 21:7–11, Deuteronomy 15:12–15, and other passages); 3) a child that dabbles in other religions is to be killed by his parents (Deuteronomy 13:6–11); 4) adulterers are to be put to death (Leviticus 20:10); and 5) anyone working on the Sabbath is to be put to death (Exodus 31:12–15). God also forbids the consumption of shellfish (Leviticus 11:9–11), wearing clothes made of two different materials (Leviticus 19:19), and, according to the most popular interpretations, eating meat and dairy products together (Exodus 23:19). God also tells us that if an individual touches a chair upon which a menstruating woman has sat, then he or she will be unclean, just as the menstruating woman is unclean (Leviticus 15:22). We are also directed by God to kill those who practice other religions (Deuteronomy 17:2–5).

Well, I could go on and on, as I have barely scratched the surface here, but these few passages should suffice. Clearly, the individual who reaches down into this cornucopia of riches known as the Christian Bible and picks out only one or two passages to build an argument around is being, *ahem*, selective. Can't we safely assume that Leviticus 20:13 (the fundamentalist homophobes' favorite verse) is just as nonsensical and abhorrent as the other passages noted above and should be ignored the way fundamentalists ignore most of the other divine laws and commandments in the Bible? (There are actually 613 *mitzvot* ["commandments"] in the Hebrew scriptures.) By the way, those fundamentalists who argue that the Old Testament has been replaced by a "new covenant" (the New Testament) or that the Old Testament is "Jewish" and not binding on Christians, might want to read what Jesus says in Matthew 5:17–19 about the Law (the "Torah" or the Pentateuch, the first five books of the Bible), especially verse 19, where he says, "Therefore, whoever breaks one of the least of these commandments, and teaches others to do the same, will be called least in the kingdom of heaven." Jesus was, after all, Jewish, and his scriptures were the Hebrew scriptures. One last point here: Those fundamentalists who wear a cotton-polyester-blend shirt, who don't kill their children for dabbling in other religions, who enjoy shrimp or lobster on occasion, and who are not actively working for a law that makes adultery a capital offense punishable by death by stoning, should stop telling the rest of us that they believe the Bible is the inerrant, literal word of God because their actions show that they, in fact, do not so believe, and should cease and desist using the Bible to demonize gays and lesbians.

Clearly, few individuals with any knowledge of what is actually written in the Bible really believe that it is the literal, inerrant word of God, although virtually all fundamentalists and evangelical Christians claim they do believe this. Only a flagrant ignorance of that ancient piece of literature could possess an individual to profess such a thing. Christians, like the adherents of other religions, are woefully under- and uninformed regarding the basic historical details of their faith. I have been teaching courses in religious studies on the college level for about twenty years now, and I am amazed at how little my Christian students know about Christianity. I can hardly remember the last time I have had a student who could state how the Bible was codified, when the Gospels were written, who the Gnostics, the Essenes, Eusebius, and Marcius were, etc., etc. And, as far as the Old Testament goes, I might as well be talking about Joyce's *Finnegan's Wake.* Sadly, however, many of them have embraced young-earth creationism, homophobia, misogyny, and other such nonsense, bequeathed to them from an older generation that is not any more informed about these things than they are.

This, then, is the sum total of contributing factors that has led to the untold suffering of homosexuals even still in today's world. Every Christian preacher who has ever spewed antigay vitriol from the pulpit has, at least in some small way, incited others to discriminate against or to attack and kill gays and lesbians. In fact, some homophobes are so blinded by their hate that they actually attack heterosexuals by mistake.[13] I can't leave this without a special "shout out" to Karl Rove and the Republican smear machine that put the gay marriage issue on the ballot in eleven states during the presidential election of 2004. It was a clever move, however, as homophobes (the large majority being conservative and Republican, two other significant predictors of homophobia[14]) turned out in droves to vote for George Bush. Now, however, some twenty years later, at least a few brave souls in the Republican Party are awkwardly attempting to make their peace with gay marriage as it is now the law of the land and a majority of the American public supports it.[15]

CHAPTER FIVE

RACE AND RACISM

The a priori, obsessively deductive mentality that gave us the myths, beliefs, and fantasies upon which religious and sexual orientation ideologies are based, are also at work in other areas as well—for example, in the myths, beliefs, and fantasies regarding race. Again, the common mainstream understanding of the relationship between human biology and human behavior is, at best, erroneous and, at worst, intentionally malicious. For example, the term "race" is still used by virtually everyone today, even though anthropologists, biologists, and geneticists have long since abandoned the term, since it is not an empirical, scientifically valid concept.

A few centuries ago, Carolus Linnaeus gave us one of the first racial classifications based on that most salient of human phenotypes, skin color.[1] Linnaeus determined that there were four basic groups or races: black (Africans), red (Native Americans), yellow (Asians), and white (Europeans). This scheme, I would suppose, was (minimally) workable during the time of Linnaeus since not much was known about the world at that time. Today, however, we know that skin color is a polygenic trait that is influenced by an adaptation to the intensity of sunlight. As it turns out, the human body needs a certain amount of vitamin D, a nutrient that needs ultraviolet rays for its production. Of course, electromagnetic radiation of this sort can be lethal if it is not controlled, and that is precisely what the melanin in our skin does. The end result, then, is a trait that is so variable as to be virtually continuous. Thus, any sort of grouping based on this trait would have to be done arbitrarily and would reveal little more than the predilection or bias of the individual who is doing the grouping and, perhaps, the geographical location relative to the equator of those being grouped. Nevertheless, skin color is still the most popular phenotypic trait used today to separate humankind into "races." This has everything to do with opportunity and nothing to do with biology, since the only reason why this trait has ever been used in this way is because it is by far the most salient. I hardly think, however, that saliency or convenience is a valid criterion upon which any sort of classification scheme of humankind should be constructed.

One might infer at this point that perhaps more phenotypic traits could be used to construct a typology of the worlds' peoples. It seems like a reasonable strategy but ultimately will lead us nowhere. There are roughly 20,500 different genes in the human genome[2] and, thus, thousands of phenotypic traits we could utilize. Unfortunately, while it is true that any sort of "scientific" classification should not arbitrarily pick and choose among the variety of phenotypic traits that exist, not doing so will only further confuse the issue, since phenotypic traits (blood groups, skin color, hair texture, body shape, stature, nasal morphology, etc., and thousands of biochemical traits) are geographically distributed in an independent fashion (i.e., the distribution frequency of one trait has no relation to the distribution frequency of another trait). What this means is that there is no "clustering" of phenotypic traits such that would allow grouping of any kind—thus, human races do not exist.

Consider, for example, the European/Central Asian landmass. Here, the frequency of the B blood allele is clinally distributed along an axis that runs from east to west. (In the case of a clinal distribution, the frequency of a trait increases or decreases gradually in an incremental fashion, much like temperatures on a weather map. Since the probability that an individual will mate with a particular person drops off gradually as a function of distance, this is just the sort of pattern that one would expect to find.) Skin color in this region, however, is clinally distributed along an axis that runs from south to north. Thus, any attempt to construct a racial classification scheme based only on these two traits (never mind the thousands that actually exist) will fail. That is not to say that the concept of race is necessarily invalid, however. There are, in fact, races of birds,[3] and at some point in human evolution, perhaps around 40,000 BCE or roughly 20,000 years after the first *Homo sapiens* left Africa, I suppose there may have been trait clustering to some degree, but that is certainly no longer the case. Race is simply not a viable biological concept when applied to humankind.

What, then, about racism? This fictive ideology actually rests on two incorrect assumptions: one, that races actually exist and, two, that race (or, more correctly, phenotype) and cultural behavior are causally related. The first assumption was summarily dispatched above. The second has been falsified on a number of occasions by social scientists (and should be obvious to anyone paying attention), yet it is still widely embraced by the general population as evidenced by the cases of blatant racial discrimination that still occur. FBI statistics show that the most common hate crime is based on racial bias, the large majority of it being accounted for by "victims of an offender's anti-black bias."[4]

There is also the rather curious "crime" referred to as "driving while black." Driving while black is not, of course, a crime, but it might just as well be in some areas of the country, including Maryland and New Jersey. Some really fine detective work by John Lamberth, a statistician, initially uncovered the tawdry mess in New Jersey.[5] He found that while African Americans, who comprised approximately 13.5 percent of the drivers on one stretch of interstate, were not breaking traffic laws any more or less than other groups, they nevertheless comprised 35 percent of those pulled over by state troopers. In Maryland, Lamberth's investigation on I-95 north of Baltimore discovered that, while 17.5 percent of the traffic violators were African American, they comprised 28.8 percent of those stopped and 71.3 percent of those searched by state troopers. Clearly these numbers reveal an appalling disproportionality that reflects an explicit racial bias on the part of the state troopers patrolling these areas. As it turned out, police were trained to target African Americans, as it was assumed that they would be guilty of some crime, especially drug crimes, far more often than other drivers. Unfortunately, this strategy was based on yet another assumption that is simply not true. A report published by the National Institute for Drug Abuse shows that African Americans use illegal drugs at a rate that is about the same as that found in whites (approximately 6 percent of the population of each group).[6] Marc Mauer, a criminologist and the executive director of the Sentencing Project, raises the value a bit to 6.4 percent but reports basically the same thing.[7] Speaking of cultural myths, I am sure that most of my readers would be surprised to hear that approximately 75 percent of those abusing illegal drugs in this country are white.[8] The blatant racial bias becomes evident when one peruses the statistics for state prison inmates incarcerated for drug offenses in 1995: 86,100 were white and 134,000 were black.[9]

Devah Pager, a sociologist, sent whites and blacks to job interviews in an attempt to uncover racial bias.[10] All of the interviewees were dressed similarly and all carried similar résumés. Also, the whites and blacks were each divided into two groups, those with criminal records and those without criminal records. (None of the participants actually had a criminal record.) The results were shocking. The group that received the highest percentage of "call-backs" was whites without a criminal record, this in itself a reflection of racial bias as the percentage of whites without a criminal record called back (34 percent) was more than twice the percentage of blacks without a criminal record who were called back (14 percent). But, wait, it gets worse. Whites *with* a criminal record were more likely than blacks *without* a criminal record to receive a call-back (17 percent vs. 14 percent). This is downright disturbing, as far as I am concerned. Oh yeah, I forgot to mention that this survey was conducted in Wisconsin . . . Wisconsin! I live in Louisiana, and I can't imagine what the results of a similar study would show in my home state, where an avowed racist and explicit race-monger who was also a former Neo-Nazi and member of the Ku Klux Klan, David Duke, received 55 percent of the white vote in the 1991 race for governor.[11] (Fortunately, he lost the election to Edwin Edwards, God bless him.) But, hey, what do you expect from a state that was the last to ban cockfighting and where state legislators passed a bill that allows Genesis-based creationism to be taught side by side with real science in the classroom? It's a package deal.

Linda Mooney and her colleagues write, "Before the 1968 Federal Fair Housing Act and the 1974 Equal Credit Opportunity Act, discrimination against minorities in housing and mortgage lending was as rampant as it was blatant."[12] Margery Austin Turner and other members of the Urban Institute reported that, in their study of the housing market in twenty-three different metropolitan areas, whites were more likely than blacks (and Hispanics) to receive information and to be allowed to inspect homes.[13]

Many more studies such as these could be cited, but they all simply point to one, undeniable, very sad fact about the United States: discrimination against African Americans, while certainly not as egregious as it was in the 1930s, when gangs of Southern white bigots could torture and murder a black man publicly and with complete impunity, nevertheless, still occurs. Excluding the time when I have been out of the country studying the worshipers of this or that religion, I have lived almost exclusively in the South. If most white Southern families are like my own, and I have no reason to think they are not, then there are a number of white folks who do not accept interracial marriage and will not vote for a black candidate for political office. And there is, no doubt, not a small number that still use the most blatantly racist, anti-black epithet (the "N-word") in casual conversation.

Clearly, then, the myth of racism is still alive and well. This artificial and contrived ideology is rather like the one constructed to provide succor to those who cannot deal with the reality of homosexuality: it can be completely and summarily deconstructed with empirical data. Not only that, these data are very accessible. One wonders how many times an assumed "theory" (like the notion that visible phenotype determines cultural behavior, for example) has to be disconfirmed before it is finally abandoned. Evidently the number is practically unattainable because such disconfirmation happens all the time. Every phenotypically East Asian person living in the United States who speaks American English, consumes an American diet, and waves an American flag at the Olympics, is a living and breathing contradiction of the myth of racism; ditto for those with an "African," "Scandinavian," or "Indian" phenotype. The clear fact of the matter is that no individual is born preadapted to speak a certain language or crave a certain diet. It was just this sort of observation that motivated me, at the age of ten or so, to question the racist ideology that was a natural part of the cultural landscape in Louisiana. I've often thought that if even a ten-year-old child can see this, perhaps the problem lies elsewhere. Perhaps what is causing so much confusion is stereotypes. After all, there is a bit of truth to many stereotypes, otherwise many stand-up comedians would be out of a job. But, while it is true that some stereotypical assumptions are somewhat valid, they are not valid in a way that would lend credence to a racist ideology. The fact of the matter is that there is nothing at all mysterious about an X or a Y who acts like other Xs or Ys. In fact, it would be surprising if they didn't since cultural behavior is, after all, learned (not inherited).

The Southern Poverty Law Center reports fifty active white supremacist groups in Texas and seventy in California, as of 2013; in fact, the number of such groups in about half of all states in the United States is in the double digits. Many of these groups—for example, the Christian Identity Movement, Neo-Nazis, the Ku Klux Klan, and White Nationalists—embrace fictive ideologies that are so ridiculous as to be downright incoherent. For example, Christian Identity folks believe that Christians, not Jews, are the "chosen people" of God, that nonwhites are "mud people," and that Jews are biological descendants of Satan.[14] It must take quite a struggle to hold onto "theories" that have been unequivocally disconfirmed by biologists, anthropologists, and geneticists. But, on the other hand, that has never seemed to bother young-earth creationists either, so I guess we shouldn't be too surprised. Many of these groups single out Jews for "special treatment," and this brings us to what has been referred to as the "longest hatred,"[15] anti-Semitism.

CHAPTER SIX

ANTI-SEMITISM

T his peculiar form of bigotry is especially preposterous given that in this case we aren't even talking about a "race," even in the way this term is generally (mis-)understood; there is no Jewish race. What we do have is a motley conglomeration of people who hardly share anything at all save for a Jewish "heritage," and even that is difficult to pin down. Thus, we have Jews by ethnicity, Jews by religion, and Jews by marriage or conversion, and these categories do not necessarily overlap—e.g., many ethnic Jews are not "observant" (do not practice Judaism). Further complicating the issue is the fact that some Jews (for example, Orthodox Israelis) are far less inclusive than, say, Reform American Jews. Recent Y-chromosomal genetic studies have shown, however, that approximately one-quarter of all Jews, regardless of location, share a common patrilineal descent that links them to the Middle East.[1] All Jews, however, share a blood-stained history marked by 2,700 years of forced migrations and exiles, discrimination, and pogroms, culminating, if you will, in the Holocaust.

The term "Jew" clearly has its origins in the Hebrew term *Yehuda*, or Judah, the name of one of Jacob's (grandson of Abraham) sons and, thus, the name of one of the twelve tribes of Israel. According to the Tanakh, the historicity of which is highly questionable the further back in time we venture, Abraham was called out of Ur (southern Iraq), traveled to Harran (present-day Syria), and finally migrated to the area of present-day Israel. His grandson's generation (Jacob and his siblings) journeyed to Egypt, where they were to spend 430 or so years. At this point, we really have no idea who we are dealing with other than some kind of generic Middle Eastern collection of ethnicities and cultural traditions.

Later, according to the Tanakh, Moses leads the "Israelites" out of Egypt back to the "promised land" (Canaan, roughly present-day Israel and the surrounding area) where, around 1290 BCE or so, Joshua leads the Israelites over the Jordan River and into Canaan. (It should be noted that there is virtually no archaeological evidence that anything like the "Exodus" ever occurred.[2]) What follows, at that point, at least according to the biblical narrative, is sheer horror for the native inhabitants of Canaan, as the Israelites, at their God's command, slaughter every living thing in one city after another (Joshua 10:28–41). The Canaanite's big "crime"? They were not Israelites but instead the dreaded "other" that has been subjected to slavery, subjugation, and slaughter for ages. What we have here is an invasion and genocide, pure and simple. To continue with the story, the Israelites settled in this land and would actually be present in significant numbers until the diaspora around 70 CE when the second temple was destroyed by the Romans. The last significant Jewish insurrection, the Bar Kokhba revolt that ended around 135 CE, was unsuccessful, and the Jewish presence in the Middle East was effectively nil from that point up until the twentieth century, with the founding of the city of Tel Aviv around 1909 and, of course, the nation of Israel in 1948.

Frankly, the somewhat tenuous genetic link to the Middle East noted above notwithstanding, I have always viewed Jewish claims on this area vis-à-vis Palestinian claims as somewhat specious. For one thing, let us not forget that we are dealing with holy scriptures, a form of literature (from any religious tradition) with a notoriously unreliable historicity. But, even if we use the Tanakh as our guide (and many Israelis do), the people who would later become known as the Jews "drifted through" Canaan during the three generations of Abraham, Isaac, and Jacob and later inhabited the land (wrested away from the native peoples of the area in a bloody, genocidal conquest) for about 1,400 years until they were dispersed in the second century CE. They were then essentially absent from the area for almost two millennia. Any native inhabitants, such as that can actually be established, whether or not that would be "Palestinians," would certainly have a more legitimate claim on the land. Nevertheless, this issue is no longer relevant today, as Israel and its 8.2 million citizens are there and their neighbors simply have to get used to it. Talk of "wiping Israel off the map" and driving Israelis into the Mediterranean Sea is little more than bombastic drivel. It's not going to happen, and Israel's neighbors need to come to grips with that reality. For one, the Israelis are far, far superior militarily than virtually all of their neighbors combined, plus they have the strong support of the United States and all the resources that brings to the table. Also, during the better part of the last three millennia, the Jews have suffered horribly at the hands of others and now, for the first time, they truly control their destiny, a control they will not relinquish to anyone.

The Jews suffered at the hands of the Assyrians and Babylonians and at the hands of the Romans before and after the time of Christ, but it would be Christianity with its strong anti-Jewish tone that would set the stage for 1,700 years of brutal persecution, discrimination, slaughter, and genocide:

> No other religion, indeed, makes the accusation that Christianity has made against the Jews, that they are literally the *murderers* of God. No other religion has so consistently attributed to them a universal, cosmic quality of evil, depicting them as children of the Devil, followers of the Antichrist or as the "synagogue of Satan." The fantasies concerning Jews that were developed in medieval Christendom, about their plotting to destroy Christianity, poison wells, desecrate the host, massacre Christian children or establish their world dominion, represent a qualitative leap compared with anything put forward by their pagan precursors. Such charges, beginning with deicide, are peculiarly *Christian*.[3]

This vehement anti-Jewish sentiment may seem odd given the fact that Jesus and all of his disciples were Jewish and that Jesus quoted the "Law" (Torah) on a number of occasions. It is not my intention to review the history of anti-Semitism here, as this has been done by other scholars, but I feel that a few comments are in order before we move on.

Perhaps the most damaging scripture in this regard is found in Matthew 27:25, where the writer of Matthew has the Jewish mob say, after Pontius Pilate has washed his hands of the matter of Jesus's guilt or innocence, "His blood be on us and on our children!" Also in this passage (Matthew 27:15–21) it is noted that a prisoner (Barabbas) was set free as per a Passover custom. As far as I am concerned, the entire episode looks contrived for a number of reasons. First, a "crowd," as if on cue, responds to Pilate's proclamation of innocence by saying "His blood be on us and upon our children" in once voice, all at the same time. This leaves us with only three options: 1) the crowd had rehearsed their line beforehand, 2) they were reading from a prepared text, or 3) the incident was fabricated in order to make a point regarding the guilt of the Jews (i.e., it was propaganda pure and simple). Clearly, option three gives us the only reasonable explanation. Second, are modern readers supposed to believe that the Romans are going to set free an insurrectionist Jew (Barabbas) who had been condemned to death? Third, crucifixion was a Roman punishment meted out by Romans; it is curious how the blame seems to be totally shifted to the Jews. And, fourth, while there is certainly a lot more that could be said about this issue, I will conclude this discussion by stating that the one element that holds the entire crucifixion story together is the "Passover custom" whereby the Romans release one prisoner of the Jews' choice. The contention that the entire episode is contrived and is either partly or wholly fictional is bolstered by the fact that no such custom exists.[4] Many other anti-Jewish passages can be found in the Gospels of Luke and John and in the book of Acts as well.

It seems odd that what was initially a "Jesus cult" of Jews gradually morphed into a blatantly anti-Jewish religion. We need to remember, however, that Jesus had come and gone long before Paul began to write his letters (about twenty years; he never actually met Jesus), long before the Gospel of Mark was written (about forty years), the Gospel of John was written (about seventy years), and the Bible was codified (about 370 years). It is certainly plausible that Jesus and his teachings were wrested away from those with Jewish interests by others who had a different agenda. In fact, according to Barrie Wilson, philosopher of religion at York University, this is precisely what happened when the "Jesus movement," led by James, brother of Jesus, no less, was politically overwhelmed by the "Christ movement," led by Paul.[5] Frankly, this hypothesis explains so much that seems peculiar, contradictory, and outright mistaken in the "orthodox" version of the story.

Well, for whatever reason, it was the "Christ movement," what Bart Ehrman refers to as "proto-Orthodox Christianity,"[6] that won the day, and it is their version of the story (recorded, as was noted earlier, diligently by Eusebius, the official church historian for many, many centuries before it was discovered that he was far from impartial) that has come down to us today. Fortunately, scholars like Ehrman, Wilson, and others are, for the first time in history, giving us a much less "Christianized" (i.e., propagandized) version of what actually happened some two thousand years ago. It is a damned shame that perhaps the most virulent anti-Jewish Christian group carried the day and not, say, the Ebionites (Jews who accepted Jesus as the Jewish messiah) or even the Gnostics (a diverse collection of religio-philosophical groups who emphasized knowledge over works and viewed the material universe and its imperfect creator, the Demiurge, as evil)—both, of course, deemed heretical by proto-Orthodox Christianity. Clearly, an Ebionite or Gnostic Christianity would not have given us almost two thousand years of mistreatment and the indiscriminate slaughter of individuals of Jewish descent. Sadly, the same cannot be said of orthodox Christianity. (In case the reader is wondering about Islam, let me state that Muslim anti-Semitism, while certainly no less repugnant, is a relatively recent phenomenon and is itself rooted in Christian ideology.)

When one reads of the things written about and done to Jews, it is hard to believe that ostensibly sane individuals are capable of such stupidity and cruelty. John Chrysostom, recognized as a saint and a Doctor of the Church by the Roman Catholic Church, writing at about 390 CE, had this to say: "the synagogue is not only a whorehouse and a theater; it is also a den of thieves. . . . The demons inhabit the very souls of the Jews, as well as the places where they gather."[7] Here is Hippolytus, now recognized as a saint, writing in the third century CE, branding the Jews as Christ-killers, a charge that would be repeated ad nauseam until the present day:

> Why was the temple made desolate? Was it on account of the ancient fabrication of the calf? Or was it on account of the idolatry of the people? Was it for the blood of the prophets? Was it for the adultery and fornication of Israel? By no means, for in all these transgressions they always found pardon open to them. But it was because they killed the Son of their Benefactor, for He is coeternal with the Father.[8]

Did Hippolytus not foresee that this dubious claim would provide the motivation for the maltreatment, hatred, and killing of hundreds of thousands of Jews throughout the ages? Every time the "Christ killer" claim is repeated in passion plays or movies, it encourages the coarsest and most ignorant among us to strike out against the Jews. In my mind, this notion that Jews as a people should be held responsible for something one small group (allegedly) did two thousand years ago is ridiculous. The Catholic Church finally recanted this ancient slander during Vatican II in the early 1960s. After almost two thousand years of horrible abuse by the church and other Christians, I suppose the church should get some credit for this apology, but nothing the church says or does today can erase the centuries of unconscionable suffering visited on innocent Jews by Christendom.

Martin Luther, the original Protestant and the eponymous founder of the Lutheran Church, was one of the most vicious anti-Semites that ever lived. Here are just a few selections from his treatise *On the Jews and Their Lies*, published in 1543:[9]

- Therefore be on your guard against the Jews, knowing that wherever they have their synagogues, nothing is found but a den of devils in which sheer self-glory, conceit, lies, blasphemy, and defaming of God and men are practiced most maliciously and veheming his eyes on them.

- Moreover, they are nothing but thieves and robbers who daily eat no morsel and wear no thread of clothing which they have not stolen and pilfered from us by means of their accursed usury. Thus they live from day to day, together with wife and child, by theft and robbery, as arch-thieves and robbers, in the most impenitent security.

- Alas, it cannot be anything but the terrible wrath of God which permits anyone to sink into such abysmal, devilish, hellish, insane baseness, envy, and arrogance. If I were to avenge myself on the devil himself I should be unable to wish him such evil and misfortune as God's wrath inflicts on the Jews, compelling them to lie and to blaspheme so monstrously, in violation of their own conscience.

- They remain our daily murderers and bloodthirsty foes in their hearts. Their prayers and curses furnish evidence of that, as do the many stories which relate their torturing of children and all sorts of crimes for which they have often been burned at the stake or banished.

In part eleven of Luther's screed, he lays out his own version of the "final solution":[10]

- What shall we Christians do with this rejected and condemned people, the Jews? . . . I shall give you my sincere advice:

  First, to set fire to their synagogues or schools and to bury and cover with dirt whatever will not burn. . . .

  Second, I advise that their houses also be razed and destroyed. . . .

  Third, I advise that all their prayer books and Talmudic writings, in which such idolatry, lies, cursing, and blasphemy are taught, be taken from them. . . .

  Fourth, I advise that their rabbis be forbidden to teach henceforth on pain and loss of life. . . .

  Fifth, I advise that safe-conduct on the highways be abolished completely for the Jews. . . ."

One shudders to think how many innocent, decent Jewish folks were ostracized, tormented, beaten, and murdered by "good Christians" inspired by Luther and his hatemongering rhetoric. The fact that there is still a Christian denomination that bears his name is disgraceful. If this was the sort of rubbish running through the minds of even the "great," learned Christian leaders of the day, can one just imagine what the peasants in the countryside were thinking?

Anti-Semitism, like all the other fictional ideologies addressed in this book, is impervious to reason, logic, and data. How else are we to understand the popularity of the "blood libel" in the Middle Ages, the ludicrous belief that Jews kidnap Christian (or Muslim) children, torture and murder them, and use their blood to make *matzah*, the ceremonial bread consumed during Passover? How else are we to understand the continued acceptance of *The Protocols of the Elders of Zion* as a valid historical document even though it has been common knowledge for decades that the pamphlet is an obvious forgery? And what of the totally unfounded and never substantiated claims that Jewish cabals control world banking and commerce? And the embarrassingly popular lie that no Jews died in the World Trade Center attacks of 2001 that is so completely impervious to refutation by empirical data that casualty lists naming hundreds of individuals of Jewish descent make no impression whatsoever?

In my mind, anti-Semitism is arguably the most repugnant fantasy of the whole sordid lot for two reasons. First, at least in the cases of religious absolutism, homophobia, and racism, individuals have at least some knowledge of the subject in question, albeit a knowledge that is far from complete and largely mistaken. But, if one wants to truly understand anti-Semitism, he must "venture" all the way back to early Christendom when this pernicious bigotry first began to take shape and follow the story over the next 1,900 or so years. The chances that your average anti-Semite will actually engage in such a study is just about equivalent to the chances that a young-earth creationist will actually read a physical anthropology textbook. Anyway, let us not forget that the "obsessively deductive" mentality does not want to be challenged, especially not with data or sound reasoning, for they already have the "truth" and the bliss (of ignorance) that comes with it. Second, this particular fantasy has arguably caused more pain, distress, misery, bloodletting, and death than all the other fantasies combined, although there is some overlap here since anti-Semitism is religiously and racially motivated.

The degree to which individuals want to be separate from and protected against the reality of the world in which they live is aptly illustrated by the willingness on the part of many individuals to embrace ideas and claims that are baseless and demonstrably mistaken. When I was much younger, I began fighting the charade that was my own conception of reality—force fed to me by my cultural "handlers"—until, as an adult, I finally prevailed. There is nothing easy about this, as one has to actually play an active role in the formation of their worldview but, by doing so, one will finally gain for himself or herself at least a small amount of autonomy and dignity that, heretofore, had been sacrificed on the altar of ignorance, ethnocentrism, and culturalism.

PART TWO

THE DELUSION OF YOUNG-EARTH CREATIONISM

CHAPTER SEVEN

THE FAITH-BASED EPISTEMOLOGY

On June 26, 2008, Louisiana became the first state in the Union to pass a law that questions the teaching of the theory of evolution. (Mississippi passed a similarly worded law a few years later.) According to the wording of this law, the so-called "Louisiana Science Education Act" will "assist teachers, principals, and other school administrators to create and foster an environment within public elementary and secondary schools that promotes critical thinking skills, logical analysis, and open and objective discussion of scientific theories." The law specifically mentions evolution and global warming and states that teachers will be able to use "supplemental textbooks and other instructional materials" in the classroom. In this context, "supplemental" materials should be understood to refer to creationist literature, not articles pulled out of legitimate scientific journals or Darwin's *Origin of Species*. That the law is essentially a stealth attack on mainstream science can hardly be denied, since it was backed by a number of religious organizations such as the Louisiana Family Forum (a Christian conservative group that seeks to "persuasively present biblical principles in the centers of influence on issues affecting the family through research, communication and networking"[1]) and the Discovery Institute, a creationist "think tank" in Seattle. According to the folks at *Ars Technica*, the Discovery Institute assisted in the writing of the law and is pushing its own antievolution, anti-mainstream-science textbook for use in science classrooms of Louisiana.

There are a number of things that are disturbing about this. First, our highly educated governor at the time, Bobby Jindal, who graduated from Brown University with honors in biology, is a seasoned political panderer who knows where his votes come from. He knows that this law has nothing to do with science, but, like any good politician, he will do virtually anything to make his constituency (religious fundamentalists and Tea Party Republicans) happy, so he signed it into law. Louisiana was already near the bottom in virtually every category that has anything to do with public education. Opening the door for creationism and science based on "biblical principles" (i.e., presumptive deductivism and a total disregard for empirical data) in our public school classrooms has done nothing to improve students' understanding of science. Second, I am afraid that our children will get the impression that state legislatures and lawmaking have something to do with science, but, fortunately, real science is not a democracy where any and every idea is considered to be a valid alternative. Third, our children will now be subjected to religious ideology even in their classrooms. Before this unfortunate law was passed, our children could at least escape from the fantasy of religious fundamentalism in their public school science classrooms, but no more. And, finally, fourth, a very scary thought: Imagine a world where the average Louisianian is even less scientifically informed than they are now!

Being an anthropologist and a citizen of Louisiana who lives and works in the state, I simply felt as if I had to do something, so I wrote a letter to the *Advocate*, the Baton Rouge newspaper, which stated a variety of reasons why this law was a very bad idea. About a week later, on May 16, 2008, a letter criticizing my views was published; the title was "Faith Offsets Lack of Doctorates." In the letter, the writer stated, "I believe the entire Bible is the inspired word of God," and, "Rockbound faith and belief in an almighty God . . . more than offset the lack of PhD's [*sic*]."[2] (I had identified myself in my letter as James Houk, PhD, college professor.) What really shocked me about this letter was not that some individual was still hanging onto the false notion that the Bible is the word of God (after all, apparently no data or evidence to the contrary will ever convince him and others like him otherwise), or even that he argued that faith is more reliable than science (admittedly an incredibly irrational position) in regard to generating knowledge of our world, but that this individual was not ashamed to state these positions publicly. What that means is that we have crossed a certain threshold that I thought was impermeable, namely the threshold of publicly avowed irrationality. What person in his right mind would draw public attention to the fact that empirical data really do not matter to him anymore? Is this what we have come to? So, do we simply put the guys with the robes and pointy hats back in charge again? If you think I am being overly histrionic here, consider the fact that young-earth creationism is quite popular today. Of course, the individual who wrote this amazing letter does not, in fact, think that faith is generally a reliable source of information as witnessed by the fact that the faith of around 5 billion people (non-Christian adherents of other religions) is, in his mind, worthless. Only his faith is reliable. Trust him.

The unfortunately misguided and irrational letter writer is suffering from what I referred to in chapter two as "obsessive deductivism"—once again, a mindset that embraces a "theory" because it is consonant with one's religious (or, more generally, cultural) beliefs and ignores all data and evidence (even future data and evidence) to the contrary that may disconfirm the "theory." (The term "theory" is placed in quotation marks to differentiate it from the standard use of the term—sans quotation marks—that refers to coherent set of hypotheses that is continuously critiqued and has withstood the test of time. A "theory," on the other hand, is simply *assumed* to be valid.) In fact, the "theory" is never tested, only believed; never critiqued, only presumed. Those who, for example, embrace a biblical or conservative idea of homosexuality are simply not interested in the anthropological, genetic, and biological data we have on sexual orientation. Just like the "young earthers," they're stuck. Once one decides to embrace the notion that the Bible is the literal, inerrant word of God (again, an assertion that cannot be defended by someone with even a passing interest in being rational, objective, and reasonable), he is forced to accept the entire package—e.g., a talking snake, a war-mongering God, virgin birth, miraculous parting seas and rivers, the just-so stories of Noah's ark and the Tower of Babel, and so on. While there have certainly been those who, on occasion, have embraced (a priori) secular fantasies and ideas, religious fundamentalism is the primary breeding ground for obsessive deductivism.

Obsessive deductivism is a by-product of what I refer to as a "mythico-deductive" epistemology, a mindset that sits at one extreme of a continuum of objective/universal and subjective/cultural epistemologies. At the opposite extreme, we find what I refer to as an "empirico-deductive" epistemology. The significant characteristics of each are as follows:

empirico-deductive epistemology	mythico-deductive epistemology
a posteriori reasoning	a priori assumption
induction ← → deduction	deduction ("obsessive")
taught in formal contexts	taught in informal contexts
"knowledge beyond culture"	cultural knowledge
production of contingent truths	blind acceptance of (presumed) absolute truths

The first item (a posteriori reasoning vs. a priori assumption) refers to the fact that the empirico-deductive approach is data-based and objective, since information is arrived at in a publicly verifiable manner; there is no room for authority, tradition, faith, mysticism, and so on—everyone will be privy to information gained in this way. With this approach, the data take precedence over theories, and the latter serve the former not the other way around, hence the descriptive phrase *a posteriori*; theory formation should, after all, be subsequent to the collection of relevant data. On the other side, the mythico-deductive approach, the mindset is manifestly assumptive and dogmatic. "Truths" are established by tradition and authority, and these "truths" are sustained by faith rather than testing and critique. Any data or evidence is, then, irrelevant to the "theory" unless the data or evidence does not falsify the "theory"; if data or evidence is found that is contrary to the "theory," it is simply ignored, explained away, or disparaged using fallacious arguments such as ad hominem attacks or association fallacies. Like the monsters in those 1950s B-grade horror movies, such "theories" never die, regardless of the weapons used against them or the damage done to them; their devoted and faithful followers simply pick them up, dust them off, and send them on their way again.

The second item refers to the temporality of both approaches, with the empirico-deductive approach being dynamic and the myth-ico-deductive approach being static. In the former, data and theories are perpetually bound to one another in an organic relationship somewhat resembling a symbiosis, since each "feeds off of" and sustains the other, thus the two-way arrow linking induction and deduction. So, for example, as our data collection methods and technology grew increasingly sophisticated and both the quality and quantity of the data increased, Aristotelian kinetics gave way to Newtonian kinetics, which gave way to Einsteinian kinetics. Likewise, a geocentric universe gave way to a geocentric solar system, which gave way to a heliocentric solar system, which gave way to the realization that our cosmological location is really not special at all. This dynamic interplay between data and theory will presumably never cease, since even "new and improved" theories will be assumed to be deficient and subject to further testing against new data.

On the other side, however, induction (the analysis of specific data that results in the derivation of general principles) is not welcome. "Obsessively" deductive reasoning simply assumes that the "theory" is, in fact, true as is; thus, there is no need to test it, which renders data collection impertinent and inconsequential. I refer to this approach as "static," since, in this case, "theories" necessarily stand the test of time. So, for example, the mountain of data that has been collected by astronomers, geologists, paleontologists, and anthropologists over the last five centuries is ignored by those who continue to accept the "young-earth" notion that was based on "information" recorded well over two millennia ago, namely the biblical chronology from which the six-thousand-year value was obtained. (This issue is addressed later in this chapter.) The "theory" is monolithic and impermeable to critique by data and reason. Unlike religious claims in general, however, this "theory" is falsifiable and, in fact, has been falsified time and again—but never underestimate the power of faith to delude believers even in the face of overwhelming evidence to the contrary.

The empirico-deductive epistemology is taught in formal contexts, primarily public schools and college classrooms, and is utilized by scientists and academics in their research. Unfortunately, the average child is not overtly instructed in this approach until their first meaningful, rigorous science class, which may not be until middle school or perhaps high school. Imagine, for the sake of argument, that a young person is not introduced to the empirico-deductive epistemology until the eighth grade. By that time, they are about thirteen years old and have been subjected to years and years of folk or cultural "theories" regarding human origins, race/ethnicity, gender, and sexual orientation, and not a small number have been taught the absolute "truths" of their parents' religion; in the United States that would be primarily Christianity, and, in many cases, fundamentalist Christianity.

I should note here that approximately 43 percent of Christian evangelicals are "born again" by the age of thirteen.[3] By the time most young people are finally taught the theory of evolution and the data and evidence that supports it, they are already preadapted to reject it. This is probably one of the reasons why only one student out of twenty-six raised their hand in my Introduction to Physical Anthropology class when I asked them near the beginning of the semester (spring 2008) to acknowledge if they were familiar with evolutionary theory and the supporting evidence. I would soon find out (exam one!) that they were being truthful. By the time the semester ended, many of my students were amazed at the data we have regarding hominin fossil evolution, mitochondrial DNA studies, the dating of rocks and human artifacts, and the fusion of chimpanzee chromosomal material that appears in humans. A few of my students (by their own admission) actually reevaluated their personal "theories" regarding the evolution of animals and humans. Children and young people will respond to science if they are given the opportunity, but it seems that this is not happening for most. The typical Louisiana native, for example, gets about fifteen years of religious instruction and the equivalent of a few months (if they are lucky) of good science instruction. If they don't actually take a course that covers evolutionary theory in college, they will probably go the rest of their lives not knowing anything about natural selection, *Homo heidelbergensis*, or Charles Darwin's trip on the HMS *Beagle*.

We will soon be facing a major crisis in this country as we fall even further in the global ranking of quality of education. Over

750,000 children[4] (those being homeschooled in Christian evangelical homes) are being taught creationism (in virtually all cases the preposterous young-earth version) instead of science, and history from a Christian perspective. Oh, and by the way, the only requirement to be a homeschool instructor is parenthood! Faith healers, psychics and other charlatans continue to bilk a gullible public out of their money, and books by "psychics" (how many times do they have to be proven wrong before people realize that these individuals are not psychic?) are given two complete shelves of exposure at my local big-box, chain bookstore. Incredibly enough, many individuals are much more inclined to get their science from their preacher or their pastor than from a biologist with a PhD and half a lifetime spent reading and conducting research in his or her field. The Bush administration was absolutely disastrous for this country, as studies and data that did not serve neoconservative ideology were disparaged or ignored (see *The Republican War on Science* by Chris Mooney) and faith-based initiatives received the highest priority. The general conservative tone of the Bush years was also very accommodating to private, Christian schools, homeschooling, creationism, and "folk" knowledge; academics and other experts were viewed as secular "elitists." As a country, we are far beyond being simply scientifically illiterate, and things are only going to get worse unless significant changes are made.

The phrase "knowledge beyond culture" was coined by Ernest Gellner,[5] and it refers to knowledge that is shared universally by all individuals regardless of geography (e.g., scientific knowledge about our world and mathematical concepts). Knowledge beyond culture is, perhaps, the most significant counterargument to (extreme) postmodernism, since its very existence belies the fact that a conceptual chasm separates us from the "other" to the extent that both parties are unable to "know" one another. In fact, if anything, it is just this sort of knowledge that binds together the various peoples of the world. Chemists, physicists, geneticists, and so on can converse quite well with their colleagues from around the planet once the trivial matter of language differences is worked out. Science is one of the important components of a postcultural world since its epistemology is distinctly acultural or universal.

Now, contrast this with the manifestly cultural knowledge of, say, religion. Since there are some 10,500 or so different versions (many of them being mutually contradictory at least to some extent) of religion, it is clear that there is no consensus and, in fact, probably never will be. This is precisely what one would predict given the fact that the various groups have serious, vested interests in the religion of their choice and that the veracity of any one religion cannot be objectively substantiated or even reasonably argued for vis-à-vis the other religions. And this is just what one would expect for belief systems that are not falsifiable; they all remain "in play" or "potentially" true forever. For these reasons, and more not noted here, the notion of the religious war is quite common in the cultural history of human beings. The monotheistic religions are particularly susceptible to this problem, since the belief in the "One True God" leaves little room for compromise. Simply because of its size and influence, no religion can touch the blood that has been shed and the individuals slaughtered in the name of Christianity; Islam ranks behind Christianity in this regard but is gaining as its fundamentalists continue to exert control over more nations and territories. With its indiscriminate slaughter of the Canaanites during the post-Mosaic occupation of Palestine (assuming that these events actually occurred), the Jews (known as the Israelites at that time) were off to a "promising" start, but the various diasporas and the relatively small number of Jews prevented them from making any sort of serious move on Christianity as history's most violent religion.

One way to contrast universal knowledge and cultural knowledge is to consider the potential for diffusion. The propagation of universal knowledge requires very little redundancy, since it generally relies on data, argument, and logic that is intuitively reasonable. Kepler's first planetary law, for example, that states that the planetary orbits are ellipses with the sun at one focus of the ellipse, is easily understood once the simple mathematics is demonstrated and provides us with the best explanation of the data. Once the problem of language and symbols are worked out, any human being at least has the potential to see the validity of Kepler's first law without much trouble.

Consider, however, the following: The most sublime spiritual gesture that an individual can make is *sallekhana*, a practice in which the individual ceases eating, drinking, moving, and eventually breathing; this practice is the only way a human being can prevent himself or herself from damaging or killing air bodies, water bodies, and other microscopic beings, insects, and other living creatures, thereby freeing the "soul" for a propitious rebirth or, ideally, an ascension into *Siddha-sila*, the abode of perfected souls.

Or this: Since the first humans disobeyed God, all subsequent humans were spiritually "stained," so God sent down a pure and perfect avatar from heaven to die in a redemptive gesture that freed humans from the primordial stain on their souls.

Or, finally, this: All humans must have their heads ceremonially "washed" and incised if they desire to be possessed by the ancient, celestial gods, since the gods can only enter the human body through the top of the head.

The first example is drawn from Jainism, the second from Christianity, and the third from the Orisha religion in Trinidad. Imagine, if you can, how preposterous these "truths" must sound to someone hearing them for the first time. Since there is nothing inherent in the claims that would make them obviously or logically true, a great degree of redundancy is required to disseminate them. Such "truths" must be culturally contextualized and explained over and over to or forced on the "target audience" if they are to be passed on. History has shown time and again that, absent the military force and political power that it takes to subjugate and dominate a group, this sort of religious diffusion almost certainly will not occur. Individuals rarely voluntarily disavow the religion of their birth and replace it with the religion of the "other."

Some Christian fundamentalists justify their exclusivist approach by claiming that eventually everyone will hear the Gospel. The cultural arrogance of this notion is shocking enough, but beyond that there is an incredible naiveté on display here. The individual Christian who makes this claim knows that she wouldn't give a Hindu or Muslim or Buddhist or Daoist the time of day; she would reject their "good news" outright. Again, we see the same problem I've alluded to before—to wit, my faith is valid, yours is not, and you should listen to me but I don't have to listen to you. Yet all these overly confident cultural warriors can offer the non-Christians are obfuscatory metaphysics and miraculous claims. Hindus, Muslims, Buddhists, and Daoists (etc., etc.) already have these things in their own religion, and that is precisely why no religion will ever achieve anything like an international consensus. Religious arguments between antagonistic parties are futile, since both parties are bereft of the sort of ammunition needed to settle such disputes.

The final characteristic that illustrates the glaring difference between the two epistemologies focuses on the type of knowledge and information that is generated. The good news regarding the empirico-deductive approach is that it does lead us to "truths" we can count on, albeit contingent truths. Thus, the study of particle physics has led us to discoveries regarding the quantized energy levels of the elusive electron, the (possibly) fundamental units of matter, and the unification of what was once known as the four fundamental forces of nature to three or, according to some physicists, two fundamental forces. But everything we know today about the world of matter and energy breaks down when we attempt to go back in time to before what is called "Planck time" (5.4×10^{-44} seconds after the initial inflation of the universe had begun) or when we attempt to go back "in space" to when the known universe was packed into a volume whose length was less than "Planck length" (6.3×10^{-34} inches). Thus, our current knowledge in this area is contingent rather than absolute. We might also consider paleoanthropological theories regarding hominin evolution. The relevant data, fossilized material that dates back some four to five million years, are hard to find but nevertheless continue to be discovered on an annual basis. Thus, today's theories are tentative and will continue to be adjusted and altered as new data come to light. Theories and interpretations change so often that I had to relearn the important evolutionary sequences of the genera *Australopithecus* and *Homo* when I taught a biological anthropology class for the first time as a college professor; much of what I learned in graduate school had changed. Such is the contingent nature of the "truths" generated by the empirico-deductive approach.

Every time a creationist criticizes evolutionary theory on the grounds that even the scientists disagree on its important points, he simply reveals his scientific ignorance. He actually has it all wrong: theories that are amenable to change (scientific theories, for example) are valid and reliable simply because they conform to and accommodate new data. Contingency is a small price to pay for validity and reliability.

It is interesting that even political conservatives apply the same sort of flawed reasoning as the creationists. So, for example, no matter how many times the charges made against the government by antiwar protesters of the sixties and seventies are proven correct, the conservative media still slander and vilify the "long haired, bead- and sandal-wearing, dope-smoking hippies" for not supporting the United States' involvement in the Vietnam War. Those who refused very early on to swallow the Bush administration's propaganda regarding the 2003 invasion of Iraq and decided that they would not support the war look like geniuses today, since their position was, as it turns out, the correct one. Nevertheless, the conservative media still continues to disparage and defame those individuals for their lack of patriotism. Never mind that they were actually right; that seems to be immaterial. There is also the issue of "flip-flopping," an "insult" that the conservative right never seems to tire of. As soon as, say, a Democratic candidate for political office changes his or her position on any issue, even when new data or information is discov- ered or uncovered, they are called "flip-floppers." That this ploy is effective for conservative right-wingers says a lot about their episte- mology. The actual, empirical truth (i.e., the way the world really is) is not as important as "theories" that serve various social, cultural, or religious biases. Exhibit A: young-earth creationism, a "theory" that is quite popular among these folks and apparently totally impervious to empirical falsification, at least in their minds.

Those who embrace the mythico-deductive epistemology claim to give us absolute truths (a claim that the empirico-deductive thinkers would never make) but offer nothing in the way of substantiation save for dogmatic proclamations and dubious reasoning generated by a faith-based epistemology. Thus, here are things as they currently stand: one can simply live with contingent "truths" or she can have faith in absolute "truths." In my mind, the reasonable choice, as I stated earlier, would be to accept a small amount of something over what could quite possibly turn out to be a large amount of nothing.

CHAPTER EIGHT
YOUNG-EARTH CREATIONISM

The so-called "young earthers" certainly do possess that "large amount of nothing" alluded to at the end of the last chapter. This so-irrational-it-is-disturbing notion of young-earth creationism is, perhaps, the best example of obsessive deductivism we have today, an example that illustrates all of the points made above regarding the faith-based, mythico-deductive epistemology. It didn't start out that way, however.

It was James Ussher who gave us the definitive, biblically based chronology of the universe in his *Annals of the World, Deduced from the First Origins of the World*, published in 1658. Lest the reader get the wrong idea, let me state at this point that I do not consider Ussher to be cut from the same cloth as today's young earthers. For one thing, he was writing in the seventeenth century and, thus, had very little sound, empirical data to work with; hominin fossils were unknown, astronomical knowledge was scant, very little was known about the geological processes that have shaped and fashioned our world, and Darwin's work was still two hundred years away. Ussher was an accomplished scholar and gifted polyglot who was working within the intellectual framework of his time. He used his knowledge of ancient languages and ancient history (both biblical and extra-biblical) in his construction of his now famous chronology that dates the Genesis creation event back to 4004 BCE. It was an amazing achievement and still stands today as the definitive biblically based chronology.

That being said, however, the fact that individuals still today accept Ussher's chronology as authoritative is preposterous. How does one simply "wave off" 350 years of data collection, scientific hypothesis testing, and theory building? Of course, the question is rhetorical, but I suppose we could answer it by simply responding that some individuals assume that the absolute truth was already known 350 years ago (or, by extension to the original source, 2,500–3,000 years ago) and, thus, all subsequent data and research are irrelevant. In other words, we are dealing with a "textbook case" of obsessive deductivism. I would guess that if Ussher were alive today he would be appalled at the blatant antiempirical and antiscientific notions of the young-earth creationists; in fact, I regret that I have to drag Ussher's good name into this mess.

In simple terms, the problem with the young earthers, like all obsessive deductivists, is that they are working backward: they begin with the assumption that their "theory" is true and then either ignore pertinent data or interpret the data in such a way so that they are consonant with their "theory." Even if at one time their "theory" were valid to some extent, it should still be subject to adjustment or alteration as new data become known. But, of course, if they proceeded in this fashion, they would be doing science rather than what they are actually doing, which is perpetuating religious dogma camouflaged as science; without this subterfuge, young earthers could not sell their "theory" to an unsuspecting and largely defenseless public. For obvious reasons, the young earthers have made virtually no headway among scientists. That is precisely why creationists and young earthers fight their battles in statehouses and school board meetings; they are well aware that the American general public and those not trained as scientists are prone to being hoodwinked by their "scientific" presentations. Even here in Louisiana, the Louisiana Science Education Act was passed over the vehement protestations of science teachers and scientific organizations, but the legislators, on the other hand, were an easy sell, especially when you factor in the usual political shenanigans of Louisiana politics. The creationists did, however, run into a buzz saw in Dover, Pennsylvania, in 2005, when a federal judge, John E. Jones (a Republican appointed by George Bush) ruled that creationism (disguised in this case as "intelligent design") was not science and, thus, not fit for the public school classroom. The good people of Dover obviously agreed, since every school board member who backed creationism in the classroom was defeated and replaced by candidates who promised not to compromise the teaching of real science in the classroom.

The young-earth creationists sometimes talk a good game and flash their (often dubious) scientific credentials, but it is all just a ruse that has been skillfully crafted to mislead the general public regarding their true motives. While they blather on about science and do their best to hide the fact that their enterprise is religiously motivated, the Creation Research Society (CRS), one of the oldest and most popular creationist organizations—which claims on its website that it is a "professional organization of trained scientists and interested laypersons who are firmly committed to scientific special creation"[1]—requires all of its members to accept and adhere to the CRS Statement of Belief.[2] According to the statement, 1) the Bible is the literal word of God, meaning that the Genesis "account of origins" is accepted as historical fact; 2) God created all living things "during the Creation Week described in Genesis"; 3) the flood described in the Genesis account of Noah and his family was an actual historical event; and 4) since "all mankind" fell "into sin" as a result of the actions of Eve and Adam in the Garden of Eden, salvation is necessary and can only be obtained through Jesus Christ, who CRS members accept as their "Lord and Savior."

There is not even a pretense of objectivity here. In fact, this statement perfectly describes the religious dogma of fundamentalist Christianity. When one peruses this statement and comes across passages regarding the historicity of Genesis, the "Creation Week," Noah's ark, Eve and Adam's "fall into sin" in the Garden of Eden, one wonders if there is anything these folks won't believe. And, as if to communicate the fact that are strict religious exclusivists, the last sentence states that only those who embrace their religion will attain salvation. Unfortunately for the children and young people of this country, CRS actually publishes a biology textbook that is used in private and Christian schools.[3]

The degree to which empirical data are reworked, selectively chosen, or flat-out ignored cannot be appreciated until one examines just how wrong the young-earth "theory" is. In the text that follows, I will discuss twenty reasons why young-earth creationism is invalid, twelve of which fall under the category heading "reasons why the young-earth hypothesis is certainly wrong," four under the category heading "reasons why the young-earth hypothesis is probably wrong," and four under the category heading "reasons why the young-earth hypothesis is dubious." Please note that these twenty reasons barely scratch the surface of this issue, as I am sure others who are schooled in, say, the natural and biological sciences would have no problem adding to this list. Nevertheless, only one entry in the category "reasons why the young-earth hypothesis is certainly wrong" is required to unequivocally disconfirm the young-earth notion.

CHAPTER NINE

TWELVE REASONS WHY THE YOUNG-EARTH HYPOTHESIS IS CERTAINLY WRONG

1. THE SIX-THOUSAND-LIGHT-YEAR BUBBLE

Many of the most obvious problems with the young-earth claim are astronomical in nature. According to astronomers (virtually every astronomer alive), the observable universe extends out to about 13.8 billion light years from our (or any) vantage point. (Measuring distances to stars and galaxies will be discussed in reason two.) Thus, we currently live in a space-time "bubble" with a radius of about 13.8 billion light years. (Please note that the universe is actually bigger than that because the universe has continued to expand since the light left the distant objects we are observing.) In this "bubble" there are approximately 100 billion galaxies, separated by an average distance of about one million light years (these are the most popular estimates). The largest major galaxy that is near our own is Andromeda, a spiral galaxy located about 2.5 million light years away from our own galaxy. The nearest star to the sun is Proxima Centauri, a red dwarf located about 4.22 light years away from the solar system; the average distance between stars in our Milky Way galaxy is estimated to be about five light years. If we reduce our space-time bubble from a "sphere" with a radius of 13.8 billion light years to one with a radius of six thousand light years, we obtain some very curious results. The following are either the young-earth point of view or implications of that point of view:

- Using a simple proportion calculation (a/b = c/d), the average distance between galaxies becomes 0.438 light years. (How nonsensical is this value? The average distance between galaxies would be anywhere from 20,000 to 200,000 times smaller than the size of the galaxies themselves. In other words, there would be no spatial separation between galaxies at all.)
- Every galaxy in the known, observable universe would be visible to the human eye; this would include even ancient quasars near the edge of the observable universe.
- The average distance between stars in our Milky Way galaxy would be about 2.190×10^{-6} light years, or about 13 million miles. (How absurd is this value? The average distance of the earth from the sun is about 93 million miles, which means that there would be, for example, a number of other stars inside the earth's orbit around the sun.)

In the interest of fairness, I should point out that the young earthers at Answers in Genesis, arguably the most popular Christian, young-earth creationist apologetics group, accept the huge distance estimates calculated by astronomers but reject the claim that any object is older than the biblical value of six thousand years. This is explained further below.

2. STARLIGHT AND OBJECTS FARTHER AWAY THAN SIX THOUSAND LIGHT YEARS

There are a number of techniques used by astronomers to measure the distances to stars and galaxies. For the closest stars, astronomers use the "parallax," or the apparent shift in the location of a star when viewed from different vantage points in the earth's orbit, and simple trigonometry; this method is accurate out to distances of about 400 or so light years. For stellar objects up to 150,000 light years away, a technique known as spectroscopic parallax can be used; the distance from Earth can be determined once a star's apparent (what we actually observe) and absolute magnitude (given by a star's location on the main sequence in the Hertzsprung-Russell diagram[1]) are known. For even larger distances to stars, and even galaxies, a special star known as a Cepheid variable, whose luminosity varies on a regular basis, can be used to measure distance with an accuracy that is approximately 99 percent of the actual value. Finally, a technique based on a shifting of light toward the red part of the visible spectrum is used to estimate distances out to the far limits of our observational capabilities; this "redshift" is caused by the expansion or "stretching" of space itself, and the shift increases as the distance to the object increases. These four methods are probably the most popular that are used today, but there are many others; Dr. Ned Wright of the UCLA Division of Astronomy and Astrophysics, for example, lists twenty-six on his website.[2] Once again, here are some of the problems with the six-thousand-year value for the universe:

- Since the observable universe is immensely large and since, according to creationists, we can only see light from objects that left those objects 6,000 years ago, as the universe gets older and continues to expand, a number of heretofore unknown stellar objects, namely those lying beyond six thousand light years from Earth, should become visible each day. (Clearly this is not happening since we have always been able to see objects much, much farther away from Earth than six thousand light years.)
- All of the galaxies in our galactic neighborhood—e.g., the Large and Small Magellanic Clouds and the Andromeda spiral galaxy—should not be visible from Earth since they are located far beyond six thousand light years from Earth. (They are visible.)

As the reader is no doubt aware, the farther away we look into space, the farther back in time we are observing. Thus, the light we observe from the sun actually left the surface of the sun about eight minutes before it reached our eyes; the light we observe from Proxima Centauri left that star over four years ago; and the light we observe from the Andromeda galaxy left that galaxy about 2.5 million years ago, and so on. Consequently, we are viewing these objects as they were when the light left them.

Many young-earth creationists either aren't aware of the starlight/time and distance problem or they assume that the scientists are simply wrong. Fundamentalist creationists assume that Genesis and the rest of the Bible must be literally correct, so if there is a discrepancy it is not religious dogma that is rejected but, rather, the empirical data. Therefore, those young earthers who are aware of the starlight/time and distance problem simply cannot accept the standard and universally accepted explanation of light travel time and distance that astronomers and astrophysicists have been using for decades. How, then, do they get around standard science? The young earthers at Answers in Genesis state four issues that they claim cast serious doubt on the standard, scientific view of light travel time and distance:

a. Light may not have always traveled at the same speed.[3]
b. Astronomers, astrophysicists, and physicists may have overlooked the gravitational time-dilation effect of Einsteinian relativity. According to relativity theory, time flows at various rates depending on the conditions of the space in question. It is possible, they argue, that light from distant objects could have arrived in a very short time.[4]
c. There is a difference between "observed time" and "calculated time," with the former being the time we observed the event and the latter being the time when the event actually happened. In regard to the creation of the universe, observed time and calculated time both give us the same result. Either God created the galaxies and stars in a staggered fashion billions, then millions, then thousands, then hundreds, then tens of years before day four of "creation week" so they all appeared in the sky simultaneously, or they were all created on day four of "creation week," with their light all reaching Earth at the same time.[5]
d. We cannot rule out supernatural intervention on the part of the Creator. God may have intervened to make light from the galaxies and stars reach the earth simultaneously during "Day 4" of "creation week." In other words, light was made to travel in a way that is not natural and not known to us today.[6]

There is ongoing research that suggests that the basic physical constants, including light speed, perhaps change over time,[7] but nothing in the literature even remotely supports the sort of change in light speed needed to rescue the young earthers. Remember, the value the young earthers are using is off by more than a factor of 10^6.

In regard to the second point, I think we can safely assume that the thousands of astronomers and astrophysicists working today are not overlooking the gravitational time-dilation effect of relativity. If the folks at Answers in Genesis know something the rest of us don't, they should publish in a peer reviewed journal. Also, again, the sort of "correction" the young earthers need (10^6) to validate their six-thousand-year value is not going to be found in any relativistic time-dilation effect.

The "observed time" and "calculated time" idea is interesting and somewhat clever, but there is no escaping the fact that light travels at a finite speed (no matter how fast or slow it actually is or was or will be), so unless one is located next to the object emitting electromagnetic radiation in the visible spectrum, the observed time will always be later than the calculated time. One could get around this problem, I suppose, by staggering the creation of stars and galaxies in the way described by Answers in Genesis, but that scenario requires creation events to be pushed back 13.7 billion years, effectively invalidating the six thousand year old universe idea. Besides, this explanation has ad hoc written all over it.

Finally, the fourth point is one that can be invoked at any time there is a discrepancy between standard science and creation "science." Virtually any claim can be "validated" by simply stating that God did it and that is precisely why it is meaningless in a scientific sense: it is not falsifiable. Also, the creationist is left with the task of explaining why an omnipotent, omniscient, and omnibenevolent God would act so capriciously, other than for the purpose of confusing humankind.

After reading the young earthers' attempts to salvage the six-thousand-year value in the face of overwhelming empirical data to the contrary, one is left wondering why they engage in such subterfuge. This issue illustrates one of the important characteristics of the obsessive deductive mindset: one begins with the assumption that a "theory" is correct (in this case, the idea that the chronology of the Bible is valid) and then interprets the data in such a way so as to make them appear that they support the "theory." Thus, the young earthers are forced to take the position that mainstream scientists and standard science are wrong; they have no other choice. Now, perhaps, we can understand the individuals who worked so hard for centuries to discourage and abolish research and reasoning based on empirical data. Galileo's problem was not that his data were insufficient to support his theories but, rather, that he dared to question the "truth" of "theories" assumed to be true.

3. STELLAR EVOLUTION

Stars begin their life with a mass value that will determine their evolutionary history. While stars spend most of their time fusing hydrogen into helium, eventually that process ceases, leading ultimately to a number of fates, depending on their mass. The atomic fusion processes are so well known today that a star's life can be plotted on a Hertzsprung-Russell (HR) diagram (with magnitude on the y-axis and temperature on the x-axis) with a very high degree of reliability. Tim Thomson, a physicist at NASA's Jet Propulsion Laboratory at the California Institute of Technology, has this to say regarding the accuracy of our current models:

> As it turns out, by building mathematical models of stars, based on straightforward physics, and allowing those models to evolve naturally in time as a star ages, we can recreate the HR diagram as it is observed. The fidelity of the agreement between theory & observation is far greater than I can communicate in this one webpage. Even small details are now the stuff of intense study in astrophysics. The ability of the theory of stellar evolution to explain the HR diagram in its finest details, singles out stellar evolution as one of the most successful and productive of scientific theories.[8]

I think that we can safely assume that the standard scientific model of stellar evolution is accurate and that is why there is virtually 100 percent agreement among scientists on the model that is currently being used. But, according to those who claim that the universe is only six thousand years old:

- All of the stellar types and phenomena we observe, including red giants, neutron stars, black holes, and supernovae formed sometime during the past six millennia.

It can take millions of years before a new star settles in on the "main sequence" (as plotted on the HR diagram) where it will spend most of its life fusing hydrogen atoms; for a star that is approximately the size of our sun, this main sequence period could last ten billion years. Now, stars do not become red giants until after this process is complete, yet many red giants exist in our galaxy, and several are visible to the naked eye. This clearly sets a lower limit on the age of the cosmos as some billions of years, certainly not thousands. When stars much more massive than our sun exhaust their nuclear fuel, they will collapse and become supernovae. Several hundred have been observed, even in other galaxies, again, effectively setting a lower limit on the age of the universe in the billions of years.

4. TREE RINGS

Trees generally add one growth ring each year, thus allowing us not only to calculate the age of trees but to date ancient wooden structures as well. By cross-dating various samples and using radiocarbon dating and statistical analysis, archaeologists can actually construct a standard chronology for a particular area. (This technique is referred to as dendrochronology.) One of the oldest standard chronologies has been constructed in Central Europe and dates back to 10,461 BCE.[9] Thus, we have here direct, organic, empirical proof that the six-thousand-year value is wrong.

5. DATING OF FOSSILIZED BONES, ROCKS, AND ARTIFACTS

A number of different techniques can be used to date ancient material. There are two popular relative dating methods that are used: stratigraphy, which uses the horizontal layers of the earth and the principle of superposition to relatively date material, and fluorine analysis, a technique that allows the relative dating of bones found in the same area based on a comparison of fluorine content. Of course, these two methods can only assign relative dates to material, but only one absolutely dated bone or artifact is needed in order to assign approximate real dates to the relatively dated material.

Several radiometric dating methods, based on the radioactive decay rates of various isotopes, are used to date material in absolute terms (i.e., we get "real" dates). Various isotopes decay at different rates, signified by a value referred to as their "half-life," a time value that signifies when one half of the original isotopes present in the material has decayed into a "daughter isotope." Thus, some radiometric techniques are appropriate for relatively young material and other techniques are appropriate for older material. The radioactive isotope carbon-14 has a half-life of 5,730 years, thus carbon-14 dating cannot be used on material that is over 50,000 years old since such a small amount of the isotope would remain in the material. Another form of radiometric dating, based on the radioactive decay of the isotope potassium-40, is used to date early hominin fossils. This isotope has a half-life of 1.25 billion years and is generally used to date materials that fall somewhere in the 100,000–2 billion year range. There are many other radioactive isotopes with various half-life values that are used as well. For example, uranium-238 decays into lead-206 and has a half-life of about 4.5 billion years, allowing for the dating of the oldest rocks.

Another dating method based on the radioactive decay of isotopes is isochron dating, a technique that uses a ratio of the daughter isotope and another isotope of the same element rather than simply the amount of the daughter isotope present. Archaeologists also use a technique referred to as thermoluminescence to date pottery shards and stone tools. Additionally, techniques such as fission-track dating, based on an analysis of microscopic fission tracks of decaying uranium-238, and paleomagnetism, a technique that analyzes the polarity of magnetically charged particles that are "captured" in rock and compares this to a known geomagnetic time scale, are used to cross-check the other dating methods.

The radiometric dating techniques are based on assumptions regarding, for example, the initial conditions at time zero for the rock, bone, or artifact; the material being dated being a closed system with regard to the increase or decrease of the parent or daughter isotopes; and a consistent decay rate for the isotope in question. Fortunately, however, there are literally thousands of individuals involved in dating these materials, and their results are checked and cross-checked, not only against a sort of universal time-reference scale (based on basically everything that has been dated thus far), but also against the work of other researchers and the results obtained by other dating methods. In regard to hominin fossils, for example, the dating of bones in one area generally agree with the dating of bones from the same genus and species in other areas.

Once again, the young earthers claim the following:

- No rock, bone, or artifact is older than six thousand years. The scientists are making assumptions that are not warranted or they are making some fundamental errors when they date these materials.

Of course, we have to allow for the possibility that errors can be made and are occasionally, but these techniques have been fine-tuned for decades and, as I noted above, dates are checked and cross-checked against other researchers' work and results obtained using a variety of other dating techniques. Basically, the young earthers are trying to convince us that, in regard to the dating of rocks, bones, and artifacts, virtually all of the geologists, archaeologists, paleontologists, and paleoanthropologists are all wrong all of the time. Not only that, but wrong by a factor of 10^3, 10^4, or more, depending on the object in question. Can 10,000 PhDs working independently, using a variety of methods, and checking and cross-checking their work on a constant basis all be fundamentally wrong all the time? Probably not.

6. INDEPENDENT DATING OF EARTH ROCKS, MOON ROCKS, AND METEORITES

In regard to the mineral matter that exists, the young earthers believe that:

- Rocks, both terrestrial and extra-terrestrial, cannot be older than six thousand years old.

One of the most definitive tests of any theory, method, technology, etc. is reliability (i.e., does the method or technique produce consistent results in independent cases). In regard to the dating methods being discussed here, the answer to this question is an unequivocal "yes." Consider, for example, these dates published by the Department of the Interior, US Geological Survey,[10] along with a date for the oldest earth rock:[11]

The oldest moon rocks

Material	Dating Method	Results (billions of yrs.)
moon rock (Apollo 17)	Rb-Sr (rubidium-strontium) isochron	4.55 ± 0.1
moon rock (Apollo 17)	Sm-Nd (samarium-neodymium) isochron	4.34 ± 0.05
moon rock (Apollo 16)	$^{40}Argon/^{39}Argon$	4.47

One moon rock sample dated two different ways

Material	Dating Method	Results (billions of yrs.)
Apollo 14 (sample #14053)	Rb-Sr isochron	3.96
Apollo 14 (sample #14053)	$^{40}Argon/^{39}Argon$	3.95

One moon rock sample dated five different ways

Material	Dating Method	Results (billions of yrs.)
Apollo 11 (sample #10072)	^{40}Argon/^{39}Argon (whole rock)	3.49 ± 0.05
Apollo 11 (sample #10072)	^{40}Ar/^{39}Ar (plagioclase)	3.56 ± 0.06
Apollo 11 (sample #10072)	^{40}Ar/^{39}Ar (pyroxene)	3.55 ± 0.05
Apollo 11 (sample #10072)	Rb-Sr isochron	3.57 ± 0.05
Apollo 11 (sample #10072)	Sm-Nd isochron	3.57 ± 0.03

The oldest meteorites

Material	Dating Method	Results (billions of yrs.)
Juvinas (achondrite)	Mineral isochron	4.60 ± 0.07
Enstatite (chondrites)	Whole-rock isochron	4.54 ± 0.13
Bronzite (chondrites)	Whole-rock isochron	4.69 ± 0.14
Krahenberg (amphoterite)	Mineral isochron	4.70 ± 0.1
Norton County (achondrite)	Mineral isochron	4.70 ± 0.1

Old earth rocks

Material	Dating Method	Results (billions of yrs.)
Amitsoq gneisses (W. Greenland)	Rb-Sr isochron	3.70 ± 0.12
A. gneisses (W. Greenland/zircons)	Lu-Hf (Lutetium-Hafnium) isochron	3.55 ± 0.22
Sand River gneisses (S. Africa)	Rb-Sr isochron	3.79 ± 0.06

The oldest earth rock

Material	Dating Method	Result (billions of yrs.)
Western Australia (zircon)	ion microprobes	4.404

These dates show a remarkable consistency even when different dating methods are used on the same sample (as with the moon rocks) and also a consistency in regard to the overall picture. Moon rocks, earth rocks, and meteorites, all dated independently using a number of different methods, confirm, beyond a shadow of a doubt, that the earth, moon, and asteroids are billions of years old. Again, for us to get anywhere near the six-thousand-year value, we would have to assume that egregious, fundamental errors are being made by many different highly qualified researchers on many different occasions, errors that result in values that are off, again, by a factor of 10^6.

7. KIRKWOOD GAPS IN THE ASTEROID BELT

Virtually all asteroids in our solar system are located in a main band between the orbits of Mars and Jupiter, but they are not distributed randomly. There are actually gaps in the main band, called Kirkwood gaps, that are relatively free of any asteroids. These gaps in the distribution of asteroids are caused by the gravitational perturbations of Jupiter. One prominent gap occurs in orbits with a semi-major axis of 2.5 astronomical units—a unit of distance based on the distance between the earth and the sun; thus, half of the longest orbital axis measures 2.5 astronomical units. At this distance, an asteroid would make three orbits for every orbit of Jupiter and, thus, would take about four earth years to orbit the sun, since Jupiter takes about twelve earth years. Therefore, this gap corresponds to a resonance of 3:1; there are others at 2:1, 5:3, and 7:2. Computer simulations have shown that it would it take hundreds of thousands of orbits before these gaps would be as "clear" as what we see today[12] or, put another way, time periods of hundreds of thousands or millions of years depending on the gap.

The young earthers claim the following:

- Since the universe is only six thousand years old, there has not been enough time for the Kirkwood gaps to form, according to astronomers, thus either the science is incorrect or the asteroids were simply created in their current orientation.

In fact, those are the only two remotely plausible explanations that will "rescue" the young earthers' hypothesis, but that's the problem: they are only remotely plausible. I seriously doubt that the fundamentals of Newtonian mechanics, Kepler's planetary laws, and computer modeling are fundamentally flawed, so they are left with the "God did it" explanation. Whenever young-earth creationists reach the point where they have to pull the "God did it" card, one can assume that they've simply run out of ideas.

8. PLATE TECTONICS

In the early twentieth century, Alfred Wegener, German astronomer and geophysicist, noted that the coastlines of South America and Africa resembled two huge puzzle pieces that could, in fact, be "matched" together quite snugly. Even more compelling, he found both fossil and lithological evidence that suggested that the two landmasses had once been connected. He proposed the notion of continental drift, but it was not well received since, at that point in time in history, there were no data concerning tectonic plates, paleomagnetic reversals, the mid-Atlantic ridge, and so on. One group that rejected Wegener's hypothesis was the "permanentists," those individuals who believed that the earth's surface was stable and that the continents and the oceans existed since creation in their current configuration. And this brings us to the young-earth creationists, whose position on this issue has never changed, even though a veritable ton of evidence to the contrary has now been amassed:

- The current positions of the world's oceans and continents have always been as they are today.

The "veritable ton of evidence" I spoke of earlier that shows beyond a shadow of a doubt that South America and Africa were once part of the same landmass includes common micro- and macrofossils of both flora and fauna found on both landmasses, the very close alignment of the continental shelves off the South American and African coasts (which "match" even better than the visible coastlines), similar rocks and geological formations, and glacial striae (caused by the friction between glaciers and bedrock) that show a shared pattern.[13]

Plate tectonics, the idea that the earth's surface is made up of seven or so large "plates" that move about atop the asthenosphere, a zone of "soft" and pliable rock that lies just below the lithosphere, the upper-most level that contains the crust, is an idea that is accepted by virtually every geologist around the world, working and teaching today. Virtually all of these geologists accept the overwhelming evidence that points to the fact that the world's landmasses were once contiguous some millions of years ago based on the age of the shared fossilized flora and fauna and the movement of the "plates." (This primordial landmass is referred to as "Pangea.") Again, the young-earth creationists are "stuck" with the "static earth" idea or the belief that the earth and the life it harbors are today as they have always been and, of course, the belief that any event or process that has occurred must have taken place sometime during the last six thousand years. There is simply no time in their scheme for continental drift to have occurred based on known rates of the movement of the "plates," so they are forced to reject what is really the only plausible explanation we have for the empirical data that exist today. Do you see a pattern here?

9. MAGNETIC-FIELD REVERSALS

In the 1950s, ships and aircraft in the Atlantic Ocean began to detect some rather odd magnetic anomalies—more specifically, field reversals in polarity. It was probably this discovery more than any other that led to a confirmation of Wegener's continental drift hypothesis. The source of the magnetic anomalies was roughly parallel "strips" of ocean crust that showed polarity reversals. Apparently, as molten rock reached the surface it would eventually cool and the magnetic polarity at that time would be "locked in" as the rock hardened. The focal point of this activity is the mid-Atlantic ridge, an underwater "mountain range" that runs roughly north to south across the Atlantic Ocean and marks the boundaries of two major "plates." The reversals occur randomly, as there may be periods of multiple reversals followed by long periods of zero reversals. According to the US Geological Survey, there have been eighteen reversals over the last five million years.[14]

Young earthers, of course, are stuck with the six-thousand-year hypothesis, so they have to reject *all* of the paleomagnetic data, research, and theorizing discovered, conducted, and generated by geologists and geophysicists. According to Answers in Genesis, magnetic reversals can occur in a matter of weeks.[15] I'll summarize their position as follows:

- Since the earth is only six thousand years old, all of the detected paleomagnetic polarity reversals have occurred during that time.

At this point, I will simply point the reader to the Answers in Genesis website if they wish to pursue the "young earth" take on this issue, but I should state that it involves some rather curious goings-on during the "Flood." In simple terms, these folks invoke mythology in an attempt to explain why the rest of us should reject science.

10. VERY OLD PLANTS

According to the young earthers:

- Since all plants were created six thousand years ago, no existing, living plant can be older than six thousand years.

I'm tempted here, right at the outset, to simply state that, according to the Genesis creation story (Genesis 1:11–19), plants

were created before the sun, a scenario that reflects a complete ignorance of photosynthesis, and be done with it. But there is more to say
here, so I'll push on.

Our task here is quite simple: simply find one example of a
plant that is older than six thousand years. We'll start with the so-
called "King Clone" creosote bush (*Larrea tridentata*). Here's how the
National Park Service describes it:

> In a few areas of the Mojave Desert clonal creosote rings have been
> found that are several yards in diameter. Near Lucerne Valley, "King
> Clone" has an average diameter of 45 feet! Using radiocarbon dating
> and known growth rates of creosote, scientists have estimated the age
> of "King Clone" as 11,700 years. Some of these common residents
> have been here continuously since the last ice age.[16]

A curious plant referred to as a "Quaking Aspen" (*Populus tremu-
loides*) found in Utah appears to be very old as well. The Quaking
Aspen is not a tree per se but rather a huge underground root system
that serves as the source or basis for the "trees" that grow out of it.
Again, from the National Park Service literature:

> Asexual or vegetative reproduction from root systems offers many
> benefits including phenomenal longevity. Aspen "clones," as the
> individual root systems are called, can live to be thousands of years
> old. The oldest known clone in existence is called "Pando" and is
> located in the Fish Lake National Forest north of Bryce Canyon
> National Park in central Utah. It has been aged at 80,000 years!
> Although 5–10,000 year-old clones are much more common, even
> these youngsters are much older than Sequoias and even Bristle-
> cone Pines.[17]

Finally, "King's Holly" *Lomatia tasmanica*, found in southwest
Tasmania, is a plant that propagates by cloning itself, a regenera-
tive process that can potentially result in very long life spans for one
plant. Researchers working out of the University of Tasmania and the
Parks and Wildlife Service in Tasmania used genetic knowledge of
the plant and carbon-14 dating to date one existing specimen back
to about 43,600 years ago.[18]

11. THE FOSSIL HOMININS

In my mind, the extremely detailed and widely documented hominin fossil record gives us some of the most impressive empirical data in support of the mainstream scientific theory of human origins. Before we go any further, however, let me state the young earthers' position on this issue:

- All creatures, extant and extinct, were created by God as they appear(-ed) on earth. Thus, no macroscale evolution has occurred on the species level. (Most young-earth creationists do not deny the Darwinian concept of natural selection, but they do argue that it is responsible only for biological change at the microscale level. In other words, in their minds, speciation does not occur. [Note: Speciation can actually be observed today, for example, in salamanders in California and warblers in northern Asia.[19] These are two examples of what are referred to as "ring species."])

The young earthers embrace the "fixity of species" idea that has been popular for centuries among those who favored the "religious explanation" (i.e., Genesis derived) of the origin and development of animals and humans. This idea has been popular since the Middle Ages and, incredibly enough, still has a relatively large number of proponents. Again, one should note that this "theory" has not been adjusted, altered, or rejected for centuries, even though mountains of new empirical data have become known to us during that time.

The theory of hominin evolution as it now stands is based on data collected and analyzed by geologists, geophysicists, geneticists, biologists, archaeologists, paleoanthropologists, paleontologists, and paleobotanists, many working independently and using analytical tools and theoretical models developed by their own field. For some sites, we have stone tools that are dated by archaeologists, plants or pollen dated by paleobotanists, geological information obtained by geologists from stratigraphy, and fossils dated by paleoanthropologists, all working more or less independently. While it is not necessarily the case that they always agree (for example, a recent fossil analysis of material from East Africa suggests a relatively early date for a common chimpanzee/human ancestor—8 million years ago [mya][20]—while molecular anthropologists argue for a much more recent date—about 5 to 7 mya[21]), their interpretations are usually consistent at least in a general sense. Anyway, and this is an important point, virtually no university- or research-based scientist disputes the fact that the general time frame is millions of years; only the young-earth creationists are working with a model that is dated in the thousands of years. (Why else do you think they put saddles on dinosaurs, for example, at the Creation Museum in Petersburg, Kentucky? Weird things like that happen when you try to squeeze hundreds of millions of years of evolutionary history into basically a few thousand years.)

The actual picture of hominin evolution is much more complicated than was once thought. (Empirical data can be "inconvenient" like that, at least if one takes them seriously.) The simple "linear" progression from one hominin genus or species to the next, with basically one "type" representing the stage of hominin development at that time, eventually gave way to a much more "messy" and complicated picture of hominin evolution; one would naturally expect that paradigm shifts such as these would generally be accompanied by disagreement and argument. Creationists have a tendency to highlight these shifts and use them as examples that ostensibly demonstrate that scientists either don't know what they are talking about or that the data are seriously flawed. In other words, the fact that scientific theories are adjusted or altered through time is used against mainstream science to show that it is not valid or reliable. Perhaps those who are not familiar with scientific epistemology may be impressed by the creationists' take on this issue, but one should simply ask himself this question: Which approach is potentially more valid and reliable, one that is amenable to change as new data become available or one that will never change, thus rendering even future data irrelevant?

Here is a (very) brief review of the raw data we have at this point (sans interpretation) regarding fossil hominins that are thought to lie in a direct line to humans. The earliest specimen we have that is part of the hominin conversation is a nearly complete skull found in Chad (north-central Africa) dated back to about 7 mya; the genus and species designation is *Sahelanthropus tchadensis*. The skull has a mixture of features that are partly apelike and partly humanlike. Unfortunately, no postcranial material has been found, but the relatively anterior placement of the foramen magnum (a large orifice in the base of the skull through which the spinal cord attaches to the head) suggests that this hominin was bipedal, at least to some extent. The cranial capacity of the skull is approximately 350 cubic centimeters (cc). (As a standard of reference, the average cranial capacity of chimpanzees is approximately 350–400 cc and for humans about 1,300–1,400 cc.) The early date for this specimen ostensibly puts it before the common ancestor of humans and chimpanzees.

The earliest fossil specimen that is generally agreed to be a bipedal hominin was found in Ethiopia. The specimen, named *Orrorin tugenensis*, has been dated back to about 6 mya. The fossil materials show some "primitive" (i.e., apelike) traits—for example, thickly enameled molars and large canines—as well as some more advanced traits—for example, postcranial material that strongly suggests bipedalism. *Orrorin* is generally recognized as the earliest definitive hominin.

Next in line (chronologically) is *Australopithecus anamensis*, which has been dated back to about 4.2 mya. Virtually all of this fossil material has been found in eastern Africa. Postcranial remains show that *A. anamensis* was definitely bipedal. The cranial remains (skull, jaws, and teeth) are quite primitive but, nevertheless, do seem to represent a transition to the more "advanced" specimens that follow it.

Fossil material representing a minimum of sixty individuals belonging to the genus and species *Australopithecus afarensis* has been found in Laetoli, Tanzania, and Hadar, Ethiopia.[22] The skull is still quite primitive, but the average cranial capacity is around 400–450 cc. The plentiful postcranial remains indicate bipedalism. Even better, however, we have actual footprints at Laetoli that date back to 3.7 mya that are "captured" in hardened volcanic ash, a material that can be easily and accurately dated. The famous specimen referred to as "Lucy" belongs to this genus and species. These trends—decreasing "primitivism" of the crania, increasing cranial capacity, and, of course, bipedalism—continue in *Australopithecus africanus*, which dates back to about 2.5 mya. The average cranial capacity of this hominin is approximately 450 cc.

The next (and last) genus in the hominin line is *Homo*, which some paleoanthropologists date back to as early as 2.4 mya, but there is certainly no scholarly consensus on that point. Most, however, agree that by 2 mya, *Homo* was present. The most important traits we see in the fossil material of this time period is an increase in overall stature and increasing encephalization. During the time period of 2.5–2 mya, there were a number of hominins coexisting, some rather primitive and some rather *Homo*-like. Some of these genera and species would die out during the next million years or so. Anthropologist Robert Jurmain and his colleagues, state that the average cranial capacity for the most evolutionarily advanced specimens during this time period is 631 cc.[23] The oldest stone tools, referred to as "Oldowan," date back to about 2.5 mya. It is thought that they are associated with the earliest species of the genus *Homo*, but we really don't know. Clearly some hominin was manufacturing and using them.

This brings us to *Homo erectus*. The earliest fossil material associated with *H. erectus* was found in East Africa and dates back to about 1.8 mya. It appears as though *H. erectus* was the first hominin to leave Africa, as *H. erectus* remains are also found in Asia and Europe, and also since no hominin fossil material older than 2 million years is found outside Africa. These hominins grew up to six feet in stature and possessed large, robust skulls, with an average cranial capacity of approximately 900 cc. A more advanced tool industry, the Acheulian, which originated around 1.7 mya, is found in association with *H. erectus* remains and living sites. From this point on, simple stone tools would become increasingly sophisticated and would eventually give way to more elaborate stone tools and composite tools (the bow and arrow, for example).

The designation *Homo heidelbergensis* is used to refer to the next *Homo* in the hominin line leading to *Homo sapiens*. Most *H. heidelbergensis* remains have been found in Africa and Europe, and the earliest specimens date back to around 800,000 years ago. The skulls are still massive and robust, but relative to *H. erectus* they are more gracile, as indicated by the reduced supraorbital torus (brow ridge), less pronounced facial prognathism, and thinner cranial bones. *H. heidelbergensis* also possessed smaller dentition than *H. erectus* and a significantly larger cranial capacity, with an average of approximately 1,200 cc.

Next in line chronologically, although not in the direct line leading to *H. sapiens*, is *Homo neandertalensis*, a hominin found only in Europe. *H. neandertalensis* began to appear in the fossil record about 130,000 years ago and actually survived until about 30,000 years ago. The average cranial capacity for Neandertals was about 1,500 cc. Thus, in absolute terms, they possessed the largest brains in the *Homo* genus; in relative terms, however, the brains of modern humans are larger, since Neandertals had a much bigger body size.

Finally, our march through the history of hominins brings us to modern *Homo sapiens*. The earliest fossil material associated with *H. sapiens* dates back to about 195,000 years ago and was found in Africa, the continent that, for paleoanthropological, genetic, and linguistic reasons, is almost certainly the origination point of modern humans. The genetic data we have suggests that *H. sapiens* left East Africa and traveled eastward about 60,000 years ago.

The brevity of this review of the hominin fossil data notwithstanding, there are some obvious trends that can be recognized. Beginning about 4 mya, a small, bipedal creature with a cranial capacity about the size of that of a chimpanzee, eventually gave way, evolutionarily, to a slightly less primitive creature with a slightly larger cranial capacity that, in turn, gave way to another hominin with more developed cranial and postcranial features possessing a slightly larger brain, and so on through the australopithecines and finally to the various species of *Homo*. There is still a lot of discussion and argument regarding precisely how all of these specimens (and some I didn't mention) are to be interpreted vis-à-vis one another—for example, did modern *H. sapiens* develop independently in Europe and Asia and Africa with the primary mechanism being gene flow (the "regional continuity model") or did they develop in Africa and then later replace the more ancient Neandertals in Europe and *H. erectus* in Asia (the "replacement model")?

While such questions are certainly significant, and will hopefully be resolved at some point, the big picture is quite clear: there has been a steady progression of hominins with gradually increasing cranial capacities, increasing stature, and cranial and postcranial material that gradually becomes increasingly modern morphologically. Also, let us not overlook hominin culture, which grows increasingly sophisticated from the earliest simple stone tools to the controlled use of fire and finally the development of composite tools and other sophisticated forms of material culture. I should also point out that literally thousands of highly trained physical anthropologists and archaeologists have been working with this material for decades, and virtually every detail, from dating to interpretation, has been looked at over and over again. Please also note that no materials, be it fossil remains or material culture, have been found that totally contradict the current picture. The reader should note that if the young earthers are correct, virtually every single fossilized hominin bone and ancient cultural artifact has been dated incorrectly. In my mind, that scenario is not even remotely possible.

One strategy that is used by young earthers is to simply claim that the fossils are not what scientists say they are. So, for example, consider a description of Australopithecus on the Answers in Genesis website. The author notes that of the various species of this genera that have been identified by paleoanthropologists, only "one remains: Australopithecus afarensis, popularly known as the fossil 'Lucy.'" He adds that Lucy is "not on the way to becoming human" and is, in fact, "very similar to the pygmy chimpanzee."[24]

This description is completely misleading in some places and flatout wrong in others. The writer makes the preposterous claim that only one fossil specimen, Lucy, represents the entire australopithecine genus. Thus, the writer is either woefully ignorant regarding the empirical data or he is lying. As noted earlier, there are at least two other widely recognized australopithecine species that are thought by many paleoanthropologists to be in the hominin line, *anamensis* and *africanus;* there are other australopithecine species, as well, that appear to be evolutionary "dead ends." You may recall that earlier I stated that the australopithecine fossil remains of *Australopithecus afarensis* (Lucy's genus and species) at only two different sites in East Africa represent approximately sixty different individuals. The writer further states that "Lucy" is "not on the way to becoming human." Again, a preposterous statement considering the habitual bipedalism of this specimen and an average cranial capacity larger than that found in chimpanzees. Finally, the writer implies that what we have here is simply a pygmy chimpanzee. For those of you who are not familiar with the subfield of physical anthropology, let me simply note that a blindfolded graduate student could easily differentiate between an australopithecine and chimpanzee skull. Note that the writer makes no comment regarding the dating of this fossil material, which consistently shows dates in the 3–4 million year range. Unfortunately, the uninformed reader could quite possibly believe that this writer actually knows what he is talking about. Here's a good rule of thumb for everyone: when it comes to science, listen to the scientists!

Another tactic long employed by young-earth creationists is to dredge up very dated examples of fossil hoaxes or misinterpreted fossils and use this to taint everything else paleoanthropologists are doing. For example, a search on the Answers in Genesis website turns up ninety-three articles in which "Piltdown Man" is discussed or mentioned. Piltdown Man was a fossil hoax perpetrated around 1912 in England. At that time, we possessed virtually no hominin fossils, so when this "fossil" turned up with an apelike jaw and humanlike cranium, the English were fooled into believing that a true "missing link" had been found, and, better yet, it was English! In 1953, an Oxford anthropology professor, Kenneth Oakley, exposed the fraud. The "fossil" was relegated to the dustbin of history and is virtually never mentioned in anthropological circles, but if one reads the creationist literature one gets the impression that it is still "exhibit A" for the theory of evolution. The websites of the Institute for Creation Research and the Creation Research Society mention Piltdown Man virtually every time the fossil evidence for hominin evolution is discussed, with the obvious intent to mislead the reader into believing that paleoanthropologists, as a matter of course, simply fabricate their data.

The creationist literature virtually never offers an interpretation of the fossil data for human evolution that would be included in any mainstream science textbook anywhere. For example, a writer at the Institute for Creation Research makes the following points regarding the fossil evidence, which he refers to as "dismal": 1) *Ramapithecus* is a "great ape"; 2) Piltdown Man was a hoax; 3) Nebraska Man was actually a pig; 4) Cro-Magnon Man is "indistinguishable from modern Europeans"; 5) *Homo habilis* is (quoting the paleoanthropologist Ian Tattersall in *Evolutionary Anthropology*) a "wastebasket taxon"; 6) Neandertals "were fully human"; and 7) Australopithecus was probably just an early ape since, after all, even the pigmy chimpanzee can walk bipedally at times; he adds that scientists cannot agree "whether or not they were the ancestors of human beings" and also that the discovery of more than one hominin at any point in time leads to "conflicting interpretations."[25]

Now, let us examine this cursory, misleading, and uninformed review of the hominin fossil record. *Ramapithecus* is so inconsequential that it is not even mentioned in one of the most popular physical anthropology texts used today.[26] Piltdown Man has already been addressed. (You will note that the author cannot resist once again flogging this dead horse.) Nebraska man was exposed as a hoax by scientists in 1927, and retractions were printed in both *Science* and *Nature*; it has never even been part of the conversation. The writer's comment regarding Cro-Magnon Man is nonsensical. Of course he is indistinguishable from modern Europeans—this fossil material dates back to 30,000 years ago, or some 165,000 years after the appearance of modern *Homo sapiens* in Africa, making Cro-Magnon Man fully *Homo sapiens*. (Do these folks read anything?) I suppose the quoted phrase ("wastebasket taxon") regarding *Homo habilis* is meant to be taken as a repudiation of the fossil record, but it is nothing of the sort. Discussions regarding nomenclature and where one genus or species ends and another begins are common in the field of paleoanthropology. In fact, many have dropped the *Homo habilis* designation. None of this, however, has any bearing on the fact that these are ancient hominins.

The writer states that Neandertals "were fully human." I cannot stress to the reader how absurd that statement is. Neandertal crania were noticeably larger than that of any other hominin, including *Homo sapiens*. Their average brain size was over 1,500 cc. A Neandertal skull is so distinctive that no trained paleoanthropologist would mistake it for anything else; the forehead sits low on the face, there is a noticeable occipital bun in the back of the skull, and exaggerated brow ridges arch over each eye. A robust postcranial skeleton indicates that Neandertals were powerful, highly muscled creatures; they also possessed a huge barrel-chested torso. Finally, and this point should confirm beyond a shadow of a doubt that Neandertals were not human, there is the genetic evidence. Thorough testing has shown that while some humans (Asians and Europeans but not Africans) possess a tiny amount of Neandertal genes, one can safely conclude that Neandertals are genetically distinct from modern humans. Here's how Jurmain et al. describe the research done with DNA derived from twelve different Neandertal fossils:

> Results from the Neandertal specimens show that these individuals are genetically more different from contemporary *Homo sapiens* populations than modern human populations are from each other—in fact, about three times as much. Consequently, Krings and colleagues (1997) have hypothesized that the Neandertal lineage separated from that of our modern *H. sapiens* ancestors sometime between 690,000 and 550,000 ya [years ago].[27]

Again, the writer of the Institute for Creation Research article is very wrong about Neandertals but, unfortunately, his uninformed readers probably won't know that.

Finally, the writer attempts to discredit the data for australopithecines by implying that some species were simply apes. (I guess we can simply ignore the cranial capacity, more humanlike dentition, and a postcranial skeleton adapted to habitual bipedalism.) His comment regarding "conflicting interpretations" only illustrates the fact that very early hominin material is difficult to classify or categorize. I fail to see how that bolsters his argument.

This attempt to discredit empirical data that support the scientific theory of hominin evolution is quite typical of the way in which creationists deal with this material. Virtually everything they write regarding fossil hominins is misleading, inaccurate, or irrelevant. Unfortunately, many individuals will never bother to pick up even an introductory physical anthropology textbook, but they will form their opinions based on commentaries like the one quoted above. How potentially damaging is this? This writer's (Frank Sherwin's) material is quoted in many creationist works, and he is a featured speaker for the Institution for Creation Research. He is not, however, a trained paleoanthropologist. Remember, though, Mr. Sherwin is working under the presumption that the young-earth creationist paradigm is correct, thus forcing him into a position of explaining to the rest of us why no data (even data not yet discovered), no matter what the data consist of, support or will support the paleoanthropological theory of hominin evolution.

12. EXTINCTION-LEVEL EVENTS

There have been five extinction-level events during the past 540 million years, catastrophic events and/or traumatic periods that have caused the extinction of at least 50 percent of all animal species alive at the time.[28] There is an impressive amount of data that support this commonly held notion, including stratigraphic and fossil evidence, all of which have been dated using both relative and absolute techniques. The young-earth creationists, of course, do not accept what they sometimes refer to as the "secular" explanation of our physical world and instead claim the following:

- There were no extinction events before the introduction of sin into our world as a consequence of Eve's and Adam's transgression in the Garden of Eden.[29]
- Dinosaurs existed at least until the flood described in Genesis, which, according to biblical chronology, would date back to around 2350 BCE.[30]
- Finally, there was only one extinction event and that was caused by the great "Flood" described in Genesis.[31]

The reader will note (again) the prominent role played by religious dogma and the assumption that the Bible can be read like a reliable history textbook. Basically, the young earthers are claiming that there was only one extinction event so (yet again) the geologists, biologists, and paleontologists simply don't know what they are talking about.

Based on what the young earthers (are forced to) believe, dinosaurs existed until 2350 BCE. If this is the case, one might wonder why no one around at the time or before knew this. For example, there is not one dinosaur painted or drawn in ancient artwork anywhere. Why is it that the early peoples of Europe and Asia were not eating these creatures? Why have paleontologists and paleoanthropologists never found a dinosaur bone in middens associated with Neandertals or early modern *Homo sapiens*? Early Egyptian hieroglyphs began appearing in the fourth millennium BCE; why is it that the Egyptians didn't have one thing to "say" about the largest land-roaming animals that ever walked the face of the earth? Ditto for the Sumerians, who developed writing sometime during the same period.

The most powerful and violent explosion on Earth during the past 2 million years or so was the Toba volcanic eruption in Sumatra about 72,000 years ago. Here's how geologists Jelle Zeilinga de Boer and Donald T. Sanders describe the aftermath of that event:

> Toba is estimated to have emitted some 2,800 cubic kilometers of magma, compared with a mere 50 cubic kilometers from Tambora [another huge volcanic eruption]. Its VEI [volcanic explosivity index] is thought to have been 8, the highest intensity known to date. Volcanologists have adopted the descriptive term *humongous* for Toba's eruption.
>
> Dust and aerosols from Toba would have been carried around the world by high-altitude winds, interfering with incoming solar radiation and leading to global cooling. Sulfur-containing gases from Toba, upon reaching the stratosphere and combining with water vapor, must have produced vast clouds of sulfuric-acid aerosols. . . . Those aerosols, which spread around the globe and reflected much sunlight, are thought to have lowered average temperatures by at least 10 degrees Celsius. Such a reduction could have led to a "volcanic winter" that may have lasted several years. This abrupt change in global climate came at a time of great stress to early humans, as tribes who had settled in the northern reaches of Eurasia were retreating southward as the ice fields advanced. The harsh climate, which lasted for several years, also affected lower altitudes and sorely taxed those migrating groups and no doubt led to a significant decline in their numbers.[32]

Anthropologist Stanley Ambrose wrote that this traumatic event could have possibly reduced the entire human population at the time to perhaps as few as one thousand pairs of breeding men and women, resulting in a classic genetic "bottleneck" in early humans.[33]

Of course, this is yet another event that must be "shoe-horned" into that four-thousand-year period that preceded the birth of Christ, at least by the creationists' reckoning. Again, how is it possible that people alive at the time didn't notice a global "volcanic winter?" There is no indication that anyone alive during this early time period was aware of this earth-shattering event. And, what about the tens of thousands that must have perished? Did no one think to write about this or even pass down stories regarding this apocalyptic event? How unlikely is that?

These twelve issues represent merely a few of the many areas where young-earth creationism contradicts standard, mainstream science, but they should suffice to illustrate just how wrong the young-earth paradigm is. Remember, if standard science is right about only one of these issues, then the young earthers must necessarily be wrong. Clearly, these arguments are not directed at the "obsessively deductive" young earthers, since no data will cause them to even question their presumptive "theory." But there are perhaps those who are relatively uninformed regarding matters of science and are traditionally religious but do not suffer from the pathology of religious fundamentalism; those are the individuals who are presumably still receptive to sound, logical, empirically based arguments and will reconsider and, hopefully, reject the dogmatic young-earth paradigm in favor of science done by real scientists who live in the real world of hypothesis testing, data collection, the conceptual circle of induction and deduction, and peer-reviewed journals.

There are other issues one might raise regarding the young-earth claim that are not necessarily of the "slam dunk" variety like those discussed in this chapter but do, nevertheless, merit some attention. Four arguments with a high degree of probability of being correct will be discussed first, followed by four arguments with a slightly lower degree of probability.

CHAPTER TEN

FOUR REASONS WHY THE YOUNG-EARTH HYPOTHESIS IS PROBABLY WRONG

1. *If the young earthers are correct, then virtually all geologists, astronomers, astrophysicists, biologists, paleontologists, paleoanthropologists, archaeologists, and geneticists teaching in our universities and/or doing research and/or publishing articles in refereed, academic journals and/or writing textbooks for classes in all these fields are fundamentally wrong about almost everything.* It seems much more likely that it is the individuals working under the assumption that that their faith-based "theory" cannot, in principle, be falsified (ever) regardless of the quantity or quality of the data collected up to this point or the quantity or quality of data that will become available in the future, who are wrong.

2. *Six thousand years is simply not enough time for every prehistorical and historical event or process to have occurred.* For example, based on the young earthers' chronology, Neandertals and *Homo erectus* peoples were coexistent with Egyptians and Sumerians and some of the early figures discussed in the Bible; one would think that they may have been mentioned by someone. The five extinction-level events discussed earlier (and others not discussed) would have to have occurred during this time. Dinosaurs are stomping around until about 2350 BCE. The continents have to "drift" away from the single landmass (Pangea) of which they were a part to their current position. Stars would have to be evolving at a rate that makes nonsense of everything we know about atomic fusion and would have to be evolving at different rates! The colossal and literally earth-shattering explosions of asteroids or meteorites that left about twenty or so huge craters with diameters measured in the tens of kilometers, would all have to

have occurred. This would also include the huge impact explosion that produced the 170 km diameter crater in the Yucatan that ended the reign of the dinosaurs (at least according to real scientists) and caused global firestorms, months of darkness around the world, and the extinction of approximately 70 percent of all plant and animal species. (One would think that event would at least be mentioned in passing by those alive at the time but, again, we have no indication that anyone at any time witnessed this event.)

3. *Analysis of human mitochondrial DNA (mtDNA) tells us that the most recent common female ancestor was alive in Africa sometime around 125,000 years ago.* The genetic material (DNA) of two different specimens can be compared and if the rate of change of the DNA (caused by mutations) is known, one can quite easily calculate at what time in the past the two specimens shared a common ancestor. This "molecular clock" idea works especially well for DNA found in the mitochondria (organelles that lie outside the nucleus of the cell) for the following reasons: the entire mtDNA genome is comprised of only 16,500 base pairs, compared to the three billion or so for nuclear DNA; mutations of mtDNA occur at a much higher rate than that found in nuclear DNA; mtDNA don't recombine (a "reshuffling" of genetic material from one generation to the next) like nuclear DNA does; and mtDNA are passed down matrilineally, allowing one to "see" a direct genetic line. Using a molecular clock that has been fine-tuned to genetic change over time in the mtDNA, it appears as though "mitochondrial Eve," the most recent common matrilineal ancestor of all human beings alive today, lived in East Africa around 125,000 years ago. (The name "Eve" was probably a poor choice, since some have mistakenly associated this individual with the biblical Eve. This has led to a popular misunderstanding that mitochondrial Eve was the original mother of all humankind. There were, however, other females with families alive at that time, but their line simply died out before the present time.)

I would be remiss here if I did not point out that while there is near unanimity among anthropologists and geneticists regarding the molecular clock idea and how it has been calibrated in this case, one study concluded that the clock actually "ticks" at a rate that is twenty times faster than what has commonly been assumed.[1] By that clock, mitochondrial Eve would have been alive about 7,500 years ago. But I don't think the young earthers should begin popping the corks on their champagne bottles just yet. For one thing, a later study[2] did not concur with the aforementioned; thus, there is virtually no credible dissenting voice remaining regarding the basic fundamentals of the process.

That, however, is the least of the young earthers' problems. The 125,000 year value is consistent with everything else we know about recent hominin evolution: it is consonant with the fossil evidence (recall that the oldest modern human specimen has been dated back to about 195,000 years ago in Africa) and it puts modern *Homo sapiens* in Africa before they migrated eastward out of East Africa—about 60,000 years ago according to other widely accepted genetic studies.

4. *Young-earth creationists have no direct empirical evidence of their claimed age of six thousand years for earth rocks or moon rocks (i.e., they have no direct dating of these materials that substantiates their claims).* As has been noted, the six-thousand-year figure that is used by the young earthers was taken directly from the scriptures of Judaism. Here is how one feature writer explains it on the Answers in Genesis website: "Since God is the Creator of all things (including science), and His Word is true ('Sanctify them by Your truth. Your word is truth,' John 17:17), the true age of the earth must agree with His Word."[3] Basically, for young earthers, empirical data always take a back seat to religious dogma. In other words, if there is a fundamental disagreement on scientific issues, it is the data or the interpretation of the data that must be wrong, not the religious presupposition.

CHAPTER ELEVEN

FOUR REASONS WHY THE YOUNG-EARTH HYPOTHESIS IS DUBIOUS

1. *Their "theory" is embraced in an a priori, deductive fashion, and the data are then interpreted so that it is consonant with the "theory."* Data that contradict their "theory" and cannot be sufficiently "massaged" to make them support their "theory" are simply ignored.

2. *Their "theory" is not falsifiable since it is assumed to be absolutely correct and no data that disconfirm the young-earth hypothesis will be accepted.* The reader should note that nonfalsifiable claims regarding the physical, tangible world we live in are nonsensical and meaningless, much like the religious dogmas of the world's religions.

3. *Young-earth creationists do little or no fieldwork of their own.* In fact, many creationists have built careers doing little more than critiquing the data obtained by geologists, paleontologists, etc. If you want to find young-earth creationists, you have to go to their websites, "museums," or church-sponsored lectures and presentations. You will not find them in departments of biology, genetics, geology, astronomy, or anthropology at accredited, mainstream colleges and universities, or on the staff at natural history museums. By the way, young-earth creationism is virtually unheard of in the universities and state-sponsored museums of Europe, Africa, and Asia.

4. *Young-earth creationists will intentionally mislead their readers by bringing up long disregarded and irrelevant specimens (e.g., Piltdown Man and Nebraska Man) and will provide analyses of fossil specimens that no practicing paleontologist or paleoanthropologist would agree with.* Here's what Robert Williams, physical anthropologist and professor of anthropology at Arizona State University has to say regarding the

way young-earth creationists continue to dredge up the now totally irrelevant Nebraska Man:

> "Nebraska Man" was never really accepted by the scientific community. The existence of the fossil (and the erroneous claim of the discoverer that the tooth was that of an ape or human ancestor) was announced in 1922, and retractions were printed in *Science* and *Nature* in 1927. The tooth turned out to belong to a peccary (a relative of pigs), an animal that does have teeth that are somewhat similar to humans. The identification of this particular tooth was made somewhat more difficult because it was badly worn. It is amazing that creationists still bring this up over seventy years after the whole thing was debunked (by other scientists, not creationists). Although a mistake was made initially, this is a perfect example of the self-correcting nature of science that helps to show how ludicrous the creationist claims that there is no evidence for an ancient earth or evolution are.[1]

One more example should suffice to illustrate just how shamelessly deceitful young-earth creationists can be. In 2001, Bill 2548, which would effectively prevent the teaching of evolutionary theory in the public schools of Arkansas, was submitted to the state legislature for consideration. The key source for the antiscience group attempting to push this bill through was "Dr." Kent Hovind. (He received his "doctorate" from the unaccredited Patriot Bible University, referred to by some as a classic "diploma mill.") Mr. Hovind was once a star witness and popular spokesman for young-earth creationism, but these efforts were interrupted by a stint in prison for tax and cash transaction offenses. He is currently on parole and is once again the featured speaker for Creation Science Evangelism. He produced an eight-DVD set titled *Creation Seminar Series*, an eight-part "scientific" documentary that was once available on Netflix, and has released numerous tapes, CDs, and DVDs and published a number of books on young-earth creationism. He founded Dinosaur Adventure Land, a creationist theme park in Florida where classes for homeschooling families were offered. Unfortunately for the bill's supporters (well, fortunately, as far as I am concerned), much of the language of the bill was provided by Mr. Hovind. And, of course, front and center are the old creationist standbys, Piltdown Man and Nebraska Man, along with a number of purposely misleading statements and dubious claims, including an inaccurate description of certain mammoth bones that Hovind stated were claimed to be from the same mammoth—in fact, that claim was not made by the researchers. Hovind continued to perpetuate this lie even after it was exposed (see, for example, his article at Fill the Void Ministries).[2] In the interest of fairness, let me state that even some creationists have parted ways with Mr. Hovind, but, nevertheless, his creationist dogmas have, no doubt, influenced thousands of individuals, many of them children. How many of them will never again even acknowledge standard science and evolutionary theory? How many of them will be teaching their own children this nonsense?

CHAPTER TWELVE

THE INTELLECTUAL DECEIT OF YOUNG-EARTH CREATIONISM

The "obsessive deductivist" is not concerned with empirical or objective truth because, as we have seen in this discussion of young-earth creationism, the data are merely inconvenient "speed bumps" on the road of religious fundamentalism—unless, of course, the data do not necessarily disconfirm their "theories," in which case they are welcomed. Young-earth creationists today operate with the same basic mindset of the Catholic Church in the seventeenth century, when it placed Galileo under house arrest for championing the idea that the solar system was heliocentric (sun-centered). (In 1616, a group of eleven Catholic theologians serving at the request of the Inquisition, voted 11–0 that the earth did not move; the sun-centered notion was deemed heretical since it contradicted scriptures.) The fact that Galileo had incontrovertible data (the phases of Venus and the moons of Jupiter) to support his theory was simply immaterial to church authorities, who had no intention of letting empirical data threaten their (assumed, a priori deductive) version of cosmology. In the early part of the seventeenth century, however, those who spoke for the church felt no compunction whatsoever to rationalize their position; they were, after all, right, and the dissenters were wrong. It is this very attitude that would impede the development of science in the Western world for some fourteen centuries or so once Christianity finally managed to subdue Greek rationalism in the fourth century CE. Today's world is, however, much different, so, unlike their religious brethren of the seventeenth century, when discussing matters of science, today's religious absolutists have to use the language of science if they want to be heard. But, while they do use the language of science, they could not care less about the epistemology of science; as far as young-earth creationists are concerned, the data exist merely to serve their "theory."

If one really desires to uncover their actual agenda, if one really wants to see what is going on behind the disingenuous veneer of (pseudo-)science creationists hide behind, she has to look for it, but it is there for all to see. Here is Mr. Hovind, again, in an article titled "Are You Being Brainwashed by Your Public School Textbooks?":

> Who Started This Lie of Evolution?
>
> Plain and simple, the devil started this lie. The Bible predicted that this would happen. In II Peter 3:3–5, the Bible says that in the last days there would be scoffers. These scoffers scoff at the Bible because of their lusts, not their science. They will teach uniformitarianism, "all things continue as they were from the beginning of the creation." They are willingly ignorant of the Creation. It is a conscious decision for them! In spite of the overwhelming evidence, they reject Creation.
>
> These scoffers are also ignorant of the Flood. They reject anything that proves that there is a God. The flood shows God's right and willingness to judge His Creation. They are rejecting God because of His rules! Rather than get right with God, they choose to deny His existence.
>
> By rejecting the Bible and God, it is easier for the scoffers to justify their sins and lusts. It makes it easier to justify abortion and euthanasia. Satan hates humanity and abortion kills people! He has been using evolutionary ideas since the Garden of Eden, and evolution is a primary method to destroy humanity. If evolution is true there are "inferior" people on Earth, and this world would be better off without them. Hitler felt this way due to his belief in evolution.[1]

Mr. Hovind is clearly a confused individual. In his world, reality is simply a matter of choice; the world really is the way you want it to be! Note that those who reject his "theory" are not simply individuals who don't agree with him but, rather, people who are morally flawed, "scoffers" who simply want to "justify their sins and lusts." In the real world that the rest of us live in, however, there are many men and women of faith who are also highly trained scientists (Vatican astronomers) who have made invaluable contributions to their particular field but who reject the young-earth paradigm because there is no empirical, objective reason to accept it. In fact, one of the key scientific witnesses who led the fight against the creationist takeover of the Dover school system in Pennsylvania was a publicly avowed Roman Catholic, Dr. Kenneth Miller, a biologist at Brown University. And, finally, there is the obligatory Hitler reference that all scoundrels trot out when they have run out of ideas. In truth, Hitler got all the motivation he needed from two thousand years of virulent and hateful anti-Semitism, courtesy of Christianity.

As I mentioned earlier, even some creationists don't have much good to say about Mr. Hovind, and they may feel as though I am not justified in my implication that he somehow speaks for them. I disagree simply because of the fact that he has been one of the most popular figures in the creationist movement and thousands have responded to his "message," as evidenced by the many books, tapes, CDs, and DVDs he has sold. And we should not forget that he was the "scientist" of note for the supporters of the Arkansas bill to undermine the teaching of evolution. Nevertheless, I am (somewhat) willing to concede that point because there are other examples I can cite to make my general point regarding the "hidden agenda" of the young-earth creationists.

Consider, for example, Ken Ham, the founder and CEO of Answers in Genesis and the Creation Museum in Petersburg, Kentucky. Mr. Ham has written a number of books (*The Lie: Evolution*; *Dinosaurs of Eden*, and others), his radio broadcasts have aired on hundreds of stations, and he has appeared on virtually every major news network. As is the case with many other creationists, his academic credentials are curious: he has a bachelor's degree in applied science from the Queensland Institute of Technology in Australia, a diploma of education, and two honorary doctorates from Christian fundamentalist colleges. Here are a few of Mr. Ham's comments on standard science found in his article titled "A Young Earth—It's Not the Issue!" on the Answers in Genesis website:

• There is no mention in the Bible of "millions or billions of years."

- The "fallible" dating methods of science should not replace the "*infallible* Word of God."
- "We should be . . . careful to let God speak *to* us through His Word, and not try to impose our ideas *on* God's Word."
- "Christian leaders" who are tempted by the knowledge of science should be trusting "the simple clear words of the Bible."[2]

I have a request to make of the creation "scientists" out there: Can we simply drop the charade? If we take a dog and put a dress and a wig on it, it is still a dog. In a more rational and objective world, the use of the term "science" by Mr. Ham and his ilk would be illegal. They should simply come clean with the American public, many of whom are, sadly, easily duped by the young earthers' "scientific" statements, and make their true intentions explicitly known. They will not, however, "come clean" because they know that once they drop the façade of science, many individuals will no longer listen to them. Anyway, they would never get the chance to present their anti-science "theories" to school boards and state legislatures if they were not dressed up in scientific garb.

There are certainly other examples of the obsessive-deductive mindset but young-earth creationism, with its overt disdain for empirical data and its willingness to proclaim a priori, presumptive "theories" as absolutely true, is one of the best illustrations of this anti-empirical, anti-objective epistemology. Other examples, however, readily come to mind: the idea that gays and lesbians choose their sexual orientation; the idea that biological races actually exist; the idea that women are in some sense inferior to men; the idea that one religion serves as the standard by which other religions should be judged; and the idea that holy scriptures are the literal, inerrant word of God. Interestingly enough, virtually all of these notions are grounded either wholly or partly in the Judeo-Christian tradition— which is not really surprising, given the fact that there are few things that can turn an individual's mind to mush like religious fundamentalism can. Individuals who are ostensibly sane and well-adjusted citizens will not tolerate irrational and nonfalsifiable claims unless, of course, they come in the guise of religion.

One would think, with the dawn of the third millennium and all that, that it is time for *Homo sapiens* to take the next step in our cognitive and conceptual evolution and recognize religions for what they truly are: geography- and culture-specific ideologies that temper and assuage our concerns with our finitude and our mortality. Nothing more, nothing less. That all religions manage to do this (for those who buy what they are selling) belies the absolutist claims of religious fundamentalists everywhere.

There is simply no good reason for the rest of us to have to put up with right-wing, antiscience, exclusivist Christians, who insist on making the world a place that accommodates their religious beliefs and biases; or with murderous, bloodthirsty, intolerant, extremist Muslims, who will kill anyone in the name of their religion; or with Jews who continue to bully the Palestinians in the Middle East; or, on the other hand, with Palestinians who strike at Israel with horrific acts of violence; or with anyone, for that matter, who uses religion to justify misogyny, homophobia, racism, xenophobia, intellectual totalitarianism, and the harming and killing of others. Religions are, for all intents and purposes, all equally right or, if you prefer, all equally wrong. Refusal or unwillingness to recognize this fact will only delay the intellectual progression and true enlightenment of our species.

PART THREE

FOUR IMPORTANT
(AND POTENTIALLY FLAWED)
SOURCES OF
RELIGIOUS KNOWLEDGE

CHAPTER THIRTEEN

QUESTIONABLE VALIDITY

I spent two years in Trinidad researching the Orisha religion, a highly syncretic, African-derived religion somewhat similar to Vodoun in Haiti; Santería in Cuba, Puerto Rico, and Miami; and Candomblé in Brazil.[1] Sometime during that period, I began to perceive and conceptualize the world in Orisha terms and, like E. E. Evans-Pritchard when he conducted fieldwork among the Azande of north central Africa,[2] I found the transition from my own "culturized" worldview, the product of a typical southern Louisiana enculturation process, to that of the Orisha worshipers to be unnervingly facile. The transition was so smooth, in fact, that at the time I was unaware that it was occurring; it's only now, in retrospect, that I can see it. What was once awkward and strange for me eventually became almost natural. Where once I had to consciously mimic appropriate social comportment, such gestures eventually became part of my standard behavioral repertoire. This would include such things as speaking and understanding an English creole (based on British English, which in itself is a bit alien to me), engaging in a proper conversation, interacting with women, dining etiquette, driving on the left side of the road, and so on; basically all those issues that can potentially induce a serious case of culture shock if not dealt with properly. In my case, being a cultural anthropologist doing fieldwork, I was faced with the additional task of learning a religion, which, given the highly culture-specific nature of religion and the personal, existential aspects of faith and belief, can be quite difficult. That I was eventually able to "clear this hurdle," probably has more to do with my initiation into the Orisha religion than anything else.

I had observed Orisha initiations and had long before decided that this was not something I wanted to do. It is, after all, quite an ordeal: three days of fasting and isolation (with the head completely wrapped) are followed by a five-hour ceremony where the head is prepared for possession by an *orisha* (the Yoruba term for god or spirit). My friends and contacts, however, told me that if I wanted to really know the religion like an insider, I would have to be initiated. So, after some cajoling on their part (all good-natured), I consented. The three-day seclusion in the small, earth-floored hut was not as bad as I thought it would be, although I was, of course, very hungry and hot, and tired, and annoyed, and anxious, and . . . well, you get the picture. After my period of seclusion, I was escorted to the *perogun* (a small structure where a handful of important *orisha* are enshrined) where the final rite would occur.

At one point during this ceremony, I had what some would describe as a religious experience. A calabash containing a repugnant but powerful medicinal concoction was passed to me with instructions to drink. I had no choice in the matter, at least not at that juncture—I was stubbornly determined to complete the ordeal, and I was so close to doing so—but, before drinking, I looked down into the calabash and had, for lack of a better term, a vision. It seemed very real to me at the time. After about five seconds or so, I closed my eyes and shook my head. When I reopened my eyes, the vision had dissipated. I was later told by my friends and contacts that this sort of thing is expected, and they all seemed genuinely pleased about it.

Sometime later, after reflecting on my experiences, I began to appreciate the power of enculturation. Now, in my case, I was an outsider and an adult with a sophisticated academic training, as opposed to an insider and a child or adolescent, as would normally be the case. Being a cultural anthropologist, it was only natural for me to interpret my experiences objectively and naturalistically; I attributed the vision to a combination of extreme fatigue, stress, malnourishment, and the consumption of a small amount of "bush rum" (pure alcohol made from molasses). In my mind, there was no doubt that what I perceived did not happen empirically (i.e., the experience was certainly real on some level but only I had access to it). But what of the fourteen-year-old who has lived his entire life in a world that is dominated by the Orisha religion? All events, thoughts, and experiences are shaped and fashioned by this "filter" before they are psychologically and intellectually internalized. In the case of this young neophyte, the ontological status of a vision such as the one I had is elevated considerably. Consequently, the Orisha religion becomes even more real, more valid, and truer than before. If, before this point, the neophyte was not a team player in the game of cultural absolutism, if he had not yet choked down a decidedly ethnocentric ideology, he would now, without question, be so and do so.

At this point, one might wonder if all religious belief is grounded on such a flimsy foundation. Perhaps not, because there are certainly other modes of "instruction" that are employed. Nevertheless, are these other modes of "instruction" as specious and questionable as the one discussed here?

There are four different instruments (broadly conceived) that are responsible for much of the religious knowledge possessed by both individuals and societies as a whole: 1) natural theology, 2) revelation (the special, historical sort that is directed at one specific individual), 3) subjective experiences (for example, being filled with the holy spirit [Protestant fundamentalism], *satori* [temporary enlightenment in Zen Buddhism], mystical experiences, and the various trance states that are part and parcel of religions everywhere), and 4) overt instruction. In the chapters that follow we will consider each in turn with a special emphasis on reliability, validity, and substance. (A fifth "instrument," holy scriptures, is, of course, a significant source of religious knowledge, the complexity of which, however, deserves special treatment and, thus, will be dealt with in Part Four.)

CHAPTER FOURTEEN
NATURAL THEOLOGY

N atural theology refers to the study of those aspects of our quotidian, tangible world that may reflect the existence of God. Some claim to see the "hand of God" in a sunset, the birth of a child (a not-so-miraculous event that occurs about 360,000 times each day), a deep-space photograph from the Hubble telescope, or a tissue sample viewed through an electron microscope. These phenomena are certainly beautiful (in a broad, aesthetic sense) and awe-inspiring, but it is clear that a general ignorance regarding the way nature works is highly (positively) correlated with the propensity to see "God's hand" in natural phenomena. If one can understand basically everything about a sunset (for example, why the sun "moves" the way it does relative to the earth, how atmospheric distortion causes the shape, size, and color of the sun to vary from time to time, etc.), there is not a whole lot of room for mystery—i.e., no need to invoke some supernatural entity or force in order to understand it. The same general argument can be made for virtually all natural phenomena. Of course, I am not suggesting that we know everything there is to know about nature—in fact, we probably never will—but if the past is any indication, we will continue to become more knowledgeable regarding the workings of nature and that will, consequently, obviate the need to invoke some preternatural entity or force to explain it.

A perfect example of this process, the elimination of ignorance (and the concomitant need to invoke the "hand of God") through scientific understanding, can be seen in our knowledge of the origins and subsequent growth and development of our world and the plants and animals that inhabit Earth. Virtually all of the oldest ideas invoked the actions of God or gods to explain the existence, form, and nature of the universe and our immediate world. This is not surprising, given the fact that little if anything was known about the physical and organic universe until just recently, historically speaking. For example, William Paley, in his *Natural Theology* (published in 1802), gave us one of the first statements of the design argument for the existence of God. His now legendary "watchmaker analogy" went something like this: One happens upon a watch and, after examining its intricate assemblage of springs, gears, and other assorted parts, concludes that such a complex mechanism surely had a designer. By the same token, the universe is complex—in fact, almost infinitely more so than a watch—and therefore must have also had a designer but, in this case, a designer capable of such a feat, or God. The intelligent-design idea today is based on similar reasoning. A comprehensive critique of the design argument is provided later, in chapter thirty-seven, but I feel a brief comment is warranted at this point.

In the most general terms, the intelligent-design idea depends almost solely on human ignorance for its utility. We no longer need to invoke invisible, cosmic forces (the "hand of God") to understand lunar and solar eclipses, tidal fluctuations, supernovae, or the evolution of the eye. (At one time, intelligent-design proponents proclaimed that the eye was "irreducibly complex," i.e., that only a fully developed human eye, for example, was useful and that the rudimentary and intermediate stages of the eye produced by the process of evolution by natural selection were not functional. This claim was quickly dropped, however, after it was met with a veritable storm of counterexamples from biologists, zoologists, and paleontologists. How could the intelligent-design folks have been so uninformed regarding the empirical data? The simple answer to that question is that those who are motivated by religious concerns to embrace a particular claim or idea aren't generally concerned with real-world data.[1]) So we don't completely understand precisely how the first amino acids developed and combined to make the proteins necessary for life—but there is certainly no reason to invoke a designer when human ignorance, a much more elegant and simple hypothesis, will suffice. Each time we increase our knowledge of the universe, the gaps in our comprehension either decrease in extent or grow fewer in number. No "God of the gaps" is necessary.

There are other, so-called "cosmological arguments" for the existence of God—i.e., arguments that attempt to invoke God as the reason for certain facts about our world, such as the first cause and contingency arguments (examined in detail in chapters thirty-six and thirty-six)—but suffice it to say that none are totally convincing since one need not necessarily invoke God to understand the phenomena in question. There is another type of argument, however, that uses the rather quotidian aspects of human reality to infer the existence of God. The sociologist Peter Berger has given us the most detailed analysis of these "signals of transcendence," roughly described as those events, qualities, and processes of everyday life that point beyond the immanent dimension of human life to a transcendent source as the ultimate reason for the precise nature and form of those events, qualities, and processes.[2] As Berger explains, "inductive faith," a term he uses liberally, "moves from human experience to statements about God."[3]

In my mind, one of the most intriguing arguments made by Berger in this regard focuses on play. Berger observes that play is so much a part of human life that it seems inherently human, but that is only if we are overlooking one very salient fact: one aspect of play—time—actually points beyond the mundane world that we inhabit. The world we live in is (with the exception of the strange goings on of general and special relativity and at "Planck lengths" and "Planck times" that represent the universe before about 5.4×10^{-44} seconds after the initial inflation began) perceived by us to pass from one moment to the next in a consistent, linear fashion. This is the world in which we grow old and die, automobiles slowly deteriorate until they are no longer useful, plants sprout, bloom on an annual basis, and eventually expire, and sickness and disease run their courses. But in play—for example, a baseball game—we can start and stop time (from the first pitch of an inning to the last out of the inning), suspend time (in between the top and bottom of innings and between innings themselves), and we can even make time eternal (if, for example, a game is suspended before the required nine innings are played and the game is never completed for some reason). In basketball and football games we can even create time, as when a referee signals to the scoreboard technician to put x number of seconds back on the clock. This idea of time as manipulable, malleable, and eternal, has no known source in the everyday world of human existence. In fact, the very idea of time as fluid, inconsistent, and interminable points away from the immanent domain we inhabit to a transcendent dimension of some sort. It is, in short, a signal of transcendence.

Berger's argument from damnation is similar. In most cases, humans are quite capable of dealing with criminals in a just fashion and in a way that does not overly offend our worldly sensibilities. A man steals a car. He is caught, convicted, and sentenced to five years in prison. Some may debate the relative fit of the punishment to the crime but, in general terms, we all agree that some specific punishment is warranted and that we are fully capable of meting out such punishment. There are a few cases, however, that so offend our sensibilities, that are so shocking, that we feel as if we are powerless to exact an appropriate justice. Berger mentions Adolf Eichmann, the "architect of the Holocaust," as one example. We might add other mass murderers of history—for example, Stalin and Pol Pot. Berger argues that, in these cases, any sort of discussion of the relative fit of the punishment to the crime is rendered superfluous, since there is only one just punitive response to heinous crimes such as these: absolute damnation; clearly, humans are incapable of meting out such punishment. Again, as in the case discussed above, we have yet another aspect of our corporeal existence that is not bounded and finite but, rather, "reaches" beyond our physical, tangible universe to a plane of existence that transcends the one we inhabit.

Berger does discuss other "signals of transcendence," but these should suffice to give the reader some idea of what he has in mind. I have always considered Berger's "cosmological arguments" to be ingenious yet ultimately not totally convincing. Of course, it is not Berger's intention to prove the existence of God in the conventional sense, but he is certainly suggesting that such arguments at least point us in that direction. I suppose a relevant question here would be whether or not such explanations are the most parsimonious, elegant, and robust available given the data. One might point out that any behavior that is driven by real-world contingencies can ultimately be explained by alluding to some aspect of the bounded, materialistic world in which we live. Manipulating time in sports contests the way we do could simply be a matter of necessity; for example, in games involving a significant degree of physical exertion it only seems reasonable that play—and, thus, time—is stopped occasionally. In regard to Berger's argument from damnation, one might point out that if we apply the same reasoning to "positive" cases—for example, individuals doing the equivalent good of thousands of individuals, such as a billionaire that funds the building of hospitals all over Afghanistan—it is not clear that we need to invoke anything other than the context of the real world we inhabit in order to understand such cases (that is, there is no need invoke a transcendent realm or the possibility of "absolute salvation" to make sense of them). And, in my mind, cases where good far surpasses what one individual can normally do, except in rare instances, are functionally equivalent to cases where the evil far surpasses what one individual is capable of, except in rare instances. In regard to Hitler, Stalin, and so on, the opportunity, means, and motivation that facilitated their heinous acts are all, regrettably, comprehensible in the context of the tangible, materialistic world in which we live. Besides, the notion that there should be perfect or absolute justice is an assumption that may tell us more about how we would like the world to be rather than how it actually is.

The theologian John Cottingham makes a similar argument, but instead of "signals" he uses the term "traces."[4] Cottingham argues that science generally employs two different forms of inquiry, experimental and observational. He writes that an argument for the existence of God can be tailored in an analogous way to investigations of the latter kind.

Cottingham points out that current ideas regarding the inflation period of the early universe (sometimes referred to as the big bang theory) are all based on "trace" evidence that point back to the event. Thus, the expansion of the universe and cosmic microwave background radiation (which is roughly the same in any direction) are offered as evidence for the initial expansion of the cosmos. In other words, he argues, the cause of these phenomena are inferred from the assumed aftereffects that are thought to be by-products of the initial event; thus, "traces" of the event are accepted as evidence for the event itself. Cottingham further argues that a faith in God buttressed by similar evidence is reasonable. Well, he certainly seems to be onto something here, but the "traces" he offers as "evidence" are dubious in my mind. Here is what he writes regarding these "traces" that are assumed to serve as some type of evidence of the Divine: ". . . the traces which are experienced in that sense of overwhelming beauty and goodness and meaning that is described in countless records of religious experience."[5]

I find Cottingham's attempt to equate cosmic expansion and microwave radiation, measurable and empirical phenomena, with religious experience, mystical and psychological phenomena, to be totally unconvincing. The reason why takes us right back to the crux of the issue: science employs a universally accepted epistemology to generate knowledge that transcends culture, whereas religion gives us 10,500 different versions of reality, all intimately linked to the cultures in which they originated. One can only imagine the many different sources of religious experience, ranging from the purely psychological to the manifestly existential. It is quite plausible to assume that religious experience, for example, is totally self-generated and has nothing to do with any sort of transcendent entity. Nevertheless, it is true that claims regarding a transcendental origin for such phenomena are not falsifiable, so such claims may be true. But, remember, that makes such claims no more true (or false) than any other nonfalsifiable claim. Long story short, the validity of such "evidence" can hardly be placed on the same epistemological level as empirical phenomena that can be measured by anyone, anywhere.

Finally, the leap from such "traces" to the cause of the "traces" is also problematic. Even if we were to substantiate that religious experiences were real in the sense that they originated outside of and beyond the individuals who underwent them, there is still the virtually impossible task of pinning down the source of those experiences, especially if that source is assumed to be transcendental. In comparison, the claims that cosmologists are making are the most reasonable claims that could be made regarding the evidence we have. We don't have to see flames to know that that ash-ridden, blackened heap of wood and bricks was once on fire. It is, however, entirely reasonable to infer the origin of those "traces" given their empirical nature. The same cannot be said for what is going on between an individual's ears—there are, no doubt, hundreds of explanations that can be offered for such phenomena.

I feel we can conclude here that, as a source of religious knowledge, natural theology is at least problematic, if not downright dubious. In regard to reliability, validity, and substance, I would argue that this mode of information transmission has very little to offer those who are seeking something a bit more compelling. Whether or not one is convinced of the validity of these cosmological or inductive arguments, we do know, with a very high degree of confidence, that these arguments do not conclusively prove anything. At best, they are merely suggestive of the conclusions they claim to reach.

CHAPTER FIFTEEN

REVELATION

In the case of revelation, a group makes the claim that God or a god has "spoken" to an individual in some way and has communicated to him some special knowledge or information that he is to disseminate to the rest of the community. Perhaps the most salient examples drawn from the three Western monotheisms would be Moses and the burning bush incident, Saul (Paul) on the road to Damascus, and Muhammad in a cave on Mt. Hira. In the case of Moses, God (allegedly) appeared to him in the form of a burning bush that was not consumed, with instructions to go to Egypt and confront the Pharaoh (Exodus chapter 3). Moses was alone at the time, tending to a flock of animals and, according to Jewish and Christian tradition, he himself wrote the account of this story, although scholars date the writing of Exodus to centuries after the time of Moses. Saul, a notorious persecutor of Christians, was traveling with companions when he was (purportedly) struck down by a blinding light on the road to Damascus. According to the written account, found primarily in the Book of Acts, only Saul heard the loud noise as the voice of the Lord and only he actually saw Christ. This account was written by the same individual who wrote the Gospel of Luke, and the scholarly consensus is that the author of Acts was not an eyewitness to Saul's experiences on the road to Damascus and he was writing about thirty years or so after Paul's death. Muhammad was meditating alone during a spiritual retreat of sorts in a cave on Mt. Hira, north of Mecca, when (supposedly) he was first contacted by the angel Gabriel. He was forty years old at the time, and he would receive these revelations from Gabriel for the next twenty-two years, until his death in 632 CE. Only Muhammad was privy to the actual revelations themselves, even though he would sometimes be "visited" while sitting with a group of individuals. What we know of Muhammad's revelations comes from the Qur'an (codified around 650 CE) and collections of the sayings and deeds of Muhammad known as *hadith*, some written centuries after his death.

If a lawyer had to go into court with this "evidence," one wonders whether she would be able to establish the veracity of these revelatory claims to the satisfaction of a judge or a jury. I think not. (Of course, this thought experiment only works if we assume that the revelatory claims are presented as if they are not associated with Judaism, Christianity, or Islam since the practitioners of these faiths on the bench or on the jury will automatically assume they are valid simply by virtue of their provenience. Remember, no evidence is required to validate matters of faith in the eyes of a true believer.) After all, in the case of Moses, no one else was present during the purported burning bush incident; in the case of Paul, it is claimed that while others were present and heard a noise, only Paul heard the voice of Christ and saw the vision of Christ; and, in the case of Muhammad, no one but Muhammad was privy to the angelic pronouncements, even when Muhammad was with other people at the time.

There is also the issue of the accounts themselves. Holy scriptures are notoriously unreliable as historical accounts, especially when one considers the many years that had passed between the time the events described occurred and the time the accounts were written down, and the fact that they are generally written by avowed and dedicated adherents of the religion in question, individuals for whom objectivity was not a primary concern. There are other issues as well. It seems at least plausible that these individuals may have had some sort of experience but misinterpreted it or perhaps embellished the story with additional details or allusions to God and angels. Finally, perhaps the primary problem with revelation is that the recognized revelations of the world's religions, when taken together, are contradictory; they can't all be speaking for the one true God or supreme spiritual entity.

On the issues of reliability, validity, and substance, this particular source of religious knowledge scores at or near zero in all three cases. Basically, without a veritable ton of trust on the part of the believers and an intense willingness to believe, these revelations are meaning-less. And another word for trust, especially in this context, is faith. Given the virtually total lack of reliable, independent documentation and empirical data, faith is the only real link between the believer and the claim. The doubter, on the other hand, has plenty to work with, not the least being the fact that incredible, miraculous claims require data that are equal to the task of confirming such claims. In this case, the basic claim is that God spoke to humans, but the sup-porting data are virtually nonexistent.

One final point. Yet another indication that religion is strictly natural and human-made is the fact that said revelations always seem to involve God or gods speaking to one individual such that only that individual is privy to the information communicated. We can cer-tainly assume, quite safely I would argue, that God could have chosen to speak to the communities in which Moses, Saul, and Muhammad lived. In the case of Muhammad, that would have spared him and his followers social ostracization and mistreatment at the hands of their fellow Meccans, and made unnecessary the many wars fought, the blood that was shed, and the lives that were lost during Muhammad's struggle to rid the Arabian peninsula of pagan religionists. Similar arguments could be made in regard to the experiences of Moses (why weren't the Egyptians included; that would have prevented the horrible suffering endured by thousands of innocent Egyptians, including the mass slaughter of infants and toddlers) and Paul (why did Jesus not also appear to his Jewish followers in Jerusalem headed by James, brother of Jesus; why sit idly by while literally hundreds of competing Christian groups fought it out for three centuries before one finally prevailed; after all, one mass appearance would have been all that was needed to establish Christ's true church). Of course, the standard fundamentalist retort here would be that God's ways are beyond the purview of human knowledge, yet God has a plan and His plan is good. But, one might reply, why do these plans so often seem to require the suffering of so many innocents? Why are there no cases (not one) of group or community revelations when even the least educated and informed among us can anticipate the certain dif-ficulties that will accompany cases where only one individual claims to speak for God?

CHAPTER SIXTEEN

SUBJECTIVE EXPERIENCES

M any of these same issues can be raised in regard to the third source of religious knowledge, subjective experiences, but in this case individual experiences of the divine are not overtly recognized by the faith community as a whole; one can read about the revelations of Moses, Saul/Paul, and Muhammad in their respective holy books, but the phenomena I am referring to as subjective experiences are literally personal. One example, drawn from fundamentalist Christianity, is "being filled with the Holy Spirit." This happens when an individual who has been "born again" is (purportedly) infused with the power and energy of the Holy Spirit. My many conversations with "spirit-filled" fundamentalists over the years have convinced me that one need not necessarily invoke the intervention of a preternatural entity—by far the most problematic and complicated hypothesis—to explain the euphoria and bliss experienced by those who claim to have had this experience. After all, practitioners of virtually every religion claim to have had similar experiences, but they contextualize the experience in terms of their own religious tradition. Also, the Christian fundamentalist believer expects that this experience will follow their conscious and willful assent to be "born again." Simply put, what we have here is a positive outcome that follows a positive expectation or, quite literally, the placebo effect. Expectation in this case refers to more than simply expecting the event to occur; it also refers to the affective behavioral aspects as well, as the newly "spirit-filled" believer will act, talk, and probably even feel the way that properly "spirit-filled" believers should.

Much the same can be said of *satori*, a state of temporary enlightenment (purportedly) experienced by practitioners of Zen Buddhism.

The great Eastern traditions themselves (Hinduism, Jainism, and Buddhism), hold that such experiences are ineffable. The Buddha himself refused on a number of occasions to even discuss *Nibbana* (Nirvana). So, as in the case of "being filled with the spirit," the observer has no way of directly validating an individual's claim that they have experienced temporary enlightenment. Much the same can be said of mystical experiences and the various trance states associated with shamans.

In this general category, I would also place (supposed) apparitions of Mary, the mother of Jesus, that Catholics say have occurred at Lourdes (France), Fatima (Portugal), Conyers (Georgia), and Medjugorje (Bosnia-Herzegovina). I place them in this category since, in every single case, Mary speaks and reveals herself only to one, two, or three individuals, the same one(s) over and over. Again, why appear only to select individuals when it is certain that, for this very reason, many will not accept their claims or the "message" of "Our Lady"? If one truly cares for human beings, a theme that is prevalent in virtually all of the "messages" from "Our Lady," then why not make an appearance on CNN or during a World Cup soccer match or during halftime at the Super Bowl? In the case of Conyers, Georgia, the scenario is particularly absurd: A middle aged woman retreats to a room, alone of course, receives the "message," and then later announces said "message" to the crowd outside; the credulous flocked there by the thousands.

The reader can no doubt see a pattern at this point: like virtually all religious claims made by believers everywhere, the alleged experiences are framed in such a way as to be nonfalsifiable. Once again, one can hide anything she wants behind the curtain of faith, and the religious fundamentalists have done just that.

On the issues of reliability, validity, and substance, the values for all three are, once again, zero or very close to it for each one. The issue of trust is actually more problematic here than in the case of revelation, since the purported claims have not been officially validated by the religious tradition itself, not that that actually counts for much anyway. Rather, what we have is individuals making incredibly improbable claims that, unless they can figure out how to make their subjectivity our objectivity, will always be considered highly suspect or simply false by those of us who need a bit more than the old fundamentalist standby, faith, to believe such things.

CHAPTER SEVENTEEN
OVERT INSTRUCTION

We now reach the last of the "mechanisms" or "processes" (to be discussed in part 3) that serves as a source of religious information: overt instruction. When it involves children, I think the proper term would be indoctrination. After all, children are intellectually and emotionally defenseless. One popular female evangelist who runs a summer camp for Christian children, states, in the excellent documentary film *Jesus Camp*, that children are "so open" and "so usable" that in a matter of minutes she can have them "seeing visions and hearing the voice of God."[1] Apparently, the peddlers of creationism are well aware of this as well:

> Evolution . . . only makes sense if you understand biology, and biology is not particularly easy to explain. As a result, most non-evangelicals don't really learn about the development of life until late high school or college, while evangelical kids start learning creationism—and anti-Darwinism—before kindergarten. By the time evangelicals are taught about evolution in school, they are well prepared to resist it.[2]

Packaged as it is and delivered by authority figures, a child really has no chance. Thus, a three year old in Muslim Egypt (as shown in the documentary *Protocols of Zion*[3]) who has never met a Jew, much less even knows what a "Jew" is, expresses her hatred for them and refers to them as "pigs," and six- and seven-year-old Christian children will babble on about being sinful and break down and cry in shame during worship services and express the need to be "born again" (*Jesus Camp*[4]). Of course, "children soldiers" who will fight and die for whatever cause they are told to fight and die for, are legendary in Asia, the Middle East, and Africa. Here's a frightening thought: those doing the "teaching" are generally the products of the very same indoctrination process. Bigotry begets bigotry, ignorance begets ignorance, and they continue unabated until the cycle is broken (if it ever is).

I use the term "indoctrination" here intentionally because the sort of education children are receiving in fundamentalist Christian private schools and in many "home schools" is "closed" as opposed to "open." (Note: In the 2000s, approximately 70 percent of families that were homeschooling their children were evangelical Christians,[5] although that proportion has dropped somewhat in the 2010s.) Closed instruction (indoctrination) is myopic (since it embraces ethnocentrism and rejects cultural relativism), obsessively deductive (since the primary concern is with the inculcation of presumed dogmas that are never tested or critiqued), and based almost exclusively on a priori assumption (virtually everything taught reflects the [assumed] moral, epistemological, and cultural superiority of the Western, Judeo-Christian viewpoint).

Just how typical the following case is, I don't really know, but I think the reader will find it quite disturbing:

> Charlie Marsh's home-schooling has included reading, writing and creationism. The New Hartford boy, who will graduate high school May 21 in a small ceremony at his family's church, is one of a growing number of evangelical Christian students to be home-schooled. Educated at home by his born-again Christian parents since he was 8, he was taught science from a creationist point of view and history from a Christian perspective.[6]

Oh, and by the way, "creationism" in this context almost always refers to young-earth creationism, arguably the most irrational popular belief in existence. (There are, sadly, quite a few competitors for this dubious distinction.) And "history from a Christian perspective" means only one thing: the virtues of Christianity are extolled in glowing terms as if it were actually a force of good for the past two thousand years. Never mind the fact that European Christians "spreading the good news" killed off, sometimes intentionally, sometimes passively, whole cultures and literally millions of indigenous peoples around the globe; never mind the fact that the overt misogyny of the Bible has made women's lives miserable as they succumbed to horrible abuses of patriarchy (one wonders how many women have been beaten and killed because of Paul—"Let a woman learn in silence with full submission. I permit no woman to teach or to have authority over a man; she is to keep silent" [1 Timothy 2:11–12]; "Wives, be subject to your husbands as you are to the Lord. For the husband is the head of the wife just as Christ is the head of the church, the body of which he is the Savior. Just as the church is subject to Christ, so also wives ought to be, in everything, to their husbands" [Ephesians 5:22–24]); never mind that the advent of Christianity in the fourth century CE marked the end of Greek rationalism and critical thought and dragged the Western world into a 1,300-year period of mind-numbing ignorance regarding the natural world; never mind that Europeans of the late Middle Ages suffered horribly under the tyranny of the church, as heretics (read: those who did not totally embrace the arbitrary "truths" of the state) were jailed, tortured, and executed by executive order of the pope, the "vicar of Christ"; and never mind that the Crusades had much more to do with political hegemony, booty, and bloodlust than anything spiritual. After all, children have no knowledge of history and are, thus, "defenseless" in the face of historical revisionism. (In the documentary *Jesus Camp*, a homeschooled child remarked, "I think personally that Galileo made the right choice by giving up science for Christ." This statement shows either an appalling ignorance of the facts or the homeschoolers' willingness to intentionally rewrite history to serve a religious agenda.)

In the interest of giving the reader some idea of what "history" from a Christian fundamentalist perspective might comprise, here is how one Christian homeschooling materials company, Notgrass History (they have been in the business for about twenty years), describes its history curriculum on their website: "Exploring World History is a one-year homeschool curriculum for high school that teaches students to understand history from a Christian perspective of faith in God and respect for the Bible."[7] In their world history textbook, history begins with the biblical creation event (assumed to be literally true, of course) that occurred a few thousand years ago. I haven't actually reviewed the text, but I must say I am curious as to how they manage to fit five major extinction events, the age of the dinosaurs, the entire cultural history of stone-aged *Homo* (the Oldowan tool technology followed by the Acheulian tool technology followed by the Mousterian followed by five other tool traditions that follow one another in time), the origin and development of plant and animal domestication, the ancient Egyptians, Sumerians, Aryans, Chinese, Greeks, etc., into a four-thousand-year time period (taking out the two thousand years since the time of Christ, since all those events took place before that time). Well, I guess most of us know the answer to that question: You simply begin by ignoring every piece of sound, valid, publicly verifiable data, including the thousands of independently derived dates obtained by various absolute-dating techniques, that plainly show, for example, that dinosaurs disappeared 65 million years ago and simply claim that they are all mistaken. This is the sort of irrationality that has given us creation "museums" that put saddles on the backs of dinosaurs. Would we allow such a thing to go on if not for the fact that a Christian justification is being invoked to defend such a preposterous rewriting of science and history? I think not.

The "closed" educational philosophy of fundamentalist Christian schooling can be clearly seen in the statement titled "Our Philosophy," found on the website of Bethany Christian School, a popular Christian private school in my hometown, Baton Rouge, Louisiana. In this statement it is noted that they desire to engrave "the Word of God on their [the children's] hearts," that the school's philosophy "centers on Jesus Christ as the focal point of all teaching and learning," that the Bible is the "infallible, divine Word of God," and that they desire that their students conduct themselves "according to biblical perspectives and principles."[8]

If the parent so desires, they can send their child to this school for ten years (six weeks through fifth grade). This sentiment is fairly typical for schools of this sort. In their "statement of faith," we find the following: the Bible is the "Holy Spirit-inspired, authoritative word of God," the "presence of angels and the reality of the devil and demonic forces," the "gifts of the Holy Spirit are operative today," the "one universal church" is "the body of Christ," "physical healing [is available] to all who will believe and receive" the redemptive act of Jesus on the cross (i.e., an affirmation of faith healing), and the virgin birth of Jesus.[9] Now, of course, any Christian private school (and homeschooling parent) has the right to teach anything they so desire but, unfortunately, the rest of us have to live in the same world with those who are the products of such schooling. If such things as virgin births, angels and demonic forces, and faith healing are simply assumed to be true and real, one really wonders about the critical-thinking ability of those who are educated in such an environment. After all, today these folks simply deny virtually everything that astronomers, biologists, and anthropologists say about the origin, development, and nature of our universe and our world. If they can so nonchalantly dismiss, for example, basically every date obtained through the various absolute-dating techniques done by thousands of highly trained scientists and technicians, one wonders what else they are capable of.

Overt instruction, then, of the sort being considered here, fails miserably in regard to reliability, validity, and substance. Of course, the major problem is that such instruction is grounded on the writings of a Bronze Age people. Thus, whatever is being taught regarding science, gender, race, sexuality, language, etc., is basically two to three thousand years out of date. The fact that this "foundational document" (the Bible) includes information about the natural world that has been proven to be false doesn't seem to faze the fundamentalists.

PART FOUR

HOLY SCRIPTURES ARE MUNDANE, FLAWED, AND UNRELIABLE

CHAPTER EIGHTEEN
SCRIPTURES

Perhaps the most popular source of religious knowledge among believers is scriptures. Unlike claims of apparitions, religious experiences, and such, here we actually have words on the printed page. Not only that, these words are the words of the "ancients" that have been passed down for centuries. For the believer, there is lots of substance here, since holy scriptures, by virtue of their canonical status, are considered authoritative. For the nonbeliever, there is, of course, much that is fascinating and informative in a cultural sense but just how reliable these works are as sources of information is highly debatable.

Many of the claims made by Christian fundamentalists regarding the Bible are patently false or dubious according to those scholars who actually work with the texts. "Moses wrote the Pentateuch": false; there were many writers and redactors, all working at different times, using different terms for God, and speaking to issues with which they were personally concerned (see. for example, Walter Houston's work[1]). "The Bible is inerrant": false; from the chapter in 2 Kings 19 that is plagiarized in Isaiah 37, or vice versa, to the two different genealogies for Jesus (found in Matthew 1:2–16 and Luke 3:23–38), to the two different versions of Jesus's last words on the cross before he died (found in Luke 23:46, and John 19:30), to the thousands of other inconsistencies, errors, and contradictions that have been catalogued in countless books and websites, the Bible is far, far from inerrant (see chapter twenty-nine). "The Gospels were written by Matthew, John, Mark, and Luke, the first two being apostles of Jesus who were actual eyewitnesses to the events they describe": false; virtually every recognized biblical scholar alive holds that the Gospels were assigned authors well after the fact and were written in the time period 70–100 CE, forty to seventy years after the death of Jesus (see, for example, Bart Ehrman's *Lost Christianities*[2]). "The Bible is inspired by God": implausible if not false; from a large collection of many "books" and other documents claimed by one Christian group or another to be canonical during the early history of Christianity, only twenty-seven were eventually selected by the politically dominant Christian group (the proto-Orthodox) about 370 years after the death of Jesus—all of the other Christian "books" and documents were rejected, including everything written by the Gnostics (see, for example, the informative and authoritative documentary *The Lost Gospels*, which details the manifestly political process that led to the acceptance of the canonical biblical books and the branding of all other writings, including those of the Gnostics, as heretical[3]).

Another problem with the Bible is the fact that we no longer possess the original manuscripts, so basically Bible scholars have to extrapolate backward from the oldest reliable manuscripts to reconstruct what might have been originally written. Bart Ehrman, one of the foremost New Testament scholars in the world today, reminds us that the original documents were copied over and over again as they were passed down from one hand to the next, and these ancient copiers were prone to making errors and even an addition or two from time to time.[4] For example, Ehrman states that the story of Jesus and the prostitute he saved from stoning was fabricated and added to the text long after the original text had been written.

It is interesting to trace back the vaunted King James Bible, perhaps the most popular Bible for English speakers around the world, from its current version to what was presumably the original texts of the "books" found in the New Testament. Separating the seventeenth century, early modern English version, and the original manuscripts written approximately 1,500 years earlier, there are a handful of different languages (each with its idioms and idiosyncrasies), many "competing" manuscripts in the same language of varying degrees of quality, and copies of copies of copies of copies of the original manuscripts. Ehrman sums it up this way:

> Someone has gone to the trouble of doing textual criticism, reconstructing the "original" text based on the wide array of manuscripts

that differ from one another in thousands of places. Then someone else has taken that reconstructed Greek text, in which textual decisions have been made . . . and translated it into English. What you read is that English translation. . . . But what if the translators have translated the wrong text? It has happened before. The King James Version is filled with places in which the translators rendered a Greek text derived ultimately from Erasmus's edition, which was based on a single twelfth-century manuscript that is one of the worst of the manuscripts that we now have available to us![5]

Clarence Darrow, writing in the first half of the twentieth century, states that the only sensible hypothesis regarding the authorship of the Bible is the obvious one:

Can any rational person believe that the Bible is anything but a human document? We now know pretty well where the various books came from, and about when they were written. We know that they were written by human beings who had no knowledge of science, little knowledge of life, and were influenced by the barbarous morality of primitive times, and were grossly ignorant of most things that men know today.[6]

In fact, his statement is even more valid today than it was eighty years ago, given what we now know.

That the Bible is a man-made document becomes increasingly clear once one is willing to critique it the way we summarily critique other written works, but that is something that Christian fundamentalists refuse to do. Once one decides that the Bible is the infallible, inerrant word of God, she has no reason or desire to treat the document as anything else. If, however, one prefers not to trust the claims fundamentalists make regarding the Bible, a reasonable position once one considers the a priori, obsessively deductive, faith-based epistemology embraced by fundamentalists, she is then free to treat it like any other book. Proceeding in this way, one quite readily stumbles upon a number of reasons why the Bible is clearly written by man (males only!) not God. In the chapters that follow, I will discuss twelve of these reasons, although many more could certainly be noted.

CHAPTER NINETEEN

THE BIBLE CONDONES SLAVERY

I am going to assume here that an omnibenevolent and infinitely just deity who reigns over all of the world's peoples would not condone the enslavement of human beings by any group. I don't think that is much of a stretch here, since slavery is condemned by virtually every country in the world today and is generally considered an egregious affront to basic human dignity.

There are multiple passages in the Bible that clearly condone slavery including the following:

- Exodus 21:2: "When you buy a male Hebrew slave, he shall serve six years, but in the seventh he shall go out a free person, without debt."
- Exodus 21:20–21: "When a slaveowner strikes a male or female slave with a rod and the slave dies immediately, the owner shall be punished. But if the slave survives a day or two, there is no punishment; for the slave is the owner's property." [According to Exodus 20:1, "God spoke all these words." It is clearly permissible in the eyes of God, then, for a master to beat his slave, as long as the slave doesn't die right away. Please note, however, that if the slaveholder should put out their slave's eye or knock out a tooth, the slave has to be freed (Exodus 21:26–27). In simple terms, then, the slaveholder is completely free to beat his slaves but there are guidelines that must be followed. One wonders how many black slaves in the South were horribly beaten to within an inch of their death by overseers who were content with the knowledge that God approved of

their actions. How could any sane person really believe that these are the words of a just and loving God?]

- Leviticus 25:44: "As for the male and female slaves whom you may have, it is from the nations around you that you may acquire male and female slaves."
- Titus 2:9-10: "Tell slaves to be submissive to their masters and to give satisfaction in every respect; they are not to talk back, not to pilfer, but to show complete and perfect fidelity, so that in everything they may be an ornament to the doctrine of God our Savior."
- 1 Peter 2:18: "Slaves, accept the authority of your masters with all deference, not only those who are kind and gentle but also those who are harsh."
- Ephesians 6:5: "Slaves, obey your earthly masters with fear and trembling, in singleness of heart, as you obey Christ."

There are many more passages that could be quoted but surely those noted here should suffice. If we accept the Bible as "the word of God" as the fundamentalists insist we do, then God's position regarding slavery is unequivocal: it is permissible. It should be pointed out here that it was not the abolitionists who were quoting Bible verses in defense of their position but the slavers! Here's what Henry Brinton, noted journalist and senior Presbyterian pastor, had to say on this issue:

> In the 1860s, Southern preachers defending slavery also took the Bible literally. They asked who could question the Word of God when it said, "slaves, obey your earthly masters with fear and trembling" (Ephesians 6:5), or "tell slaves to be submissive to their masters and to give satisfaction in every respect" (Titus 2:9). Christians who wanted to preserve slavery had the words of the Bible to back them up.[1]

It's the same old problem that has muddled social and cultural issues for ages in the West. There are some—unfortunately, in many cases those who wield power and authority—who insist on reading the Bible literally and applying it absolutely, firmly convinced as they are that the words are the "word of God." Clearly they are not.

It is a bit ironic, don't you think, that slavery is repulsive to decent, law-abiding folks in today's world but is (purportedly) condoned by God and, I assume by logical extension, Christian fundamentalists as well? If one is bothered by that observation, he might consider the alternative explanation: that these works of literature were written by ancient men living in a world where slavery was the norm.

CHAPTER TWENTY

THE BIBLE IS MISOGYNISTIC

The following passages can be used to illustrate the misogynistic ideology of the Bible:

- Deuteronomy 22:28–29: "If a man meets a virgin who is not engaged, and seizes her and lies with her, and they are caught in the act, the man who lay with her shall give fifty shekels of silver to the young woman's father, and she shall become his wife. Because he violated her he shall not be permitted to divorce her as long as he lives." [Again, this is God talking. Notice how the woman is treated like a mere commodity that can be abused—raped—and bought off with fifty pieces of silver. Question: Who is more likely to write a law that says if a man rapes a young woman he gets to keep her, an omnibenevolent God or a man who has internalized a Bronze Age mentality?]
- Deuteronomy 22:20–21: "If, however, this charge is true, that evidence of the young woman's virginity was not found, then they shall bring the young woman out to the entrance of her father's house and the men of her town shall stone her to death, because she committed a disgraceful act in Israel by prostituting herself in her father's house." [If one wonders where the blatant double standard that favors men over women originated, this is certainly one of the primary sources. Notice that it is the woman's virginity not the man's that is an issue. In fact, it is entirely possible that the man who took away the woman's virginity would be right there with the rest of them, stoning a young woman to death. It is sentiments like this one that have

given us the morally repugnant custom of "honor killings"—
really just a culturally sanctioned institution that facilitates
the disposal of "inconvenient" women—in traditional Muslim
countries that has led to the murder of tens of thousands of
innocent young women. It seems quite reasonable to assume
that this passage was written by men who lived in a brutal,
ancient world where misogyny was the norm.]

- Exodus 20:17: "You shall not covet your neighbor's house; you
  shall not covet your neighbor's wife, or male or female slave,
  or ox, or donkey, or anything that belongs to your neighbor."
  [Women, then, are merely property of men and count no more
  or no less than a donkey or an ox.]

- Exodus 21:4: "If his master gives him a wife and she bears him
  sons or daughters, the wife and her children shall be her master's and he shall go out alone." [Again, women (and children)
  are merely property of males.]

- Leviticus 12:2, 5: "If a woman conceives and bears a male child,
  she shall be ceremonially unclean seven days. . . . If she bears
  a female child, she shall be unclean two weeks." [The reduced
  relative worth of females vis-à-vis males is recognized even at
  birth.]

- Exodus 22:18: "You shall not permit a female sorcerer to live."
  [Note: The King James Bible translates "female sorcerer" as
  "witch." During the fifteenth, sixteenth, and seventeenth centuries, tens of thousands of women—roughly four or five times
  the number of men—were horribly tortured and/or burned
  alive for committing the fictional crime of "witchcraft." Of
  course, virtually all of them were completely innocent of
  any crime. One wonders how many innocent women—many
  of them midwives and/or elderly—were burned at the stake
  because of this one line in the Bible. It was certainly not a small
  number.]

- Colossians 3:18: "Wives, be subject to your husbands, as is
  fitting in the Lord."

- 1 Corinthians 14:34–35: "Women should be silent in the
  churches. For they are not permitted to speak, but should
  be subordinate, as the law also says. If there is anything they

desire to know, let them ask their husbands at home. For it is shameful for a woman to speak in church."

- 1 Timothy 2:11–14: "Let a woman learn in silence with full submission. I permit no woman to teach or to have authority over a man; she is to keep silent. For Adam was formed first, then Eve; and Adam was not deceived, but the woman was deceived and became a transgressor." [The reasoning employed here is circular and self-serving for males since it was males who fashioned the Edenic narrative.]

There are many, many other passages that could be cited here but these should suffice. Christian fundamentalists will protest and claim that I am taking passages out of context or that I really don't understand the "true message" of the scriptural passage or that males have restrictions too, etc., etc. Once again, however, the Bible says what it says; the fundamentalists insist on a literal reading, and I am giving it to them.

In today's world, good, decent, enlightened people do not put up with the foolish notions described in these biblical passages. No, women are not more unclean after giving birth to females than they are after giving birth to males (in fact, they are not "unclean" at all!); no, women are not and should not be told to keep their mouths shut at public gatherings; no, women are not and should not be considered property; no, women who have lost their virginity are not "defiled" and should not be subject to execution; no, women are not inherently inferior to their husbands; no, no, no, no, and no. And, of course, the contrived story of Eve and Adam in the Garden of Eden has Eve leading Adam into sin. This all makes perfect sense if we simply grant that the Bible was written by misogynistic males who were the products of a Bronze Age culture.

CHAPTER TWENTY-ONE

WRITERS OF THE BIBLE SHOW AN IGNORANCE OF BASIC SCIENTIFIC KNOWLEDGE

There are a number of passages in the Bible that perfectly reflect the knowledge of people writing during a time in which virtually nothing was known about the natural world. Here are just a few examples:

- Genesis1:9–19: "Plants yielding seed" and "fruit trees of every kind" are created on the third day and the sun ("the greater light to rule the day") is created on the fourth day. [As was noted earlier, the individual who wrote this passage was obviously not aware that plants and trees require sun-powered photosynthesis to survive.]
- Genesis 2:19: "So out of the ground the Lord God formed every animal of the field and every bird of the air, and brought them to the man to see what he would call them; and whatever the man called every living creature, that was its name." [The total number of species of which we are aware increases yearly as new animals are discovered but, according to the International Union for Conservation of Nature and Natural Resources, current estimates of known species are as follows—mammals: 5,416; birds: 9,956; reptiles: 8,240; and amphibians: 6,199.[1] According the UK Natural History Museum, there are 331 known dinosaur genera,[2] although the literature suggests that the actual number is certainly much greater than that value. If we assume, again conservatively, that there were at least two

species per genera, we get a value of 662. Finally, according to Bruce Roberts and M. E. J. Newman,[3] and to David Raup,[4] distinguished paleontologist at the University of Chicago, approximately 99.9 percent of all species that have ever existed are now extinct, a value commonly cited by biologists and paleontologists. So how many species did Adam name? This number can be obtained by calculating the existing number of species, adding that to a number that represents those species that are now extinct, and then adding to that value the number of dinosaur species:

$$5,416 + 9,956 + 8,240 + 6,199 +$$
$$(5,416 + 9,956 + 8,240 + 6,199)/.001 + 662 = 29,841,473$$

(The reader will note that I did not include in my total any insects, which would include the 350,000 existing species of beetles and who knows how many extinct beetle species. We are never told who named the beetles, but it was presumably someone with a lot of time on his or her hands.) If we assume that Adam named these species at a rate of one per minute, nonstop, which, again, will give us a very conservative value (if we factor in time to sleep and eat, and the logistics of the sort of observation required to make such determinations, it is doubtful that Adam could actually accomplish this task at anywhere near that rate), and then convert the value obtained to years, the final result is 56.77. (Of course, if we were to factor in the very reasonable accommodations that would have to be made, we would get values far greater than that.) Now, according to Genesis 2:20, Adam completed his task before Eve was created, thus, the naming of all the living creatures occurred during the literal creation week. Even if my estimate is a way off for some reason (which is doubtful, especially considering the fact that I have used the most conservative reasoning possible in my calculations), such a scenario is clearly not possible. I should add that, according to creationists, all living things were created by God in their distinct form; no speciation is allowed. Again, the creationism paradigm, based on a literal reading of the Bible, is nonsensical. Clearly, the individual who wrote this part of Genesis, like everyone else living in the first millennium BCE, (understandably) knew very little about the faunal diversity of the world and virtually nothing of extinct species or dinosaurs.]

- Genesis 30:37–39: "Then Jacob took fresh rods of poplar and almond and plane, and peeled white streaks in them, exposing the white of the rods. He set the rods that he had peeled in front of the flocks in the troughs, that is, the watering places, where the flocks came to drink. And since they bred when they came to drink, the flocks bred in front of the rods, and so the flocks produced young that were striped, speckled, and spotted." [So Jacob managed to affect the phenotypes (thus, genotypes) of his animals by having them gaze at an object that was colored in the way he wanted his animals to look. If one wants to manipulate the phenotypes of animals he is breeding, there are, of course, ways to do that. Gregor Mendel, for example, illustrated this with his famous experiments on garden peas (by the way, one will find real genetics in a biology textbook, not the Bible). This passage could only have been written by someone with virtually no knowledge of genetics; in other words, an individual living in the first millennium BCE. Of course, that is totally understandable for some of us but, let us not forget, fundamentalists claim this is the word of God.]

- Leviticus 11:13–19: "These you shall regard as detestable among the birds. They shall not be eaten; they are an abomination: the eagle, the vulture, the osprey, the buzzard . . . and the bat." [Bats are mammals, not birds, an understandable mistake for an individual living in the first millennium BCE to make, but not for God.]

- Psalm 104:5: "You set the earth on its foundations, so that it shall never be shaken." [This is, again, an understandable error; in fact, one that used to be made all the time, but the statement is still, nevertheless, inaccurate. By the way, the same claim is made in Psalm 93:1 (the earth "shall never be moved") and 1 Chronicles 16:30 ("The world is firmly established; it shall never be moved.") Actually the earth undergoes

all sorts of movement from the daily rotation, annual revolution around the sun, and even a very long term axial preces-
sion, just to mention a few.]

- Ecclesiastes 1:5: "The sun rises and the sun goes down, and
  hurries to the place where it rises." [Again, another common
  misconception but, nevertheless, "common knowledge"
  among many in the ancient world.]

- 2 Chronicles 4:2: "Then he made the molten sea; it was round,
  ten cubits from rim to rim, and five cubits high. A line of thirty
  cubits would encircle it completely." [The term "round" is a
  translation of the Hebrew term "*ogul*," which can also be translated as "circular." The writer is clearly not aware that the value
  of π (circumference ÷ diameter) is 3.14159 . . . not 3.]

- Matthew 17:14–18: "When they came to the crowd, a man
  came to him, knelt before him, and said, 'Lord, have mercy on
  my son, for he is an epileptic and he suffers terribly; he often
  falls into the fire and often into the water. And I brought him
  to your disciples, but they could not cure him.' Jesus answered,
  'You faithless and perverse generation, how much longer
  must I be with you? How much longer must I put up with you?
  Bring him here to me.' And Jesus rebuked the demon, and it
  came out of him, and the boy was cured instantly." [In ancient
  times—in fact, up until quite recently historically—dissociative
  behavior of virtually any sort was attributed to demonic possession. Today, such individuals are diagnosed as suffering from
  Tourette's, schizophrenia, epilepsy, or a number of other maladies; such individuals are treated successfully for the most part,
  with psychoactive pharmaceuticals and therapy. They are not
  demon possessed. Jesus's diagnosis in this case was incorrect,
  and the treatment he provided was efficacious only in a psychotherapeutic sense, if it was effective at all. If Jesus was (and is)
  what Christians say he was (and is), he would have knowledge
  that far surpasses our own. The Jesus depicted here, however,
  was just as ignorant as everyone else of his time. By the way,
  Jesus reacts this way every time he is confronted with an individual manifesting symptoms of some mental disorder.]

- Matthew 24:29: "Immediately after the suffering of those days the sun will be darkened, and the moon will not give its light; the stars will fall from heaven, and the powers of heaven will be shaken." [Whoever wrote or spoke this statement was working with an ancient and very inaccurate understanding of the cosmos. The claim that "the stars will fall from heaven" is non-sensical. For example, if one is in the northern hemisphere and the stars appear to "fall," then in the southern hemisphere they will appear to "rise" in the sky, and vice versa if the situation is reversed. This does make sense, however, if one believes that the stars are points of light in the heavenly sphere above a flat earth, a common belief in the first millennium BCE. Also, the moon doesn't produce light, it merely reflects it.]

- James 3:7: "For every species of beast and bird, of reptile and sea creature, can be tamed and has been tamed by the human species." [Clearly, this ancient writer was oblivious of the thousands of species of creatures that existed during his time. In regard to the statement, no they cannot all be tamed, and no they had not all been tamed. The statement is false on both counts.]

- Joshua 10:13: "And the sun stood still, and the moon stopped, until the nation took vengeance on their enemies. Is this not written in the Book of Jashar? The sun stopped in midheaven, and did not hurry to set for about a whole day." [This verse shows beyond a shadow of a doubt that the writer believed that the sun moved around the earth. This was, of course, a common belief in ancient times, illustrating, once again, that the Bible was neither written nor inspired by an omniscient God.]

As was the case with misogyny and slavery, there are many other passages that could be noted here, but these should certainly suffice. The Bible, taken literally as the creationists and fundamentalists insist, is full of inaccurate or nonsensical statements that sound precisely as if they were written by men living in the first millennium BCE (Old Testament) or the first century CE (New Testament).

CHAPTER TWENTY-TWO

THE BIBLE IS HOMOPHOBIC

W e'll begin once again with passages from the Bible:

- Leviticus 18:22: "You shall not lie with a male as with a woman; it is an abomination."
- Leviticus 20:13: "If a man lies with a male as with a woman, both of them have committed an abomination; they shall be put to death; their blood is upon them."
- Romans 1:26–27: "For this reason God gave them up to degrading passions. Their women exchanged natural intercourse for unnatural, and in the same way also the men, giving up natural intercourse with women, were consumed with passion for one another. Men committed shameless acts with men and received in their own persons the due penalty for their error."
- 1 Corinthians 6:9-10: "Do you not know that wrongdoers will not inherit the kingdom of God? Do not be deceived! Fornicators, idolaters, adulterers, male prostitutes, sodomites, thieves, the greedy, drunkards, revilers, robbers—none of these will inherit the kingdom of God."

There are actually very few homophobic references in the Bible, and some of these passages are prone to misinterpretation. Probably the best example of this is the story of Sodom in Genesis, chapter 19, a topic that I discussed earlier, in chapter four. Unfortunately, Christian fundamentalists jump all over this story and use it as exhibit A, if you will, in their argument that homosexuality is an abomination to

God. As I suggested in chapter four, there is no need to quibble here since the Bible itself has already decided the issue for us in Ezekiel 16:49. This is particularly interesting since "sodomites" has come to be used to refer to those who engage in gay male sexual activity but, at least according to Ezekiel, that is clearly an inappropriate use for this term. A true sodomite is one who is arrogant, antipathetic, greedy, etc., or, if we interpret the account literally, a male who violently gang rapes another male, nothing more, nothing less.

Another important issue here involves the term "homosexual." The term, actually a hybrid comprised of the Greek *homos* and the Latin *sexualis*, is only about 150 years old. Of course, there has always been same-sex sexual activity, and those who generally prefer to enjoy intimacy with members of their own sex have always been around; it's just the term that is relatively new. Given the recent provenience of the term the reader might find it curious that it is used in 1 Corinthians 6:9 in the following English versions of the Bible: Revised Standard Version Catholic Edition, New English Bible, New King James Version, Amplified Bible, World English Bible, International Standard Version, Living Bible, Tree of Life Version, Good News Translation, God's Word Translation, New American Standard Bible, New Living Translation, English Standard Version, Holman Christian Standard Bible, and the New Testament for Everyone. This is clearly a significant issue since these translations include a term that didn't even exist when the biblical texts were written. One would naturally wonder what other "adjustments" might have been made through the years.

As was noted earlier, the intensity of Christian fundamentalists' obsession with homosexuality is not commensurate with the fact that this subject receives very little treatment in the Bible. Nevertheless, this doesn't stop today's fire and brimstone preachers from embellishing things a bit. Here's what one writer had to say about this:

> We have noticed a practice of a few fundamentalist and other evangelical Christian pastors which appear to be inconsistent, unethical and/or dishonest. We use the word "*appear*" because we are not certain that the pastors are consciously aware of their practices:

- Some pastors cite Genesis 19, a passage that condemns homosexual rape, as proof that God hates all homosexual behavior. Yet they would never quote a verse that condemns heterosexual rape and state that it applies to all heterosexual activity.
- We have noticed some pastors switching between Bible translations in order to find the version that is most critical of homosexual behavior. When quoting Deuteronomy 23:17 some deviate from their usual usage of the New International Version (NIV). It accurately translates the original Hebrew condemnation of male and female prostitution in the temple (a common Pagan practice). They prefer the King James Version (KJV) which incorrectly translates the passage as condemning female prostitutes and male "sodomites."[1]

On one level, it is difficult to imagine the infinitely capable and infinitely endowed Creator of the universe even being concerned about the sexual activity of creatures on a tiny rock located next to an ordinary star (one of billions in this galaxy) in the backwaters of an ordinary spiral galaxy (one of billions in the universe). The "sin" of homosexuality is not really a moral issue at all in my mind; two adult males, for example, engaging in consensual sexual activities is about as trivial and inconsequential as it gets in a world where genocide, torture, child abuse, poverty, and starvation are common. In fact, here's what Rabbi Shmuley Boteach has to say about this issue:

> Homosexuality and sodomy are not ethical sins. No one is being hurt, no one is being cheated, nobody's rights are being infringed upon. Homosexuality is a religious sin, analogous to other Biblical prohibitions, like not eating the carcass of a dead animal, or not sleeping with a woman during her menstrual cycle. In many ways, adultery is even worse, because it does transgress ethics. It involves deception and lying. But we don't prosecute people for adultery.
>
> I don't mean to minimize these prohibitions. I am an observant Jew who takes the Bible seriously. But a man who eats shellfish— which the Bible calls an abomination (Leviticus 11:12: "Whatsoever hath no fins nor scales in the waters, that shall be an abomination unto you") is not immoral so much as irreligious. Likewise, a

man or a woman who works on the Sabbath is not unethical. They haven't stolen from anyone. But they have contravened a Biblical injunction.[2]

In fact, I would put homosexuality right beside all of the other strange and goofy "sins" of the Bible—for example, planting two different types of seeds in your field (Leviticus 19:19), eating the fruit of a tree before the tree is five years old (Leviticus 19:23–25), shaving the edge of your beard (Leviticus 19:27), cross-dressing (Deuteronomy 22:5), and boiling a kid in its mother's milk (Exodus 23:19, Exodus 34:26, Deuteronomy 14:21). (Note: This latter prohibition appears in identical form three times in the Pentateuch and refers to a pagan custom practiced at the time.[3] This is clearly a prohibition that was directed at individuals living in the ancient Middle East and was obviously written by a man living in that time and place.)

When one reads of such prohibitions as these, it becomes immediately obvious that virtually no one really believes that the Bible is the literal, inerrant word of God, since these prohibitions and many others like them are routinely ignored by Jews and Christians, even the fundamentalists. Basically, the Bible is used to justify prejudices that are popular, especially those that reflect a patriarchal bias (e.g., misogyny and homophobia). The passages that condone slavery were also quite useful (again, for slaveholders) until just recently historically. One would think, however, given the vitriol, hate, and hysteria Christian fundamentalists show toward homosexuality, that the Bible is one massive homophobic tome, when, in actuality, it barely says anything at all about the issue. In regard to the issue at hand, however, one would have to agree that, at least when the topic is raised, the Bible does condemn homosexuality. Which, then, is more believable, that God has a problem with homosexuality or that the males of the ancient Middle East had a problem with homosexuality? Again, I will err on the side of reason and common sense and choose the latter.

CHAPTER TWENTY-THREE

THE BIBLICAL TEXT CONTAINS ABSURD AND NONSENSICAL FOOD PROHIBITIONS

There are many passages to choose from here, including the following:

- Leviticus 11:4–7: "But among those that chew the cud or have divided hoofs, you shall not eat the following: the camel, for even though it chews the cud, it does not have divided hoofs; it is unclean for you. The rock badger, for even though it chews the cud, it does not have divided hoofs; it is unclean for you. The hare, for even though it chews the cud, it does not have divided hoofs; it is unclean for you. The pig, for even though it has divided hoofs and is cleft-footed, it does not chew the cud; it is unclean for you."
- Leviticus 11:10–12: "But anything in the seas or the streams that does not have fins and scales, of the swarming creatures in the waters and among all the other living creatures that are in the waters—they are detestable to you and detestable they shall remain. Of their flesh you shall not eat, and their carcasses you shall regard as detestable. Everything in the waters that does not have fins and scales is detestable to you."
- Leviticus 11:20–21: "All winged insects that walk upon all fours are detestable to you. But among the winged insects that walk on all fours you may eat those that have jointed legs above their feet, with which to leap on the ground."

- Leviticus 11:29–30: "These are unclean for you among the creatures that swarm upon the earth: the weasel, the mouse, the great lizard according to its kind, the gecko, the land crocodile, the lizard, the sand lizard, and the chameleon."

I should point out that virtually the same food prohibitions are repeated again in Deuteronomy 16; this is a common occurrence in the biblical text. So, either God is forgetful, or God assumed that human beings were stupid and forgetful, or this is precisely the kind of thing one would expect of a collection of texts written by many different authors that was compiled over many centuries. Again, I will go with the latter.

Dietary prohibitions, like religions, are forged in a matrix of environmental factors, historical accident, and opportunity—i.e., they are culture-relative. In the case of the biblical food taboos, however, we need to add another component to this matrix: the need to differentiate one's own tribe and people from the "others." The "chosen people" versus the unclean and pagan "others" is a consistent theme throughout the Hebrew Scriptures.

In regard to dietary preferences, it is well-known in anthropological circles that cultural groups never consume everything that is palatable, nutritious, and digestible in their local environment. As was noted in chapter two, human beings "culturize" the overwhelming, mysterious, and threatening world they live in by reducing that which is possible to that which is permissible, thus allowing them some measure of control over nature; dietary prohibitions are examples of this tendency. Thus, when viewed from a panhuman or global perspective, food taboos are nonsensical, since what is prohibited in one culture might well be savored in another.

Probably the best example of the cultural relativity of food is the pig. For some (Jews and Muslims) it is reviled as "unclean"; for others, it is craved and consumed with gusto. This particular dietary taboo has been discussed for centuries, and many theories abound regarding the origin of this prohibition. One theory that has been abandoned is the claim that pork is somehow unhealthy and dangerous. It is actually no more dangerous than any other meat as long as it is properly handled and prepared. The pig is certainly not "unclean"; this idea was popular until it was learned that pigs cover themselves in mud and sometimes their own feces in an attempt to stay cool since they have no sweat glands. The best explanation of the pork taboo attributes it to the ecology and animal domestication practices in the ancient Middle East.[1]

In regard to the bizarre and sometimes ridiculous dietary taboos in Leviticus and Deuteronomy, it is obvious that, like all other food taboos, they are distinctly culture-relative. In other words, they are no less or no more bizarre and ridiculous than many other dietary prohibitions associated with cultural groups around the globe. There is certainly no need to invoke the special wisdom and omniscience of God to understand and explain them. The food taboos of the peoples and cultures of the ancient Middle East, like those found anywhere around the world, were conceived of and popularized by the peoples and cultures of the ancient Middle East. The only reason we are even talking about this particular set of food taboos is because the colonizing Europeans possessed technology, nautical skills, and a military proficiency that surpassed that of the people they conquered. Otherwise, another completely different set of food taboos would be the focus of our discussion.

CHAPTER TWENTY-FOUR

THERE ARE "JUST-SO STORIES" IN THE BIBLE

A again, there is a lot of material I might access here, but I will confine myself to some of the most popular stories. We'll begin with one of my favorites, the Tower of Babel (Genesis 11:1–9).

THE TOWER OF BABEL

> Now the whole earth had one language and the same words. And as they migrated from the east, they came upon a plain in the land of Shinar and settled there. And they said to one another, "Come, let us make bricks, and burn them thoroughly." And they had brick for stone, and bitumen for mortar. Then they said, "Come, let us build ourselves a city, and a tower with its top in the heavens, and let us make a name for ourselves; otherwise we shall be scattered abroad upon the face of the whole earth." The Lord came down to see the city and the tower, which mortals had built. And the Lord said, "Look, they are one people, and they have all one language; and this is only the beginning of what they will do; nothing that they propose to do will now be impossible for them. Come, let us go down, and confuse their language there, so that they will not understand one another's speech." So the Lord scattered them abroad from there over the face of all the earth, and they left off building the city. Therefore it was called Babel, because there the Lord confused the language of all the earth; and from there the Lord scattered them abroad over the face of all the earth.

It seems as though the Tower of Babel story was simply inserted into the biblical text at the beginning of Genesis 11, and fundamentalists generally do not date the incident with their standard biblical chronology. After all, in Genesis 10 (verse 5), the chapter before the one that describes the Tower of Babel incident, we are told of various "coastland peoples," each "with their own language"; thus, many languages were already being spoken before the Tower of Babel incident if the text is chronological. Nevertheless, we can certainly come up with a time period in which the incident must have occurred (according to a fundamentalist understanding of history).

In regard to pinning down a date for the Tower of Babel incident, Genesis 10:1–5 gives us an important clue:

> These are the descendants of Noah's sons, Shem, Ham, and Japheth; children were born to them after the flood. The descendants of Japheth: Gomer, Magog, Madai, Javan, Tubal, Meshech, and Tiras. The descendants of Gomer: Ashkenaz, Riphath, and Togarmah. The descendants of Javan: Elishah, Tarshish, Kittim, and Rodanim. From these the coastland peoples spread. These are the descendants of Japheth in their lands, with their own language, by their families, in their nations.

So, at least according to this passage in Genesis, the descendants of Noah's grandsons were in their own lands speaking their own languages.

Now, using a biblical chronology, the date of the great flood of Genesis involving Noah and his family has been placed variously at 2497 BCE, 2348 BCE, and 2304 BCE.[1] I feel we can use the date 2400 BCE as a valid estimate for the biblical date of the flood. Clearly, one common language was spoken by Noah and his family, but at some later point many different languages are present globally. At least based on what is written in Genesis, I suppose we could set the earliest date for the appearance of different languages sometime during the lifetime of the sons of Javan, Noah's grandson. That would move the date up from 2400 BCE to around 2300 BCE or so. So, if a number of different languages are being spoken by 2300 BCE, then the Tower of Babel incident occurred sometime between 2400 BCE and 2300

BCE. Answers in Genesis places the date at 2242 BCE,[2] which very nearly lies within this time period. I see no reason why we couldn't use 2250 BCE as a rough estimate for the (biblical) date of the Tower of Babel incident.

Now let us shift our attention to the real world of empirical data, archaeology, and historical documentation. There is incontrovertible evidence that establishes the existence of the written languages of the Sumerian and Egyptian cultures by around 3200 BCE. There were other advanced civilizations that existed during that general time period as well—for example, the Harappans in the Indus River Valley region (beginning sometime in the fourth millennium BCE) and early European civilizations (dating back to the fifth millennium BCE). There were also, of course, thousands of tribal/indigenous cultures with their own native tongues that can be traced back many millennia. Given the geographical spread of these cultures and the nature of the languages that eventually come to be spoken in these areas, it is obvious that even during these earliest periods each group had its own language. Thus, according to the empirical data we have, different written languages were in existence by around 3200 BCE and, thus, given what we know today about the historical development of language, many different spoken languages existed at least centuries if not millennia before that time. The biblical account of the origin of languages then, is clearly absurd since it is not even remotely possible that only one language was being spoken in the world around 2400 BCE and that all the languages of the world were present only a century or two later. In fact, the only way we can understand the world of ancient languages is to assume the existence of thousands of native tongues many millennia before the time of Christ. I should also note that not a single piece of empirical data has been presented to support the fact that only one language was spoken by all humanity anytime during the last 10,000 or so years. In fact, research in both the evolution of human anatomy and phonemic diversity tells us that we can push the date back much, much farther than that.

Finding the date when human language began is, of course, a daunting task, but we certainly have some interesting evidence that we can use to at least estimate when this may have happened. There are three pieces of empirical evidence suggestive of the presence of spoken language that all seem to converge about 400,000 years ago or so: the size of the hypoglossal nerve, throat morphology, and cranial capacity.[3]

The hypoglossal nerve controls the movements of the tongue, thus, larger nerves allow for more complex movements of the tongue, the sort needed for human speech, for example. Based on the relative sizes of the bony canal in the skull through which this nerve passes, it appears as though chimpanzees are not able to move their tongues like humans do, since this bony canal in chimpanzees is only about one-half the size of those found in humans. The size of this bony canal in australopithecines (early hominins that date back to over 4 mya) is about the same size as that found in chimpanzees but, according to anthropologist Matt Cartmill, the bony canals found in *Homo* about 400,000 years ago are comparable in size to those of modern humans.[4]

The chimpanzee larynx is located at a relatively high point in the throat compared to humans. This is the primary reason why chimpanzees are not capable of making the wide range of sounds that humans make. According to linguist Philip Liebermann, modern human throat morphology doesn't appear in the hominin fossil record until about 500,000 years ago.[5]

Finally, as we move evolutionarily through the various species of *Australopithecus* and *Homo*, we can see a gradual growth in cranial capacity. As noted in chapter nine, there was a substantial increase with the appearance of the first *Homo* around 2 mya, and by around 500,000 years ago *Homo heidelbergensis* possessed a cranial capacity that was approaching modern values. Thus, it appears that around 400,000 years ago, *Homo* at least possessed the important physiological traits required for human speech. Speech, of course, does not fossilize, so all we can really say is that the potential was there.

The reader will recall from chapter nine that modern *Homo sapiens* appeared in Africa about 195,000 years ago. These anatomically modern individuals were using fire, building shelters, crafting relatively sophisticated tools, and living in cooperative groups; they were almost certainly speaking some sort of language. As humans began to leave East Africa about 60,000 years ago, the various groups dispersed, some moving eastward and (later) some moving north-ward. By about 50,000 years ago, there certainly existed an even greater number of distinct language communities than had hereto-fore existed. Today, approximately seven thousand "living languages" exist around the globe.[6]

If we consider the fantasy-like, fairy tale beginning (Genesis 11:1: "Now the whole earth had one language and the same words."), the sketchy details regarding time and place, the lack of information regarding who these people were, the obvious insertion of the Babel tale almost completely out of context, the empirical impossibility of having only one language being spoken in the world as of only a few thousand years ago, and our linguistic knowledge regarding lan-guage and language change and evolution, it seems clear that the Tower of Babel narrative is strictly a mythical "just-so story" totally devoid of historicity.

EVE AND ADAM IN THE GARDEN OF EDEN

In Genesis 2:4–3:24, one will find the second creation story. This account was written at an earlier time than the first creation account found in Genesis 1:1–2:3,[7] uses the term "YHWH" for God rather than "Elohim," and is much more anthropocentric. A careful cri-tique of this second creation story uncovers a number of significant problems.

In this second version of the Eden creation story, Adam is created alone before plants, animals, and birds, and Eve is the last thing to be created; in the Genesis chapter 1 version of the creation story, Eve and Adam are created together after the creation of everything else.

In Genesis 2:16–17, God, speaking of the tree of the knowledge of good and evil, states that Adam will die on "the day that you eat of it." This, in fact, does not happen, since Adam does eat from the tree and he lives to an age of 930 years (Genesis 5:5). In an ironic twist, the serpent actually told Eve the truth when he told her that "you will not die" on that day, and, in fact, she did not. I suppose the funda-mentalists might quibble with my (overly) literal interpretation, but, frankly, context or intention cannot bail them out here.

God tells Adam that he will die if he eats of the tree of the knowledge of good and evil; later Adam eats from the tree. Not only does he not die (as noted above) but, near the end of the Eden account, God is concerned about Adam eating from the tree of life and living forever and exerts not a small amount of effort to prevent that from happening. Why? If, in fact, Adam was to die after eating from the tree of the knowledge of good and evil, why should God be concerned about Adam eating from the tree of life? There is a clear and certain contradiction here.

Many scholars have noted the obvious Sumerian, Babylonian, and Egyptian influences on the Genesis creation stories, and it is common knowledge today that the Genesis accounts borrowed heavily from these more ancient sources.[8] In the *Oxford Companion to the Bible*, for example, biblical scholars Bruce Metzger and Michael Coogan note that the similarities between the Genesis creation accounts and the older Sumerian and Babylonian accounts clearly show that Genesis is at least partly derived from those sources.[9] Gary Greenberg describes one Sumerian myth regarding plants that were not to be eaten:

> The best known of these stories, The Myth of Enki and Ninhursag, tells of two important deities known as Enki and Ninhursag, who were brother and sister and who lived in an earthly paradise named Dilmun. On one occasion, Ninhursag managed to trap some of her brother's sperm and used it to create eight previously unknown plants, which were to remain untouched by others. Her brother, curious to know what these plants were, tasted each of them. When his sister saw the damaged plants, she cursed her brother, saying, "Until he is dead I shall not look upon him with the eye of life."[10]

Greenberg then describes the influence of this myth:

> In this major Mesopotamian myth, which would have been well-known to the Hebrew scribes in the Babylonian era, we find the motif of forbidden fruit in an earthly paradise coupled with a curse of death upon eating the fruit, themes presented in the Genesis story. Ninhursag's curse against Enki provided the motif to challenge the Egyptian idea of "eating moral order," leading to the biblical theme of "forbidden fruit."[11]

Now, the fact the ancient literature of one cultural tradition is derived from the even older sources of another is not that surprising or unexpected, since this practice is quite common around the world. But it is problematic if one is claiming that a particular written work is "special" in some way—in this case, the "word of God." If we attribute nonbiblical mythologies and stories to "earthly" sources, then we would have to do the same in regard to the Genesis creation stories, since they are derived from them. One cannot insist on "divine authorship" for the Genesis accounts of creation if the stories are derived from sources that one does not consider to be divine in origin. Again, the most obvious explanation here, one that solves a number of problems, is simply the notion that the Hebrew accounts of creation are no more or no less "the word of God" than all the other creation accounts one finds associated with the other cultures and peoples of the ancient Middle East.

Like many other "just-so" stories, this one also includes an animal that talks, in this case a serpent. Before I go any further, let me state that I am well aware than many Christians and virtually all Jews do not believe that there was a talking snake in the Garden of Eden. Nevertheless, it is not the point of view of moderate or liberal Christianity or mainstream, orthodox Judaism that is being critiqued here but, rather, Christian fundamentalism. As has been noted many times, their approach to the Bible is strictly literal and, thus, they are stuck with a talking snake. Besides, here is what one of the staff writers with Answers in Genesis says about the serpent in the Garden of Eden: "It needs to be noted from the outset that Satan certainly did use a real, literal, physical snake as his instrument for tempting Eve. Satan is the master at posing himself as something else and not tempting someone with his full identity exposed."[12] One might understandably suggest that the talking snake was an obvious "plant" by the original writer to ensure that future readers would not read and interpret the creation story in a literal fashion. Apparently it didn't work.

We are told in the Garden of Eden story that Eve and Adam were originally naked but they "were not ashamed." Later, after eating from the forbidden tree, "the eyes of both were opened, and they knew that they were naked." The obvious implication here is that humans (post-Eden) have a natural shame of their nudity and, since all humans are descended from Eve and Adam, it is a shame that is inherent to our species. But this is contradicted by the hundreds of tribal/indigenous cultures around the globe that wear little or no clothing. Of course, the ancient writers of Genesis did not know about these peoples, virtually all of whom live in hot and humid rain forests, so we cannot expect them to be aware of this problem, but certainly God knew about them.

After God creates all the cattle, birds, and wild animals, it is written "but for the man there was not found a helper as his partner." Are we to assume this was a real issue, that the fact that Adam found no suitable partner among the cattle, birds, and wild animals was problematic? Wouldn't an omniscient God already know this?

Eve and Adam already possessed free will before they ate from the forbidden tree since a choice was made to do evil as opposed to doing good. It is written that after eating from the forbidden tree "Then the eyes of both were opened. . . ." Opened how? Eve and Adam were already aware of the difference between good and evil. The comment is at least confusing and arguably nonsensical in this context.

I have noted earlier that the punishments meted out by God to Eve and Adam, the pain of childbirth and strenuous manual labor to obtain food respectively, are routinely overcome today with anesthesia and a trip to the supermarket. Again, the writers living in the ancient Middle East could not have anticipated this, but God could have.

There is an obvious patriarchal bias in the Garden of Eden story. According to the writers, it is Eve who takes the initiative to disobey God and eat from the forbidden tree and later tempts Adam to do the same. Eve is said to be created from a rib of Adam, a claim with obvious implications regarding both the ontological and social status of females vis-à-vis males. And, finally, Eve is told by God that her husband "shall rule over you." While it is true that there is nothing necessarily contradictory or erroneous here, the tone and content of the text almost perfectly reflects the patriarchal bias of the ancient world (for that matter, today's world to some extent). Even a cursory reading of world history reveals the horrible implications of patriarchy, especially when it is said to reflect "the word of God" or holy scriptures or claimed that it is simply the "will of God." Included in this long and tragic list are bride-burnings in India, honor killings in traditional Islamic cultures, and the brutality women suffer from the hands of men virtually everywhere, including the United States, where the primary cause of physical injury to women is intimate partner violence.[13] The fact that an omniscient, omnibenevolent God would actively encourage patriarchy while being fully aware of the horrible consequences of doing so is simply not believable.

NOAH'S ARK (GENESIS, CHAPTERS 6, 7, AND 8)

There are so many contradictions and errors in the account of Noah's ark that I will simply focus on those that are the most glaring and obvious.

The great number of species that existed at the time (roughly around 2400 BCE according to biblical chronology) invalidates the story of Noah's ark for two reasons: they would not fit inside the craft and Noah and his seven companions (his wife, his three sons, and their three wives) could not care for such a large number of species. According to Genesis 6:19–20, Noah was to load two "of every living thing" inside the ark. Earlier, in chapter twenty-one, I calculated the total number of species that existed during the time of Adam (29,841,473) and I will use that number here. (Remember, the "Noachian" flood is the first and only extinction event according to Christian fundamentalists. Thus, virtually all species created by God are alive at the time Noah begins loading his ark.) Keep in mind that fundamentalists reject the concept of speciation and believe that God created all creatures in their existing form, whatever that may have been for those that are now extinct. I point this out since some fundamentalists attempt to get around the large number by counting families (referring to the Linnaean taxonomy) rather than species, but families do not exist in reality, only species do since that is the most fundamental unit of reproduction and fertility.

Let us now examine the space inside the ark. The Bible states that the ark is 300 cubits long, 50 cubits wide, and 30 cubits high. The cubit is a relative measurement based on the distance between a human elbow and the tip of the middle finger. Of course, such a measurement can vary quite a bit, but, in the interest of erring on the side of the fundamentalists, I will use the largest estimate commonly given for the cubit, 22 inches. Thus, a cubit measures about 1.83 feet. The resulting width and height of the craft would then be approximately 92 ft. x 55 ft.; I have (generously) rounded these numbers up to the nearest whole number. If we imagine the craft as being shaped something like a rectangular block (which the original dimensions imply), then a one-foot-wide cross section would consist of 5,060 cubic feet. Now, let us allot one cubic foot on the average for the storage of one species (this would include two creatures, male and female). Again, I would argue that this is extremely generous since even the smallest creatures would probably need at least that much space and others (large land mammals) would need much more space than that. If we divide the storage area of a one-foot-wide cross section (5,060 cubic feet) into the total number of species (29,841,473), that will give us the length needed to store all the creatures. That number is 5,898 feet (rounded up to the nearest whole number since a "partial foot" is nonsensical in this context), which is equivalent to approximately 1.12 miles, or almost eleven times longer than the length (300 cubits = 549 feet) the biblical text calls for. Considering the fact that I haven't even discussed food storage space, dung maintenance, and living quarters for the eight humans, it is obvious that the story as related to us in the Bible is pure fantasy and cannot be literally true. Again, we have yet another case that illustrates the (understandable) ignorance on the part of the Bronze Age writers of the Bible. The ancient writer who wrote this may have known of a couple of hundred species at most and was probably careful to allow more than enough space for all the creatures he assumed existed at the time. Nevertheless, the details do not stand up in light of today's knowledge.

Because of their insistence on a literal reading of the Bible, Christian fundamentalists are forced to accept the story as it is written. So they do what anyone else would do when forced to deal with a reality that does not agree with their claim: they "explain away" and "rationalize" the data. For example, in regard to the number of species, fundamentalist apologists will typically use a much smaller value than the one I have calculated here. An article on the Answers in Genesis website states that as few as two thousand creatures may have been loaded on the ark: "For land animals and birds, the created 'kind' most often corresponds to the scientific rank of 'family,' which includes many species. If we relate created kinds to scientific families, estimates as to the number of animals on Noah's Ark might be as few as 2,000 or as high as 16,000."[14]

According to the first Genesis account, God created all living things according to their "kinds." By simply arguing that "kinds" are not species but rather families, the apologist can drastically reduce the total number of different animals. But, as I pointed out earlier, creationists do not allow speciation because to do so would be equivalent to concurring with the standard scientific model of evolutionary theory. Using the standard and widely accepted definition of a species as an interbreeding population (the "biological species concept"), then, it is clear that God created species or, put another way, "kinds" are species. The only way to get around this issue is to claim that the standard definition of species is not valid, which, considering the ease and willingness with which fundamentalists routinely dismiss or ignore much of the rest of mainstream science, would not be much of a stretch.

The writer quoted above claims that "kinds" are roughly equivalent to biological families, which is even more generalized and inclusive than genera in the Linnaean classification system. Thus, in some cases, hundreds or even thousands of different species can be combined into one using this "clever" device. How then do we get the huge number of species that exist in today's world? The writer would simply have to accept that they were all generated in the last few thousand years. Unfortunately, not one shred of tangible evidence exists that would validate such a notion. If this were true, we would have to accept that hundreds of thousands of speciation events have occurred in the last four thousand years. Speciation events are measured in terms of millions or hundreds of thousands or tens of thousands of years, not four thousand.[15] As far as I am concerned, this writer has to resort to another "just-so story" in his attempt to iron out the serious wrinkles in the original one. Real science is done in the context of data collection and hypothesis testing leading, in some cases, to theories that stand the test of time; one cannot just redefine species as this writer has done in an effort to make his "theory" more plausible. As we have seen, however, this seems to be standard operating procedure in young-earth creationism circles; simply put, they believe nothing can be as science has actually shown it to be (all the dating methods are inaccurate, there really is no hominin fossil record, etc., etc.).

Another popular strategy found in the creationist literature to deal with the storage issue is to simply claim that the largest animals (large land mammals and dinosaurs, etc.) were represented by very young and consequently very small versions of their adult selves. This blatantly ad hoc "repair" makes their case even less credible, if that is possible, for two reasons. First, the notion of loading the ark with very young, physically and biologically immature animals is never mentioned anywhere in the Bible, but it seems clear that the historically recent discovery of dinosaurs has brought this issue to a head for ark apologists. Fundamentalists have made such ad hoc adjustments before. When it finally became clear to those claiming inerrancy and demanding a literal reading of the "word of God," that there were, in fact, many errors, inconsistencies, mistakes, and contradictions in the Bible, many Christian schools and colleges, when referring to the divine perfection of biblical texts, began including the phrase "in its original autographs" in their mission statements to address the issue. The point being, of course, that the original autographs no longer exist so virtually any faith-based claim could be made about them. Second, any plan that is designed to repopulate the world using only two young and biologically immature members of each species will be doomed to failure given the fairly high probability that the members of that species will not both survive to reproductive age.

Finally, there is the issue of extinct species, an issue that is virtually ignored in the creationist literature. As was noted earlier, if God created all living things around six thousand years ago, then, according to fundamentalist biblical chronology, the great flood during the time of Noah was the first (and only) major extinction event; it follows, then, that virtually every species that has ever existed was present at that time. Thus, extinct species have to be counted. Given that this number is many, many times the number that currently exist, the fundamentalists' estimates for the number of species that existed during Noah's time is incorrect by as much as a factor of 10^3.

Many of these animals are carnivores, some quite large, requiring food (lots of it) in the form of other creatures, yet nothing is mentioned in the creationist literature regarding extra storage space required for these creatures or, for that matter, precisely how the carnivores were to be separated from the other animals. Even the smaller carnivores cannot be handled by humans without sophisticated technology and tranquilizers, none of which Noah possessed. Once again, since there were no extinction events before the great flood, Noah and his family had to deal with huge bears, tigers, and other animals that were considerably larger than even today's large versions, not to mention the massive and dangerous *Tyrannosaurus rex* and its even larger cousin the *Giganotosaurus carolinii.*

There are approximately 150 species of marsupials, a rather curious infraclass of mammals (the so-called *metatheria*), that are indigenous only to Australia. In regard to the discussion at hand, two pertinent questions come to mind: 1) how did Noah distribute or redistribute the marsupials in Australia, and 2) if it was a matter of redistribution, how did Noah manage to retrieve these animals from seven thousand miles away in the first place? The only reasonable answer to both questions is, of course, "he didn't."

The biblical text blatantly contradicts itself regarding the number of each "kind" of animal that was to be placed on the ark. According to Genesis 6:19–20, "And of every living thing, of all flesh, you shall bring two of every kind into the ark, to keep them alive with you; they shall be male and female. Of the birds according to their kinds, and of the animals according to their kinds, of every creeping thing of the ground according to its kind, two of every kind shall come in to you, to keep them alive." But here's what one reads a few verses later, in Genesis 7:2–3: "Take with you seven pairs of all clean animals, the male and its mate; and a pair of the animals that are not clean, the male and its mate; and seven pairs of the birds of the air also, male and female, to keep their kind alive on the face of all the earth." Finally, in Genesis 7:8–9 one reads, "Of clean animals, and of animals that are not clean, and of birds, and of everything that creeps on the ground, two and two, male and female, went into the ark with Noah, as God had commanded Noah."

There is a clear contradiction here that context and/or intention cannot rescue. But later in the narrative we finally learn why God commanded that "seven pairs" of some animals were to be brought aboard the ark: "Then Noah built an altar to the Lord, and took of every clean animal and of every clean bird, and offered burnt offerings on the altar" (Genesis 8:20). Clearly, the "extra" animals were to be sacrificed. Greenberg writes that we are simply dealing with two different writers, one ("J") who recognized the art of sacrifice and another ("P") who did not.[16]

The Noah's flood story has its origins in Egyptian, Sumerian, and Babylonian mythology. For example, in the New English Bible (Oxford Study Edition), a commentary below the flood story reads, "The story was adapted from the Babylonian Gilgamesh Epic."[17] Robert Best persuasively argues that six popular Middle Eastern flood stories all draw from an actual flood that occurred around 2900 BCE and the exploits of a Sumerian king named Ziusudra.[18] Gary Greenberg argues that the flood story in Genesis draws heavily off of Egyptian and Babylonian mythologies.[19] And Ralph Ellis writes, "I am relatively certain that the story [Noah's flood story] is based upon Egyptian mythology rather than an actual flood."[20]

The fact that the ancient story of Noah's flood is partially or totally derived from other similar ancient stories is neither surprising nor unexpected. But it does cast a negative light on fundamentalist claims that the biblical text is literally the word of God. If this very popular and commonly accepted notion regarding an Egyptian, Sumerian, or Babylonian provenience is accurate, and it certainly appears to be, then the story of Noah's ark is simply yet another "take" on a popular Middle Eastern mythological tale and has nothing to do with God.

As I noted earlier, I have only discussed a few of the many contradictions and errors found in the Genesis account of Noah's flood. Like so much of the biblical text, the story clearly does not hold up under the scrutiny of today's scientific knowledge of our world. Again, it appears as though it was written by ancient writers who lacked an understanding of how big the world actually is, the huge number of biological species, the many major extinction events that have occurred, and so on. You will note that I have said virtually nothing of the fundamentalist claim for a worldwide flood, even though there are a number of problems there as well; for example, only a few plants and virtually no freshwater fish would survive being submerged in salt water for days on end.

Most educated and well-read individuals are, no doubt, surprised and perhaps shocked that there are some who consider the tale of Noah and his family marching all the beasts, birds, reptiles, and dinosaurs two by two (or seven by seven) aboard a wooden ark that they built themselves, to escape a worldwide flood caused by a wrathful God who is fairly incensed at His creative handiwork, an accurate, literal, historical account. But if history has taught us anything it is that even reasonable, decent people can be driven to irrationality if it is thought to serve some religious "good."

Finally, in regard to "just-so" stories, it should be noted that not only has the Exodus story never been confirmed by either historical or archaeological data but the Pharaoh in Exodus is not named. The (supposed) epic struggle that pitted Moses against the Pharaoh, the plagues, and the consequent exodus of the Israelites from Egypt is one of the greatest and most significant stories in the Bible. Thus, it is quite curious that the Pharaoh is not identified anywhere in the text. As I see it, there are only a few logical options here:

Either God is responsible for the content of the Bible or man is.

If God then:

a)   God did not know Pharaoh's name.
b)   God did know Pharaoh's name but chose not to reveal it.

If man then:

c)   the writer did not know Pharaoh's name.
d)   the writer did know Pharaoh's name but chose not to reveal it.

Options b and d are, of course, possible but not probable. Not revealing Pharaoh's name adds nothing to the credibility of the story (in fact, it does just the opposite) or the credibility of the Bible itself. Not revealing Pharaoh's name can only lessen claims made regarding the story and the book in which it is written. Option a is not a viable option since God is said to be omniscient. That leaves us with option c, by far the most probable and reasonable choice.

So the question now is why the ancient writer did not know the Pharaoh's name. Again, the most reasonable response to that question is simply that the whole episode never happened as described in the Bible. According to Egyptologist William A. Ward, "There are hints here and there to indicate that something like an exodus could have happened, though on a vastly smaller scale, but there is not a word in a text or an archaeological artifact that lends credence to the Biblical narrative as it now stands."[21] Again, let us not forget that the Bible chronicles the Israelites' history, not the Egyptians' or the Canaanites' or the Babylonians'. Thus, even if the story is based on some sort of historical event, the chances range somewhere between slim and none that the Bible would give us a reliable account of it.

CHAPTER TWENTY-FIVE

THE BIBLE CONTAINS NO INFORMATION THAT GOES BEYOND WHAT PEOPLE KNEW AND UNDERSTOOD AT THE TIME IT WAS WRITTEN

O f the many reasons one might cite as being evidence for the fact that the Bible was conceived, written, and codified by humans rather than God, this is perhaps the most convincing. I find it curious that a book of some 750,000 words, which is purportedly the literal, inerrant word of an omniscient God, tells us nothing beyond what the ancient writers knew and thought about the world. In fact, not only is the text totally devoid of information that is common knowledge today, but, as was noted earlier, the scientific information that is in the Bible is often inaccurate and nonsensical. Instead, what we get is a steady diet of ancient, antiquated notions of a wrathful God who causes droughts (1 Kings 8:35) and leprosy (Numbers 12:9–10), the efficacy of astrology (Judges 5:20), the healing of disease (leprosy) by bathing in a river (2 Kings 5:14), a fixed, immovable earth (1 Chronicles 16:30 and many other passages), a sun that moves around the earth (Psalms 19:4–6 and many other passages), and so on. And, as was noted earlier, even Jesus gets in on the act as he misdiagnoses various dissociative disorders as demonic possession, a practice that, unfortunately, would lead to the social ostracization, torture, and deaths of untold numbers of innocent people in Christian, pre-Enlightenment Europe.

This huge book of (purportedly) God's wisdom does not give

us one single cure for the various sicknesses and disease that afflict humanity; the fundamentalists should ponder that fact for a few minutes, as it pretty much invalidates virtually everything they claim is true about the Bible and the nature of God. Such cures would have to wait (ironically) for the secular worldview of the Enlightenment and the advent of science some seventeen centuries after the time of Christ. The heliocentric theory of the solar system would have to wait for Copernicus (sixteenth century); a simple vaccination for smallpox, an infectious disease that has killed hundreds of millions of people, many of them innocent children who suffered horribly, would have to wait for its discovery in the eighteenth century; Kepler's planetary laws and Newton's laws of motion, the seventeenth century; the basic laws of genetics, the nineteenth century; quantum mechanics and the theory of relativity, the twentieth century; and so, so much more that could be listed. Next to these impressive feats of discovery and learning that have drastically increased our quality of life, the Bible and its contents offer virtually nothing in this regard.

Somewhere in this analysis, we need to visit the Bronze Age conception of menstruation, and this is as good a place as any, as it perfectly reflects the ignorance of the time in regard to a basic and necessary biological function. We'll start by letting the Bible speak for itself:

- Leviticus 15:19–24: "When a woman has a discharge of blood that is her regular discharge from her body, she shall be in her impurity for seven days, and whoever touches her shall be unclean until the evening. Everything upon which she lies during her impurity shall be unclean; everything also upon which she sits shall be unclean. Whoever touches her bed shall wash his clothes, and bathe in water, and be unclean until the evening. Whoever touches anything upon which she sits shall wash his clothes, and bathe in water, and be unclean until the evening; whether it is the bed or anything upon which she sits, when he touches it he shall be unclean until the evening. If any man lies with her, and her impurity falls on him, he shall be unclean seven days; and every bed on which he lies shall be unclean."

- Leviticus 15:26–27: "Every bed on which she lies during all the days of her discharge shall be treated as the bed of her impurity; and everything on which she sits shall be unclean, as in the uncleanness of her impurity. Whoever touches these things shall be unclean, and shall wash his clothes, and bathe in water, and be unclean until the evening."

It is clear from these passages as well as others (e.g., Ezekiel 18:5–6, 22:10, 36:17, Leviticus 20:18) that menstruation is "unclean" and "impure." The fanatical prohibitions involving menstruation are almost comical, but I'm sure women of the time did not feel that way.

To the Bronze Age peoples, these practices were not merely physically hygienic but spiritually hygienic as well:

- Leviticus 15:28–30: "If she is cleansed of her discharge, she shall count seven days, and after that she shall be clean. On the eighth day she shall take two turtledoves or two pigeons and bring them to the priest at the entrance of the tent of meeting. The priest shall offer one for a sin offering and the other for a burnt offering; and the priest shall make atonement on her behalf before the Lord for her unclean discharge."

And there it is, arguably exhibit A regarding why the Bible was certainly written by (not particularly well-informed) men living in the ancient world and not an omniscient God: the Bible claims that menstruation is a sin for which a woman must atone. Today, of course, we know all this is foolishness, as menstruation is a completely normal, in fact necessary, biological act, no different in that way from breathing, defecation, or sneezing. So why would this very human writer pen such an account? Because it perfectly reflected his understanding of menstruation. Unfortunately for the "the-Bible-is-the-literal-and-inerrant-word-of-God" folks, the ignorance of the ancient world becomes the ignorance of God. Or, they could simply accept the fact that God had nothing to do with it.

CHAPTER TWENTY-SIX

THE BIBLICAL GOD IS A LOCAL, TRIBAL GOD WHO FAVORS ONLY THE ISRAELITES

Of the many biblical passages that could be cited here, Deuteronomy 7:1–6 probably says it best:

> When the Lord your God brings you into the land that you are about to enter and occupy, and he clears away many nations before you—the Hittites, the Girgashites, the Amorites, the Canaanites, the Perizzites, the Hivites, and the Jebusites, seven nations mightier and more numerous than you—and when the Lord your God gives them over to you and you defeat them, then you must utterly destroy them. Make no covenant with them and show them no mercy. Do not intermarry with them, giving your daughters to their sons or taking their daughters for your sons, for that would turn away your children from following me, to serve other gods. Then the anger of the Lord would be kindled against you, and he would destroy you quickly. But this is how you must deal with them: break down their altars, smash their pillars, hew down their sacred poles, and burn their idols with fire. For you are a people holy to the Lord your God; the Lord your God has chosen you out of all the peoples on earth to be his people, his treasured possession.

If the reader is, perhaps, still wondering what could make ostensibly sane, God-fearing Christians despise, socially ostracize, beat, torture to death, or burn alive other human beings for a) worshiping the wrong God, b) embracing the wrong religious beliefs,

c) accepting empirical data and objective analyses rather than religious dogma, d) having the wrong sexual orientation, e) speaking
the wrong language, f) having the wrong color skin, g) being female,
etc., etc., ad nauseam, now you know. And it should be noted that
the foregoing passage is merely one of many that could be cited in
this context.

We might pause here to ponder how many innocent people have
been mistreated, tortured, or slaughtered because of this particular
passage in the "Good Book." The number certainly runs into the
millions. Let us not forget that since the greatest causal factor by far
regarding religious affiliation is geography (see chapter one), many
of these individuals were killed for the "sin" of being born in the
wrong place. Is it really that simple, one might wonder? Yes, it is.
And no one should rationalize or attempt to justify these detestable,
xenophobic biblical passages and the bigotry they encouraged by
claiming that it is anything more than that.

How easy it is for so many individuals to overlook the fact that
the Hebrew scriptures were conceived of and written by men who
were speaking on behalf of the Hebrews/Israelites. Robert Deffinbaugh, a pastor and church elder at the Community Bible Chapel
in Richardson, Texas, and a regular contributor to the website Bible.
org, justifies the wrath of God by claiming that pagans, the people of
Sodom, and the Canaanites were all "wicked." Here's what he has to
say about the Canaanites:

> The Israelites were to be the instrument of God's wrath toward
> these Canaanites. They were to show no mercy. They must not
> allow any of the Canaanites to live. This was for Israel's own good.
> If allowed to live, the Canaanites would most certainly intermarry
> with the Israelites and also teach them to sin, duplicating the very
> sins for which God was pouring out His wrath upon them.[1]

Deffinbaugh's comments and attitude are actually typical among
fundamentalists. One would think that those who believe this have
no grasp of the concept of propaganda. Of course, they are working
under the mistaken assumption that the author of the Bible is God,
thus, whatever it says must be the absolute truth. The passage from

Deuteronomy and many other similar passages show clearly that it is men who wrote the Bible, not God.

The fundamentalists soothe their consciences by assuming that the invading Israelites were right to slaughter the Canaanites (including women and children) because they were a wicked people who practiced incest, human sacrifice, idolatry, and so on. Similar claims have been made at one time or another by virtually all cultures toward the hated and despised "other," whoever they happen to be. Fundamentalists who are seduced by this tactic are no better than European anti-Semites who actually believed the absurd "blood libel" accusation made against the Jews.

If one desires to actually learn something about Canaanite religion, there are a number of serious and objective sources one can turn to.[2] With the discovery of the Ugarit cuneiform tablets some eighty years ago and archaeological data, we are no longer hampered by the decidedly one-sided, self-serving, propagandistic interpretation of Canaanite religion that is found in the Bible. Canaanite religion was a somewhat typical fertility-based, polytheistic religion that was rather common to many peoples and cultures of the time. In my mind, the primary "problem" with the Canaanites, from the perspective of the invading Israelites, was the fact that they occupied land that the Israelites wanted to occupy.

Let us not forget the reasons why the Israelites' biased interpretation of Canaanite religion is even relevant to any discussion today: European colonialism, the Battle of Tours, the destruction of the second Jewish Temple in Jerusalem, the suppression of Marcionism and Gnosticism, Paul's wresting Christianity away from Peter and James (which effectively ended any chance that Jesus would be recognized as a Jewish messiah), and so on. Had even one of these historical events unfolded differently, the Western religious landscape today would be far different. In a real sense, we have what we have. Thus, the Christian fundamentalist feels compelled to defend the virgin birth of Jesus but scoffs at the virgin birth claims made for Nataputta Vardhamana (Jainism), Genghis Khan, Siddhārtha Gautama (Buddhism), and many figures from pagan mythology; defends the violence inspired and led by God in the Old Testament but points to the battles and skirmishes of Muhammad's life as evidence that Islam is a violent religion; and accepts all miraculous claims made by Christianity no matter how absurd yet rejects all the miraculous claims made by adherents of other faiths. Thus, Christians quite easily, and apparently without compunction, simply assume that the Israelites' claims regarding the Canaanites are valid even though if we were to change the name of the book they are reading such claims would be dismissed as blatant propaganda.

The warlord God depicted in the Hebrew scriptures is not unlike similar figures found in the legends and mythology of many peoples. But because of a variety of historical accidents, present-day Christians believe one of these accounts and vehemently reject the others. The only sober conclusion that one might draw is that the various claims of divine intervention that are part and parcel of the mythology of any culture are all equally dubious at best and manifestly false at worst.

CHAPTER TWENTY-SEVEN

THE BIBLICAL GOD IS A VIOLENT KILLER

Let us begin with the slaughter of children:

> He [Elisha] went up from there to Bethel; and while he was going
> up on the way, some small boys came out of the city and jeered at
> him, saying, "Go away, baldhead! Go away, baldhead!" When he
> turned around and saw them, he cursed them in the name of the
> Lord. Then two she-bears came out of the woods and mauled forty-
> two of the boys. From there he went on to Mount Carmel, and then
> returned to Samaria (2 Kings 2:23–25).

Lest one think that perhaps there are other translations that state
things differently, it should be mentioned that various English translations state that "little boys," "little children," "youths," or "young
lads," "mocked," "jeered," or "made fun of" Elisha. I'm guessing most
Christian readers do not recall a sermon based on this story of a
prophet who called forth bears to slaughter children for making fun
of him.

There is nothing in the context of this story that would lead us to
believe that it is anything other than what it appears to be. This is not
a "teaching story" or a dream or a fantasy. And, according to biblical
literalists, it is true. In my mind, this would make Elisha one of the
most despicable, murderous, and bloodthirsty human beings that has
ever lived. I wonder if he watched as the children screamed in terror
as they were butchered and eaten alive by the bears? Since it would
take a while for the bears to actually maul forty-two children, did

Elisha prevent some of them from escaping while the bears worked their way through all forty-two? Did he hold some of them down to keep them from escaping? As the children were cut to pieces by the bears, did Elisha look on with satisfaction at his handiwork? The reader will also note that after the bears completed their slaughter of the children, Elisha, this great prophet of the Bible, simply went on his way; there were no doubt a number of children screaming and suffering from their wounds, since it probably took a while for all of them to succumb to their injuries, and he simply left them there to suffer and die. There is no indication whatsoever that he was bereaved or remorseful so we can assume that he felt vindicated. This brief analysis shows what happens when one actually applies reason and empathy to the many absurd stories found in the Bible.

Let's stay with the murder of children theme since there is a fair amount of biblical material to work with. In this example, God decides to punish the obstinate Pharaoh by killing children:

> At midnight the Lord struck down all the firstborn in the land of Egypt, from the firstborn of Pharaoh who sat on his throne to the firstborn of the prisoner who was in the dungeon, and all the firstborn of the livestock. Pharaoh arose in the night, he and all his officials and all the Egyptians; and there was a loud cry in Egypt, for there was not a house without someone dead (Exodus 12:29–30).

So God murders children in an attempt to subdue the recalcitrant Pharaoh. Why didn't God simply kill Pharaoh rather than thousands (tens of thousands?) of innocent children who knew virtually nothing of the events around them? And did God really think that thousands of ordinary, decent folks should have their child murdered for Pharaoh's stubbornness? Are we to believe that the murder of thousands of children was necessary for God to carry out His plans?

In this next passage, God tells us how the "wicked" people of Babylon, including, of course, the children, will be dealt with: "Whoever is found will be thrust through, and whoever is caught will fall by the sword. Their infants will be dashed to pieces before their eyes; their houses will be plundered, and their wives ravished" (Isaiah 13:15–16). Leaving aside for the moment the fact that God is sanctioning if not encouraging the rape of Babylonian women, the children, including the tiniest neonates and toddlers, will be smashed against the ground until dead.

If we leave behind those passages that focus only on children and move on to those that focus on both women and children, again we will find a lot of material. Here is Samuel speaking to Saul, the first king of the United Monarchy: "Thus says the Lord of hosts, 'I will punish the Amalekites for what they did in opposing the Israelites when they came up out of Egypt. Now go and attack Amalek, and utterly destroy all that they have; do not spare them, but kill both man and woman, child and infant, ox and sheep, camel and donkey'" (1 Samuel 15:2–3). Note that the prophet is quoting God verbatim. Saul would go on to slaughter every human being as he was told to do, but he did spare some animals and a king. It should be noted that Saul was strongly rebuked by both God and Samuel for sparing the Amalekite king and some of the animals. The king, Agag, was later butchered ("hewed . . . in pieces before the Lord" [1 Samuel 15:33]) by the prophet Samuel.

As one reads through the many Bible verses such as those cited here, one begins to wonder about God's obsession with killing children. (Remember, we're reading this like a fundamentalist.) To call these simply war crimes is a crime in itself. At least according to the Bible, it appears as though the ancient Israelite armies were arguably among the cruelest and most bloodthirsty armies that have ever existed and, let us not forget, working at the behest of a (purportedly) omniscient, omnipotent, and omnibenevolent God.

Here is another example: "So when Sihon came out against us, he and all his people for battle at Jahaz, the Lord our God gave him over to us; and we struck him down, along with his offspring and all his people. At that time we captured all his towns, and in each town we utterly destroyed men, women, and children. We left not a single survivor" (Deuteronomy 2:32–34). (Moses was speaking here of what the Israelites had done while in the wilderness.) It was, no doubt, verses such as these that inspired the Crusaders as they slaughtered Jews, Eastern Orthodox Christians, and anybody and everybody in old Jerusalem during the first Crusade.

Here is the word of the Lord as spoken by Hosea: "Samaria

shall bear her guilt, because she has rebelled against her God; they shall fall by the sword, their little ones shall be dashed in pieces, and their pregnant women ripped open" (Hosea 13:16). Thus, pregnant women are to be sliced open. This may not put Yahweh in the company of Vlad the Impaler, but it comes pretty damned close.

In Numbers 31:13–19, Moses meets his "gallant" warriors when they return from the latest God-inspired slaughter with women, children, and animals in tow. Moses is incensed that they have "allowed all the women to live," and commands his soldiers to "kill every male among the little ones, and kill every woman who has known a man by sleeping with him" but "all the young girls who have not known a man by sleeping with him, keep alive for yourselves." So, Moses, a "great man of God," perpetrated one of the most cowardly, detestable criminal acts ever committed in the annals of human history (assuming, of course, that this historical event actually occurred). I guess those women who had children (and, thus, were not virgins) were simply deemed "unclean" or some such foolishness and murdered for the crime of being mothers. As for the little boys ("every male among the little ones"), what exactly was their crime? I wonder if these brave soldiers for the Lord simply ran the defenseless and helpless women and children through with their swords, butchered them, or decapitated them? Can you imagine the terror of the children?

If we take the fundamentalists at their word, then, the God of the Israelites was hateful, wrathful, and sadistic almost beyond what any decent person can grasp. (One writer, on his blog *Dwindling in Unbelief*, did a count of individuals killed by God—biblical references included—and came up with a value of 2,476,633 [not including the flood or Sodom and Gomorrah or, in some cases, women and children].[1]) There is never a good reason for slaughtering children, and it makes me nauseous when the biblical literalists attempt to justify the murder of innocents. In this supposed "word of God," we see everything that is inhumane, immoral, and evil in human beings, but in this case they are acting at the behest of God. Many of humankind's worst atrocities are found right here in the Christian Old Testament. Given the popularity of this book and the way it has been force-fed to so many individuals over the last 1,700 years or so, one can be certain that these murderous and bloody tales have inspired thousands upon thousands of people to commit the most unconscionable acts.

There is only a problem here if one insists on the historicity of and the influence of God on the Christian Old Testament. A much more reasonable interpretation, however, exists and it is the one I am arguing for here: If we simply assume that these stories of war and conquest were written by men who lived in a time when such things were more common, the Old Testament makes a lot more sense. Basically, it comes down to one question: who is more likely to have sanctioned the rape and killing of women and the slaughter of children in wars of conquest, an omniscient deity who created and oversees the universe or man?

CHAPTER TWENTY-EIGHT

THE BIBLE CONTAINS MANY PASSAGES THAT ARE PREPOSTEROUS AND ABSURD

One could literally write a book on this topic alone, but I will confine myself to a few bits of wisdom imparted to us (supposedly) by the creator and supreme ruler of the cosmos:

- Exodus 21:33–34: "If someone leaves a pit open, or digs a pit and does not cover it, and an ox or a donkey falls into it, the owner of the pit shall make restitution, giving money to its owner, but keeping the dead animal." [This is certainly a pressing issue and God was right to address it. After all, what would we have done without God's guidance on this problem?]
- Exodus 23:4–5: "When you come upon your enemy's ox or donkey going astray, you shall bring it back. When you see the donkey of one who hates you lying under its burden and you would hold back from setting it free, you must help to set it free." [Again, where would humanity be without God's guidance?]
- Leviticus 13:29–30: "When a man or woman has a disease on the head or in the beard, the priest shall examine the disease. If it appears deeper than the skin and the hair in it is yellow and thin, the priest shall pronounce him unclean." [This entire chapter is a long, rambling discourse on whether or not an individual is "clean" or "unclean" based on the appearance of the skin disease from which the individual is suffering. One never gets even the slightest indication that an omni-

scient being is talking here; so much could have been said if it actually were an omniscient God speaking—for example, a description of the various skin afflictions, their etiologies, and how one might go about treating them. That the writer of this piece is clearly ignorant regarding even the basics of human medicine is obvious. Imagine how much good could have been done if the writer had told us something about smallpox or the plague; for one thing, tens of millions of innocent lives could have been spared and tens of thousands of Jews would not have been slaughtered by ignorant and hateful Christians who blamed the Jews for these problems (and basically everything else as well). The intense hatred and anti-Semitism of Christian Europe notwithstanding, it would have been difficult for someone to argue against "the word of God," especially in the Middle Ages when religious fanaticism was the norm.]

- 2 Chronicles 7:5, 8: "King Solomon offered as a sacrifice twenty-two thousand oxen and one hundred twenty thousand sheep. . . . At that time Solomon held the festival for seven days." [For those of you scoring at home, the sacrifice of 22,000 + 120,000 = 142,000 animals during one week works out to 14.1 animals per minute! Mind you, this goes on hour after hour seven days straight. One can imagine the sheer chaos that would have ensued after only one hour, during which time 846 animals would have already been slaughtered. This story is clearly a fabrication of the worst kind.]

- Deuteronomy 13:6–10: "If anyone secretly entices you—even if it is your brother, your father's son or your mother's son, or your own son or daughter, or the wife you embrace, or your most intimate friend—saying, 'Let us go worship other gods,' whom neither you nor your ancestors have known, any of the gods of the peoples that are around you, whether near you or far away from you, from one end of the earth to the other, you must not yield to or heed any such persons. Show them no pity or compassion and do not shield them. But you shall surely kill them. . . . Stone them to death." [The nicer terms that are used today to describe someone with such views are "religious fanatic" and "kook." Such views would place God squarely in a group that includes the most ignorant, bigoted, and xenophobic among us. Imagine this scenario: One night in Anytown, USA, at the dinner table, a fifteen-year-old girl begins telling her parents that she attended a meditation session at a Tibetan Buddhist temple in the neighborhood and found it to be quite interesting and suggests that the rest of the family may want to accompany her on her next visit. Her father picks up the large butcher knife being used to cut the roast and thinks about plunging it into her chest because, as God commanded in no uncertain terms, she must die. He catches himself, however, and recalls that God's word calls for stoning. He goes to the garage, retrieves some rope, returns to the dining room, and begins tying her up. The young girl is screaming in terror and the rest of the family is in tears, screaming at their father and husband to stop what he is doing. He recalls, however, that God's word demanded that no pity be shown, and he continues with the task at hand. He drags the girl into the backyard and, having no stones available, he decides to use the bricks he has purchased to build the addition to the house. Not wanting the girl to suffer any more than is necessary, he aims a large brick at her head and throws it, caving in her left eye socket; blood is gushing and brain tissue is seeping out of the horrible wound. The young girl is screaming hysterically in pain and terror as he throws the second brick, which caves in her forehead, and the cries stop. The young girl loses consciousness and in two minutes she is dead, as her brain and brain stem have ceased functioning. Like Moses who ordered the murder of children and mothers by his soldiers returning from battle, this father is also a great man of God who follows the literal, inerrant word of God without hesitation. Clearly, virtually no decent, humane individual who has actually read the Bible believes that it is the literal word of God.]

- Exodus 12:37: "The Israelites journeyed from Rameses to Succoth, about six hundred thousand men on foot, besides children." [If we use the figure of 600,000 men as a reference, the total population would have been at least two to three million. Given the huge size of the group, the Exodus account is rendered nonsensical. For example, in Exodus 14:19–31, we are told that the Israelites crossed "the sea" (probably "Sea of Reeds") in one night. This is absurd. It would take literally weeks for such a group and all of their belongings and their animals to cross the sea. Also, each day, millions of gallons of water would be required. What we get, however, in Exodus 17, is a quaint story of Moses striking a rock at the command of God and water flowing forth for the people to drink. It would take literally weeks to organize and execute the dispersion of millions of gallons of water to two or three million people. Literally hundreds of thousands, those "at the back of the line" so to speak, would die of dehydration in the meantime while waiting on water flowing from the rock.

We've seen this basic problem already on a number of occasions. The men who wrote the Bible really had no idea what a group of two to three million people would look like nor how absurd it would be to speak of them as if they were a small group of a few thousand people. If the exodus involved as many people as the writers say it did, the entire story would have to be rewritten to accommodate the incredibly huge number of people.]

Even Jesus gets in on the act:

- Mark 8:34: "He [Jesus] called the crowd with his disciples, and said to them, 'If any want to become my followers, let them deny themselves and take up their cross and follow me.'" [Jesus clearly did not say this at that point in time since the notion of "taking up the cross" would be nonsensical before the crucifixion. No one would know what he was talking about.]
- 1 Timothy 6:10: "For the love of money is a root of all kinds of evil." [This claim reflects a complete misunderstanding regarding what motivates people to do what they do. Certainly money is potentially problematic in this regard, but it doesn't hold a candle to the evil wrought by religious, cultural, and political ideologies that have caused and encouraged hatred, discrimination, ostracization, torture, and killing throughout the ages.]

CHAPTER TWENTY-NINE

THE BIBLE CONTAINS NUMEROUS CONTRADICTIONS, ERRORS, AND FALSEHOODS

I n the following section, I have noted forty-eight contradictions and twenty-five mistakes and falsehoods found in the Old and New Testaments.[1] Please note that those contradictions and errors noted here are but a tiny sample of the many hundreds that can be found in the Bible.

Contradictions (Tanakh [Old Testament])

Explanation	Verses
The world contains no man who is perfectly righteous vs. Job is a "blameless and upright man."	Eccl. 7:20–21 vs. Job 1:8
God does not change his mind vs. God does change his mind.	Numbers 23:19 vs. Exodus 32:9–14
David killed 700 Aramaeans in chariots vs. David killed 7,000 Aramaeans in chariots.	2 Samuel 10:18 vs. 1 Chron. 19:18
Solomon had stables for 40,000 chariot horses vs. Solomon had stables for 4,000 chariot horses.	1 Kings 4:26 vs. 2 Chron. 9:25
Zerubbabel's father was Pedaiah vs. Zerubbabel's father was Shealtiel.	1 Chron. 3:19 vs. Ezra 3:2
Ahaziah died in Megiddo vs. Ahaziah died in Jehu.	2 Kings 9:27 vs. 2 Chron. 22:9

420 talents of gold were brought back from Ophir and delivered to Solomon vs. 450 talents of gold were brought back from Ophir and delivered to Solomon.	1 Kings 9:28 vs. 2 Chron. 8:18
The world contains no man who is perfectly righteous vs. Job is a "blameless and upright man."	Eccl. 7:20–21 vs. Job 1:8
God does not change his mind vs. God does change his mind.	Numbers 23:19 vs. Exodus 32:9–14
David killed 700 Aramaeans in chariots vs. David killed 7,000 Aramaeans in chariots.	2 Samuel 10:18 vs. 1 Chron. 19:18
Solomon had stables for 40,000 chariot horses vs. Solomon had stables for 4,000 chariot horses.	1 Kings 4:26 vs. 2 Chron. 9:25
Zerubbabel's father was Pedaiah vs. Zerubbabel's father was Shealtiel.	1 Chron. 3:19 vs. Ezra 3:2
Ahaziah died in Megiddo vs. Ahaziah died in Jehu.	2 Kings 9:27 vs. 2 Chron. 22:9
420 talents of gold were brought back from Ophir and delivered to Solomon vs. 450 talents of gold were brought back from Ophir and delivered to Solomon.	1 Kings 9:28 vs. 2 Chron. 8:18
Joab reports to David that there were 800,000 arms-bearing men in Israel and 500,000 in Judah vs. Joab reported that there were 1,100,000 in Israel and 470,000 in Judah.	2 Sam. 24:9 vs. 1 Chron. 21:5–6
Joshua captured Debir vs. Othniel captured Debir.	Joshua 10:38–39 vs. Judges 1:11–13
Sisera is killed in his sleep by Jael vs. Sisera was killed while standing by Jael.	Judges 4:21 vs. Judges 5:27
Children shall be held accountable for their father's sins vs. a child shall not be held accountable for their father's sins.	Exodus 20:5 vs. Ezekiel 18:20
The "Sea" in Solomon's temple held 2,000 baths vs. the "Sea" held 3,000 baths.	1 Kings 7:26 vs. 2 Chron. 4:5

Solomon had 3,300 foremen in charge of work vs. Solomon had 3,600 foremen in charge of work.	1 Kings 5:16 vs. 2 Chron. 2:2
David buys property for 50 shekels of silver vs. David buys the (same) property for 600 shekels of silver.	2 Sam. 24:24 vs. 1 Chron. 21:25
David captured 1,700 horsemen from King Hadadezer vs. David captured 7,000 horsemen from King Hadadezer.	2 Samuel 8:4 vs. 1 Chron. 18:4
1,222 people of the family of Azgad returned from Babylonian exile vs. 2,322 people of the family of Azgad returned from Babylonian exile.	Ezra 2:12 vs. Neh. 7:17
One should not make a carved or graven image of anything vs. Moses is told "You shall make two cherubim of gold."	Exodus 20:4 vs. Exodus 25:18
God created birds before man vs. God created man before the birds.	Gen. 1:20–28 vs. Gen. 2:7–19.
God created man and woman at the same time vs. God created man first and woman later.	Gen. 1:27 vs. Gen. 2:7–22
Baasha began his reign over Israel in the third year of King Asa's reign (over Judah) and reigned for twenty-four years (Baasha's reign lasted twenty-four years) vs. in the thirty-sixth year of King Asa's reign, Baasha, king of Israel, built Ramah (Baasha's reign lasted at least thirty-three years).	1 Kings 15:33 vs. 2 Chron. 16:1
Saul kills himself with his own sword vs. the Philistines killed Saul .	1 Samuel 31:4 vs. 2 Samuel 21:12
David killed the giant Goliath from Gath vs. Elhanan kills the giant Goliath from Gath.	1 Samuel 17:48–51 vs. 2 Samuel 21:19

Contradictions (New Testament)

Explanation	Verses
Mary Magdalene's first visit to Jesus's tomb occurred "when the sun had risen" vs. "it was still dark" when she visited Jesus's tomb.	Mark 16:2 vs. John 20:1
Mary Magdalene, Mary mother of James, and Salome all visited Jesus's tomb vs. only Mary Magdalene visited the tomb. (Note: each of the four Gospels has different women visiting Jesus's tomb on that morning.)	Mark 16:1 vs. John 20:1
Jesus's tomb was closed when the women arrived vs. Jesus's tomb was open when they arrived.	Matthew 28:2 vs. Luke 24:2
The women saw one angel at Jesus's tomb vs. the women saw two angels at Jesus's tomb.	Matthew 28:2-5 vs. John 20:12
Mary Magdalene did recognize Jesus when she first saw him after the resurrection vs. she did not recognize him	Matthew 28:8-10 vs. John 20:14
Jesus's dying words on the cross were "Father, into your hands I commend my spirit" vs. Jesus's dying words on the cross were "It is finished."	Luke 23:46 vs. John 19:30
Jesus claims he will be "three days and three nights" in "the heart of the earth" vs. he is crucified on a Friday and is arisen by Sunday morning or two days and two nights.	Matthew 12:40 vs. all four Gospels
The father of Joseph (father of Jesus) was Jacob vs. the father of Joseph (father of Jesus) was Heli.	Matthew 1:16 vs. Luke 3:23
One is saved only by faith and grace not works vs. one is saved by works and not only by faith.	Eph. 2:8-9 vs. James 2:24
One must do good works so that they can be seen vs. one must not do good works where they can be seen.	Matthew 5:16 vs. Matthew 6:1-6

Jesus was crucified at 9 a.m. vs. Jesus was crucified sometime after 12 noon.	Mark 15:25–26 vs. John 19:14–18
Satan entered Judas before the Last (Passover) Supper vs. Satan entered Judas during the Last (Passover) Supper.	Luke 22:3–7 vs. John 13:27
The "women" prepared spices and perfumes to anoint the body of Jesus but were not able to vs. Joseph and Nicodemus brought the spices and perfumes to the tomb and anointed the body of Jesus.	Luke 23:55–56 vs. John 19:38–40
No one would be filled with the Spirit until after Jesus was glorified vs. John the Baptist was filled with the Spirit before Jesus was even born.	John 7:39 vs. Luke 1:15
Mary Magdelene entered Jesus's tomb vs. Mary Magdelene did not enter the tomb.	Mark 16:5 vs. John 20:1–2, 11
Jesus instructs his disciples to bring him one animal (a colt) for his fateful ride into Jerusalem vs. Jesus instructs his disciples to bring him two animals (a donkey and her foal) for his ride into Jerusalem.	Mark 11:2 vs. Matthew 21:2
Jesus attacks the money-changers in the Temple during the Passion Week vs. Jesus attacks the money-changers in the Temple near the beginning of his ministry, well before Passion Week.	Mark 11:15 vs. John 2:15
A woman anoints Jesus's head with oil at Simon's house vs. a woman anoints Jesus's feet with oil at Simon's house.	Mark 14:3 vs. Luke 7:38
Matthew traces Jesus genealogy back to David through David's son Solomon vs. Luke traces Jesus's genealogy back to David through David's son Nathan.	Matthew 1:6–7 vs. Luke 3:31
The inscription on the cross over Jesus's head read "The King of the Jews," vs. the inscription on the cross over Jesus's head read "This is Jesus, the King of the Jews."	Mark 15:26 vs. Matthew 27:37

Matthew quotes Jesus as saying "Go therefore, and make disciples of all nations," vs. Luke, writing in Acts, states that Paul and his companions were "forbidden by the Holy Spirit to speak the word in Asia."	Matthew 28:19 vs. Acts 16:6

Contradictions (Old and New Testaments)

Explanation	Verses
All individuals are held accountable for the sin of Eve and Adam as it is passed down through the generations vs. individuals are not held responsible for the sins of their fathers.	Romans 5:12, 19 vs. Deut. 24:16, Ezekiel 18:20
God has never been seen by any man vs. the Lord spoke to Moses face to face like one speaks to a friend.	1 John 4:12 vs. Exodus 33:11
Jesus claims, "No one has ascended into heaven" vs. Elijah "ascended" into heaven.	John 3:13 vs. 2 Kings 2:11
It is written that all men must die once yet Enoch and Elijah did not die before they were taken up into heaven.	Hebrews 9:27 vs. Genesis 5:24 and 2 Kings 2:11
God tempts no one vs. God tempted Abraham.	James 1:13 vs. Genesis 22:1

Mistakes and Falsehoods (Tanakh [Old Testament])

Explanation	Verses
Adam did not die on the day he ate of the tree of good and evil as God said he would; he dies at 930 years of age.	Genesis 2:17 vs. Genesis 5:5

God said that he will no longer call Jacob "Jacob" but, instead "Israel," but later God calls out to him, "Jacob, Jacob" and Jacob answers "Here I am."	Genesis 35:10 vs. Genesis 46:2
All the kings of the earth sought out Solomon for his wisdom. (False. Clearly the writer of this passage knew nothing of the kingdoms and peoples of North and South America, the Far East, and Africa.)	2 Chron. 9:23
The earth is stationary and cannot be moved. (False. This notion reflects the understanding of men in the first millennium BCE.)	Psalms 93:1
The moon shines as it gives off its own light. (False. The moon passively reflects the light of the sun.)	Isaiah 13:10
A woman is unclean for forty days after birthing a male child and for eighty days after birthing a female child; it will take this long for the blood to be purified. (False. This is nonsense. The longer period for females reflects Bronze Age misogyny not biological principles.)	Leviticus 12:1–5
The total number of all males at least a month old of the Gershon, Kohath, and Merari clans is incorrectly totaled to give an incorrect sum.	Numbers 3:21–34, Numbers 3:39
The total number of people of the tribes and families returning from exile in Babylon is incorrectly summed as 42,360 in Ezra 2:64; the actual total based on the numbers provided in Ezra 2 is 29,818. Virtually the same account is also found in Nehemiah 7. Also, the numbers used for the various tribes and families. while similar in magnitude, differ in both accounts.	Ezra 2 and Nehemiah 7

Different numbers for those returning from Babylonian exile are provided in Ezra and Nehemiah for the same tribes and families, for example Azgad: 1,222 (Ezra 2:12) vs. Azgad: 2,322 (Nehemiah 7:17), Adin: 454 (Ezra 2:15) vs. Adin: 655 (Nehemiah 7:20), Bigvai: 2,056 (Ezra 2:14) vs. Bigvai: 2,067 (Nehemiah 7:19), and so on. Please note that there are many other discrepancies in this list that could be added to those specified here.	Ezra 2 vs. Nehemiah 7
Fifteen cities are listed and the total given is fourteen.	Joshua 15:33–36
The earth is flat. (Both passages describe phenomena that would be possible or true only if the earth were flat.)	Daniel 4:10-11, Matthew 4:8
God says that all plants bearing seed and every tree bearing fruit shall be food for humans. (False. Many of these are fatal.)	Genesis 1:29
The rainbow first appears after Noah's flood. (False—that is unless the laws of physics were not operable before that time, which is unlikely since it would change the universe to such an extent that it would not be recognizable.)	Genesis 9:12–16
The snake does not eat dirt.	Genesis 3:14

Mistakes and Falsehoods (New Testament)

Explanation	Verses
The (purported) prophecy found in the Gospel of Matthew, namely ". . . so that what had been spoken through the prophets might be fulfilled, 'He will be called a Nazorean,'" is not found in the Old Testament.	Matthew 2:23
A crowd of people asks Jesus a thirty-one word question, presumably all speaking extemporaneously and in unison (not believable).	John 12:34

The Gospel of Christ had been heard by everyone in "all the earth" in the time of Paul. (Not true: There were tens of millions occupying lands in the western hemisphere and the far reaches of Asia and Africa who were totally unaware of Paul, his teachings, or Jesus.)	Romans 10:18
Those who have faith in the Lord will be able to handle snakes or drink deadly poison and no harm will come to them. (False. There are a number of documented cases of members of Pentecostal Holiness churches and similar snake-handling faiths dying after handling snakes, including the Church of God with Signs Following founder George Hensley.)	Mark 16:18
Matthew incorrectly attributes a scriptural passage to Jeremiah, but it is actually from Zechariah.	Matthew 27:9-10 vs. Zech. 11:12-13
A (purported) scripture from the Hebrew scriptures (Old Testament) is quoted. This scripture does not exist.	Luke 24:46-47
Matthew writes that Jesus is the "son of David." This cannot be true since David is in Joseph's ("father" of Jesus) line and, since Mary was not impregnated by Joseph, Joseph's ancestral line is irrelevant.	Matthew 1:1
Matthew mistakenly refers to Zechariah as the "son of Berachiah," but in the Old Testament, Zechariah is said to be the son of Jehoiada.	Matthew 23:35 vs. 2 Chron. 24:20
In a number of New Testament verses, Jesus is quoted as saying that the end times or his second coming will occur in the lifetime of his listeners as in, for example, Matthew 16:28, where he says, "Truly I tell you, there are some standing here who will not taste death before they see the Son of Man coming in his kingdom." This is clearly a false prophecy.	Matthew 16:28, 23:36, 24:34, Mark 9:1, 13:30, Luke 9:27

Mark claims, "When it was noon, darkness came over the whole land until three in the afternoon." Yet no astronomical records of the time, chronicler, or historian makes any mention of this amazing event. It has presumably been added to the account in order to make an impression on the reader.	Mark 15:33
According to Acts, Paul says that Moses and the prophets prophesied "that the Messiah must suffer, and that, by being the first to rise from the dead, he would proclaim light both to our people and to the Gentiles." This prophecy regarding Christ is an obvious example of "prophecy historicized,"[2] as no such verse is found in the Tanakh (Old Testament).	Acts 26:22-23

For some Christians, and most Jews for that matter, in regard to the Tanakh, such contradictions and errors are probably somewhat interesting but not really that troubling. After all, what would one expect of a text that has been cobbled together by many different men, drawing off of a variety of sources, over a period of about 1,200 years or so? Such errors are to be expected in any ancient document produced by humans. And that, my friends, is precisely my point. I would hope by now that it is clear to the reader that the Bible is not the literal, inerrant word of God, in fact not even close. Considering the data I have cited thus far, one wonders how anyone could make such an obviously baseless claim when even a cursory reading of the Bible is enough to invalidate beyond a shadow of a doubt the claims of divine literalism and inerrancy. But let us not forget, in matters of faith, anything and everything is possible.

The Qur'an, by the way, is easily just as problematic as the Bible. First, let us not forget that the sole source of the information that comprises the 114 suras of the Qur'an is Muhammad who (allegedly) received them from an angel (Gabriel). There are varying stories regarding precisely when and how the text was actually codified, some claiming that this happened during the reign of the first caliph (successor of Muhammad), Abu Bakr, some claiming that it happened later. Either way, Muhammad was illiterate, so clearly at some point the text had to be committed to memory and then later written down. Just how authentic or true the text is to the original revelations of Muhammad is another issue:

> Arabic script itself was not standardized until the later part of the ninth century, and in the meantime the undotted and oddly voweled Koran was generating wildly different explanations of itself, as it still does. This might not matter in the case of the *Illiad*, but remember that we are supposed to be talking about the unalterable (and *final*) word of god. There is obviously a connection between the sheer feebleness of this claim and the absolutely fanatical certainty with which it is advanced. To take one instance that can hardly be called negligible, the Arabic words written on the outside of the Dome of the Rock in Jerusalem are different from any version that appears in the Koran.[3]

Another problem regarding the authenticity of the Qur'an is that the oldest surviving manuscripts date back to about 100 or so years after the death of Muhammad. The most complete manuscript that survives today is found in the British Library and, according to many Islamicists, dates back to about 160 years after Muhammad's death. Though these time periods are actually shorter than the time periods separating the earliest existing biblical manuscripts from the dates when they were reputed to have first been written, it is nevertheless troublesome that, as in the case of the Bible, we do not know for sure precisely what the original manuscripts said.

The casual Jewish or Christian reader of the Qur'an will notice that much of the content seems similar to the stories and tales found in the Bible, but there are significant differences between the two versions. For example, the Bible (Genesis 22:1–2) claims that Abraham was commanded to sacrifice Isaac (Abraham and Sarah's son), whereas the Qur'an never names the child but Islamic tradition holds the child was Ishmael (Abraham and Hagar's son); the Qur'an comments at length on the person of Jesus but it claims that he was not crucified (sura 4:157); the Qur'an contains the story of Eve and Adam, but the text claims that both were equally at fault for disobeying God and that God eventually forgave them for their transgression, thus, there is no textual support for the concept of original sin; the Qur'an mentions the Decalogue but it scatters the commandments throughout the text and does not state them as a combined unit; and the story of the birth of Jesus in the Qur'an (suras 3 and 19) does not mention Joseph (Muslims believe that Jesus had no human father) and Jesus's birth took place at the trunk of a palm tree rather than in a stable as per the New Testament. I could go on and on, page after page, adding examples to those noted here, but suffice it to say that the Qur'an contains many of the stories and personalities found in the Bible but with differences that are sometimes glaring and sometimes subtle. (It should be pointed out that there are many chapters in the Qur'an, such as many of the Madinan suras, that reflect the fact that they were revealed to Muhammad in Medina during the later stages of his "ministry,"[4] and, for this reason, bear little similarity to biblical writings.)

Now, if we were to take this same information, remove any association with Judaism, Christianity, and Islam, and present it to an impartial audience, the consensus would be that one version of the text, the most recent one (Qur'an), was clearly plagiarized (at least in part) from the older version (Bible) or it simply borrowed from the body of mythology and traditions common to the area, *à la* the Bible. The former is entirely plausible, since Muhammad and his mates certainly had access to Jewish and Christian scriptures as well as many Jews and Christians in the flesh. In fact, the great respect Muhammad had for the grand old religion of Judaism is evidenced by the fact that he first instructed his followers to pray facing Jerusalem. Later, however, after realizing that the Jews of Yathrib (Medina) were not going to accept his revelations, he established the *Ka'bah* in Mecca as the focal point of prayer. Unfortunately, the entirely reasonable hypotheses discussed here are unnecessarily problematic, since we cannot remove faith-based sentiments from this exercise; those who claim absolutism for their version of religion (in this case Muslims) will be outraged at my suggestion that the Qur'an is plagiarized (at least in part) from the Bible. Nevertheless, the plagiarism hypothesis is immensely more robust, elegant, and concise than the other popular hypothesis, which states that the Qur'an contains the words of God relayed through the angel Gabriel to Muhammad. Only a (collective) mind that has been beaten down for ages by the tyranny of religious absolutism could embrace that extraordinary claim without question.

The scriptures of eastern religions are highly problematic as well, although virtually no claims are made in this case for the literal, historical veracity of the texts, although they are, of course, considered to be authoritative in matters of dogma. The scriptures of Hinduism are voluminous and were written over a period of about two thousand years (approximately 1500 BCE–500 CE). The *Upanishads* contain many of the teachings that revolutionized Hinduism around 500 BCE, and here one will find teachings regarding issues such as the Brahman (the supreme spiritual reality in the Hindu universe), the relationship between humans and the Brahman (humans possess *atman* or a tiny piece of the Brahman, an idea immortalized in the Sanskrit phrase "*tat tvam asi*" or "you are that"), karma and reincarnation, and *samsara* (the birth/death cycle that humans are trapped in until they achieve *moksha* or liberation). The "truths" contained in these ancient writings are assumed to be valid but, of course, they are, not surprisingly, manifestly nonfalsifiable. No specific authors for these texts are mentioned (the one exception being the traditional claim that Vyasa, an avatar of Vishnu, wrote down the *Vedas* sometime around the eighth millennium BCE) and the provenience, especially of the oldest texts, is unknown. The scholarly consensus is that many of these sacred teachings were passed down orally for centuries before being written down since such a high premium was placed on sound and the spoken word rather than writing.

The oldest texts of Buddhism, the "Pali canon" (Pali is a dialect of Sanskrit), were codified and written down about four hundred years after the death of Buddha. As in the cases of Jesus and Muhammad, the Buddha left no writings of his own but, according to tradition, his many followers and assistants purportedly memorized and then recorded the teachings of the Buddha, which were initially assigned to one of three categories: the discourses of the Buddha, the rules and general dos and don'ts of monastic life, and special, advanced teachings; this collection is known as the *Tripitaka* or "three baskets." There are other collections of Buddhist scripture that postdate the Pali canon, for example the Chinese canon (generally associated with Mahayana Buddhism) and the Tibetan canon (generally associated with the somewhat peculiar form of Buddhism first practiced in Tibet).

The scriptures of Jainism, an ancient religion founded in India that became popular at about the same time as Buddhism, were probably written down some nine hundred or so years after the life of Nataputta Vardhamana ("Mahavira"), the twenty-fourth and final *Tirthankara* of this spiritual cycle. According to Chinese tradition, the *Dao De Jing*, the primary scriptures of Daoism, was written by Daoism's most famous proponent, Lao Tzu, in about the sixth century BCE. Most scholars, however, believe that no such individual existed and that the *Dao De Jing* was probably written down sometime around the fourth or third century BCE.

It should be stated that practitioners of the Western monotheisms generally do not read and understand their scriptures like the followers of the Eastern religious traditions. Whereas Westerners tend to consider their scriptures as either being directly inspired or literally dictated by God and, thus, are inclined to interpret these writings dogmatically, the followers of the Eastern traditions generally do not. Nevertheless, the scriptures of the Eastern traditions are considered to be important sources of instruction and spiritual insight.

The brevity of this cursory review of the sacred writings of some of the world's "great" religions notwithstanding, we can see that using these ancient texts as sources of teachings and dogma is clearly a problematic endeavor. Remember, the claim is that these texts are the sources of absolute truth but, frankly, reliability, validity, and substance are, again, dubious to a fault. In reality, no one alive today knows very much at all regarding the authorship or authenticity of these writings. There is simply no way we can assume that these texts have been passed down to us without error or redaction. And, then, this issue isn't even relevant unless it can be shown that the words are actually what the faith traditions say they are, namely the thoughts and utterances of God or some similar authoritative, transcendental source.

There are many, many good reasons to reject the claims that believers make regarding their scriptures, not the least of which is the sheer ignorance many of these folks display regarding even the most basic historical and linguistic knowledge regarding these texts. Muslims are by far the least likely group as a whole to critique their scriptures or even question the claims and assumptions of orthodoxy, as evidenced by the hysterical behavior over cartoon drawings and the death sentence placed on Salmon Rushdie for his novel *The Satanic Verses*. In fact, there is virtually no tradition of Qur'anic criticism in the Islamic world. If there were, however, it probably wouldn't take very long to totally deconstruct the Qur'an and expose it for what it actually is: yet another work of literature written by men, attributed by men to God, and then forced on everyone else as "God's word."

CHAPTER THIRTY

DIVINE(?) ORIGIN
OF THE BIBLE

The notion that the Pentateuch (first five books of the Bible) was written by Moses was a common and popular belief for ages until the nineteenth century when Bible scholars, after studying the text impartially, popularized the "documentary hypothesis." Since that time, it has been strongly argued that the Pentateuch had at least four different authors, referred to as J (the Jahwist), E (the Elohist), D (the Deuteronomist), and P (the priestly source). The time period in which they were writing and both the style of writing and content of what was written are noticeably different in each case. For example, J and D referred to God as "YHWH," and E and D referred to God as "Elohim"; J uses the term "Sinai," but E uses the term "Horeb"; E focuses on Northern Israel, P focuses on Judah, and D focuses on the Temple; and J relates to and discusses God using anthropomorphic language but P relates to and discusses God in cultic and transcendental terms.[1] Christian fundamentalists, however, ignore the empirical data and refuse to reject the dogma of Mosaic authorship for the Pentateuch, but, according to Richard Elliott Friedman, professor of Jewish Studies, there is little doubt among biblical scholars that Moses was not the author of the Pentateuch:

> Until the past generation there were orthodox Christian and Jewish scholars who contested the Documentary Hypothesis in scholarly circles. At present, however, there is hardly a biblical scholar in the world actively working on the problem who would claim that the Five Books of Moses were written by Moses—or by any one person. . . . But the hypothesis itself continues to be the starting

point of research, no serious student of the Bible can fail to study it, and no other explanation of the evidence has come close to challenging it.[2]

Today, there is by no means a consensus among Bible scholars regarding the documentary hypothesis, and, in fact, other hypotheses to account for the duplications and contradictions in the Pentateuch have been put forward. Nevertheless, complete Mosaic authorship for the entire Pentateuch is rejected outright by virtually all scholars. Christian fundamentalists, however, over and against a solid body of evidence to the contrary, continue to insist on the traditional claim of Mosaic authorship. Do you see a pattern here? Fundamentalists will always reject good data and sound scholarship if it means giving up on a matter of faith or tradition. An old earth? No. Biological evolution? No. The Bible is simply a work of literature like any other book? No. An uncertain authorship of the Gospels? No. Non-Mosaic authorship of the Pentateuch? No. Faith, tradition, and authority will always trump empirical data and sound reasoning in the world of religious fundamentalism.

The general consensus seems to favor the view that the Hebrew Scriptures were written, compiled, and edited sometime between about the tenth and second centuries BCE. If we use the rough chronology provided by the Bible, then Abraham was alive around 1900 BCE, Noah's flood occurred about five hundred years before the time of Abraham, and, finally, the time period from Noah's flood back to the time of Eve and Adam was another 1,600 years or so. This means, of course, that the parts of the Hebrew Scriptures that cover Eve and Adam in the Garden of Eden, the destruction of Sodom, the Tower of Babel, Noah, and Abraham were written some one thousand to four thousand years after the fact. Unless one is willing to accept a scenario that involves God actually writing the scriptures or God whispering in the ears of the early scribes, what we have is a fascinating and ancient collection of lore, legends, and mythology, rather than a historical account of the ancient Middle East.

Young-earth creationists will often invoke the (purported) fact that the biblical creation account in Genesis is historically accurate since it is based on God's eyewitness account. Well, if that is in fact the case, then God was clearly confused. Here is the order of creation as recorded in the first creation account, found in Genesis 1:1–2:4: sky ("dome") → earth and plants → sun and moon → aquatic creatures and birds → animals → man and woman. Now, here is the order as recorded in the second creation account, found in Genesis 2:5–25: earth and sky → water → man → plants → animals and birds → woman. Please note that there are clearly stated time markers that separate these various creation events. This is precisely what one would expect to find if Genesis was, in fact, the result of a decidedly human compilation of stories from various sources over a long period of time. The scholarly consensus is that the second story, written by the "J" source who uses "YHWH" to refer to God, is simply older than the first, written by the "E" source who uses "Elohim" to refer to God. Biblical literalists, however, simply cannot accept what is written as is and insist on explaining why what one reads in the first two chapters of Genesis is really not what it seems to be. As far as I am concerned, it is not my problem; after all, they are the ones who demand a literal reading of the Bible.

If we turn to the Christian New Testament, we see much of the same, although the time periods are, of course, not nearly as long. The scholarly consensus today is that Paul's letters were the first material to be written (beginning around 50 CE) and that the four Gospels were written between about 70 CE to 100 CE, with Mark being the oldest and John being the last one written. Mark, the shortest Gospel, served as a sort of template for Matthew and Luke, and these two Gospels also drew off of an unknown source usually identified as "Q," the first letter of the German term "*Quelle*," which means "source." The similarity of the three Gospels is reflected in the term "synoptic" that is used to refer to all three.

The four Gospels, then, were written anywhere from about forty to seventy years after the death of Jesus and, according to biblical scholar Bart Ehrman, not only were the writers not eyewitnesses to what was written about in the Gospels but we actually do not know who wrote them:

The four gospels that eventually made it into the New Testament, for example, are all anonymous, written in the third person *about*

Jesus and his companions. None of them contains a first-person narrative . . . or claims to be written by an eyewitness or companion of an eyewitness. Why then do we call them Matthew, Mark, Luke, and John? Because sometime in the second century, when proto-orthodox Christians recognized the need for *apostolic* authorities, they attributed these books to apostles (Matthew and John) and close companions of apostles (Mark, the secretary of Peter; and Luke, the traveling companion of Paul). Most scholars today have abandoned these identifications, and recognize that the books were written by otherwise unknown but relatively well-educated Greek-speaking (and writing) Christians during the second half of the first century.[3]

The proto-orthodox Christians would eventually manage to overcome and dominate the many other competing Christian groups to the extent that after the Council of Nicaea (325 CE) they essentially controlled all things Christian, including doctrines, dogmas, and liturgy. So, for example, today Arius (256–336 CE) is known as a "heresiarch," the founder of a heretical notion known as Arianism, the belief that God and Jesus were not "consubstantial" (of the same substance), in contradistinction to the belief held by the more powerful faction (supported by Constantine for reasons that had much more to do with politics than theology) that God and Jesus were of the same substance. It would be this very same proto-orthodox faction that would make decisions regarding the canonization of some Christian writings and the rejection of others, with the former comprising the New Testament as we know it today. Ehrman describes the influence of this group:

> But virtually all forms of modern Christianity, whether they acknowledge it or not, go back to *one* form of Christianity that emerged as victorious from the conflicts of the second and third centuries. This one form of Christianity decided what was the "correct" Christian perspective; it decided who could exercise authority over Christian belief and practice; and it determined what forms of Christianity would be marginalized, set aside, destroyed. It also decided which books to canonize into scripture and which books to set aside as "heretical," teaching false ideas.[4]

Lest the reader assume that only a handful of works were rejected and ignored and conclude that this is a trivial issue, in his *Lost Christianities: The Battles for Scripture and the Faiths We Never Knew*, Ehrman lists the following "major Christian apocrypha": sixteen Gospels, six "Acts," thirteen "epistles and related literature," and nine "apocalypses and related literature."[5] These works were all used by one Christian group or another at some point but were not included in the "official" collection that came to be known as the New Testament. The first church council to canonize the twenty-seven books we now recognize as the New Testament was the Council of Hippo in 393 CE, some four hundred years after the birth of Jesus.

There is, of course, much more to this story, but I think it should be clear that a careful reading of history certainly does not suggest that there is anything divine or miraculous about the origin and development of the Bible. Those who continue to insist that the Bible is God-given must argue the following, at least in regard to the New Testament: Yes, it is true that certain books were chosen and certain books were not, but the hand of God was at work making these decisions; these men were led by God to choose the correct books. This is simply another variation of the "God did it" hypothesis that can be invoked to explain anything, but the probability that this hypothesis is correct is inversely proportional to the quantity and quality of the documentation and empirical data that support a more mundane explanation; as far as I am concerned, in this case, the "God did it" hypothesis is untenable.

CHAPTER THIRTY-ONE

THE PUTATIVE DIVINE LITERALITY AND INERRANCY OF THE BIBLE

T he one foundational idea upon which all other Christian fundamentalist principles, dogmas, and doctrines are grounded, the
one notion that has figured quite prominently in this commentary
on the sources of religious knowledge, is the belief that the Bible is
the literal, inerrant word of God. This assertion is part and parcel
of the mission statements of fundamentalist Christian schools everywhere and even some colleges as well (the Bob Jones University's
statement of beliefs notes that "the account of origins in Genesis
is a factual narrative of historical events"[1]), even though it can be
"deconstructed" quite easily.

There are two basic issues to consider here. One involves the
reasons why such a belief exists in the first place (i.e., if one should
ask a Christian fundamentalist why she embraces such a claim, what
reasons would she give?). Issue two focuses on the truth or falsity of
the assertion itself (i.e., is the Bible, in fact, the literal, inerrant word
of God?). We will consider both in turn.

The primary, and by far the most popular, justification for this
claim of literality and inerrancy is that the "Bible says" or "it is in
the Bible";[2] those who don't make the argument for strict literality
and inerrancy nevertheless still use this justification for the notion
that God is the source of all the writings. Thus, they will point to 2
Timothy 3:16, where it is written, "All scripture is inspired by God and
is useful for teaching, for reproof, for correction, and for training in
righteousness." (Some translations read "God-breathed" instead of

"inspired by God.") So, the Bible does, indeed, "say"; at least that can't be denied. But what about the logic? One believes the Bible is the literal, inerrant word of God or has its source in God because it contains a statement that, based on their interpretation, affirms that fact. But how does one defend that reasoning? She simply claims that any statement found in the Bible must be true. The reasoning strategy being employed here is, of course, manifestly circular. Besides, the average Christian fundamentalist unwittingly rejects this reasoning herself by virtue of the fact that she will dismiss all such claims made in other books. So, a more ingenuous statement of the belief would go something like this: The Bible is the literal, inerrant word of God or has its source in God because Christian fundamentalists believe this is the case. In truth, the literalism, inerrancy, and Divine provenience of the Bible are simply unwarranted assumptions without any basis in fact. These claims are actually no more or less credible or compelling than all other such claims made about the scriptures of any religion.

Now, what of the second issue, namely the veracity of the claim that the Bible is inerrant? Basically what is being claimed here is that the entire book is without error. Thus, if only one error is located in the thousand-plus pages of your typical Bible, then the claim is refuted. In chapter twenty-nine, I cited just a few of the hundreds of errors found in the Bible. There is one flub, however, that is particularly noteworthy, and that is the rather curious case of plagiarism (alluded to earlier) found in 2 Kings 19 and Isaiah 37. The two chapters are so similar that one may not notice any dissimilarities unless she compares the two chapters word for word. If any individual were presented this information regarding any other book that consisted of a compilation of materials from various authors, she would immediately conclude that one author overtly (and, apparently, shamelessly) stole someone else's work and claimed it as his own (but how did it get past the editor?!?). The impartial observer would plainly see that there was a serious oversight here. But, remember, we are dealing with the Bible, a book that is assumed (for no good reason, as argued above) to be infallible. For those individuals who have no intention whatsoever of allowing any data to falsify their belief, they must "explain away" this problem—they have no real choice in the matter. They are stuck with this strategy for the same reason that they are stuck with the unfortunate (and preposterous) six-thousand-year value for the age of the universe: they are working backward from an (assumed) theory to the data (which are ignored, dismissed, or denigrated if the facts do not fit the theory) instead of the other way around.

Here's what the *Oxford Bible Commentary* says about this plagiarism issue:

> It is likely that the final redactors of the book of Isaiah drew on something akin to our present 2 Kings as one of their sources, and the modern reader who wishes to find out how much we can know about Judah in the second half of the eighth century BCE must do the same. By the time Isaiah reached its final form the time of the monarchy, the pre-exilic period, was a distant memory.[3]

In other words, the final editors of Isaiah, working much later than the events being described, had to "refer back" to an older document (2 Kings) to make sure they got the story right. I guess in this case they borrowed a bit too literally. Of course, this explanation makes perfect sense, and it is totally understandable, but it must be rejected outright by the fundamentalists because it hardly describes a text that is "inspired by God" or "God-breathed" (2 Timothy 3:16) unless God sometimes suffered from lapses of memory.

In the interest of fairness, I should note that some in the Christian fundamentalist community have "adjusted" their inerrancy claim, perhaps in response to arguments such as those found in this book. After all, all one has to do is open a Bible; the inconsistencies, mistakes, and contradictions are everywhere for anyone to see. Here, for example is a statement lifted from the website for Patrick Henry College, in a section labeled "Statement of Faith": "The Bible in its entirety (all 66 books of the Old and New Testaments) is the inspired Word of God, inerrant *in its original autographs,* and the only infallible and sufficient authority for faith and Christian living" [my emphasis].[4] Liberty University posts a similar statement on its website: "We affirm that the Bible, both Old and New Testaments, though written by men, was supernaturally inspired by God so that all its words are the written true revelation of God; it is therefore inerrant *in the originals* and authoritative in all matters" [my emphasis].[5]

At least we can see some frank recognition of the empirical data here, since these schools, and others as well, have finally recognized what many scholars and skeptics recognized a long time ago: the claim of strict infallibility and inerrancy for the Bible is simply not credible. The administrators at these two institutions of higher learning have cleverly taken a claim that is patently false and turned into one that is patently nonfalsifiable. Why is the claim nonfalsifiable? Simply because the original manuscripts do not exist; they are all copies[6] or, more accurately, copies of copies of copies . . . etc. Bart Ehrman, a noted authority in the area of New Testament studies, writes, "Not only do we not have the originals, we don't have the first copies of the originals. We don't even have copies of the copies of the originals, or copies of the copies of the copies of the originals."[7] Thus, the clever fundamentalists get to have their cake and eat it too.

Too bad the Mormons didn't think about this when the Lamanite brouhaha surfaced a few years back. The older editions of the book of Mormon claimed outright that the Lamanites (people of Middle Eastern Jewish origin) were the ancestors of Native Americans. Of course, archaeologists had long ago established that said ancestors were clearly Asian. The Mormons continued to ignore reality for some time, but recently, with the thorough DNA analyses that have been conducted on Native Americans that establish definitively, beyond a shadow of a doubt that the Mormon claim was incorrect, they have backed up on the claim and now qualify it by stating that only some of the Native Americans were descended from Lamanites (even that is not true). Some sort of contrived story (similar to those giving rise to this religion in the first place) regarding a mistake in the original texts (the ones that were transcribed directly from the "golden tablets") would have worked out much better for them. As a result of this issue, the Mormon religion is truly experiencing a crisis, with some having left the church. What can you really expect, however, from a religion that dropped their blatantly racist stance against allowing African Americans to be ordained by simply announcing that the president of the church had received a new revelation from God (conveniently in 1978, when such views were beginning to be regarded as racist) that stated that African Americans could, in fact, be ordained. This raises a few questions: Are professing Mormons that credulous? How high is their threshold for gullibility? What will they not believe?

Let me conclude this discussion by asking the reader to ponder the fact that many of the instructors of evangelical homeschooled children are they themselves the products of the woefully misguided and inept pedagogy discussed above. But, it may be argued, surely these homeschool instructors are receiving some sort of training? After all, public school teachers must be degreed and certified. Unfortunately, as I noted earlier, the only qualification required for a homeschool instructor is parenthood. Imagine a typical home-schooled child going through what is essentially a glorified Sunday school curriculum for twelve years, then becoming an instructor of their own children.

Let me state here that I am fully aware of the studies that show how well homeschooled students do on various standardized tests vis-à-vis students that attend public school, but these data are patently misleading. Public schools have to take everyone who shows up, so we're not talking apples and apples here; when one considers afflu-ence and ethnicity, it is clear that we are comparing two totally dif-ferent demographics. Also, it's not that difficult to "teach to a test." But this discussion of comparative test scores totally misses the point. What sort of critical thinking skills are being engendered in homes where the Bible is considered the inerrant word of God, Christianity is considered to be the only true religion, history is taught from a "Christian perspective," and virtually all biologists, geologists, astron-omers, and anthropologists are thought to be almost totally incom-petent? It may not happen in one year, in ten years, or even in twenty years, but one of these days, this country, once the world standard bearer of education and scientific inquiry, will reap what it is now sowing. You can't put millions of children through curricula that are rife with half-truths, unfounded assumptions, myths, and fanta-sies without eventually realizing the negative consequences. Home-schooling will be the educational scourge of the twenty-first century, and we have Christian fundamentalists to thank for it.

CHAPTER THIRTY-TWO

EITHER FALSE OR
NONFALSIFIABLE

I t seems clear that all five mechanisms, processes, and sources of religious knowledge (natural theology, revelation, subjective experiences, overt instruction, and scriptures) are seriously flawed in some way, as each one fails (miserably) to measure up to standards of reliability, validity, and substance. There is certainly nothing about any of the five that an impartial or objective party would find compelling. In reality, the only individuals who are swayed by claims and beliefs generated and disseminated by the five sources are those who are already believers. One might argue that, given the fact that approximately 85 percent or so of the world's population embraces a religious belief of some sort, there are a whole lot of folks that seem to have a great deal of confidence in the five sources. Such an argument, however, is specious at best. One must not forget that said believers accept only the beliefs and dogmas generated by their own religion and not those generated by another religion, even though the "mode of transmission" of religious knowledge is basically the same in both cases. Thus, it is incorrect to posit that, say, believer X acknowledges the validity of revelation because he does not; in fact, believer X rejects 99 percent of all information (supposedly) gained by revelation, namely those of all the other religions. The average believer, then, by his own actions and behavior, demonstrates his utter lack of "faith" in revelation by virtue of the fact that he deems virtually all information obtained this way to be dubious if not completely spurious.

If one is ingenuous and objective regarding the sources of religious knowledge, I think it will become quite clear that all the major claims, beliefs, and dogmas of the world's religions can be placed in one of two categories: 1) they are false or 2) they are nonfalsifiable.[1] In category one, we would place any proposition that has been proven incorrect—e.g., Mormonism's dogma regarding a Lamanite ancestry for Native Americans, the Christian fundamentalist young-earth dogma, the tribal/indigenous belief that a sorcerer can kill an individual using metaphysical means (these "voodoo deaths" are attributed to physiological and psychological trauma), and the Jain claim that Nataputta Vardhamana, or Mahavira, lived for long periods of time on one grain of rice per day.

Then there are other claims that push the envelope of credulity to such an extent that we should probably throw them out as well, for example, any claim of virgin birth (believers of many religions believe—or believed—that their founder or prophet was conceived and birthed in a distinctly nonhuman way), (putative) revelations from God (see above), demonic possession, apparitions of the Virgin Mary, and many, many others.

Nevertheless, no matter how questionable, unreasonable, or even preposterous a claim is, if it is not an objective claim (i.e., if it is neither testable nor publicly verifiable), then we must label it "nonfalsifiable." If there is a God (a hypothesis that is widely recognized as being untestable), then there is certainly no reason why such an entity could not suspend natural law from time to time. Thus, it appears as though the bulk of religious claims and dogmas can be labeled nonfalsifiable, which would technically mean that, given our current understanding of the world we live in, we simply cannot know if they are true or false. This leads us, then, to what I consider to be the most defensible position on issues of faith, doubt, and religious knowledge, namely, agnosticism.

PART FIVE

AGNOSTICISM AND THE OBJECTIVE ARGUMENTS FOR AND AGAINST THE EXISTENCE OF GOD

CHAPTER THIRTY-THREE

AGNOSTICISM

Any discussion of agnosticism should begin with Thomas Henry Huxley, who, if he did not actually coin the term, certainly popularized it. After many years of study and contemplation, Huxley finally came to the same realization that all truly wise and reasonable thinkers come to: he knew for sure that he didn't know and was quite sure that he could not know:

> When I reached intellectual maturity and began to ask myself whether I was an atheist, a theist, or a pantheist; a materialist or an idealist; Christian or a freethinker; I found that the more I learned and reflected, the less ready was the answer; until, at last, I came to the conclusion that I had neither art nor part with any of these denominations, except the last. The one thing in which most of these good people were agreed was the one thing in which I differed from them. They were quite sure they had attained a certain "gnosis,"—had, more or less successfully, solved the problem of existence; while I was quite sure I had not, and had a pretty strong conviction that the problem was insoluble.[1]

Thus, Huxley rejected the idea that we could know anything with certainty regarding spiritual and metaphysical issues, a very reasonable position that is quite popular today.

In his description of agnosticism, Bertrand Russell explicitly addresses the limits and the potential of human knowledge: "An agnostic is a man who thinks that it is impossible to know the truth in the matter such as God and a future life with which the Christian religion and other religions are concerned. Or, if not for ever impossible, at any rate impossible at present."[2] Russell also comments on the degree of confidence one has in the ability of humans to at least potentially know everything there is to know about all things corporeal and ethereal. If we consider this issue, two basic types of agnosticism become evident:

- **absolute agnosticism**: The idea that we currently do not know anything about spiritual/religious matters of a supernatural sort and that, given our objective reality in an empirical world, we never will know.
- **qualified agnosticism**: The idea that we currently do not know anything about spiritual/religious matters of a supernatural sort but that such knowledge may be attainable in the future.

Curiously enough, some have even constructed definitions of agnosticism around the notion of faith. Thus, "agnostic theism" is the view that although one has no knowledge of spiritual/religious matters of a supernatural sort, one believes in such things anyway (i.e., one has no certain knowledge of God's existence but he nevertheless believes in God). "Agnostic atheism" is the view that since one has no knowledge of spiritual/religious matters of a supernatural sort, he does not believe in such things (i.e., one has no certain knowledge of God and, for this reason, does not believe that God exists).

There is clearly a lot of room here for hope, desire, and other emotive responses to uncertainty regarding things metaphysical; one can be optimistic or pessimistic regarding our ability to know the world we live in, and one can choose either to believe or not believe. Nevertheless, there is one common thread that runs through all conceptions of agnosticism—namely, the contention that we don't really know anything (with certainty) about such matters. In my mind, everyone is technically an agnostic in this regard, since no one has certain knowledge of spiritual/religious/supernatural phenomena, whether or not one believes he does. Agnosticism, in other words, is materially inherent to our species and belief or a willingness to believe doesn't change that.

There is, however, another form of "awareness" that needs to be addressed here, namely subjectivity. If my aforementioned comments are valid in regard to objective awareness, that does not necessarily make them so in regard to subjective awareness. There are, no doubt, quite different ways of "knowing," as Søren Kierkegaard reminded us. In chapter three it was noted that Kierkegaard argued that "objective reflection" would certainly lead to knowledge regarding empirical, worldly matters but that such reflection was, at best, an "approximation process," since it would lead to better and better versions of the "truth" but it would never uncover Absolute Truth.[3] Actually, that is a pretty good assessment of the potential of science, and no responsible scientist would claim any more than that. When we turn away from empirical matters to spiritual/religious matters, objectivity is useless and ineffectual. If we are to grasp the admittedly implausible claims of incarnating gods and virgin births, we have no other recourse but "subjective reflection." Now, by virtue of the fact that these claims are nonempirical, one never simply "gets it" in an Archimedean paroxysm of certainty, but rather one becomes increasingly aware of the chasm that separates their desire to know and the subject they are trying to know. In this view, the realization of spiritual or religious truth involves "becoming" not "knowing."

Kierkegaard, then, is certainly pessimistic regarding our ability and potential to know spiritual/religious matters of a supernatural sort using "objective reflection," but, unlike some of us, he is perfectly willing to employ "subjective reflection" in this task. Thus, his approach is only valid to the extent that such a strategy can lead us to a realization of religious truth. Clearly, even if it can, it will still be (obviously) a subjective truth (i.e., one individual's truth). And this is where it will remain unless this individual can figure out how to make his subjectivity our objectivity, which is a logical and practical impossibility. No matter how excited my friend is after "being born again in the Holy Spirit," I can only relate to him or her the way I relate to any other object, and that is objectively.

Obviously, without trust, this whole process breaks down; without trust, "subjective reflection" is stillborn. If I am to engage in this sort of subjective reflection, I must begin with both a desire to eventually realize the truth and an awareness that I cannot know the truth objectively. Now, since I am a native of Louisiana, born and raised Catholic, this will mean some sort of tentative or tacit acknowledgement (or at least as much "acknowledgement" as I can muster at the time) of

Mary's assumption into heaven, Jesus as both one hundred percent human and one hundred percent God, transubstantiation, the infallibility of the pope in matters *ex cathedra*, and other assorted claims that fail every test of a rational, empirical, objective epistemology. We have now arrived at what I consider to be the most serious flaw in Kierkegaard's approach. Imagine, if you will, that, instead of being born in Christian Denmark, Kierkegaard was birthed to Muslim parents in Turkey and, like virtually everyone else born in Turkey, he was raised as a Sunni Muslim and was taught the appropriate Islamic beliefs and practices. It seems clear that Kierkegaard's brilliant and passionate writings on faith and subjectivity would have been contextualized in an Islamic religious context, rather than Christian, and that we would be encouraged to search inwardly for Allah and that subjective truths would now include Muhammad's "Night Journey," the Qur'an as the literal spoken word of Allah, and Islam as the only absolutely true religion. I don't see how it could be otherwise, since the objective status of Christian beliefs and Islamic beliefs is identical; the issue of the objective truth of one faith versus that of another is unresolvable.

Now, the reader might point out (quite reasonably in my mind) that Kierkegaard was the unique product of a nineteenth-century, Scandinavian politico-historico-socio-religious context and that his thinking reflected that fact. But the issue of whether or not the Turkish Kierkegaard would have been a different thinker with different ideas is not relevant. The important point is that religious belief in both the generic and specific sense, in the context of this discussion, is something that cannot be maintained and engaged in objectively, irrespective of the fact that the religious belief in question is Eastern, Western, tribal, or whatever. The same sort of trust is required at the outset regardless of whether the individual is a Wiccan, Hindu, Daoist, or Parsi. Clearly, then, since it is true that the various claims and beliefs of the world's religions are largely mutually exclusive, then at least most, if not all, of them are wrong and such trust is unwarranted. Besides, we have no way to evaluate the various beliefs and dogmas of one religion vis-à-vis the others, so even if one religion is true, or some are partially true, we will never know.

So, faith, in Kierkegaardian terms, calls for trust and lots of it; some, in fact, would argue an inhuman amount of trust. (Kierkegaard, of course, recognized this. For him, faith was a default position with which he was not altogether happy.) Another Christian theologian, C. S. Lewis (discussed briefly in chapter three), also argues that trust is the most significant component of faith. Lewis describes faith ("belief in the strongest degree") as an "assent to a proposition which we think so overwhelmingly probable that there is a psychological exclusion of doubt, though not a logical exclusion of dispute."[4] The first part of the statement reflects the emotive investment a believer makes when she accepts a religious creed or dogma. I use the term "investment" because, just like real-world investments, this investment may or may not pay off for the believer, since she cannot know for certain whether or not the creed or dogma in question is true. (Either Allah spoke [through Gabriel] to Muhammad or "He" did not. Either Jesus was resurrected from the dead or he was not. Either the pope is the "vicar of Christ" or he is not.) The second part of the statement reflects the rational aspect of faith; it would clearly be irrational to continue to embrace a creed that has been subsequently disconfirmed by data that were not available when the believer first assented to the creed. In fact, this has already happened. Many beliefs embraced by traditional Christianity—for example, the Mosaic authorship of the Pentateuch and the geocentric orientation of our solar system—have been refuted as new data became available. At any point in time, any rational individual must recognize the fact that certain data that invalidate a particular creed or belief may come to light. (Although, many important religious claims, dogmas, and beliefs are, as has been noted on several occasions, nonfalsifiable.) But what is it, then, according to Lewis, that compels us to believe in the first place? This will sound familiar . . . trust. In fact, he describes the relationship one has to God as being similar to a relationship built on the trust one has with a close friend or a spouse.[5] It is incorrect, he says, to consider a belief in God a scientific hypothesis that may simply be disregarded at the first sign of trouble. One should continue to trust in God much as one would continue to trust in a good friend, otherwise there is no relationship with either God or one's friend. As he writes, "To love involves trusting the beloved beyond the evidence, even against much evidence. No man is our friend who believes in our good intentions only when they are proved."[6]

So, again, the primary component of faith and belief is trust. And, again, one might rightly raise the same issues I raised earlier in regard to Kierkegaard. Lewis's comments regarding faith and belief would have probably been applied by him to Brahman, had he been Hindu, Avalokiteśvara had he been a Tibetan Buddhist, or Obatala, had he been an Orisha worshiper in Trinidad. How, then, does one justify his or her trust? And doesn't this again push us toward agnosticism, a response that seems immanently reasonable especially when compared to the (potentially) empty promises of faith and belief? As was noted earlier, in chapter three, there is also a strong element of trust in Augustine's "believe that thou mayest understand."[7]

Fine, one might respond, but how do I know where to start? A Parsi in India, would tell us to begin with a belief in *Ahura Mazda* and the active role humans play in assisting him in his struggle against chaos and evil. A Daoist in China would tell us to begin with the belief that there is a true, natural principle, the Dao, upon which the order of all things is based, and that this natural order must not be disrupted. A Scientologist in Florida might tell us to begin with the belief that human beings can reach a godlike status through the practice of Scientology. A Yanomamo in Brazil might tell us to begin with the belief that only aggressive and belligerent males are the true descendants of the First Beings. Of course, when Augustine urged us to have faith if we desire understanding, what he meant was faith or trust in the basic creeds, dogmas, revelation, and principles of Christianity (as these were understood during his time). Thus, Augustine's approach, like that of Kierkegaard and Lewis, can be faulted for not being applicable in a general sense; what we are talking about is something like phonemics (with its focus on specific language sounds) rather than phonetics (with its focus on universal language sounds). In anthropology, we would say that Augustine's, Kierkegaard's, and Lewis's analyses of faith (or trust) and belief were "emic" rather than "etic" and, thus, described faith (or trust) and belief in only a culture-specific sense; this poses serious difficulties when the topic in question is religion. I seriously doubt that it was, say, Lewis's intention to lead individuals to a better understanding of Vishnu, Amitabha Buddha, Gao!na, or Zeus.

Again, since the primary attributes of these various "gods" and the nature of the universe they govern are mutually exclusive for the most part, the basic problem here for true believers is that the faith and trust approach will (potentially) lead them to embrace a false notion and their faith will not ultimately be rewarded with understanding in anything. In fact, it can be stated that if all the world's peoples were to embrace the faith and trust approach, then the majority (if, for example, only one religion is valid) or perhaps all (if the truth claims of all religions are false) of the world's population would be engaged in a mass delusion. The contention that we should begin with belief or faith or trust in some creed or dogma or the reliability of revelation, is, in my mind, potentially problematic since it could lead the unsuspecting believer almost anywhere in a conceptual sense.

Certainly, there has to be something better than the faith and belief approach, grounded as it is on trust and hope regarding things unknown and unknowable. Well, there is, but we have to move away from subjectivity to objectivity to find it. While it is indeed true that the "objective process" can only offer us approximate answers to the big questions, let it be stated one last time: Kierkegaard notwithstanding, perhaps a small amount of something is better than what is quite probably a very large amount of nothing. For this reason, then, in the next four chapters we will explore the best objective arguments for what is probably the most significant religious belief, the notion that God exists.

By leaving subjectivity behind we may be giving up on our only true chance at gaining absolute certainty, in a Kierkegaardian sense, regarding things religious, but even if after an extended period of hoping, trusting, and believing we should reach the point where we feel we "have" the truth or we "know" (with certainty) the truth, there is still room for doubt for two reasons: 1) it cannot be determined if one subjective experience is qualitatively different from another (is the provenience mundane or transcendental?), thus, the subjective "knower" can never disprove that the experience is not simply "in their head," giving it virtually the same status as a daydream or fantasy, and 2) the "knower" can never transform his subjectivity into another's objectivity, thus disallowing the possibility of independent confirmation. So, let us turn, then, to objectivity. And, while it is true that such "truths" are contingent or tentative, at least they do come with a high degree of certainty.

CHAPTER THIRTY-FOUR

MORAL ARGUMENTS FOR THE EXISTENCE OF GOD

I suppose most of my readers are familiar with some form of the moral argument, which is, according to many, the best argument for theism. Our focus in this chapter will be on the two basic types of moral argument, the classic form and the Kantian version. These moral arguments will then be anthropologically deconstructed, which means that I will critique them using global ethnographic data and the concepts of kinship, altruism, and reciprocity.

All classic moral arguments have the same basic structure. They begin by first recognizing the existence of objective moral principles or the existence of a moral consciousness in all humans and the fact that the limitations of human beings are such that they cannot be the ultimate source of these things. In fact, so goes the argument, only an omniscient and omnipotent God has the ability and capacity to be totally and solely responsible for the existence of objective moral principles or a moral consciousness, and since humans possess these things, then God must be the source, thus God exists. We will begin our analysis by examining this classical form of the moral argument. Later, we will look at a Kantian version, which proposes that a rational, moral world requires the existence of God.

Before I move on to an anthropological critique of the basic premises of the classical version of the argument, I should briefly discuss a (potentially) devastating philosophical critique of the notion of the existence of objective moral principles. The critique draws its inspiration from an exchange between Euthyphro and Socrates, as recorded in Plato's eponymous dialogue, *Euthyphro*. According to "divine command theory," an action is moral because God wills us to do it and it is evil if God wills us to avoid it; after all, God is, according to the various forms of the moral argument, the source of human morality. But, if we apply this logic consistently, we must necessarily state that the reason why, say, murder is evil is because God prohibits it, not because the act is intrinsically evil; and charity is good because God sanctions it, not because it is intrinsically good. Thus, by logical extension, it necessarily holds that if God sanctioned child abuse, then child abuse would be good. But this is a *reductio ad absurdum*; thus, there must exist a system of moral principles quite apart from God (i.e., God sanctions and prohibits certain actions because they are intrinsically good or evil and, since a system of moral principles exists independent of God, the moral behavior of humans can have their source in something other than God). Thus, the existence of a moral awareness or a moral consciousness in humans does not necessarily lead us to the existence of God, since the source of such awareness can lie elsewhere.

The first time I read the classical version of the moral argument as an undergraduate, it seemed to me as if the originator of this argument immediately jumped to a rather facile conclusion— namely that humans do not possess the ability or capacity to create or evolve, quite independently of some transcendental entity, a moral awareness or a moral consciousness. I feel that there are other more reasonable conclusions that can be drawn from the foundational premise of the argument. It seemed to me that the proponent of this argument gave up rather too quickly on humans. This is, no doubt, largely due to the fact that most individuals cannot envision a moral world that is not overseen by an omnipotent, omniscient, and omnibenevolent God; without his presence, even in a deistic form, the argument goes, humans would not be capable of ethics and morality. In simple form, this very common assumption can be worded as follows: without the guidance of God and religion, there would be no rule of law and humans would simply act as they will, usually in their own self-interest, leading to chaos and anarchy. This notion is so popular that, outside of the literature authored by agnostics and atheists, it is rarely critiqued, if ever.

As far as I am concerned, this common assumption is driven as much by ignorance and intellectual indolence as it is by fallacious reasoning. Those who are willing to gaze dispassionately at religion from time to time can see that religion easily has as much potential to do harm as to do good. Consider, for example, the millions of Jews slaughtered by Christians over the last 1,700 or so years for the ridiculous charge of deicide (the Christian reader should ponder the "God-breathed" scripture penned by "Matthew" (27:25) ["Then the people as a whole answered, 'His blood be on us and on our children!'"] and ask himself if God simply decided that the slaughter of millions of innocent people was a fair price to pay for the inclusion of this line in the Gospels); the millions of women who have suffered all over the world at the hands of males who simply assumed, based on scripture and tradition, that God sanctioned patriarchy; the 11 million or so Africans who were crammed into the holds of slave ships bound for the New World by European Christians who, no doubt, took to heart the biblical "curse of Ham" and the fact that the Bible condones slavery; the many individuals who have been imprisoned, beaten, and executed for the "crimes" of adultery and homosexuality by those who claim a biblical or Qur'anic mandate; the tens of thousands (many of them elderly females) tortured and executed (many burned alive) by the Catholic Church in Europe for the preposterous "crimes" of heresy or witchcraft; and the wars that have been fought in the name of this or that God or sect or denomination, and the millions who have died horrible deaths in these religious conflicts.

Of course, I could go on and on, as I have barely scratched the surface of evil wrought in the name of religion. (See works by Michel Onfray[1] and Christopher Hitchens[2] for comprehensive treatments of this topic.) Also, quite apart from the physical abuse suffered by millions in the name of religion, there is the psychological abuse that many (especially children) have suffered as they tried to reconcile their "inherently sinful natures" with a God who will condemn them to hell for eternity lest they "repent." The Judeo-Christian obsession with human sexuality (in a negative way) has ruined many a psyche and has given us "prime-time" television programming that is rife with torture, murder, and violence but nary a female nipple in sight; thus, killing and bloodshed are acceptable but the very wheels of Western civilization will come off if, God forbid, a man lovingly caressed a woman's breasts on prime-time network television. If those who embrace the moral argument are correct, then the individuals (virtually all "God-fearing" men of God by their own admission) who were involved in the aforementioned killings, subjugation, physical abuse, torture, etc., all received their moral consciousness from God. So we either accept the fact that God is the source of a "perverted" morality or simply throw out the assertion that humans must receive their moral awareness from God. (Since these actions were perpetrated by the religiously orthodox and not a few "bad apples," I don't think the free will issue is germane in this context.) Clearly, the latter option is the more reasonable of the two.

There is also another issue that needs to be addressed, and that is the disturbingly common assumption that religious folks are somehow more "decent" and "moral" than atheists, agnostics, and freethinkers. The Pew Research Center, for example, reports that 53 percent of those polled stated that they would not vote for an atheist for political office,[3] the largest negative value measured in sixteen different categories. Again, there is virtually no data or evidence that supports this assumption regarding atheists, agnostics, and freethinkers. For example, no study or survey has ever been done that shows a greater propensity for crime among atheists than believers. The opportunistic and anecdotal evidence we do have show that religious folks are well represented (perhaps disproportionately so?) in jails and prisons. In fact, this preference for "faith-based" candidates is so strong that an avowed and practicing Mormon (Mitt Romney) won the Republican nomination for the presidency of the United States in the 2012 election. When one considers the golden tablets, angelic translators, revelations from God that come at just the right time to change a racist policy, posthumous baptism, and the Lamanite debacle (and I suppose we should throw in the infamous "magical underpants"), it seems unbelievable to me that an individual who embraces such notions should be favored over an atheist. In fact, once again opportunistic and anecdotal evidence and some actual data-based research generally reveal that atheists, agnostics, and freethinkers tend to be more intelligent, well-read, and educated than the average believer; they also certainly seem to know more about religion. The Pew Research Center reported in 2010 that atheists and agnostics scored higher than any other category in a religious knowledge survey.[4] In a rational world (one that we sadly do not live in), atheists, agnostics, and freethinkers would be chosen over faith-based candidates for political office, all things being equal.

Now, what of another commonly held assumption that is implicit in the moral argument—namely that without God and religion humans are incapable of fashioning a moral world? Let's take this one step at a time. First, what of a world without God? Here's what Jean-Paul Sartre had to say:

> Dostoyevsky once wrote: "If God does not exist, everything is permissible." This is the starting point of existentialism. Indeed, everything is permissible if God does not exist, and man is consequently abandoned, for he cannot find anything to rely on—neither within nor without. For if it is true that existence precedes essence, we can never explain our actions by reference to a given and immutable human nature. In other words, there is no determinism—man is free, man is freedom.[5]

It seems to me that Sartre has pushed this notion about as far as reason will take it. Certainly, in the absence of God, there is no *pre-existing* system of ethics, and thus nothing *preexistent* of humans on which to ground morality and moral principles. Thus, to the extent that such a system exists, it will be humankind that creates it. It is not at all clear to me, however, that humans are incapable of generating such a system themselves. In fact, if it is true that God does not exist, that is precisely what we have done. One might rightly claim at this point that there is really no difference between the actual existence of God and the belief that God exists; since the hypothesis that God exists is not falsifiable, the statement "God exists" means nothing. Thus, it follows that if a belief in God is functionally equivalent to the actual existence of God—i.e., if both scenarios (God actually does or does not exist) are characterized by the assumption that an absolute, God-given system of ethics and morality exists, then humans, albeit deluded humans, are, in fact, the source of (an assumed) absolute system of ethics and morality. Thus, the contention that without God there is no ethics and morality is unwarranted on these grounds by the fact that another source is possible, namely (deluded) humans.

There is another way to consider this issue of whether or not humans can generate their own system of ethics and morality and that is to consider other motivations for "proper" moral comportment. Consider, for example, an economic exchange system found among some indigenous/tribal peoples, the !Kung of southern Africa for example. The !Kung are a hunting and gathering people with a very simple material culture, which often makes living in the harsh and arid conditions of the Kalahari desert quite a challenge. In the !Kung culture, generosity in the form of reciprocity is one of the highest virtues. Thus, everyone shares what they have with the entire community and no one "owns" anything. It doesn't take much imagination to realize that any sensible individual will trade off the "luxury" of gorging himself on occasion but facing starvation on other occasions for a system where he will always have something to eat, if not ever enough to gorge himself. It is quite possible to build an ethical and moral system atop this foundation of reciprocity, since it calls for sharing, generosity, humility, and honesty. Not only that but the ubiquitous "golden rule" is an unspoken assumption. No God or gods, angels, religious dogma, holy scriptures, etc., are necessary. All that is necessary is a survival instinct that will encourage congenial and cooperative participation in a collective enterprise. (By the way, the generous and ethical !Kung do recognize a supreme, creator god, but this god is distant and withdrawn and plays virtually no role in !Kung ideology. I should also point out that in the egalitarian !Kung society, men and women are virtually equal and they have no history of the ugly misogyny one finds in the Judeo-Christian tradition.)

Immanuel Kant expressed a similar idea when he wrote, "There is but one categorical imperative, namely this: *Act only on the maxim whereby thou canst at the same time will that it should become a universal law.*"[6] Thus, any reasonable individual will agree to a certain rule or law that protects his or her interests as long as everyone else does the same. The !Kung system begins to break down as soon as someone challenges it with his greed and selfishness. But a potentially greedy and selfish individual realizes that she will unnecessarily risk her own demise if she should challenge the system. Clearly, many peoples around the globe intuitively grasped the good sense of Kant's categorical imperative long before the notion became an integral part of his epistemology.

What about the origin of ethics and morality in humankind? Any sort of information along these lines would certainly be helpful here. Unfortunately, however, no matter how far back we look in the *Homo* line (which extends back to the first appearance of the *Homo* genus in eastern Africa around two million years ago), we can see that these individuals are social creatures, hunting together, living together. A *Homo neandertalensis* specimen, dated back to about 70,000 years ago, found in Iraq, lived to old age (for Neandertals) even though he was blind in one eye, was missing part of his right arm, and had suffered trauma to both legs. Scholars Erik Trinkaus and Pat Shipman noted that his survival can be attributed primarily to the "compassion and humanity" of his mates.[7] One *H. erectus* found in Dmanisi, Georgia, dated back to about 1.8 mya, had survived several years with only one tooth in his mouth. Archaeologist David Lordkipanidze suggests that this individual needed considerable assistance to survive.[8] We can even push the envelope back further than that to one of the earliest hominin genera, *Australopithecus*, which takes us back past 4 million years ago, and we can still see clear signs of cooperative, social living in small groups. That these pre-stone-aged and stone-aged peoples lived in small, cooperative social groups is not surprising; after all, apes, monkeys, and many other animals do so as well. One might ponder the good sense of allowing apes, monkeys, etc., to be capable of "constructing" a viable, cooperative social system (clearly without the assistance of God and religion) yet deny the same capability in humans.

Here's another way to attack this issue regarding the alleged inability of humans to "construct" an ethical and moral system by which to live. Atheists do stop at red lights just like everyone else. They do so because if they do not there is the potential for death, dismemberment, months spent in the hospital with the consequent draining of one's assets, a totaled automobile, an insurance claim that will cause one's monthly payments to rise, maybe going without an automobile for a few days, and so on. Of course, I could continue this list but, since this individual is an atheist, I would not include this reason: because God expects us to obey the laws of men and live cooperatively with our fellow citizens. (See, for example 1 Peter 2:13–17, where we are told to submit to authorities, "Honor everyone," and "Honor the emperor.") Now, I suppose we should allow the possibility that a fundamentalist Christian might, in fact, be influenced by the Good Book to stop at a red light, but that is entirely beside the point. What is important in the context of this discussion is that, again, we can see that humans are quite capable of regulating and governing themselves even in the total absence of any divine mandate. Also, don't forget that humans constructed the system of traffic laws from scratch just recently, and it is sufficient to provide order for and obedience from millions of drivers.

We can also look to sociobiology for yet another way to account for the existence of ethics, morality, and order among human beings but, admittedly, the validity of this explanation is only as good as the paradigm upon which it is grounded. The basic tenet of sociobiology is that an individual will behave in such a way so as to maximize their potential to pass on their DNA to the next generation. Thus, dominant males, lions for example, will sometimes kill the offspring of a female and then sire their own. Sociobiology easily explains this behavior since, on the average, each offspring carries 50 percent of the DNA of its parents. Clearly the male lion is acting in its own self-interest. Sociobiology also helps us understand the intense bond between parents and progeny, since each offspring obviously represents a huge genetic investment on the part of the mother or father. It can also help us understand why chimpanzees will guard their territory and fight other groups of chimpanzees if challenged, since close kin all share some percentage of DNA. Sociobiology is not, however, without its critics, especially when it is applied to human behavior. One sticking point is the presumption that behavior can be naturally selected for or against. Passing down a genetic propensity for brown eyes or sickle-cell anemia is one thing but passing down behavioral traits is quite another. Frankly, when one contemplates a spermatozoon and an ovum coming together to form a zygote, one might wonder exactly where the ideas are. Nevertheless, sociobiology, again to the extent that it is valid, does give us yet another way to understand the genesis and development of order and morality in human societies.

Now that we have seen that the contention that humans would be morally adrift without God and religion is presumptuous at best, there is one more assumptive premise of some forms of the moral argument that is at least questionable—namely, the notion that all humans share the same general ethical and moral system. Of course, no one can deny that virtually all human societies around the world recognize a certain core set of moral principles—e.g., murder (nevertheless, defined in different ways from culture to culture) and pilfery are wrong, personal space should be respected, and bravery in battle is good, just to mention a few. There is also some form of what Westerners call the "golden rule" that is recognized by all societies in one form or another. So there is clearly a common moral "baseline," if you will, from which all societies are working. But, not only can this moral baseline be explained in terms of kinship, reciprocity, altruism, and the Kantian categorical imperative as I have done above, but it should be noted that ethnographic data collected from around the globe shows, in fact, that human behavior cross-culturally can be quite dissimilar. In some groups living around the Arctic circle, for example, a male guest is offered the woman of the house for the night to keep him warm, and for sexual intercourse should she so desire.[9] The preferred form of marriage among many tribal/indigenous groups is matrilateral, cross-cousin marriage (i.e., first cousin marriage); clearly definitions of incest differ from group to group. Puberty rituals among the Sambia in Papua New Guinea involve an adolescent fellating an older boy to completion.[10] In some parts of Tibet and Nepal, a woman marries a man and his brothers (a custom referred to as fraternal polyandry). Speaking of marriage, we find the following: people marrying deceased individuals ("ghost marriage" among the Nuer[11]), individuals who haven't been born yet, and children,[12] just to mention a few. The youngsters in many societies are encouraged to engage in sexual play. Many other examples could be cited, but these should suffice. So is this issue settled one way or another? Do the similarities "outweigh" the differences? Perhaps not, but clearly the contention that humans are morally the same or even similar is debatable.

The moral argument examined here, then, is questionable for a number of reasons. Many of the assumptions upon which the argument is built are, if not unwarranted, at least dubious. Clearly, the moral argument does not come close to "proving" anything other than, perhaps, a lack of confidence in the ability of human beings to live and prosper in a secular, humanistic world.

We cannot leave this discussion of the moral argument without assessing and critiquing what is generally considered to be the strongest argument of this type, namely the version conceived by Immanuel Kant. The basic form of the argument begins by assuming that morality is only rational if there is absolute justice to go along with it. Only an omniscient, omnipotent, and omnibenevolent God, however, can be the source of absolute justice. It follows then, that a truly rational, just world requires the existence of God. In other words, the concept of morality becomes nonsensical in the absence of absolute justice.

While this is a popular and common statement of Kant's position, it should be noted that Kant never suggested that this argument was any more than simply suggestive of the existence of an omnipotent, omniscient, and omnibenevolent being. He might say it would provide those so inclined with a practical reason to believe in the existence of God but nothing more than that. In my mind, he is suggesting that one can quite easily imagine a reasonable and just world if it is assumed that the grounding of all being is an omnipotent, omniscient, and omnibenevolent being.

That being said, and using the Kantian-type argument as stated as our starting point, it implies that a godless world is an irrational, chaotic place where evil people might prosper and good people might suffer for no good reason, and that is the end of it. The human world does appear to be nonsensical in this regard because individuals who choose to act immorally often do benefit from their actions. Nevertheless, most individuals are law-abiding, at least somewhat generous, and respect the autonomy of others. Why? Because, while perfect justice is not to be found in this world, it is found in a transcendent realm beyond this one since God is capable of meting out rewards and punishments that are absolutely commensurate with the deed in question. What is being alluded to here is something like a "zero balance" on the scales of justice. It is quite clear that humans are not capable of such a thing. How do we punish a Hitler? Could we have reestablished a zero balance by executing him? No. Could we have reestablished a zero balance by torturing him the rest of his natural life? No. There was simply nothing that could have been done in this case. The same could be said of Stalin, Pol Pot, serial killers, and many others whose evil deeds cannot be appropriately punished in this world. If, however, there is another world, a world where the scales of justice can, in fact, be balanced, where absolute justice can be effected, then the unconscionable crimes of the worst human monsters that have ever lived can at least be understood in a rational way. We would, then, also be able to understand and rationalize the suffering of the good and the innocent.

It seems to me that the Kantian form of the moral argument is based as much on hope as it is on reason. To be honest, I see no reason why the world must be a place that we can understand or that it must be palatable in regard to justice or fairness or that there must be some reason why things are as they are. A common question asks "what is the meaning of life?" But the question itself presupposes that there is one. Maybe the world is as absurd as Camus said it was. According to Camus's philosophy of the absurd, the tragedy of human existence is that we insist on finding meaning and purpose in what is a totally indifferent, materialist world that has no inherent meaning or purpose.[13] It appears as though that is precisely what the Kantian form of the moral argument is attempting to do.

There is another issue that must be addressed here and that is our "compunction" to do good. As I argued earlier, I don't think we need to appeal to a God or any transcendent entity to find a foundation for ethical and moral behavior in this world. Much more often than not, "being good," or acting morally is the wise choice that benefits the individual more so than acting in a fashion that runs contrary to what is considered socially "proper." It seems to me that humans have always had a tendency to deemphasize or disparage the ability of humans in a way that is almost inversely proportional to the credit given to God or gods. There are simply too many reasonable alternative hypotheses that can be invoked to explain ethical and moral behavior among humans for the moral arguments to be anything more than interesting and, perhaps, somewhat compelling to some. There is certainly nothing here that definitively proves the existence of God.

While the moral arguments are generally agreed to be the strongest arguments for the existence of God, there are certainly other so-called "classical arguments" that are quite popular. In fact, some assume that these arguments are so commonsensical as to be obviously correct but, as we have seen, that can be a poor justification for the validity or lack thereof of any argument or explanation. There are three more such arguments that warrant examination here, the argument for the existence of God based on causation, the argument based on contingency, and the design argument.

CHAPTER THIRTY-FIVE

THE ARGUMENT FROM UNIVERSAL CAUSATION

There are many forms of this argument, but the following form could be considered to be an accurate and appropriate rendering:

1. All effects, events, beings, etc., have causes, and these causes, in turn, have causes.
2. This chain of cause and effect began at some point (i.e., there must have been a "first cause" or a "prime mover").
3. The only uncaused cause is God.
4. Therefore, God exists.

One might immediately think of a line of dominos placed on end. Clearly, it is the domino preceding the one that just fell that is responsible for its movement, but to get back to the "ultimate cause" one must go back to the individual who pushed over the first domino. By the same token, all of the causes at work in the universe can be traced back to a "primal cause," and, of course, most assume that primal cause was God. There are a number of problems with this argument, but I will focus on the three most serious problems.

1. *This classical form of the "first cause" argument deals with the generic notion of cause and effect but real events are specific and, thus, have specific causes.*

It strikes me that those who first penned this type of argument had in mind beforehand where they were going and how they wanted to get there. But could the chain of cause-and-effect links be described differently—i.e., must all events necessarily be traced back to one necessary and sufficient cause? It seems apparent to me that a totally different argument might be made. While events (with rare exceptions) do have causes, some specific events can be explained without tracing their (ultimate) origins back to a specific and necessary beginning point or cause, as I will illustrate.

I am a Louisiana native, so I will use the Louisiana State University (LSU) Fighting Tigers football team in my example. (It is not necessary for the reader to know anything about college football to follow the example.) The LSU Tigers won the national championship in 2007. Why? Because they beat the Ohio State Buckeyes in the Bowl Championship Series (BCS) national championship game. Period. Regardless of what transpired before this event, this was the last link in the chain, the last "cause." Of course, there are other events or causes that have to be invoked; after all, there was a reason why the Tigers were in the championship game in the first place. Well, yes; for example, if they had not won at least eleven games during the regular season that year they would not have played for the championship. (Obviously, they probably still would have played in the championship game if they had won more games, but let's stay with the events that actually took place.) Now, the Tigers played thirteen games during the regular season. So which eleven did LSU have to win? It can't be stated with certainty. Presumably, if they had won a different eleven games, they might still have been in the championship game, but maybe not; we cannot know this for certain. Clearly, we are speaking here of a cause that is certainly relevant but only in the general sense; its precise nature cannot be determined since we don't know which of the seventy-seven other combinations of eleven wins would have done the trick. Or one may point to team personnel and recruiting. If LSU did not have this or that player on the team, they may not have been as successful. But, on the other hand, they may have been. We simply cannot say for certain, and note that here there are probably tens of thousands of potential combinations of players. Thus far, the only thing we can say with certainty is that the Tigers had to win the BCS national championship game; that is the only specific cause that we could label as "necessary" at this point.

What we have here are primary and secondary causes. Only the primary cause is necessary in and of itself; the secondary causes are necessary only in a vaguer and more general sense, since the influence of these causes on the ultimate outcome could range anywhere from zero to one hundred percent, depending on the cause in question. If one were to continue taking this progression to its logical extreme, we can even imagine tertiary causes (i.e., those events that caused the secondary causes). So, for example, the reason why this or that athlete plays for the Tigers can be attributed to those experiences that influenced (caused) a player to sign with the team. We can again take this further by imagining the various causes that influenced these experiences (quaternary causes) and the causes that caused these causes (quinary causes) and so on. Eventually, if one proceeds in this fashion from the primary cause to secondary causes and the causes of those causes and so on, the result is a tree whose number of branches grow exponentially until one reaches causes or events that are so removed from the original event so as to be virtually negligible, a veritable "cloud" of causes that grows increasingly dense the further back in time we go. Nevertheless, there is still only one primary cause that is necessarily responsible for the original event in question.

Now, the argument from universal causation claims that all events ultimately have necessary and sufficient causes and claims that, in this case, the necessary and sufficient cause of the existence of the universe is God. But, in the case just discussed, when we move back in time we reach causes that may or may not be necessary, like, for example, a different set of eleven victories that may have put the Tigers in the championship game. The further back we go, the situation becomes increasingly diffuse.

Thus, by proceeding in this fashion, identifying the primary cause of a thing or event, then the secondary causes of that thing, and then the tertiary causes (or the primary causes of all the secondary causes), etc., etc., the various causes diverge to greater and greater numbers as we follow the various chains back in a causal fashion. This is precisely the opposite of what the believer is arguing for—which is, namely, that the various causes and events of the universe converge to a single point, God.

2. *Problems with causality.*

In the realm of the very, very small, quantum mechanics is used to describe and predict the behavior of subatomic particles. This new, more sophisticated, and more accurate paradigm replaced the older, classical Newtonian model in the first half of the twentieth century. It just so happens that on this level of the infinitesimal, the classical laws of motion, energy, cause, and effect no longer hold. For example, in a curious phenomenon known as quantum tunneling, electrons may disappear in one location and appear in another instantaneously without traversing the distance between; it would be analogous to a ping pong ball falling through a table. It was also discovered that, when working with particles at the subatomic level, we can only calculate the probability that an electron, for example, will do this or that; we cannot know for certain until after the event occurs. The physicist Michio Kaku notes that in certain settings gas molecules might move around forever without any apparent cause that produced the motion.[1] I realize, of course, that the argument from universal causation is dealing with large-scale events and causes, but my point here is that the world does not always work in an expected or "common sense" fashion; what seems so obviously true may not be. The classical "first cause" arguments were constructed in such a way so as to be compatible with Newtonian mechanics, but Newtonian mechanics only gives an adequate description of motion and activities at the level of the very large. The classical assumptions made about cause and effect in our world are simply not warranted.

And then there is the Scottish philosopher David Hume and his skepticism regarding the cause and effect relationship. If we were to observe cause X followed by effect Y over and over without fail, we would simply assume that the relationship linking X and Y was necessary (i.e., there is a fundamental nexus that binds them together such that it would always be active). But Hume argued that this was only a common-sense assumption on our part.[2] The only knowledge we have of this relationship or nexus is based on whatever we can observe now and past experiences. This is not enough, however, to assume the action or presence of some fundamental regularity of nature; neither inductive reasoning (data analysis leading to theory building) nor deductive reasoning (using theories to understand the data), Hume argued, will allow us to discover any sort of fundamental regularity of this sort. Now I am far from a philosopher, and I will certainly defer to my colleagues in the philosophy department on this one, but I feel as though Hume's comments cannot be easily dismissed. One may want to argue Hume on this point, but if we keep this in the realm of the practical, all we could say is, "Well, Y follows X, always has, always will." Hume would probably respond that "always has" is qualitatively different from "always will." The former we know for certain because it is based on past experience (albeit, "past experience," which covers an immensely long time period the critic may point out), but the latter we can only predict or guess. What is important for us, however, is that, again, assumption and common sense don't necessarily make it so.

3. *Assuming a first cause, it does not necessarily have to be the Judeo-Christo-Islamic God.*

With perhaps a few exceptions, those who have championed the argument from universal causation have implicitly assumed that at the terminus of the links comprising the cause/effect chain we would find the Judeo-Christo-Islamic God. I have added reference to the Islamic God because this is the same God as is worshiped by Jews and Christians. Many evangelical Christians, however, disagree with this fact but, as has been shown time and again in the earlier chapters, their grasp of history and world cultures is specious at best. Pat Robertson, in a blatant attempt at slandering Islam, refers to Allah as "The Moon God of Mecca."[3]

Pardon the digression but, in my mind, this is one of the silliest "debates" occurring today. Believe it or not, some folks get tripped up over the appellation "Allah." Let's dispense with this issue by simply stating that Allah in Arabic means "the God." Let us also not forget that Jews, Christians, and Muslims all worship the God of Abraham, a figure accepted by Jews, Christians, and Muslims as being the father of both Isaac and Ishmael and thus the "father" of all three faiths. Sure, God in an Islamic context has different character attributes and seems concerned with issues relevant only to Muslims but, on that basis, Christians in certain sects and denominations should reject the God of other Christian sects and denominations, and all of them should reject the God of the Tanakh (Old Testament) who has almost nothing in common with the God of the New Testament. Even in the Tanakh, God is initially (during the time of the Patriarchs) a much more personable, approachable, and humble character than the belligerent, blood-thirsty, irascible, jealous God we find later in the time of Moses and Joshua. Basically the only reason Christian evangelicals refuse to equate God and Allah is because they simply don't like the idea. After all, this is how they treat science; anything that runs counter to their (assumed) notions regarding how the world is supposed to be according to their understanding of the Bible, is simply rejected. Thus, theories are evaluated on the basis of emotive criteria rather than on the quality of the data supporting them.

Okay, back to the discussion at hand. All the argument from universal causation requires is some force, entity, or being that serves as the "prime mover." There is nothing in the argument itself that necessarily points to the Judeo-Christo-Islamic God as the "uncaused cause." For all we know, this first cause could be something that is naturalistic yet totally unknown to us at the present time. (This issue will be discussed further below.) Thus, even if the argument is logically unassailable and valid in a practical sense (which it apparently is not), it still has not "proved" the existence of God. In the words of physicist Victor Stenger, "But, as we have seen, movement does not require a mover, and modern quantum mechanics has shown that not all effects require a cause. And even if they did, why would the Prime Mover need to be a supernatural anthropomorphic deity such as the Judaeo-Christian God? Why could it not just as well be the material universe itself?"[4]

In sum, then, this argument is unsatisfactory for a number of reasons, most of which have been described here. And, besides, even if the argument were sound (which it is not), it still doesn't address why the "first causer" must be God in the Judeo-Christo-Islamic sense.

CHAPTER THIRTY-SIX

ARGUMENT FROM CONTINGENCY

This brings us to another argument that has a very long pedigree as well, the contingency argument. This argument is the famous "third way" of thirteenth-century theologian and *Doctor Angelicus* of the Church, Thomas Aquinas, in his five arguments for the existence of God. While the basic premise of the argument—namely, that contingent things must ultimately have been created by a noncontingent thing—is straightforward, the forms of the argument range from the simple to the very complex. Anticipating the various issues that are generally germane to this discussion and retaining the spirit of the ancient forms, I have constructed the argument as follows:

1. Things (matter, energy, and events) are not self-caused (which is logically contradictory) but rather dependent on something else for their existence.
2. Things (matter, energy, and events) do exist.
3. Thus, some contingent or noncontingent thing caused their existence.
4. If this thing is contingent, then there exists an infinite regress of contingent things.
5. But, since an infinite number of actual things (an "actual infinite") cannot exist, the thing that causes the existence of contingent things must itself be noncontingent (not dependent on anything else for its existence).
6. The only noncontingent thing in the universe is God.
7. Thus, God exists.

There are two major problems with the argument: the contention that an infinite regress, and, thus, an infinite number, of actual things cannot exist and the assumption that God's nature and existence require no explanation. The infinite regress issue is crucial since, without it, statement five is erroneous, thus rendering the entire argument fallacious. The general strategy utilized by those who argue that the assertion is valid is to show, by means of hypothetical examples, that the assumption that an infinite regress (infinite number) of actual things (an "actual infinite") can exist leads us to absurd conclusions. So, for example, imagine that we have an infinite number of balls in a box, the balls are all colored red, white, and black, and there are an infinite number of balls in each color. If we should remove the infinite number of red balls from the box, we would still have an infinite number of balls in the box. Thus, since infinity equals infinity, the two quantities would be equal. But, this is nonsense since for each red ball, there is one white ball and one black ball; intuitively, at least, the red balls comprise 1/3 of the total, thus, the quantities cannot be equal. This contradiction invalidates the notion that an infinite number of actual things might exist. There are other thought experiments that demonstrate that an infinite regress or an infinite number of actual things cannot exist, including mathematician David Hilbert's famous hotel example.[1] Essentially, they all simply demonstrate that an assumption of the reality of an actual infinite can be shown to be absurd based on real world scenarios. Not everyone agrees, however.   .

Philosophy professor Bruce Reichenbach notes that Cantorian set theory states that many intuitive and practical notions regarding the behavior of finite sets simply do not apply to infinite sets.[2] So, for example, let us say set A consists of all natural numbers and set B consists of all positive even numbers. Both are, by definition, infinite sets. Nevertheless, if we were to match up the two sets we would get 1:2, 2:4, 3:6, 4:8, 5:10, and so on. If we apply intuitive assumptions regarding finite sets, we might say that there is a paradox here because even though both sets are infinite, set A contains many more numbers than set B. Thus, the sets are both equal and not equal. Cantorian set theory, however, states that as long as any item in one set can match up with some item in another set (in a one-to-one correspondence such that each item in set A matches only one item in set B and vice versa) we have infinite sets. The precise nature of the members of each set is irrelevant. So, for example, consider two sets containing days that are counted without end. Let's say the days in set X are counted from the day that Siddhārtha Gautama died (in 483 BCE) and the days in set Y are counted from the beginning of the third millennium (January 1, 2001). If the days of both sets are to be counted forward without stop, the two sets are both considered to be infinite sets. The fact that for set X the counting began about 2,500 years before the counting for set Y is irrelevant.

It appears that the crucial assumption regarding the existence of an actual infinite—namely that such a thing cannot exist—is at least questionable if not incorrect. If the latter, then the argument fails and the existence of nothing more than a natural universe need be invoked to explain the existence of contingent things. The physicist Victor Stenger is a proponent of the naturalistic genesis notion:

> What this example illustrates is that many simple systems are unstable, that is, have limited lifetimes as they undergo spontaneous phase transitions to more complex structures of lower energy. Since "nothing" is as simple as it gets, we would not expect it to be completely stable. In some models of the origin of the universe, the vacuum undergoes a spontaneous phase transition to something more complicated, like a universe containing matter. The transition nothing-to-something is a natural one, not requiring any external agent.[3]

And, apparently, according to cosmologist Stephen Hawking, nothing is what we began with:

> There are something like ten million million million million million million million million million million million million million million (1 with eighty zeroes after it) particles in the region of the universe that we can observe. Where did they all come from? The answer is that, in quantum theory, particles can be created out of energy in the form of particle/antiparticle parts. But that just raises the question of where the energy came from. The answer is that the total energy of the universe is exactly zero. The matter in

the universe is made out of positive energy. However, the matter is all attracting itself by gravity. Two pieces of matter that are close to each other have less energy than the same two pieces a long way apart, because you have to expend energy to separate them against the gravitational force that is pulling them together. Thus in a sense, the gravitational field has negative energy. In the case of a universe that is approximately uniform in space, one can show that this negative gravitational energy exactly cancels the positive energy represented by the matter. So the total energy of the universe is zero.[4]

Now, what of the other problem—namely that God's nature and existence require no explanation. Cosmological arguments use various premises to reach a conclusion that God exists and stop there. It is simply assumed that the argument should terminate there and that no further explanation is required. But, as many philosophers have pointed out, a God who is without cause and eternally existing is just as problematic as a universe that is without cause and eternally existing. The philosopher B. C. Johnson argues that there are only three explanations that can be invoked here.[5] First, one could simply claim that God's existence is a "brute fact," but this would result in simply replacing one brute fact (the existence of the universe) with another and would still have to be explained. Second, God may have been created by something else, an explanation that would require us to explain this Super God and the God who created that God and the God who created that God, *ad infinitum*; this infinite regress of greater and greater Gods really doesn't explain anything. And third, one might simply state that God is noncontingent, self-sustaining, and eternal by God's very nature. But such notions are presumptive, at best, as no such thing is known to exist. Besides, the ontological status of God in cosmological arguments is intrinsically linked to a definition that was itself created to describe an assumed entity.

Finally, let us not overlook the fact that we have much more information about our physical universe today than existed even twenty years ago, much less some 750 years ago when Aquinas penned his argument. All of the classic arguments for the existence of God, in fact, were developed and championed by individuals who had basically no cosmological data relative to today's knowledge. Today, for example, we know, with a very high degree of confidence, that the expansion of space that we call our universe began approximately 13.7 billion years ago. The evidence for this is overwhelming and includes the following: 1) the expansion of the universe that tells us that in the past the universe was denser than it is now, 2) the detection of cosmic background radiation measured at about three degrees Kelvin that is the remnant "echo" of an early universe that began "radiating" about 400,000 or so years after the initial "inflation" (expansion) began, 3) the homogeneity of the universe at very large scales, 4) the ratio of light to heavy elements that is precisely what we should see today based on predictions of this model, and 5) very distant and, thus, very old galaxies that are structurally different than the galaxies that are relatively near to us; this is a clear indication of galactic evolution and, thus, some sort of beginning point.

One might guess that if, for whatever reason (say, one of these putative God-inspired or God-dictated holy books would have actually contained knowledge regarding something we didn't know at the time), the ancient and medieval creators of the cosmological arguments had been privy to this information, they would have been far less likely to invoke metaphysics in an attempt to figure out where things come from or why things exist at all. Consequently, I would guess that most of these folks, being men of intelligence and reason, would have probably pursued careers in one of the natural sciences rather than theology. I would also guess that they, like the vast majority of our physicists and other natural scientists today, would have found the argument from contingency dubious at best and flat out unconvincing at worst.

CHAPTER THIRTY-SEVEN

ARGUMENT FROM DESIGN

T he final popular objective argument for the existence of God that we will consider is the design argument. Like the other arguments being discussed here, the design argument, too, has a long history, stretching back to the latter part of the first millennium BCE. Also, like the other arguments, there are various forms of the argument, but they are all based on the assumption that there are some features of our natural world that reflect a design and purpose that cannot be accounted for by reference to any natural thing or process. Thus, a supernatural cause (God) is inferred to explain these features. We will examine the two most popular forms of the argument, the "classical" version and the "anthropic" version that is quite popular today.

CLASSICAL ARGUMENT FROM DESIGN

This argument begins with the observation that there are certain things that exhibit a degree of complexity and purpose that cannot be accounted for by the actions of natural processes, a watch for example, and, thus, must have been created or designed by an intelligent agent. Now, in the case of a watch, we are obviously dealing with a human artifact, but what of things like trees, planets, and stars? Clearly, in this case, an intelligent agent, assuming there is one, must have characteristics and attributes that are commensurate with the task of creating things that are far beyond the capacity of humans. That intelligent agent, so the argument goes, is God. A slightly more sophisticated version was developed by William Paley, who gave us the famous watch and watchmaker account in his 1802 classic, *Natural Theology*.[1] According to Paley, there are certain features of some things that can be accounted for only by invoking an intelligent designer, namely function and complexity. Thus, a watch accomplishes some task (has a purpose that the designer had in mind when it was created, i.e., it is "functional") and it was designed just so in order to accomplish that task (any other arrangement of the parts or the loss of one part would make the watch dysfunctional). Likewise, an infinitely complex and functional world also calls for an intelligent designer but, in this case, one who is infinitely capable of creating such a world, namely God. Thus, Paley's argument uses certain observations of our natural world to infer some (supposed) fact regarding the supernatural world.

Clearly, one of the reasons design arguments of this sort are so popular is because they seem immanently commonsensical. But, of course, it could be pointed out that a cursory examination of the area around one's residence would lead one to the "commonsensical" conclusion that the world is flat; or, given the nature of our winters and summers in the northern hemisphere, that the earth is closer to the sun in the latter. Wrong on both counts. The problem with common sense is that it is prone to overly facile observations.

Another reason regarding why such arguments are so popular is that they provide an alternative to scientific hypotheses and theories that many evangelical/fundamentalist Christians reject out of hand, generally without any study or investigation at all, since they assume, a priori, that any notion or idea that runs counter to Genesis is wrong. Thus, many design argument proponents are not driven by a desire to understand the natural universe; rather, they are motivated simply by a desire to demonstrate what is already assumed by them to be true, namely that God created the universe *à la* Genesis. If this issue were to be settled only by an examination of the data available, virtually no one would feel compelled to invoke a "great creator in the sky" hypothesis except, perhaps, to explain certain phenomena we currently don't understand; even then, however, the rational individual would probably just defer to the future, assuming that if we wait long enough and look hard enough, we will eventually understand those phenomena as well. (Note: "data" do not include an ancient literary work penned by a Bronze Age people whose scientific knowledge was roughly equivalent to that of, at best, a fifth grader in today's world.) These design arguments were, after all, created and written long before we had even one one-thousandth the amount of information we have today regarding our natural world.

These comments are not necessarily meant to be taken as criticisms of the argument itself. I am well aware that any argument should be evaluated based on the merits of the argument, and that the motivation, character, or ability of those who created the argument are generally irrelevant. But, in this case, where, especially in regard to many of the current proponents of the argument, one of the primary motivations involves finding an alternative to scientific arguments that have been rejected outright because they are inconsonant with religious belief, I feel these comments are warranted.

There are many legitimate criticisms of this basic form of the design argument. The more significant criticisms are as follows:

- The simple observation that since a watch implies a watchmaker then the universe requires a universe maker (God) is an analogy, and all analogies are flawed to the extent that they compare (assumed) like things and processes that are themselves dissimilar. To wit, a watch is mechanical, inanimate, and non-self-sustaining, whereas a dog, for example, is organic, animate, and self-sustaining. Also inferred in this analogy is that the creative process that links humans and watches is similar to the creative process that links the universe and God. This reasoning is clearly assumptive. The basic structure of this particular argument is A (watch) is to B (watchmaker) as C (universe) is to D (God). But A is mechanical, not too complex, and was created from existing materials. C, however, is organic, complex beyond our comprehension, and was, according to Judeo-Christian orthodoxy, created *ex nihilo* ("from nothing"). Also, B is contingent upon another source (his father and mother) for his existence, whereas D, again, according to Judeo-Christian orthodoxy, is a noncontingent being. Then there is the structure of the analogy itself. It basically states that since A is X (complex) then B and, thus, since C is also X, then D (which is assumed to have the same relationship to C as B does to A). Consider this analogy using the exact same strategy: humans possess a complex atomic structure and are sentient, thus a one-celled archaeobacterium that possesses a complex atomic structure is also sentient. Clearly, the last statement is false. Further, Hume points out that, in regard to things in our world, we can clearly differentiate between, say, a pile of bricks and a brick wall since we have a basis for comparison, but we have only one universe with nothing to compare it to.[2] Are we to assume that our universe is the categorical standard for designed universes? What would an undesigned universe look like? And would the relationship between a designed and an undesigned universe be similar to the relationship between a brick wall and a pile of bricks? It is amazing (and disturbing) that the very argument (intelligent design) that is being used by fundamentalists in the United States today to undermine the teaching of standard science in public schools is built upon fallacious reasoning. The fact that so many are swayed by such an argument is an indication of either gross ignorance or intellectual indolence.

- If the probability that the natural universe was crafted by natural processes is infinitesimally small, as these arguments imply, then what of the probability of a universe designed by God? We know nothing of such a process. What is the probability of that happening? On what grounds can we simply infer that the probability of a natural design is so much smaller than that of a divine design? I suppose that if "God" is perceived of in a certain way, then the inference is congruent with the perception. But one commits the logical fallacy of "begging the question" if she assumes the existence of this creator God simply by virtue of the fact that she has assigned certain attributes to God that would allow God to create the universe as we see it. In fact, that is the fundamental problem with many of these arguments. They all appear to be constructed with one goal in mind and that is to terminate in a conclusion that requires the existence of a personal, Judeo-Christian God. No attempt is actually made to substantiate the various claims made about the nature of this God. Thus, the arguments are rendered meaningless unless one happens to be a true believer in a certain faith community and, for this reason, have no objective, universal validity.

- There is nothing inherent in the design argument itself, other than, perhaps, an implicit assumption on the part of theists, that logically precludes the existence of two or more creators. The existence, then, of a pantheon of equally capable gods would itself require explanation, and the existence of a henotheistic pantheon (*à la* many tribal/indigenous religions) would raise all sorts of issues such as the precise nature of the relationship between the "high god" and the "lesser gods," and the extent to which the various gods were involved in the creation process.

- Some qualities generally attributed to God (e.g., omnibenevolence) cannot be logically inferred from the argument. The general point here is that the argument claims to take us back to something that was active at the very beginning of time (and space, according to cosmologists) but exactly what cannot be determined by the argument.

- In many of its variations, the design argument assumes that the universe is infinite in extent and complexity, thus implying that its creator must be likewise. This is yet another assumption that is unfounded. Once again, Hume pointed out that we have nothing to compare this universe to. Might this version that we live in be somewhat flawed? If that were the case, God would not be omnipotent and omniscient but rather simply very powerful and very wise. In fact, certain design features of the universe and the various forms of life found in it appear to be flawed. Here are just a few:

  ° When the male prostate expands in size, a fairly common occurrence, it closes around the urethra, thus shutting off the flow of urine; this could be avoided simply by having the urethra pass outside the prostate.[3]
  ° The poorly designed spinal cord is the source of numerous problems; if the vertebral discs were just a bit more robust, many of these problems could be avoided.[4]

° 99.9 percent of all the species that have ever existed are extinct today; one might think that even 30 percent or 40 percent would be wasteful, but 99.9 percent?

° Whales and dolphins have lungs and obtain oxygen from the air the same way land mammals do; this is a preposterous "design" for aquatic creatures.

° The bone structure of the forelimbs of dogs, whales, humans, crocodiles, salamanders, and many other animals are structurally nearly identical (which, by the way, is an obvious indication of common descent), whereas each creature could have greatly benefitted from designs specifically adapted to their needs.

° The human eye has a form and structure that are more easily explained by a natural and imperfect process such as evolution as opposed to being designed by an infinitely capable designer; for example, because of the "reverse" orientation of the retina, the photoreceptor cells of the retina are aimed away from the light source, and nerve fibers pass in front of the receptors, partially occluding the incoming light.[5]

The point here is that these flaws are not problematic for a natural universe but they are problematic for a universe supposedly created by an omniscient and omnipotent Creator.

• The mere existence of complex and ordered natural things is not sufficient grounds to invoke an infinitely capable supernatural designer. There is evidence of complex and ordered natural things that we know are solely the result of natural processes— e.g., heavier, denser material is closest to the earth's core; the intricate, symmetrical design of a snowflake; the fact that water follows the path of least resistance; and the perfectly concentric wave patterns produced by dropping a rock in a pond.

• A "designer" does not necessarily imply a "creator" *ex nihilo.* The designer could have merely been a Platonic demiurge, fashioning the universe out of existing materials.

• One might just as well infer from the data that nature is intelligent. Anthropologist Jeremy Narby, in fact, offers compelling data that seem to suggest that this is the case.[6] Bacteria, plants, and other forms of nonhuman life often behave as if they were ordered, purposive, and self-deterministic. The strength of this hypothesis is that the "designer" is nature (which exists and can be discussed in a rational way) as opposed to God (which is conjectural and totally unknown to us).

- The explanation of the nature and design of the universe provided by the argument is unnecessarily complex and untestable. The sciences of cosmology, biology, genetics, and physical anthropology provide more elegant, robust, and testable hypotheses for the nature and design of the universe. In particular, the impressive fossil hominin data that have been accumulated over the past one hundred or so years unequivocally show that the small-brained bipedal creatures of the genus *Australopithecus* are the evolutionary ancestors of the larger-brained *Homo* that followed them.

In my estimation, this "classical" form of the design argument is no longer tenable today. The "modern" version of the design argument, however, based on the "anthropic" principle, is probably the most popular argument currently invoked to "prove" the existence of God.

ARGUMENT FROM DESIGN BASED ON THE ANTHROPIC PRINCIPLE

There are a couple of different variations of the "anthropic principle," but the general idea can be described as follows: The universe we live in, from the precise nature and form of subatomic particles, the fundamental forces of nature, the many physical constants that describe space-time and the matter/energy found in it, to the location and nature of the earth itself, must be precisely as they are in order to support life as we know it. So, for example, the ratio of the electron mass to the proton mass and the difference in the mass of the neutron and the proton must be precisely what they are if we are to have stable atomic structures; if the earth's orbit were more eccentric, its axis tilted a bit more, or if the distance between the earth and the sun were increased or decreased slightly (effectively taking it out of the "Goldilocks Zone" where conditions are "just right"), our life on Earth would not be possible; and, according to cosmologist Martin Rees,[7] there are six universal fundamental constants that must have their precise values if life is to develop: the ratio of the fine structuring constant to the gravitational coupling constant, the strong force that holds together quarks and gluons, the number of electrons and protons in the observable universe, the cosmological constant, a "ratio of fundamental energies," and the number of spatial dimensions. Other necessary constants and features of the universe have been cited as well.

At first glance, the anthropic principle seems tautological. After all, if we were not sentient and consciously aware, we would not be thinking about this, or anything else for that matter. But, we are, in fact, sentient and aware, and so it is quite obvious that conditions have to be conducive to our existence before we can ponder this issue. Thus, in a way, the probability that the universe and the properties and features that characterize it will be conducive to life is one (certainty) since we are here. Here's how Nobel Prize–winning physicist Stephen Weinberg, commenting on research on the value of vacuum energy, the background energy present in a vacuum, sees it: "On the other hand, if [the vacuum energy] takes a broad range of values in the multiverse, then it is natural for scientists to find themselves in a subuniverse in which [the vacuum energy] takes a value suitable for the appearance of scientists."[8] According to scientist Jürgen Schmidhuber, the anthropic principle simply states that the probability of finding oneself in a universe compatible with one's existence is one.[9] Finally, Richard Dawkins adds, "The great majority of planets in the universe are not in the Goldilocks zones of their respective stars, and not suitable for life. None of that majority has life. However small the minority of planets with just the right conditions for life may be, we necessarily have to be on one of that minority, because here we are thinking about it."[10]

When science writer Robert Lawrence Kuhn considers the vastness of the cosmos and our "human friendly" abode in the outskirts of the Milky Way galaxy, he is not that impressed:

What we can expect to observe must be restricted by the conditions necessary for our presence as observers. Such expectations then suggest, perhaps inevitably, the startling insight that there could be infinite numbers of separate regions or domains or "universes," each immense in its own right, each with different laws and values—and because the overwhelming majority of these regions, domains, or universes would be non-life-permitting, it would be hardly remarkable that we do not find ourselves in them nor do we observe them. One could conclude, therefore, that while our universe seems to be incredibly fine-tuned for the purpose of producing human beings, and therefore so specially designed for us, it is in fact neither.[11]

Kuhn's comments are especially pertinent when one considers human life on Earth. Our planet may, in fact, be the only habitable one in our solar system but, according to a paper published in the *Proceedings of the National Academy of Sciences*, there are 8.8 billion habitable Earthlike planets in our Milky Way galaxy.[12] Again, though, whatever the number, it is irrelevant since we are here.

Those who apply the anthropic principle specifically to life on Earth are overlooking the fact that Darwinian evolution by natural selection is a cumulative, systematic, and methodical (not teleological) process that can quite easily and convincingly account for the existence of *Homo sapiens*, for example. We must not forget that the evolution of humankind was accomplished through countless "steps" that brought us to where we are today. Thus, the earth was not fine-tuned to be conducive to human existence, rather the various forms of life that comprise our branch of the evolutionary tree merely adapted themselves to the laws of nature and the parameters of our earthly environment. Ostensibly, these laws and parameters could have been different (if the earth had a greater mass, for example, our stature would presumably be shorter and bulkier) and a different form of "human" would have resulted. Or, if the laws and parameters were not conducive to life, we simply would not exist at all. Not much mystery here.

There is another, perhaps even more problematic issue for the anthropic principle argument: those who attempt to use the anthropic principle to account for the existence of a God who fine-tuned the cosmos for humans are guilty of anthropocentrism. Humans, particularly those who feel as if they are the central focus of God's creation, like to think that "it's all about them," that the world we live in is simply a backdrop to human existence and activity. Such an orientation, of course, leads quite naturally to the notion that the earth is the way it is because that is how it had to be in order to be conducive to human existence. If we humble ourselves, however, and assess the situation critically and objectively, it appears as though it is humans who have been "adjusted" or "fine-tuned" by our world (the earliest and most "primitive" bipedal human ancestors appeared around 5 million years ago) and there is really nothing special about human life at all. In fact, if one insists on arguing that the world has been designed so that it is conducive to human life, she has to consider that there are other forms of life that are arguably more successful than humans (e.g., the 350,000 species of beetles, an extant shark species [the "goblin shark"] that has been around 125 million years,[13] and extant horseshoe crab species—sometimes referred to as "living fossils"—that date back to around 445 million years ago and have remained relatively unchanged during that time[14]). In fact, the oldest surviving type of mammal is the platypus, which dates back to the age of the dinosaurs. One could just as easily say that the universe has been fine-tuned for beetles or horseshoe crabs if the criterion by which we measure success is simply biological survival or Darwinian fitness. Of course, beetles and horseshoe crabs are not consciously aware of themselves as humans are, but I don't doubt for a second that, if they were, they would refer to our anthropocentrism as delusional.

Those who attempt to use some form of cosmological argument for the existence of God will often argue that there are only two possible explanations for things as they are: either God made them that way or they were caused by the blind, random action of natural forces and processes. Many creationists, in fact, will characterize the "debate" (this debate exists only in the minds of Christian fundamentalists) as one involving good against evil or theism vs. atheism. Unfortunately, many Americans are so scientifically illiterate that they are vulnerable to the influence of these foolish notions. The design argument based on the anthropic principle is often represented the same way, as ultimately coming down to a choice between an omniscient and omnipotent God on the one hand and blind, random chance on the other. According to Kuhn, "Since the 1970s, theists have invoked this fine-tuning argument as empirical evidence for a creator by asserting that there are only two explanations: God or chance. However to pose such a stark and simplistic choice is to construct a false and misleading dichotomy."[15] Kuhn goes on to suggest twenty-seven different explanations for the supposed fine-tuned-for-humans universe we live in, and he groups them into four different categories: "one universe models," "multiple universe (multiverse) models," "nonphysical causes," and "illusions."[16]

One of the more interesting hypotheses discussed by Kuhn, one he labels the "necessary/only way" model, suggests that the universe simply has to be the way it is or it would not exist at all. He states, "There has been and is only one universe and its laws seem fine-tuned to human existence because, due to the deep essence of these laws, they must take the form that they do and the values of their constants must be the only quantities they could have."[17] Theologians have long used this notion to tackle the problem of evil, a strategy often referred to as "the best of all possible worlds" argument—i.e., yes there is evil in the world, but it is simply a by-product of the necessary conditions of a physical, tangible world. (This notion is discussed further in the next chapter.) In a similar vein, Dawkins notes that perhaps the values of these constants can only be what they are (for example, the ratio of a diameter of a circle to its circumference).[18] This is an intriguing idea and certainly a viable hypothesis, both in the practical and logical senses but, unfortunately, it is not now falsifiable, although, I suppose if the popular multiverse idea should turn out to be correct, perhaps we will one day be able to test it.

The physicist Victor Stenger points out that some of the fundamental constants are misused and perhaps misunderstood by theists who use the anthropic principle as evidence of God's existence:

> Many of the examples of fine-tuning found in theological literature suffer from simple misunderstandings of physics. For example, any references to the fine-tuning of constants like the speed of

light, c, Planck's constant, h, or Newton's gravitational constant, G, are irrelevant since these are all arbitrary constants whose values simply define the system of units being used. Only "dimensionless" numbers that do not depend on units, such as the ratio of the strengths of gravity and electromagnetism, are meaningful.[19]

Stenger adds that some will exaggerate the probabilities involved by assuming that various parameters are independent of one another when that is not necessarily the case. It is also at least theoretically possible that a different group of values for these fundamental constants might produce a universe that at least resembles our own in some or all aspects. Stenger notes physicist Anthony Aguirre's research that shows that when six different cosmological parameters are changed, even substantially, other cosmologies result that would allow the formation of stars, planets, and intelligent life.[20]

One of the most active and capable critics and debunkers of the notion that the universe is fine-tuned for human existence is Richard Carrier.[21] He has reviewed the literature thoroughly and argues that he sees the same errors over and over, including the following: 1) not distinguishing between the probability that a finished product would spontaneously form in its present form—usually resulting in probabilities that are totally improbable—and the probability that the finished product is the result of a very long series of graduated, cumulative, and "directed" change, resulting in probability values that are generally within the realm of the possible; 2) calculating the odds that, for example, a full human DNA molecule will form rather than calculating the odds for the origination of a simpler form of life; and 3) making certain assumptions about what would entail life, assumptions that tend to involve complex life forms, thus causing the probabilities to skyrocket (for example, the assumption that life must be based on twenty amino acids).

Carrier cites an example of points 2 and 3:

In *The Anthropic Cosmological Principle* (Oxford, 1986), John D. Barrow and Frank J. Tipler exhaust over 600 pages trying to prove their point, yet a single sentence is sufficient to destroy their whole project: "The odds against assembling the human genome spontaneously," argue the authors, "is even more enormous: the probability of assembling it is between $(4^{180})^{110,000}\ldots$ and $(4^{360})^{110,000}.\ldots$ These numbers give some feel for the unlikelihood of the species *Homo sapiens*" (p. 565). They fail to realize that this is a *non sequitur*, as already noted by Sagan, for it only establishes such an unlikelihood if we assume, borrowing from their own words "spontaneous assembly." But no one has ever claimed this of the human genome, and the facts establishing evolution demonstrate that this absolutely did not happen. Thus, like [David] Foster and [Fred] Hoyle, Barrow and Tipler completely ignore the fact of evolution and the role of natural selection in their calculation, and consequently their statistic (which has already been cited by [William Lane] Craig in a debate with [Paul] Draper) has absolutely no relevance to the real question of whether man *evolving* is improbable.[22]

Carrier finds a similar error in Mark Ludwig's *Computer Viruses, Artificial Life and Evolution* (1993):

The odds against the spontaneous assembly of the E. Coli bacterium are assumed to be equivalent to the odds against the formation of life, calculated as 1 in $10^{3,000,000}$, or perhaps as 'low' as 1 in $10^{2,300,000}$ (p. 274). But no one believes E. Coli is the first organism or anything like the first organism—it is a highly advanced creature, the end result of over a billion years of evolution.[23]

This line of reasoning is, in my mind, seriously flawed and misleading, and Carrier is right to point it out. One could generate an enormous improbability by calculating the probability that, for example, a fully functioning human eye would form spontaneously from the various parts that constitute its structure. Such a probability would, however, be meaningless, since that is not how the human eye formed. The many examples of "eyes" and "eyelike" structures in nature clearly show that the evolution of the eye involved many, many different cumulative steps or "advances," virtually all of which were functional in some capacity. This example illustrates two of the errors Carrier is referring to, since it is assumes that the eye must be the relatively complex human eye and that it must be formed as it is spontaneously rather than cumulatively.

The latter error is often represented in the creationist/intelligent-design literature with some sort of humorous reference to a group of monkeys banging on typewriters. The reader is asked to ponder just how long it might take our monkeys to bang out, for example, the first paragraph of *War and Peace.* But that is not an accurate representation of biological evolution, since it assumes that the monkeys are starting from scratch each time. Evolution, however, is cumulative, so a better analogy would have the monkeys using a new template each time, a template that would include all the correct letters and, perhaps, words that have been cumulatively obtained up to that point. In other words, each evolution event is not totally independent of those events that preceded it. It should be pointed out, however, that even the corrected version of this analogy is unsatisfactory, since evolution is not teleological so, in this case, the first paragraph of *War and Peace* should not be understood as a goal that the evolutionary process is striving for but, rather, simply the "biological form" that is reached at some point in the evolutionary process.

The argument from design based on the anthropic principle is certainly intriguing and, as expounded upon by its various supporters and champions, appears to be at least somewhat valid, but, in my mind, the objections that have been raised by the argument's critics, some of which have been discussed here, seriously undermine if not totally refute the argument. One cannot escape the feeling that, once again, it is an argument that is born of ignorance—to wit, since we cannot figure out how or why the various fundamental constants got this way, then a designer (usually assumed to be the Judeo-Christo-Islamic God) must be responsible. But humankind has been engaging in this sort of reasoning since the beginning of time. Eons ago, we attributed even thunder and lightning, wind, rain, eclipses, the tides, comets, meteors, planetary motion, you name it, to the activities of this or that god. Little by little, however, objective and empirical thinking have chipped away at this edifice of ignorance until now there is hardly a reason to invoke a supernatural agent as being the cause of anything.

One last point regarding the putative designer: Theists who invoke God as the designing agent argue back to God and simply stop there as if no further explanation is needed. But it is ironic that these very same individuals who argue that an incredibly complex cosmos requires an explanation merely drop the matter once God appears in the argument. If the universe is so complex that it needs explaining, what about its creator that, by logic alone, would have to be considerably more complex than what it created? Here's how one philosopher sees it:

> For all of these reasons, G [the God hypothesis] can be seen to be a very poor explanation for the fact to be explained. It is incomplete, incomprehensible, obscure, unreasonable, anomalous, and counter-intuitive. It also appeals to still greater mysteries than the fact to be explained, so it hardly qualifies as an adequate explanation. It fails to illuminate anything or to enlarge our understanding. This may be called the Inadequacy Objection. To be "the very best" among competitors, an explanation needs to be at least minimally adequate, but G does not qualify in that respect.[24]

THE PROBLEM OF EVIL

While there are a number of arguments (both classical and modern) that have been offered as "proofs" of God's existence, most of which were reviewed above, it is generally thought that the problem of evil is the most serious issue that must be addressed and overcome by those who believe that God exists, at least a personal God in the Judeo-Christo-Islamic mold. The problem becomes evident as soon as one ponders four basic affirmations recognized by Jews, Christians, and Muslims:

1. God exists.
2. God is omnipotent.
3. God is omnibenevolent.
4. Evil exists.

The problem arises when one attempts to reconcile these affirmations that, by the way, must all be true from the perspective of Judeo-Christo-Islamic theology. The problematic issues can be stated as follows: if God is omnipotent and evil exists, then God chooses not to stop it (this questions God's omnibenevolence), or if God is omnibenevolent and evil exists, then God cannot stop it (this questions God's omnipotence). Clearly, neither of these is satisfactory for the traditional, Western theist, since both would radically change the definition of God and, thus, the Judeo-Christo-Islamic God would not exist. All four of the affirmations are viewed by Western theists as being nonnegotiable (i.e., they must all remain "in play"). What we need, then, is a theodicy, or an explanation that reconciles the four affirmations in a manner that is satisfactory to Jews, Christians, and Muslims. Thus, the defender of traditional, Western theism will have to explain why evil exists in a world created by God. Such explanations are referred to as "harmony theories," since they ostensibly explain how evil is simply a natural part of the world we live in—in other words, everything is really okay (from God's perspective) although it doesn't appear that way to us.

One approach invokes a pedagogical strategy by arguing that the world is a sort of training ground for souls. The prominent Christian apologist, John Hick, argues that the world is just as it should be and just as God intended it to be, for otherwise how might humankind progress from a purely biological state to one that is spiritual and Christlike, from *bios* to *zoe* as he would say? According to Hick, "The question that we have to ask is rather, Is this the kind of world that God might make as an environment in which moral beings may be fashioned, through their own free insights and responses, into 'children of God'"?[1] He adds that the "value [of the world] is to be judged, not primarily by the quantity of pleasure and pain occurring in it at any particular moment, but by its fitness for its primary purpose, the purpose of soul-making."[2]

Hick's "solution" to the problem of evil is intriguing and clever and, I guess, convincing enough for some, but for others it fails miserably. Perhaps some other world, very different from ours, harbors the type and magnitude of evil that could be rationalized in this way but not our own. Consider, for example, the following evils that, following Hick's scheme, God either allows or directly causes in order to build souls:

- One child dies an excruciating, slow death of starvation every five seconds; thus, while God builds souls, 16,000 children suffer horribly and die of starvation every day.[3]
- Tens of thousands were killed by an earthquake in China in 2008, including thousands of children who were crushed to death in schools.
- In 2003, an average of over four children per day were killed in the United States as a result of some form of child abuse.[4]
- Tens of thousands of innocent and defenseless elderly women were tortured and executed, many burned to death, for the fic-

tional crime of witchcraft in Europe from the fifteenth through the seventeenth centuries.
- Six million Jews and five million others, including Gypsies, homosexuals, and the handicapped, were murdered by the Nazis; among these numbered approximately 1.5 million children.

Of course, I could go on and on and on, as I've barely scratched the surface, but certainly my point has made itself by now. If not, let me state it clearly: An infinitely capable God allows a child to die a horrible death from starvation every five seconds in order to build souls. Or, an infinitely capable God allowed 11 million people to be murdered in Nazi extermination camps in order to build souls. But, you know what, there is no need to be that dramatic. Consider this: God decided that the kidnapping, rape, and murder of a twelve-year-old girl, Polly Klaas, was an acceptable part of this soul-building world. Shouldn't just that be enough to shut the whole thing down? Ivan Karamazov, one of the characters in Dostoyevsky's novel *The Brothers Karamazov* thought so, and expressed it this way: "And if the sufferings of children go to swell the sum of sufferings which was necessary to pay for truth, then I protest that the truth is not worth such a price."[5] But, what, then, would be the alternative for Ivan, or for anyone else who finds Hick's explanation not only unconvincing but distasteful? Nonexistence plain and simple. Hick's God certainly had the choice not to create. The cretins who enjoy dog-fighting and cock-fighting could certainly choose not to play the game, thus sparing these animals intense pain, suffering, and death. But Hick's God decided to go on and play the game anyway, and that is the basic flaw with the "harmony theory" approach: all the evils of the world are supposedly not enough to prevent God from creating anyway, and the alternative, nonexistence for humans and animals, a decidedly "neutral" state, is rejected.

Again, the major problem here is the sheer amount and intensity of the evil that exists. Much of it, in fact, Hick notwithstanding, ostensibly has no pedagogical purpose at all—for example, the suffering of animals and the suffering of children, who cannot begin to comprehend what is happening to them. I can certainly imagine a world where all animals are herbivores or humans have bodies that are not so hyper-sensitive to pain. There is much about this world we live in that seems impossible to reconcile with the "harmony theory" approach. Let us consider an event that, in my mind, brings to mind just the kinds of questions that doubters, agnostics, and atheists alike raise regarding the problem of evil.

After a cyclone hit Myanmar on May 3, 2008, well over 100,000 people were either missing or dead. Those that remained endured almost unimaginable suffering; diarrhea, malaria, and dengue fever were rampant, food was scarce, potable water was practically nonexistent, and tens of thousands of orphaned children were without aid or comfort of any sort. According to BBC News, on May 11, a Red Cross aid ship carrying food and clothing, including five hundred bags of rice and five thousand liters of drinking water, sank after it hit some debris in the water. Clearly, the suffering of many was prolonged as a result of this event and many, no doubt, died for want of food and water. In the context of the discussion we are having here, it is hard to imagine evil that is more unnecessarily cruel and pointless. God has intervened before, at least according to Jews, Christians, and Muslims, so why not now? These individuals were suffering horribly already; it is hard to believe that the evil that had already been done was not enough to build souls or teach spiritual lessons. Besides, when one is delirious from fever or dying of dehydration or starvation, there is not a whole lot of "soul-making" going on.

In my mind, the sheer intensity, ubiquity, and extent of evil present in our world effectively rules out any sort of pedagogical explanation for the problem of evil. I can imagine the sort of world where that might be the case, but as I noted above it is not this one. A father does not torture his son for breaking curfew and a mother does not beat her daughter until she can no longer walk for telling a lie. When considering pedagogical explanations of the problem of evil, it is important to keep in mind the fact that, as I stated earlier, the alternative would simply have been nonexistence for us; God certainly had the option not to create. One might be tempted to argue that one's life in the suburbs of Chicago is not so bad even though he has suffered from depression on occasion and is currently battling a heart condition. Yes, but what about the Rwandan mother who watched as Hutu killers armed with knives and machetes hacked to death her five-year-old child and then was viciously raped before being gutted like a fish? I am guessing she would have a different take on things. Certainly, if she had had the choice, she would have chosen nonexistence for her child and, perhaps, for herself as well.

The prominent Christian apologists, J. P. Moreland and William Lane Craig, however, have a different take on this issue.[6] According to Moreland and Craig, there are two primary reasons why God and evil do, in fact, coexist (my response follows each one):

1. "Christian theism entails doctrines that increase the probability of the coexistence of God and evil."[7] The first doctrine
   is stated as follows: "the chief purpose of life is not happiness,
   but the knowledge of God."[8]

It is not clear to me why the doctrines of Christianity (or any other religion, for that matter) are relevant here. Religious doctrines hardly constitute empirical, logical, or objective truth. "The chief purpose of life is not happiness, but the knowledge of God?" Unless one simply assumes that the doctrine that he is embracing is true or that the religion from whence it came is the one true religion (both highly questionable assumptions at best), then such a statement is nonsense. The reader is not told exactly how this "truth" has been determined; it is merely described as "Christian doctrine," which, ostensibly, is good enough for the writers, and, no doubt, their readers as well.

According to Moreland and Craig, while it is true that millions have suffered horribly in places like China during the cultural revolution and in Ethiopia during droughts and famines, many people have, nevertheless, been won over for Christ, thus expanding the kingdom of God on Earth. They write, "It is not at all improbable that this astonishing growth in God's kingdom is due in part to the presence of natural and moral evils in the world."[9] There are a number of problems with this line of argument. First, it is manifestly arrogant (and insensitive) to assume that the horrible suffering of individuals in, for example, China and Ethiopia, is somehow meaningful only in the context of a Christian ideology. Second, the statement comprises an *argumentum ad populum* (i.e., assuming that there is a correlation between the numbers of individuals who embrace an idea and the probability that that idea is correct); lots of people can certainly be very wrong about whatever cause they all support or belief they may all embrace. And, third, Moreland and Craig might want to double-check their facts; while it is next to impossible to determine the fastest-growing religion, since statistics and percentages can be manipulated in various creative ways, there seems to be at least a general consensus that Islam is the fastest-growing religion. If that can be shown definitively, I wonder if Moreland and Craig would be willing to argue that the spread of Islamic doctrine is sufficient to explain the horrible evils of our world? I seriously doubt it.

> The second doctrine that "increase[s] the probability of the coexistence of God and evil" is stated as follows: "mankind is in a state of rebellion against God and his purpose."[10]

This incredible claim (how could we possibly know this even if it were true?) is argued by referring to "man's depravity" (which actually seems to be decreasing according to Steven Pinker[11]) "spiritual alienation from God," "demonic creatures," and Bible verses. These things have no relevance to an objective treatment of the subject at hand, virtually zero appeal to a universal audience, and involve so many assumptions that I will simply move on to the third doctrine.

> The third Christian doctrine that supposedly increases the probability that God and evil coexist is stated as follows: "God's purpose is not restricted to this life but spills over beyond the grave into eternal life."[12] Morehead and Craig explain that "when God asks his children to bear horrible suffering in this life, it is only with the prospect of a heavenly joy and recompense that is beyond all comprehension."[13]

Again, this point is valid if and only if one simply assumes that the orthodox teachings of Christianity are correct and, of course, this takes us back to all the problems discussed earlier regarding the sources of religious knowledge. If one is simply willing to believe that

Christian assumptions regarding God and eschatology are valid, then I suppose this may mean something to him, but it certainly does not constitute an objective argument that would appeal to a universal audience. To say this third doctrine is manifestly nonfalsifiable, and thus meaningless, would be an understatement.

If the time spent suffering on Earth will, in retrospect, eventually be "infinitesimal" compared to eternity, as Moreland and Craig claim, then why does God force us to endure it? Individuals who have happy childhoods often go on to enjoy fulfilling marriages and loving families later in life. If that is true of earthly happiness, then it can certainly be true of the absolute happiness of heaven.

> Finally, the fourth doctrine that Moreland and Craig invoke in an attempt to reconcile the existence of God and evil is stated as follows: "the knowledge of God is an incommensurable good."[14] Moreland and Craig explain that knowing God is the "fulfillment of human existence." They add that "the person who knows God, no matter what he suffers, no matter how awful his pain, can truly say, 'God is good to me!' simply in virtue of the fact that he knows God, an incommensurable good."[15]

Some individuals would argue, contra Moreland and Craig, that knowledge of the self is an incommensurable good since the self is real, whereas "God" is quite possibly a metaphysical construct generated by humankind and that, even if God does exist, it is certainly plausible that we do not and, in fact, cannot know anything of God's nature. It may turn out that "God" is an energy field or simply an indifferent creative force.

Again, I sense a degree of insensitivity in their statement, especially when I ponder the thousands of Saxons who were impaled, anus first, onto large wooden stakes by Vlad III (the "Impaler"), where they suffered unimaginable pain sometimes for days until they expired, or the Chinese citizens who were used for bayonet practice by the invading Japanese during the "Rape of Nanking."

There is nothing here in this fourth doctrine that a non-Christian (and perhaps some Christians as well) would find compelling. Again, the sheer number of assumptions being made invalidates their assertion. Acceptance of this doctrine is simply a matter of blind faith of the most egregious sort.

>   2. The second reason proffered by Moreland and Craig to explain the coexistence of God and evil is stated as follows: "we are not in a good position to assess with confidence the probability that God has no morally sufficient reasons for permitting the evils that occur."[16] Moreland and Craig explain that we are finite creatures bounded by the limitations of a corporeal existence and, thus, we simply cannot see things the way an infinitely capable God does. They add that even the most ostensibly pointless evils are all part of God's plan, a plan that will come to fruition at some time in the distant future.

I find it quite ironic that Moreland and Craig claim that human ignorance prevents us from understanding God and the necessity of evil in our world, but then turn around and make authoritative statements regarding the nature of God, God's plan, eternal life, and so on. Logically and practically, I don't see any difference between Moreland and Craig's assumptions regarding the purpose of evil in God's providential plan and the assumptions that others make regarding the incommensurability of the existence of God and the existence of evil as we know and experience it here on Earth. They offer us no data or reason or rhyme that would support their contention that evil is part of God's plan, other than, of course, presumptive Christian doctrine that in my mind is, categorically, no more valid than Hindu or Islamic or Jain doctrine.

Before leaving this issue, I would like to rebut their comment regarding human ignorance. I suppose we could simply put our tail between our legs and slouch off to a corner and brood and mindlessly embrace the "answers" that authority and tradition force on us, but I much prefer a "response" fashioned after Sartre, Camus, Nietzsche, Ernest Becker, and other heroes of the human condition, which is to take some initiative and do something about our predicament, give it meaning on our own terms, and then take responsibility for our actions. We certainly should not simply throw our arms up and say, "Oh well, it is how it is and we shouldn't bother ourselves regarding why." We are denizens of this earth; we do have to live in it. Living involves thinking, and we think by virtue of human reason. Besides, all we have to do is look around us to realize that humans do have the ability to think rationally and correctly about their world—we can fly, spend time underwater, put men on the moon, etc. So, while it is true that a humanistic epistemology ("science") only gives us contingent knowledge, this knowledge is comprised of reliable and valid insights regarding the world in which we live. Also, according to the tradition that gave us the God we are discussing here, humankind was created in the image of God. Thus, if one questions our ability to think about the human world in which we live, that would be tantamount to asserting that God is somewhat dimwitted, even a tiny bit. Of course, that is all that is needed to subtract from God's infinite qualities.

Others have turned away from pedagogical or "naturalistic" solutions to the problem of evil and have embraced a decidedly biblical (Old Testament) notion that evil is punishment from God for being sinful, the so-called "penal" explanation of evil. So, to cite one example (though, quite possibly, mythological), after Moses convinced God not to kill every Israelite for the sin of idolatry at Mt. Sinai, the Levites were dispatched to slaughter approximately three thousand people. This is, perhaps, the most notorious case, although there are many others that could be noted as well.

Some of our current "spiritual leaders" do not hesitate to invoke the penal explanation to justify death and suffering. On September 13, 2001 (only two days after the horrifying events of 9/11), Jerry Falwell made the following comments during an interview with Pat Robertson on a *700 Club* telecast:

> And I agree totally with you that the Lord has protected us so wonderfully these 225 years. And since 1812, this is the first time that we've been attacked on our soil and by far the worst results. And I fear, as Donald Rumsfeld, the Secretary of Defense, said yesterday, that this is only the beginning. And with biological warfare available to these monsters—the Husseins, the Bin Ladens, the Arafats—what we saw on Tuesday, as terrible as it is, could be minuscule if, in fact—if, in fact—God continues to lift the curtain and allow the enemies of America to give us probably what we deserve.[17]

And again:

> And, I know that I'll hear from them for this. But, throwing God out successfully with the help of the federal court system, throwing God out of the public square, out of the schools. The abortionists have got to bear some burden for this because God will not be mocked. And when we destroy 40 million little innocent babies, we make God mad. I really believe that the pagans, and the abortionists, and the feminists, and the gays and the lesbians who are actively trying to make that an alternative lifestyle, the ACLU, People For the American Way—all of them who have tried to secularize America— I point the finger in their face and say "you helped this happen."[18]

By the way, Pat Robertson concurred with Falwell's comments.

Overlooking the incredible insensitivity of these comments, coming as they did only two days after approximately three thousand individuals perished in the collapsing World Trade Center buildings, there is the preposterous claim that God directly willed or caused the disaster as punishment for "sin," or at least what Falwell and Robertson call sin. Actually, it's not that difficult to figure out why there have been so few attacks on American soil. For one thing, the United States is geographically isolated. Also, consider the fact that we have one of the world's strongest economies and the mightiest military force. This is not, however, a blessing from God, but, rather, the by-product of generations of manipulating foreign nations to further our interests, manipulation that often involved installing and backing brutal totalitarian regimes. In regard to our wealth and welfare, the United States uses (and wastes) a disproportionate amount of the world's resources. Since our invasion of Iraq in 2003, somewhere between 178,442–199,849 Iraqi civilians (as of August 16, 2017) have been killed to protect our oil interests in the Middle East.[19] The "Lord has protected us"? Hardly. Our prosperity has been gained at the expense of hundreds of thousands of innocents who have suffered horribly because of our hegemonic and imperialistic foreign policies.

As for "pagans," "gays," and "feminists," there is simply no room for them in the perfect world of the Christian fundamentalist—only obsequious, obedient, gullible, God-fearing, Christian, conservative Republicans need apply. And apparently God doesn't like the ACLU and other "secularists" either. The real problem folks like Falwell and Robertson have with the ACLU is that they defend the constitution of the United States to the letter—not just the parts they like, but all of it. That includes, of course, the first amendment that states in unequivocal language that the government is to stay out of the religion business. When I look back to the "giddy" days of the Bush administration when Karl Rove and Dick Cheney were simply out of control (2002–2005 or so) or consider the influence of Christian fundamentalists in politics today and a president that coddles them, I shudder to think what would have or might become of this country if not for the first amendment and, for that matter, many of the other amendments as well.

One of the reasons so many people no longer attend church or involve themselves with organized religion is comments such as those made by Falwell. His God, and the God of so many on the Christian fundamentalist right is homophobic, misogynistic, xenophobic, cruel, and belligerent. I guess this should not be surprising since the Bible these folks read and understand literally champions a warlord God who led the Israelite rampage through Canaanite (the hated and despised "other") lands where whole villages of people, including children and even animals, were slaughtered, or a God who demands death by stoning (a death that is akin to being slowly beaten to death with a ball-peen hammer) for the "crimes" of idol worship, working on the Sabbath, dabbling in other religions, and adultery (by the way, this is a short list). How much more evidence is needed to demonstrate that this God was created by men, the same men who wrote the Bible?

This penal interpretation of evil was again on display after Hurricane Katrina devastated New Orleans. On September 18, 2006, on the National Public Radio's show *Fresh Air,* John Hagee, founder and pastor of Cornerstone Church in San Antonio, Texas, and popular religious conservative, had the following to say regarding Katrina and New Orleans:

> All hurricanes are acts of God, because God controls the heavens.
> I believe that New Orleans had a level of sin that was offensive to

God, and they are—were recipients of the judgment of God for that. The newspaper carried the story in our local area that was not carried nationally that there was to be a homosexual parade there on the Monday that the Katrina [*sic*] came. And the promise of that parade was that it was going to reach a level of sexuality never demonstrated before in any of the other Gay Pride parades. So I believe that the judgment of God is a very real thing. I know that there are people who demur from that, but I believe that the Bible teaches that when you violate the law of God, that God brings punishment sometimes before the day of judgment. And I believe that the Hurricane Katrina [*sic*] was, in fact, the judgment of God against the city of New Orleans.[20]

Rev. Bill Shanks, pastor of New Covenant Fellowship of New Orleans had this to say about Katrina:

New Orleans now is abortion free. New Orleans now is Mardi Gras free. New Orleans now is free of Southern Decadence and the sodomites, the witchcraft workers, false religion—it's free of all of those things now. God simply, I believe, in His mercy purged all of that stuff out of there—and now we're going to start over again.[21]

Walter Russell, religious conservative commentator, posed the question "Is it really a coincidence that a city known for depravity was condemned (literally) by God?"[22]

These three comments barely scratch the surface, but they should suffice to get the point across. Personally, I find it repulsive that so-called "religious leaders" and "men of God" practically fell over one another as they attempted to use the devastation of September 11th or Hurricane Katrina to make some fundamentalist point regarding a God who has clearly been fashioned in their own image. What would Jesus do? For that matter, what would the Buddha do? Of course, we can't really answer these questions, but I am guessing that their first response would have been sadness and compassion for the loss of innocent life and the thousands who lost everything. If one wants to find mean-spiritedness and insensitivity, there are examples aplenty in the world of fundamentalist Christianity.

If we could move back to the real world of empirical data for just a moment, I would like to direct your attention to the fact that the "sinful" French Quarter (which, by the way, sits five feet above sea level—didn't God know this?) experienced only minor flood damage during the Katrina devastation. Not only that but Bourbon Street, the focal point of "licentious activity" and home to a number of gay bars, suffered no flood waters and little water damage. The 9th ward, home to predominately black working class families, most of them good, decent, "God-fearing" folks, was, however, devastated. I should also note that many of those who perished were the elderly and infirmed who simply could not get out. How could any sane person actually believe that this is how God would punish sin? Is God really that incompetent?

The penal interpretation of evil fails for a number of reasons. In many cases, the innocents are killed along with the "sinful," so the logic that God is punishing evil simply doesn't follow. Also, using this line of thinking, this interpretation could be applied to every instance of natural evil (storms, earthquakes, mudslides, etc.) since there would always be at least a handful of sinful individuals that are affected. But, then, an "explanation" for everything is really no explanation at all, since there would be no specific reason to invoke it—it's sort of like the "God did it" explanation. Finally, this is the twenty-first century and we no longer have to invoke the invisible hand of God to understand the workings of nature.

The contention that such evil is part of God's plan would, by logical extension, ostensibly include all such evils, which brings us back to a point made earlier: why is an omnibenevolent God so willing to cause us to suffer, in some cases horribly and for extended periods of time, to bring about whatever plan God has in the works? And, as I suggested earlier, if our suffering is "infinitesimally" negligible compared to what is planned for the future of humankind, why subject us to it? Or, why force us to go through anything at all?

There are more reasonable "solutions" to the problem of the coexistence of (an omnipotent and omnibenevolent) God and evil than those discussed thus far—namely, the "best of all worlds" explanation for natural evil and the free will explanation for moral evil. Both explanations potentially appeal to both believers and nonbelievers since they are not based on the dogma and doctrines of any specific religion, a plus as far as I am concerned. As soon as one invokes the dogma and doctrines of a particular religion, *à la* Moreland and Craig above, he or she is burdened with all the assumptions, half-truths, and fantasies that are part and parcel of that religion. Only when one can establish the validity of their belief system vis-à-vis the thousands of other belief systems that exist (and are accepted as absolute truth by their adherents), can one then proceed to build an argument based on that belief system. Since no one has even come close to doing this, at least not to the satisfaction of a universal audience, such arguments are woefully unconvincing.

The German philosopher Gottfried Leibniz first used the phrase "the best of all possible worlds" in his 1710 work *Theodicy*.[23] Leibniz's reasoning was as follows:

1. An omnipotent, omniscient, and omnibenevolent God could have created any type of world God wanted to create.
2. Thus, it follows that, at least theoretically, this world could have been very different since it potentially could have been any one of a number of possible worlds.
3. But, if the world we are living in is not the best possible world then one of the following must be true:
   a. God has neither the ability nor the will to create the best world.
   b. God does not know which would be the best world.
   c. God is not the creator of this world.
   d. God was constrained to create only this world—i.e., God could not exercise "His" free will.
4. But if God is omnipotent, omniscient, and omnibenevolent, then 3a, 3b, and 3d must be false. For the sake of argument and by definition, 3c is assumed to be false. Thus, we are living in the best possible world.

This "best of all possible worlds" contention effectively leaves us with the task of understanding how and why this apparently flawed world is the "best." In other words, a "harmony theory" strategy will have to be utilized since we will have to reconcile the Judeo-Christo-Islamic God and the evil world we live in. Any sort of explanation along these lines must recognize that the world we live in is a tangible, organic world with limitations and physical restraints and, thus, it follows that it cannot be perfect the way God is perfect. In other words, it is quite possible that the best physical, tangible world must be like this one. Consider, for example, that God decides to create a circle. Descartes reminded us that a circle possesses certain "essences" that are necessary to the existence of circles (and triangles possess certain "essences" that are necessary to the existence of triangles, etc.), including the fact that all points on the circle are equidistant from a common center point, the longest line one can draw connecting two points on the circle is the diameter, and the circumference divided by the diameter equals the irrational number 3.141592—commonly symbolized with the Greek letter π. These properties will be present in any circle that God draws; in fact, they must be present. So, God cannot draw a circle where $\pi = 4$, for example, or for that matter a triangle (in Euclidean space) whose interior angles sum to a value greater than 180 degrees.

In an analogous sense, in regard to our world, consider what it would take to eliminate the evils of cancer. This would require a serious manipulation of the fundamental principles and laws of biology, genetics, human physiology, and biochemistry. Thus, cancer may simply be a necessary by-product of the physical nature of our world, i.e., perhaps it can't be any other way. The same would hold true for cholera, dengue fever, and epidermolysis bullosa, a horrible genetic disorder that causes the skin to blister and peel off. Gravity is one of the fundamental forces of nature and it functions as the "glue" that holds things together, so to speak; unfortunately, it is also the primary cause of plane crashes and avalanches.

I am not implying that God is unable to do something due to a lack of power or knowledge. What I am explicitly arguing here is that God cannot do the logically impossible or the nonsensical. If the physical world we live in is, in fact, the only one possible in that there are certain properties or "essences" that must necessarily be present, then the world we have is the only one God could make once God decided to create a world. Nevertheless, this still leaves us with the problem of rationalizing or explaining the evil that is present in our world. Clearly, God foresaw the evils of this world and created it anyway. Thus, one might question the omnibenevolence of a God who decided that the greater good that he had in mind more than counterbalanced the evils of this world. This "best of all possible worlds" argument assumes that the existence of such evils is not sufficient to prevent God from creating this world and carrying out his Grand Design, whatever that may be. This "best of all possible worlds" argument is one of the best explanations for the existence of natural evil, even though, like all the other musings on God and the nature of this world, it leaves many questions unanswered.

Of the two basic types of evil, it is moral evil (the evil that humans do to one another) that is the most troubling. In fact, if we were to take moral evil out of the picture, the problem of evil would not be so vexing; minus the pogroms, torture, enslavement, the mass murderers, the serial killers, child abuse, and the like, the evil that remains would be a lot closer to something we could stomach. Well, we cannot, in fact, take moral evil out of the picture, so how do we explain it? The most popular strategy is built around the notion that moral evil is simply a by-product of free will. So, for example, one might state that free will is a necessary component of God's Grand Design and that creatures with free will sometimes choose to do evil rather than good. The Christian apologist Alvin Plantinga proffers a subtler, and, according to some, more convincing version than the one stated here.[24] Plantinga argues that it is at least logically possible that God allows moral evil to exist in order for free will to be an inherent part of the world God created (i.e., free will is the greater good here and moral evil is a necessary means to that good). Important here is Plantinga's notion of "transworld depravity," the idea that (expressed in its most general and comprehensive form) it is possible that all individuals will freely choose to do at least one evil act. Thus, while God can certainly create a world where morally good actions far outnumber morally evil actions, God cannot create a world where individuals have free will yet morally evil actions do not occur. Therefore, God retains "His" omnipotence and omnibenevolence and the world retains the evil as we know it.

Some interesting objections to Plantinga's argument have been raised. Philosopher Andrea Weisberger argues that the range of actions that humans might possibly engage in could be neutral, good, and supererogatory, where only the neutral actions would not be worthy of praise.[25] Weisberger also suggests that God, knowing beforehand precisely which individuals would choose to act morally bad, could simply choose not to "instantiate" those individuals, and since God's prescience does not logically exclude free will on the part of those whose lives "He" foreknows, the result would be a world where free will is present and moral evil is absent. I will again raise the point regarding God's decision to create this world. Since we live in this world, be it the best or the worst or whatever, we know precisely the nature of the evil that is present. Even if we give Plantinga his basic point, that, basically, this is the way this world has to be regarding free will and moral evil, one still questions the omnibenevolence of a God who allows, for example, tens of thousands of women and children to be murdered or physically abused every day as the world marches on toward the denouement of "His" Grand Design.

We might also critique the free will defense in terms of Christian theology and doctrine as well. This seems appropriate since Christian apologists seem to generate much (most?) of the literature on this topic. Consider, for example, Eve and Adam. (Please note that I do not believe this story is literally true but, for the sake of argument, I need to use the narrative in my analysis. In fact, it almost appears as though certain details were "planted" in the story by the original writers solely to prevent individuals in the future from believing that the story is historical, to wit, the first human being created from dust, a talking snake, a woman created from a rib of man, a tree of knowledge of good and evil, and so on. The original story also describes a God who is not omnipotent or omniscient since, as I noted earlier, God's punishment of Eve and Adam, childbirth pains and the manual labor of tilling the soil respectively, are easily circumvented today with anesthesia and a trip to the supermarket. There is also the bogus issue of nudity, something that clearly distressed the original writers of Genesis but hardly registers at all on the cultural oscilloscope of tribal peoples living in the rainforests around the globe. In other words, it appears certain that the document was written by men—not God—with a first millennium BCE mentality.) In regard to the question of whether or not the primal couple had free will before "the fall," an issue that has been raised by some philosophers and apologists, it seems clear that they did since they were punished for choosing to do evil (eating from the tree of knowledge), an action on the part of God that would be illogical and unreasonable unless Eve and Adam could be held responsible for their transgression. Clearly, they were punished for not choosing to do good, thus, they certainly possessed free will.

Now, before "the fall," according to Augustine and others, Eve and Adam lived in a perfect world. In fact, Augustine builds a theodicy around that notion by claiming that before "the fall," Eve and Adam were perfect creatures living in a perfect world (i.e., there was no evil), just as God had intended, but humans corrupted this idyllic paradise when they ate of the forbidden tree and, thus, introduced evil into the world. One can rightly conclude, at this point, that God did, in fact, have the ability to create a world in which humans had free will yet chose not to do evil, as this is precisely the sort of world that existed before "the fall."

We might also consider angels. (Remember, once again, I am speaking "emically" here simply for the sake of argument. I think a substantial cash prize—funded by Christian fundamentalist churches?— should be awarded to any individual who can explain how one might falsify the ostensibly nonfalsifiable and, thus, meaningless assertion that angels exist.) The general understanding of angels is that there are good angels who do not sin, namely the ones who did not rebel against God. Angels are not beasts or robots and, thus, possess free will. This gives us another example of creatures with free will who choose only to do good. The important point here is that, using Christian doctrine, we can find examples where God created perfectly good creatures who also possessed free will. This seriously undermines the claim that evil must be present when free will is present.

Finally, there is one last problem with the standard free will defense of the problem of moral evil. Again, referring to Christian doctrine for the sake of argument, God sometimes overrides free will. Here are two examples: The first involves Saul (Paul) on the road to Damascus, where Saul was on his way to persecute Christians, but God stopped him from doing so. Then there is the example involving God overriding the free will of the Pharoah by controlling his behavior; in the Exodus story we are told that God "hardened" the

Pharaoh's heart (Exodus 9:12). In yet another example, in Genesis 20 we find the story of king Abimelech who had sexual designs on a married woman but God came to him in a dream exhorting him not to lay with her, thereby preventing him from doing so. Why does God actively intervene only in these isolated cases? And, in fact, given that there is a precedent of him so intervening, how difficult would it have been for God to override the will of the small number of individuals (one, two, four, ten?) whose ideology, charisma, and political power led to the Holocaust? One would think that 11 million lives would have been worth the effort.

Given this analysis of the problem of evil and the various attempts that have been made to "rescue" the four affirmations (God exists, God is omnipotent, God is omnibenevolent, evil exists), I feel we can safely conclude that the existence of a Judeo-Christo-Islamic God in a world where evil as we know it exists, is problematic at best and unlikely at worst. The problem of evil remains, in my mind, a formidable obstacle for Christian apologists who argue for the existence of a God who possesses the attributes ascribed to him by Jews, Christians, and Muslims. Bart Ehrman reviewed the problem of evil in his book, *God's Problem*, and summed up his feelings this way:

> If there is an all-powerful and loving God in this world, why is there so much excruciating pain and unspeakable suffering? The problem of suffering has haunted me for a very long time. It was what made me begin to think about religion when I was young, and it was what led me to question my faith when I was older. Ultimately, it was the reason I lost my faith.[26]

THE BURDEN OF PROOF

T he foregoing review of the popular objective arguments for the existence of God was not meant to be comprehensive or even authoritative, but, rather, it was my intention to demonstrate that even the best arguments for God's existence are dubious and unconvincing. The reader should be aware that these arguments represent the most popular attempts by many learned men over the centuries to prove or at least make credible the notion that God exists. Nevertheless, in the minds of many, they have failed; there is certainly nothing close to a universal consensus regarding this issue. Philosopher C. Stephen Evans writes that it is the sheer complexity of the subject in question, namely God, that makes the task of saying anything definitive very difficult:

> Few philosophers today would view a single argument for God's existence as a *proof*. This is partly because of a recognition that even good philosophical arguments rarely amount to a proof, and partly because of a recognition of the complexity of belief in God. "Theism" does not refer to a single proposition but a complex web of assertions about God's reality, character, and relations with the universe. It is unreasonable to think that a single argument could establish such a complicated theoretical network. Rather, particular theistic arguments should be seen as providing a lesser or greater degree of support for the web as a whole only indirectly.[1]

Speaking in a similar vein, the prominent Catholic apologist, Peter Kreeft, notes that even if we assume that the arguments prove what they say they do, they still give us only "slices" of God.[2]

Apologists from the Jewish, Christian, and Islamic traditions are in the unenviable position of attempting to use objective reasoning on a subject—God—that is, by definition, beyond the purview of the objective method. Kierkegaard writes that it is the frustration of the "approximation process" of the objective method that will actually lead one to the awareness that (absolute) truth can only be grasped subjectively.[3] As we have seen, however, subjectivity brings with it a host of problems as well. All this does not bode well for the theist, especially since it appears as though the burden of proof is on the believer to demonstrate or prove that God exists.

Burden of proof can be understood a few different ways, but it comes to us from the study and practice of law, so a quick review of precisely what the term means in that context is in order here. According to *Black's Law Dictionary*, burden of proof involves both a burden of production and a burden of persuasion.[4] A burden of production refers to the requirement on the part of the claimant party to produce sufficient data or other evidence to the "fact-finder" (a judge or a jury) so that they are able to render a decision. The burden of persuasion refers to the responsibility of the claimant party to convince the "fact-finder," using the data or evidence that has been presented, that the issue should be resolved to the satisfaction of the claimant party. The evidence or data provided must be "preponderant" in civil cases or "beyond a reasonable doubt" in criminal cases. In short, the individual making a claim must provide evidence or data that are at least minimally sufficient to allow the other party to decide the issue by a preponderance of the evidence, or, applying the strictest standards of the concept of burden of proof, beyond a reasonable doubt.

The burden of proof here clearly lies with the claimant party (i.e., the party that claims that God exists). After all, belief in God is a cultural idea that one is taught during the enculturative process; religions, languages, customs, norms, and values are all learned. Atheism, or at least agnosticism, is, in my mind, clearly the "default belief." I should also point out that it is belief in God that is extraordinary rather than disbelief, since transcendental claims are being made by the theists whereas the materialist or the atheist is not forcing us to push the envelope of credulity past the point where empirical data can take us. And, as has been noted on many occasions, extraordinary claims require extraordinary evidence. The notion that something does not exist is not an extraordinary claim. It is basically the absence of any belief (or, better, knowledge) whatsoever. Besides, the notion that it is incumbent upon the atheist to prove that God does not exist is preposterous both on practical and logical grounds. One can never prove a negative of this sort since, as has oft been said, absence of evidence is not evidence of absence. Besides, one who commits this "false criteria fallacy" would logically, by extension, necessarily hold that unicorns must exist since we are unable to disprove their existence.

So, the burden of proof clearly lies on the side of the believers and theists. Now, we might ask ourselves whether they have met the standards stated above (i.e., have the believers and the theists provided data and evidence that is preponderant or that is sufficient to settle the issue beyond a shadow of a doubt and, further, have they used this evidence or data to convince us that their claim is valid). Well, as my brief review of the objective arguments for the existence of God demonstrated, one could hardly claim that these arguments are very persuasive or convincing. Many scholars continue to write and publish fairly convincing critiques of these objective arguments for the existence of God. Now, of course, I am not suggesting that there is truth in numbers or anything like that (a fallacious strategy itself), but the fact that so many can quite easily rebut the arguments does show that they are at least dubious at best.

The common idea of God popular among the general public today was bequeathed to us by the foggy mists of pseudo-history, tradition, authority, and scripture, all of which were hegemonic vis-à-vis those whose voices we will never hear. What survives of the idea is little more than the propaganda conceived of and perpetrated by the politically powerful, the landed, the militaristic, the privileged, the aristocratic. Consider, for example, the sort of God whose existence theists and believers would be attempting to prove if the Gnostics would have survived being purged by the proto-Orthodox Christian group. (The Gnostic God was understood to be the eternal source of all things but was not thought to have created anything; rather all things "emanated" from him, including the "lesser gods" referred to as Aeons.) On the other hand, it may be that, given the problematic ontology of the Gnostic God, there would be no arguments for his existence, or his existence would simply be assumed, since I can't see much in the Gnostic concept that would be an issue today. Who really knows? Or what if Flavius Claudius Julianus (known more commonly by the ridiculous anachronistic moniker Julian the Apostate), Roman emperor in the fourth century CE who attempted to restore Hellenic paganism to prominence in a rapidly Christianizing world, had been successful? I am guessing that many believers today would be engaged with the task of proving the existence of Jupiter or Zeus. In this case, we would clearly be dealing with an entirely different list of "attributes," with serious implications for virtually everything that has been said thus far about God in this book.

In a way, it is absurd to think how contingent this entire "conversation" on the existence of God is on the happenstance of history. If, for example, *Homo sapiens* should be struck with some sort of collective religious amnesia, I wonder if we would even bother with the idea of a God. It could be quite possible that, even were the idea conceived and propagated, it would fade away due to lack of necessity or popularity. Or, if the idea were to gain some traction, one wonders what "His" attributes would be. Would we simply dispense with omnibenevolence due to lack of evidence? Probably.

Finally, it should be noted that the idea of God that is popular in the West today is primarily a Judeo-Christian concept, and this religious tradition has a woeful track record regarding the basic facts of our world. A tradition that is largely responsible for the irrational mindsets of misogyny, homophobia, xenophobia, religious absolutism, and young-earth creationism, and holds that menstruation is a sin for which a woman must seek out a priest for atonement (Leviticus, chapter 15), is, as far as I am concerned, not one that can be trusted when it comes to the important questions we have about our world. It is not clear to me that we should trust this tradition when it comes to the concept of God either. In my mind, agnosticism is simply the most honest "comment" we can make regarding this issue. After all, who can honestly say anything more than that they know they don't know?

CONCLUSION

CHAPTER FORTY

THIS ILLUSION
HAS NO FUTURE

I f one were to list the various ills and problems that have plagued humanity for millennia and, in fact, continue, for the most part, unabated even today, one would certainly include war, genocide, oppression, tyranny, misogyny, and xenophobia among them. History, sociology, and anthropology have shown, quite clearly in my mind, that religion, especially in the guise of fundamentalism, is the most common and most significant causal factor responsible for these various problems; this is especially true in regard to the three Western monotheisms. Just to cite one example, *The State of Religion Atlas* notes that there were eighteen active wars in 1992–93 where religion was either "a significant factor" or was "directly involved."[1] I have no reason to assume that this time period is that much different than any other time period. As I have noted in this book, the Christian tradition is directly and solely responsible (i.e., it is a necessary and sufficient cause) for anti-Semitism (and, by extension, the Holocaust and all of the pogroms, banishments, discrimination, and general mistreatment that Jews have been subjected to during the last two millennia), homophobia, and misogyny in the Western world, was a major influence in the establishment and perpetuation of the Atlantic slave trade, has played a role in the spread of racism in general and the creation of various Christian white supremacist hate groups prevalent in the United States and Europe, and, finally, has encouraged individuals to reject mainstream, data-based science.

Unfortunately for those of us who do not affiliate with any fundamentalist belief system, religion is sort of like the alcoholic uncle the family next door keeps sequestered in their guest room—yes, he is unruly; yes, he is unkempt and smelly; yes, he is often an embarrassment, but, nevertheless, he is family and they love him anyway because they feel some compunction to do so. Actually, in an intellectual and conceptual sense, religious fundamentalism is much worse than the drunk uncle next door, since its generally unacceptable behavior (to continue with the analogy) is defended and explained away without the least bit of shame or embarrassment. Religious fundamentalism decrees virtually anything and everything in the name of God, and it is blindly accepted without question for that reason; religious fundamentalism engenders such fantasies as guardian angels, resurrection of the dead, virgin births, embryo transplants, heavens, hells, witches, demon possessions, etc., etc., and elevates them to the status of "divinely inspired" dogma, which then makes them necessarily true in the eyes of the believers; religious fundamentalism convinces its adherents to hate, kill, and maim in the name of its God or gods and its followers do so with conviction and gusto; and religious fundamentalism can do all this and much more simply because the majority of the human race actually believes that "faith" is a reliable epistemological tool that can be used to establish knowledge and truth.

The cold, hard, and brutal facts of reality, however, tell quite a different story. Even a cursory glance at the history of science and human culture reveals that the application of the faith-based epistemology has not led to the discovery of one single empirical fact regarding the world we live in. (Let us also not forget that all the supposedly "divinely inspired" holy books of the world's religions do not contain one piece of data or information not already known to the relatively scientifically uninformed peoples in the ancient world who wrote them.) Furthermore, as I noted earlier in the book, as a tool of discovering knowledge and truth, faith is so unreliable that it seemingly never produces the same result twice, as evidenced by the 10,500 religious ideologies around the globe.

One thing the faith of religious fundamentalism has given us in spades, however, is ignorance; mind-numbing, stultifying, honest to goodness I-can't-believe-what-he-just-said ignorance. If it were my task to choose a good example of such ignorance, there would be hundreds of excellent candidates I would have to sift through, but for sheer, slam-dunk stupidity that just takes your breath away, the saddle on the dinosaur at the Creation Museum in Petersburg, Kentucky, takes the prize. This, my friends, is the price the ostensibly sound human mind pays for faith. In this case, faith requires the individual to ignore damned near everything that virtually every geologist, biologist, paleontologist, and astronomer says about our universe and essentially everything that is printed in every science textbook used at every accredited, mainstream college or university around the world. It is quite a feat. Heck, in comparison, virgin births and guardian angels are a piece of cake. In short, there is no idea or claim, no matter how absurd or preposterous, that would potentially tax the gullibility of the fundamentalist, "faith-based" individual. Anything and everything is at least potentially true since it can be made a matter of faith.

Here is a sobering and embarrassing fact that true fundamentalist believers simply have to come to grips with: if eons ago someone, somewhere had decreed, in the name of religion, that God X was the creator and sustainer of all things, and the champions of God X had managed to wrest control of political and social institutions, and, thus, history, away from competing groups, today millions would dutifully and uncritically worship God X, its apologists would passionately argue for the existence of this god, and its theologians and priests would defend the various dogmas and doctrines that had been created to sustain belief in God X. This is true because the existence of such an entity is no more or no less falsifiable than any other deity that is currently worshiped by some group somewhere in the world today. If the reader is tempted to doubt or even reject this argument, she should consider this: the great majority of individuals are perfectly happy with the religion they are born into—and there are, after all, Mormons, millions of them. Incredibly enough, a majority of the American people still desire a "faith-based" candidate for political office.

Now, while the flaws of religious fundamentalism are many, with ignorance and the encouragement of the faith-based mentality being prominent among them, there is another problem I would like to address. This flaw is more subtle, latent, and implicit but, in many ways, no less significant and harmful than the others. What I am referring to here is the loss of personal autonomy that occurs as a result of an intense period of enculturation during which time the individual is relentlessly and ceaselessly bombarded with (putative) absolute truths that must be embraced lest she suffer dire consequences, in both this world and especially the (assumed) next one. As I noted earlier in the book, simple statistics and the religious "law of geography" prove that very few individuals who undergo this period of intense religious indoctrination survive with their individual autonomy and personal integrity intact.

In the disturbing and eye-opening documentary film *Jesus Camp* discussed earlier in the book, six- and seven-year-old children are seen wailing and crying during a religious service after they have been driven by psychologically abusive adults to believe that they are sinful in the eyes of God and need to repent for their "reprobate" behavior. One cannot say for certain that these children will carry this trauma with them the rest of their lives, but it doesn't take a genius to figure out that they have been psychologically crippled at least to some extent. I may not necessarily agree that there is a high positive correlation between religious enculturation and psychosis, but at least one practicing psychiatrist and medical doctor, Henry Jones, in his book *Religion: The Etiology of Mental Illness,* argues that the religious indoctrination of children leads to mental illness later in life.[2] How many American children raised in Christian homes were not utterly ashamed of themselves and terrorized by thoughts of demons and hellfire after having their first sexual experience, even simply masturbation? It can take some individuals years to get over being traumatized for engaging in an act that is about as natural as sneezing, and this is assuming that they do.

This childhood experience is, for most of us, the first significant, overt attack on our individuality, although the general foundation that will serve to facilitate the usurpation of our autonomy was constructed long ago. This attack on our autonomy will continue as we are constantly threatened with eternal perdition lest we scrupulously follow the dictates of God and Church at all times. And there is no respite from this twenty-four-hour surveillance—God knows and sees all! No action, no idea, no thought is truly private. It is annoyingly ironic that these very same fundamentalists who embrace this theology can use the term "free will" with a straight face. In the context of their intractable and exclusivist theology, "free will" simply means the opportunity to follow (what they assume are) the dictates of their God or being horribly punished for not doing so.

I am guessing that my upbringing is somewhat typical for individuals raised in Christian homes in the United States. My own religious enculturation occurred within the context of Catholicism which, unfortunately, embraces as dogma the belief that since Eve and Adam sinned some six thousand years ago by Bible reckoning, all humans (even those not yet born) are inherently sinful. By the way, Jesus is given a pass here for obvious reasons—he is God after all—and, by virtue of a declaration of Pope Pious IX in 1854, as was noted earlier in chapter three, Mary, mother of Jesus, also gets a pass. The Vatican powers determined that a sinless human, Jesus, could not, after all, be birthed by a sinful human, so it was decided that Mary herself must also necessarily be sinless. Religion is not anything if not ideologically convenient. "But wait," the poor unsuspecting bystander might say, "what about Mary's parents? If the basic premise at work here is the notion that sin begets sin and sinlessness begets sinlessness, there seems to be a problem here." Well, my son, Catholicism giveth and Catholicism taketh away. Clearly, the application of logic and reason here would result in a regression of pardons for Original Sin leading all the way back to Eve and Adam, and that would seriously gum up the entire Catholic enterprise. Without the doctrine of Original Sin, the entire theological construct would implode; everything from the sacrifice of Christ, to baptism, to the mediatory role of Catholic clergy from priests all the way up to the pope himself, would be seriously compromised at best and rendered moot at worst. Thus, the line is steadfastly drawn at Mary; a dogma—the Immaculate Conception—is created, and then is declared a matter of faith. End of story.

Well . . . not exactly. Not for me and not for many others like myself who, at some point in their lives, decided that they desired to live in the real world, where mature, rational individuals can make their own way through this journey we call human existence without the fantasies, fallacies, and falsehoods of fundamentalist ideologies conceived, for the most part, by woefully uninformed and culturally myopic individuals living in the Bronze Age. And, more importantly, not for me and not for many others like myself who resent being made to feel guilty for simply having been born. No doubt the Catholic dogma of Original Sin takes this concept about as far as theology can, but it is in the very nature of religion itself, especially the big three Western monotheisms, to burden individuals with the notion that they are intrinsically flawed and simply do not measure up to God, the gods, or their (alleged) earthly representatives. Two of the more extreme manifestations of this guilt are the medieval flagellants who beat themselves bloody for failing to measure up to a standard of piety in vogue at the time or, more generally, anyone who suffers in their own way for the same reason, and celibacy, arguably the most anti-human response to our (assumed) religious and theological shortcomings.

In a postcultural world that embraces humanism, an immanently natural, organic, empirical, and realistic ideology, as opposed to the absolutist, exclusivist, faith-based, metaphysical musings of religious fundamentalism, humankind is not inherently guilty of anything. It is truly as Sartre tried to tell us, "We are alone, with no excuses."[3] If one takes as his starting point that God does not exist (Sartre's approach) or simply that religion is irrelevant, that Sartrean window of opportunity that follows axiomatically from his dictum "existence precedes essence" immediately opens. Whereas Kierkegaard tells us that an awareness of the futile uncertainty of the "objective process" forces us to take the leap toward subjectivity (which itself, as I argued earlier, brings with it a whole host of problems, not the least of which is trying to determine precisely whose version of subjectivity one should leap toward), Sartre offers, in my mind, a much more mature approach, which deals honestly, realistically, and forthrightly with the fact that the world is a frightening, mysterious, overwhelming place and that simply pretending that it is not so doesn't make it so.

Perhaps Camus's advice to cease trying to find some meaning in a world that is ultimately meaningless is a bit harsh for most folks, but I suspect that he is onto something. One could certainly do much worse than simply accepting the materialistic world we live in as no more than that. Anthropologist Ernest Becker was a master at driving home the point that the ground beneath our feet, the air we breathe, defecation, procreation, and death constitute reality, relentless and undeniable, whereas gods, angels, heavens, hells, virgin births, and resurrections constitute hope, nothing more, nothing less.[4] Are we ready as a species to trade in our faith-based illusions for a decidedly more intellectually mature and realistic postcultural ideology? Perhaps a rephrasing of the question will clarify the issue: What would humankind be willing to trade for a world where discourse is guided by objective, empirical, data-based inquiry rather than the irrationalism of faith-based religious fundamentalism?

Postculturalism, then, is a clarion call for humanism. In a postcultural world, individuals are not simply obsequious mouthpieces for the cultural/religious status quo but speak for themselves disencumbered by the necessity of answering to tradition and authority. In a postcultural world, there is dignity and grandeur in the human species that is inherent and not assumed by association with some metaphysical standard. In a postcultural world, the alterity of the heretofore dreaded and hated "other" fades into obscurity as the idea of cultural and religious normativity becomes a thing of the past. In a postcultural world, the often "inconvenient" and harsh light of empiricism and objectivity shines forth brightly, exposing the fallacies of misogyny, homophobia, xenophobia, racism, and creationism. And, finally, and most importantly in my mind, in a postcultural world, individuals are no longer forced or feel compelled to exchange the freethinking spirit of ingenuous and unfettered inductive reasoning for the a priori pathology of an obsessively deductive, fundamentalist, faith-based epistemology.

There is certainly nothing easy about steeling ourselves against the existential angst of finitude and annihilation armed only with the humanistic desire to survive and prosper on our own terms, rather than relying on assumed proclamations from assumed metaphysical beings recorded in assumed sacred writings by individuals who believed that the sky was a canopy above the earth and who were prone to believe tales of giants, virgin births, and humans who lived for centuries. But it could be that our very survival as a species depends on it. After all, it is quite probable that religion will be the primary cause of a nuclear exchange sometime in the next few decades, if not somewhere in the Indian subcontinent then, perhaps, somewhere in the Middle East.

As significant and horrible as that threat is, however, we are also facing another threat, albeit one that is a bit more subtle and latent but no less potentially damaging to our species, and that is intellectual stagnation. It is time for *Homo sapiens* to reject the failed paradigms of the past, founded largely on cultural sectarianism and religious absolutism, and embrace a world with neither physical nor conceptual borders, a world where a postcultural humanism truly unites us all in a common enterprise founded on tolerance, compassion, reason, empiricism, and dignity for one and all. We had best not drag our feet here; not only our happiness but the very survival of humankind may be at stake.

NOTES

PREFACE

1. Christopher Hitchens, *God Is Not Great: How Religion Poisons Everything* (New York: Twelve, 2007).

2. Alana Horowitz, "Paul Broun: Evolution, Big Bang 'Lies Straight from the Pit of Hell,'" *Huffington Post*, October 6, 2012, http://www.huffingtonpost.com/2012/10/06/paul-broun-evolution -big-bang_n_1944808.html (accessed August 22, 2015).

3. Jillian Rayfield, "House GOPer: Biblical Flood Proves Climate Change Isn't Man-Made," *SALON*, April 10, 2013, http://www.salon .com/2013/04/10/house_goper_biblical_flood_proves_climate _change_isnt_man_made/ (accessed August 22, 2015).

4. John Whitehead, "The Passing of the Christian Right," *Liberty*, January/February 2008, http://www.libertymagazine.org/ article/the-passing-of-the-christian-right (accessed August 22, 2015).

5. Henry Morris, *The Remarkable Birth of Planet Earth* (Bloomington, IN: Bethany House, 1972), p. 94.

6. Kenneth M. Pierce, "Education: Putting Darwin Back in the Dock," *Time* 117 (March 1981): 80.

7. Robert S. McElvaine, *Grand Theft Jesus* (New York: Three Rivers, 2009), p. 35.

8. "Religious Landscape Study," Pew Research Center, Washington, DC, 2015, http://www.pewforum.org/religious-landscape -study/ (accessed August 22, 2015).

CHAPTER ONE: INTRODUCTION

1. C. S. Lewis, "On Obstinacy in Belief," in *They Asked for a Paper: Papers and Addresses* (London: Geoffrey Bles, Ltd., 1962), pp. 183–96.

2. Phil Zuckerman, "How Secular Family Values Stack Up," *Los Angeles Times,* January 14, 2015, http://www.latimes.com/nation/la-oe-0115-zuckerman-secular-parenting-20150115-story.html (accessed August 11, 2016).

3. Susie Allen, "Religious Upbringing Associated with Less Altruism, Study Finds," UChicagoNews, November 5, 2015, https://news.uchicago.edu/article/2015/11/05/religious-upbringing-associated-less-altruism-study-finds (accessed August 11, 2016).

4. Michel Onfray, *Atheist Manifesto: The Case against Christianity, Judaism, and Islam,* trans. Jeremy Leggatt (New York: Arcade, 2007), pp. 38–39.

5. Joseph Ratzinger, "Cardinal Ratzinger on Europe's Crisis of Culture," Catholic Education Resource Center, translation of lecture, April 1, 2005, http://www.catholiceducation.org/en/culture/catholic-contributions/cardinal-ratzinger-on-europe-s-crisis-of-culture.html (accessed August 11, 2016).

6. Barry A. Kosmin and Ariela Keysar, *American Religious Identification Survey (ARIS 2008)* (Summary Report; Hartford: Trinity College, March 2009), http://livinginliminality.files.wordpress.com/2009/03/aris_report_2008.pdf (accessed October 2, 2014).

7. "America's Changing Religious Landscape," Pew Research Center, Washington, DC, May 12, 2015, http://www.pewforum.org/2015/05/12/americas-changing-religious-landscape/ (accessed February 3, 2016).

8. Barna Group, "Unchurched Population Nears 100 Million in the US," March 19, 2007, https://www.barna.com/research/unchurched-population-nears-100-million-in-the-u-s/ (accessed October 1, 2014).

9. Loek Halman and Veerle Draulans, "How Secular Is Europe?" *British Journal of Sociology* 57, no. 2 (2006): 263–88.

CHAPTER TWO: THE ETIOLOGY OF THIS PATHOLOGY

1. Émile Durkheim, *The Elementary Forms of Religious Life*, trans. Karen E. Fields (New York: Free Press, 1995), p. 2.

2. Friedrich Nietzsche, *On the Genealogy of Morals/Ecce Homo*, trans. Walter Kaufman and R. J. Hollingdale (New York: Random House, 1967); Friedrich Nietzsche, *The Antichrist: A Criticism of Christianity*, trans. Anthony M. Ludovici (New York: Barnes and Noble, 2006).

3. Sigmund Freud, *Future of an Illusion* (New York: W. W. Norton, 1989); *Civilization and Its Discontents* (New York: W. W. Norton, 2005).

4. Karl Marx, *Critique of Hegel's "Philosophy of Right"* (Cambridge, UK: Cambridge University Press, 1977).

5. Richard Dawkins, *The God Delusion* (New York: Houghton Mifflin, 2006).

6. Christopher Hitchens, *God Is Not Great: How Religion Poisons Everything* (New York: Twelve, 2007).

7. Ernest Becker, *The Denial of Death* (New York: Free Press, 1973).

8. Stewart Elliot Guthrie, *Faces in the Clouds* (Oxford, UK: Oxford University Press, 1995).

9. Humphrey Taylor, "The Religious and Other Beliefs of Americans," Harris Interactive, Rochester, NY, November 29, 2007, http://media.theharrispoll.com/documents/Harris-Interactive -Poll-Research-Religious-Beliefs-2007-11.pdf(accessed July 27, 2017).

10. William Howells, *The Heathens* (Garden City, NY: Doubleday, 1962).

11. David Kinsley, *Health, Healing, and Religion: A Cross-Cultural Perspective* (Upper Saddle River, NJ: Prentice Hall, 1996), p. 66.

12. James Cowan, *The Maori: Yesterday and Today* (Auckland, NZ: Whitcombe and Tombs, 1930).

13. "Marriage," Gallup, Washington, DC, May 8–11, 2014, http://www.gallup.com/poll/117328/marriage.aspx (accessed October 17, 2014).

14. David C. Lindberg, "Galileo, the Church, and the Cosmos," in *When Science and Christianity Meet*, eds. David C. Lindberg and

Ronald L. Numbers (Chicago: University of Chicago Press, 2003), p. 49.

15. George Peter Murdock, *Social Structure* (New York: Macmillan, 1949), p. 265, cited in Ira L. Reiss, *Premarital Sexual Standards in America: A Sociological Investigation of the Relative Social and Cultural Integration of American Sexual Standards* (New York: Free Press of Glencoe, Collier-Macmillan, 1960).

16. Max Bearak and Darla Cameron, "Here Are the 10 Countries Where Homosexuality May Be Punished by Death," *Washington Post,* June 26, 2016, https://www.washingtonpost.com/news/worldviews/wp/2016/06/13/here-are-the-10-countries-where-homosexuality-may-be-punished-by-death-2/?utm_term=.5555eef61fd9 (accessed July 13, 2017).

CHAPTER THREE: RELIGION

1. Søren Kierkegaard, *Concluding Unscientific Postscript to* Philosophical Fragments (Princeton: Princeton University Press, 1941).

2. C. S. Lewis, "On Obstinacy in Belief," in *They Asked for a Paper: Papers and Addresses* (London: Geoffrey Bles, 1962), pp. 183–96.

3. Augustine, "In Joannis Evangelium Tractatus," in *An Augustine Synthesis,* ed. Erich Pryzywara (New York: Harper and Brothers, 1958), pp. 58–59.

4. Eusebius (of Caesarea), *Ecclesiastical History* (Peabody, MA: Hendrickson, 1998).

5. Bart Ehrman, *Lost Christianities: The Battle for Scripture and the Faiths That We Never Knew* (New York: Oxford University Press, 2003).

6. "In US, 42% Believe Creationist View of Human Origins," Gallup, Washington, DC, June 2, 2014, http://www.gallup.com/poll/170822/believe-creationist-view-human-origins.aspx (accessed October 1, 2014).

7. Peggy R. Sanday, *Female Power and Male Dominance: On the Origins of Sexual Inequality* (Cambridge, UK: Cambridge University Press, 1981).

8. Karl Marx, *A Contribution to the Critique of Political Economy*, trans. N. I. Stone (Chicago: Charles H. Kerr, 1904), pp. 11–12.

9. Ludwig Feuerbach, *The Essence of Christianity* (1841; repr., Amherst, NY: Prometheus Books, 1989).

10. Sigmund Freud, *Future of an Illusion* (New York: W. W. Norton, 1989).

11. Alfred Adler, *Social Interest: A Challenge to Mankind*, trans. J. Linton and R. Vaughan (London: Faber and Faber, 1938).

12. Marvin Harris, *Cultural Materialism: The Struggle for a Science of Culture* (New York: Random House, 1979), p. 57.

13. James Houk, *Spirits, Blood, and Drums: The Orisha Religion in Trinidad* (Philadelphia: Temple University Press, 1995).

14. Barrie Wilson, *How Jesus Became Christian* (New York: St. Martin's, 2008).

15. John Young, "Transubstantiation and Reason," Real Presence Eucharistic Education and Adoration Association, http://www.therealpresence.org/eucharst/realpres/transubstantiation.htm (accessed October 4, 2014).

16. Christopher Hitchens, *God Is Not Great: How Religion Poisons Everything* (New York: Twelve, 2007), p. 64.

CHAPTER FOUR: SEXUAL ORIENTATION

1. "Section 3: Religious Belief and Views of Homosexuality," Pew Research Center, Washington, DC, June 6, 2013, http://www.people-press.org/2013/06/06/section-3-religious-belief-and-views-of-homosexuality/ (accessed October 2, 2014).

2. Linda Mooney, David Knox, and Caroline Schacht, *Understanding Social Problems*, 6th ed. (Belmont, CA: Wadsworth, 2009).

3. Kenneth S. Kendler et al., "Sexual Orientation in a US National Sample of Twin and Nontwin Sibling Pairs," *American Journal of Psychiatry* 157, no. 11 (2000): 1843-46.

4. Niklas Långström et al., "Genetic and Environmental Effects on Same-Sex Sexual Behavior: A Population Study of Twins in Sweden," *Archives of Sexual Behavior* 39, no. 1 (February 2010): 75–80, http://www.ncbi.nlm.nih.gov/pubmed/18536986 (accessed January 14, 2015).

5. Sandra F. Witelson et al., "Corpus Callosum Anatomy in Right-Handed Homosexual and Heterosexual Men," *Archives of Sexual Behavior* 37, no. 6 (2008): 857–63.

6. Brian S. Mustanski et al., "A Genomewide Scan of Male Sexual Orientation," *Human Genetics* 116, no. 4 (2005): 272–78.

7. Richard C. Pillard and J. Michael Bailey, "Human Sexual Orientation Has a Heritable Component," *Human Biology* 70, no. 2 (1998): 347–65.

8. Ibid., p. 351.

9. Anne Fausto-Sterling, "The Problem with Sex/Gender and Nature/Nurture," in *Debating Biology: Sociological Reflections on Health, Medicine and Society*, eds. Simon J. Williams, Lynda Birke, and Gillian A. Bendelow (London: Routledge, 2003), pp. 123–32.

10. Pillard and Bailey, "Human Sexual Orientation."

11. "Iran: UK Grants Asylum to Victim of Tehran Persecution of Gays, Citing Publicity," *Telegraph*, February 4, 2011, http://www.telegraph .co.uk/news/wikileaks-files/london-wikileaks/8305064/IRAN-UK -GRANTS-ASYLUM-TO-VICTIM-OF-TEHRAN-PERSECUTION-OF -GAYS-CITING-PUBLICITY.html (accessed October 3, 2014).

12. Augustine, *On Marriage and Desire*, in *Answer to the Pelagians II*, trans. Roland J. Teske, ed. John E. Rotelle, The Complete Works of St. Augustine: A Translation for the 21st Century, vol. 1/24 (Hyde Park, NY: New City, 1998), p.75.

13. National Coalition of Anti-Violence Programs, *Anti-lesbian, Gay, Bisexual and Transgendered Violence in 1997* (New York: New York City Gay and Lesbian Anti-Violence Project, 1998).

14. Mooney, Knox, and Schacht, *Understanding Social Problems.*

15. "Marriage," Gallup, Washington, DC, May 8–11, 2014, http://www.gallup.com/poll/117328/marriage.aspx (accessed October 17, 2014).

CHAPTER FIVE: RACE AND RACISM

1. Carolus Linnaeus, *Caroli Linnaei Systema Naturae Sistens Regna Tria Naturae, In Classes et Ordines Genera et Species (1748)* (Whitefish, MT: Kessinger, 2009).

2. Broad Institute of MIT and Harvard, "Human Gene Count Tumbles Again," *Science Daily*, January 15, 2008, http://www.science daily.com/releases/2008/01/080113161406.htm (accessed October 17, 2014).

3. Jared Diamond, "Race Without Color," in *Applying Anthropology: An Introductory Reader*, ed. Aaron Podolefsky and Peter J. Brown, 6th ed. (Mountain View, CA: Mayfield, 2001), pp. 200–206.

4. "Hate Crime Statistics 2011," FBI (Federal Bureau of Investigation), http://www.fbi.gov/about-us/cjis/ucr/hate-crime/2011/narratives/victims (accessed October 17, 2014).

5. John Lamberth, "DWB Is Not a Crime: The Numbers Show That Police Unfairly and Unconstitutionally Pull Over More Cars Driven by Blacks," in *Reading Between the Lines: Toward an Understanding of Current Social Problems*, ed. Amanda Konradi and Martha Schmidt, 3rd ed. (Boston: McGraw-Hill, 2004), pp. 526–29.

6. National Institute on Drug Abuse, *Drug Use among Racial/Ethnic Minorities*, rev. ed. (Bethesda, MD: US Department of Health and Human Services, 2003), http://www.nida.nih.gov/pdf/minorities03.pdf (accessed October 19, 2014).

7. Marc Mauer, *Race to Incarcerate*, 2nd ed. (New York: New Press, 2006).

8. Ibid.

9. Ibid.

10. Devah Pager, "The Mark of a Criminal Record," *American Journal of Sociology* 108, no. 5 (2003): 937–75.

11. Tyler Bridges, *The Rise of David Duke* (Oxford, MS: University of Mississippi Press, 1995).

12. Linda Mooney, David Knox, and Caroline Schacht, *Understanding Social Problems*, 6th ed. (Belmont, CA: Wadsworth, 2009), p. 365.

13. Margery Austin Turner et al., *Discrimination in Metropolitan Housing Markets: National Results from Phase I HDS 2000* (Washington DC: Urban Institute, 2002), http://www.urban.org/sites/default/files/publication/60776/410821-Discrimination-in-Metropolitan-Housing-Markets.PDF (accessed July 31, 2017).

14. "Christian Identity," Apologetics Index, last updated February 7, 2001, http://www.apologeticsindex.org/c106.html (accessed October 17, 2014).

15. Robert S. Wistrich, *Antisemitism: The Longest Hatred* (New York: Pantheon Books, 1991).

CHAPTER SIX: ANTI-SEMITISM

1. Doron M. Behar et al., "Multiple Origins of Ashkenazi Levites: Y Chromosome Evidence for Both Near Eastern and European Ancestries," *American Journal of Human Genetics* 73, no. 4 (2003): 768–79; Ornella Semino et al., "Origin, Diffusion, and Differentiation of Y-Chromosome Haplogroups E and J: Inferences on the Neolithization of Europe and Later Migratory Events in the Mediterranean Area," *American Journal of Human Genetics* 74, no. 5 (2004): 1023–34.

2. William Dever, *Recent Archaeological Discoveries and Biblical Research* (Seattle: University of Washington Press, 1990); William Dever, "Archaeology and the Israelite Conquest," in *The Anchor Bible Dictionary*, ed. David Noel Freedman (New York: Doubleday, 1992); Israel Finkelstein and Neil Asher Silberman, *The Bible Unearthed: Archaeology's New Vision of Ancient Israel and the Origin of Its Sacred Texts* (New York: Free Press, 2001).

3. Robert Wistrich, *Antisemitism: The Longest Hatred* (New York: Pantheon, 1991), pp. xvii–xix.

4. John Dominic Crossan, *Jesus: A Revolutionary Biography* (San Francisco: Harper, 1995); Lynn Picknett and Clive Prince, *The Masks of Christ: Behind the Lies and Cover-Ups about the Life of Jesus* (New York: Simon and Schuster, 2008); Michael Cook, *Modern Jews Engage the New Testament: Enhancing Jewish Well-Being in a Christian Environment* (Woodstock, VT: Jewish Lights, 2008); Max I. Dimont, *Appointment in Jerusalem* (New York: E-Reads, 1999).

5. Barrie Wilson, *How Jesus Became Christian* (New York: St. Martin's, 2008).

6. Bart Ehrman, *Lost Christianities: The Battles for Scripture and the Faiths We Never Knew* (New York: Oxford University Press, 2003).

7. Cited in Mordecai Paldiel, *Churches and the Holocaust: Unholy Teaching, Good Samaritans, and Reconciliation* (Jersey City, NJ: Ktav, 2006), p. 16.

8. Hippolytus, *Expository Treatise against the Jews*, 7, available online at http://www.newadvent.org/fathers/0503.htm (accessed July 13, 2017).

9. Martin Luther, *Excerpts from Martin Luther's Book: "On the Jews and Their Lies"* (1543), available online at http://www.excellent-valley.org/Martin_Luther/Luther_Antisemitism.htm (accessed October 20, 2014).

10. Martin Luther, *On the Jews and Their Lies* (1543), http://www.preteristarchive.com/Books/1543_luther_jews.html (accessed October 20, 2014).

CHAPTER SEVEN: THE FAITH-BASED EPISTEMOLOGY

1. "A Few Words about Us," Louisiana Family Forum, 2017, http://www.lafamilyforum.org/about (accessed August 1, 2017).

2. "Faith Offsets Lack of Doctorates," Letters to the Editor, *Advocate* (Baton Rouge, LA), May 16, 2008, p. 8B.

3. *Jesus Camp*, directed by Heidi Ewing and Rachel Grady (Colorado Springs: Magnolia Pictures, 2006).

4. There are approximately 1.5 million young people being homeschooled in the United States according to *USA Today* (Janice Lloyd, "Home Schooling Grows," *USA Today*, January 5, 2009, http://www.usatoday.com/news/education/2009-01-04-homeschooling_N.htm [accessed October 22, 2014]), and a little over one-half of all families that are homeschooling their children are evangelical Christians (Dan Gilgoff, "As Home Schooling Surges, the Evangelical Share Drops," *US News and World Report*, January, 9, 2009, http://www.usnews.com/news/religion/articles/2009/01/09/as-home-schooling-surges-the-evangelical-share-drops [accessed October 21, 2014.]). The stated figure of "over 750,000" is a rough estimate based on this information.

5. Ernest Gellner, *Postmodernism, Reason, and Religion* (London, UK: Routledge, 1992).

CHAPTER EIGHT: YOUNG-EARTH CREATIONISM

1. "About CRS," Creation Research Society, 2017, https://www
.creationresearch.org/about-crs (accessed August 1, 2017).

2. "Statement of Belief," Creation Research Society, 2017,
https://www.creationresearch.org/about-crs/statement-of-belief
(accessed August 1, 2017).

3. Leslie Mackenzie et al., eds., *Biology: A Search for Order in Complexity*, 2nd ed. (Chicago: Christian Liberty Press, 2004).

CHAPTER NINE: TWELVE REASONS WHY THE YOUNG-EARTH HYPOTHESIS IS CERTAINLY WRONG

1. Refer to this website, created by an astronomy group at the
University of Nebraska–Lincoln, for a thorough explanation of the
Hertzsprung-Russell diagram: http://astro.unl.edu/naap/hr/hr
_background3.html.

2. Edward L. Wright, "The ABCs of Distance," Edward L. (Ned)
Wright, last modified July 25, 2016, http://www.astro.ucla
.edu/~wright/distance.htm (accessed August 1, 2017).

3. Jason Lisle, "Does Distant Starlight Prove the University Is
Old?" Answers in Genesis, December 13, 2007, https://answersin
genesis.org/astronomy/starlight/does-distant-starlight-prove-the
-universe-is-old/ (accessed August 5, 2017).

4. Ibid.

5. Robert Newton, "Distant Starlight and Genesis: Conventions
of Time Measurement," Answers in Genesis, April 1, 2001, https://
answersingenesis.org/astronomy/starlight/distant-starlight-and
-genesis-conventions-of-time-measurement/ (accessed August 5,
2017).

6. Ibid.

7. John D. Barrow and John K. Webb, "Inconstant Constants:
Do the Inner Workings of Nature Change with Time?" *Scientific American* 292, no. 6 (June 2005): 32–39; John K. Webb et al.,
"Search for Time Variation of the Fine Structure Constant," *Physical Review Letters* 82, no. 5 (1999): 884–87.

8. Tim Thompson, "Hertzsprung-Russell Diagram and Stellar Evolution," Tim-Thompson.com, last modified April 15, 2003, http://www.tim-thompson.com/hr.html (accessed October 22, 2014).

9. Michael Friedrich et al., "The 12,460-Year Hohenheim Oak and Pine Tree-Ring Chronology from Central Europe: A Unique Annual Record for Radiocarbon Calibration and Paleoenvironment Reconstructions," *Radiocarbon* 46, no. 3 (2004): 1111–22.

10. G. Brent Dalrymple, *Radiometric Dating, Geologic Time, and the Age of the Earth: A Reply to "Scientific" Creationism* (Menlo Park, CA: US Geological Survey, 1986), (Open-File Report 86-110), https://pubs.usgs.gov/of/1986/0110/report.pdf (accessed August 2, 2017).

11. Obtained from Simon A. Wilde et al., "Evidence from Detrital Zircons for the Existence of Continental Crust and Oceans on the Earth 4.4 Gyr Ago," *Nature* 409, no. 6817 (2001): 175–78.

12. Alessandro Morbidelli, "Modern Integrations of Solar System Dynamics," *Annual Review of Earth and Planetary Sciences*, 30 (May 2002): 89–112; Prasenjit Saha, "Simulating the 3:1 Kirkwood Gap," *Icarus* 100, no. 2 (December 1992): 434–39.

13. Peter Goldblatt, ed., *Biological Relationships between Africa and South America* (New Haven, CT: Yale University Press, 1993); Philip Kearey and Frederick J. Vine, *Global Tectonics*, 2nd ed. (Boston: Blackwell Sciences, 1996); Anne Weil, "Plate Tectonics: The Rocky History of an Idea," University of California Museum of Paleontology, 1997, http://www.ucmp.berkeley.edu/geology/techist.html (accessed October 22, 2014).

14. Edward A. Mankinen and Carl M. Wentworth, *Preliminary Paleomagnetic Results from the Coyote Creek Outdoor Classroom Drill Hole, Santa Clara Valley, California* (Menlo Park, CA: US Geological Survey, 2003), (Open-File Report 03-187), https://pubs.usgs.gov/of/2003/of03-187/of03-187.pdf (accessed August 2, 2017).

15. Andrew Snelling, "More Evidence of Rapid Geomagnetic Reversals Confirms a Young Earth," Answers In Genesis, January 8, 2015, https://answersingenesis.org/age-of-the-earth/more-evidence-rapid-geomagnetic-reversals-confirms-young-earth/ (accessed August 5, 2017).

16. Harold DeLisle, "Creosote Bush," National Park Service, last

updated February 28, 2015, http://www.nps.gov/jotr/nature
science/creosote.htm (accessed July 13, 2017).

17. "Quaking Aspen," National Park Service, last updated February
24, 2015, http://www.nps.gov/brca/naturescience/quakingaspen
.htm (accessed July 13, 2017).

18. René E. Vaillancourt et al., "Is *Lomatia tasmanica* a 43,000
Year Old Clone?" (presented at the Royal Botanical Gardens Com-
memorative Conference, Proteaceae Symposium, Melbourne, Australia, September 29–October 5, 1996).

19. Carl G. Thelander, "Ring Species: Salamanders," *Life on the
Edge: A Guide to California's Endangered Natural Resources* (Berkeley,
CA: Ten Speed Press, 1994), on *Evolution*, PBS, 2001, http://www
.pbs.org/wgbh/evolution/library/05/2/l_052_05.html (accessed
August 5, 2017); Darren Irwin, "The Greenish Warbler Ring
Species," Irwin Lab, Department of Zoology, University of British
Columbia, http://www.zoology.ubc.ca/~irwin/GreenishWarblers
.html (accessed August 5, 2017).

20. Shigehiro Katoh et al., "New Geological and Paleontological
Age Constraint for the Gorilla-Human Lineage Split," *Nature* 530, no.
7589 (February 11, 2016): 215–18.

21. James Houk, *Introduction to Anthropology: An Interactive Text*
(El Cajon, CA: National Social Science Press, 2013).

22. Robert Jurmain et al., *Introduction to Physical Anthropology*,
11th ed. (Belmont, CA: Thomson/Wadsworth, 2008), p. 274.

23. Ibid., p. 280.

24. Answers in Genesis, "Is There Really Evidence that Man
Descended from the Apes?" January, 21, 1998, https://answersin
genesis.org/human-evolution/ape-man/is-there-really-evidence-that
-man-descended-from-the-apes/ (accessed October 23, 2014).

25. Frank Sherwin, "'Human Evolution': An Update," *Acts &
Facts* 26, no. 9, Institute for Creation Research (1997), http://www
.icr.org/article/823/ (accessed October 23, 2014).

26. Jurmain et al., *Introduction to Physical Anthropology*.

27. Ibid., p. 343.

28. David M. Raup and J. John Sepkoski Jr., "Mass Extinctions in
the Marine Fossil Record," *Science* 215, no. 4539 (March 19, 1982):
1501–503.

29. Terry Mortenson, "Death Is Not Good," Answers in Genesis, July 1, 2014, https://answersingenesis.org/death-before-sin/death -not-good/ (accessed August 6, 2017).

30. Ken Ham, "What Really Happened to the Dinosaurs?" Answers in Genesis, October 25, 2007, https://answersingenesis. org/dinosaurs/when-did-dinosaurs-live/what-really-happened-to -the-dinosaurs/ (accessed August 6, 2017).

31. Andrew Snelling, "Five Mass Extinctions or One Cataclysmic Event?" Answers in Genesis, February 12, 2017, https://answersin genesis.org/geology/catastrophism/five-mass-extinctions-or-one -cataclysmic-event/ (accessed August 6, 2017).

32. Jelle Zeilinga de Boer and Donald Theodore Sanders, *Volcanoes in Human History: The Far-Reaching Effects of Major Eruptions* (Princeton, NJ: Princeton University Press, 2002), p. 156.

33. Stanley Ambrose, "Late Pleistocene Human Population Bottlenecks, Volcanic Winter, and Differentiation of Modern Humans," *Journal of Human Evolution* 34, no. 6 (1998): 623–51.

CHAPTER TEN: FOUR REASONS WHY THE YOUNG-EARTH HYPOTHESIS IS PROBABLY WRONG

1. Thomas J. Parsons et al., "A High Observed Substitution Rate in the Human Mitochondrial DNA Control Region," *Nature Genetics* 15, no. 4 (1997): 363–68.

2. Graziano Pesole and Cecilia Saccone, "A Novel Method for Estimating Substitution Rate Variation among Sites in a Large Dataset of Homologous DNA Sequences," *Genetics* 157, no. 2 (2001): 859–65.

3. Mike Riddle, "Does Radiometric Dating Prove the Earth Is Old?" Answers in Genesis, October 4, 2007, https://answersin genesis.org/geology/radiometric-dating/does-radiometric-dating -prove-the-earth-is-old/ (accessed October 23, 2014).

CHAPTER ELEVEN: FOUR REASONS WHY THE YOUNG-EARTH HYPOTHESIS IS DUBIOUS

1. Robert Williams, "The Evidence against Creationism," Evolution Education Site Ring, January 3, 2002, http://www.gate.net/~rwms/crebuttals.html (accessed October 23, 2014).

2. Kent Hovind, "Are You Being Brainwashed by Your Public School Textbooks? What All Students Should Know about the Evolution-Creation Controversy," Fill the Void Ministries, http://www.fillthevoid.org/Creation/Hovind/Brainwashed.html (accessed December 16, 2014).

CHAPTER TWELVE: THE INTELLECTUAL DECEIT OF YOUNG-EARTH CREATIONISM

1. Kent Hovind, "Are You Being Brainwashed by Your Public School Textbooks? What All Students Should Know about the Evolution-Creation Controversy," Fill the Void Ministries, http://www.fillthevoid.org/Creation/Hovind/Brainwashed.html (accessed December 16, 2014).

2. Ken Ham, "A Young Earth—It's Not the Issue!" Answers in Genesis, January 23, 1998, http://www.answersingenesis.org/docs/1866.asp (accessed December 16, 2014).

CHAPTER THIRTEEN: QUESTIONABLE VALIDITY

1. James Houk, *Spirits, Blood, and Drums: The Orisha Religion in Trinidad* (Philadelphia: Temple University Press, 1995).

2. E. E. Evans-Pritchard, *Witchcraft, Oracles and Magic among the Azande,* abr. ed. (Oxford, UK: Clarendon, 1976).

CHAPTER FOURTEEN: NATURAL THEOLOGY

1. For an authoritative and exhaustive account of the religious underpinnings and the flawed epistemology of intelligent design, see Barbara Forrest and Paul R. Gross, *Creationism's Trojan Horse: The Wedge of Intelligent Design* (New York: Oxford University Press, 2007).

2. Peter Berger, *A Rumor of Angels: Modern Society and the Rediscovery of the Supernatural* (New York: Doubleday, 1969).

3. Peter Berger, "Starting with Man," in *Exploring the Philosophy of Religion*, ed. David Stewart (Englewood Cliffs, NJ: Prentice Hall, 1980), p. 51.

4. John Cottingham, *The Spiritual Dimension: Religion, Philosophy, and Human Value* (Cambridge, UK: Cambridge University Press, 2005).

5. Ibid., p. 135.

CHAPTER SEVENTEEN: OVERT INSTRUCTION

1. *Jesus Camp*, directed by Heidi Ewing and Rachel Grady (Colorado Springs: Magnolia Pictures, 2006).

2. Daniel Radosh, *Rapture Ready!: Adventures in the Parallel Universe of Christian Pop Culture* (New York: Scribner, 2008), p. 278.

3. *Protocols of Zion*, directed by Marc Levin (HBO/Cinemax Documentary Films, 2005).

4. *Jesus Camp*, dir. Ewing and Grady.

5. "Trends 2005," Pew Research Center, January 20, 2005, Washington, DC, http://www.pewresearch.org/2005/01/20/trends-2005/ (accessed February 7, 2015).

6. Angela Valenzuela, "Home-Schooling Drawing More Evangelical Christians," Texas Educational Equity, Politics, and Policy in Texas, May 1, 2005, http://texasedequity.blogspot.com/2005/05/home-schooling-drawing-more.html (accessed February 7, 2015).

7. "*Exploring World History*," Notgrass History, https://history.notgrass.com/high-school/exploring-world-history (accessed August 4, 2017).

8. About Our School: Our Philosophy," Bethany Christian

School, http://www.bethanychristianschool.com/about (accessed February 7, 2015).

9. "About Our School: Statement of Faith," Bethany Christian School, http://www.bethanychristianschool.com/about (accessed February 7, 2015).

CHAPTER EIGHTEEN: SCRIPTURES

1. Walter Houston, *The Pentateuch* (London: SCM Press, 2013).

2. Bart Ehrman, *Lost Christianities: The Battles for Scripture and the Faiths We Never Knew* (Oxford: Oxford University Press, 2003).

3. *The Lost Gospels*, dir. Annie Azzariti, *Biblical Mysteries Explained* (Silver Springs, MD: Discovery Channel, 2009), available online at https://www.youtube.com/watch?v=4-RKypi8y6o (accessed August 16, 2017).

4. Bart Ehrman, *Misquoting Jesus: The Story Behind Who Changed the Bible and Why* (New York: HarperSanFrancisco, 2005).

5. Ibid., pp. 208–209.

6. Clarence Darrow, "Why I Am an Agnostic," in *Why I Am an Agnostic and Other Essays* (1929; Amherst, NY: Prometheus Books, 1995), p. 15.

CHAPTER NINETEEN: THE BIBLE CONDONES SLAVERY

1. Henry G. Brinton, "In Civil War, the Bible Became a Weapon," *USA Today*, editorial, February 27, 2011, http://usatoday 30.usatoday.com/news/opinion/forum/2011-02-28-column28 _ST_N.htm (accessed January 19, 2016).

CHAPTER TWENTY-ONE: WRITERS OF THE BIBLE SHOW AN IGNORANCE OF BASIC SCIENTIFIC KNOWLEDGE

1. International Union for Conservation of Nature and Natural Resources, "Estimated Number of Animal and Plant Species on Earth," Fact Monster, 2007, http://www.factmonster.com/ipka/A0934288.html (accessed December 18, 2014).

2. "Dino Directory," Natural History Museum (UK), http://www.nhm.ac.uk/nature-online/life/dinosaurs-other-extinct-creatures/dino-directory/name/a/gallery.html (accessed January 12, 2015).

3. Bruce W. Roberts and M. E. J. Newman, "A Model for Evolution and Extinction," *Journal of Theoretical Biology* 180, no. 1 (May 7, 1996): 39–54, https://ecommons.cornell.edu/bitstream/handle/1813/5556/95-220.pdf?sequence=1&isAllowed=y (accessed August 9, 2017).

4. David M. Raup, *Extinction: Bad Genes or Bad Luck?* (New York: W. W. Norton, 1991).

CHAPTER TWENTY-TWO: THE BIBLE IS HOMOPHOBIC

1. B. A. Robinson, "The Bible and Homosexuality: Detailed Introduction, Part 2," Ontario Consultants on Religious Tolerance, last updated January 10, 2011, http://www.religioustolerance.org/hom_bibi1.htm (accessed January 12, 2015).

2. Shmuley Boteach, "Homosexuality Is a Religious Sin, Not an Ethical One," BeliefNet, 2008, http://www.beliefnet.com/News/2003/07/Homosexuality-Is-A-Religious-Sin-Not-An-Ethical-One.aspx (accessed January 12, 2015).

3. Geoffrey Wigoder, "Dietary Laws," in *The Illustrated Dictionary and Concordance of the Bible*, ed. Geoffrey Wigoder, rev. ed. (New York: Sterling, 2005).

CHAPTER TWENTY-THREE: THE BIBLICAL TEXT CONTAINS ABSURD
                         AND NONSENSICAL FOOD PROHIBITIONS

1. See, for example, Marvin Harris, *Cows, Pigs, Wars, and Witches: The Riddles of Culture* (New York: Vintage Books, 1989).

CHAPTER TWENTY-FOUR: THERE ARE "JUST-SO STORIES" IN THE BIBLE

1. See, for example, John Osgood, "The Date of Noah's Flood," Creation Ministries International, http://creation.com/the-date -of-noahs-flood (accessed August 10, 2017); "Years of Noah's Life," Bible Chronology, https://www.biblechronology.com/events/15 (accessed August 10, 2017); David Wright, "Timeline for the Flood," Answers in Genesis, March 9, 2012, https://answersingenesis.org/ bible-timeline/timeline-for-the-flood/ (accessed August 10, 2017).

2. Bodie Hodge, "How Does Man's History Fit with the Biblical Timeline?" Answers in Genesis, June 30, 2006, https://answersin genesis.org/bible-timeline/how-does-mans-history-fit-with-the -biblical-timeline/ (accessed August 10, 2017).

3. Matt Cartmill, "The Gift of Gab," *Discover Magazine* 19, no. 11 (November 1998): 56–64.

4. Ibid.

5. Philip Lieberman, *Eve Spoke: Human Language and Human Evolution* (New York: W. W. Norton, 1998).

6. Gary F. Simons and Charles D. Fennig, eds., "Summary by World Area," *Ethnologue: Languages of the World*, 20th ed. (Dallas: SIL International, 2017), available online at http://www.ethnologue .com/statistics (accessed August 7, 2017).

7. Samuel Sandmel, M. Jack Suggs, and Arnold J. Tkacik, eds., *The New English Bible*, with the Apocrypha, Oxford Study Edition (New York: Oxford University Press, 1976), p. 2.

8. James K. Hoffmeier, "Some Thoughts on Genesis 1 & 2 and Egyptian Cosmology," *Journal of the Ancient Near Eastern Society* 15 (1983): 39–49; A. S. Yahuda, *The Language of the Pentateuch in Its Relation to Egyptian* (London, UK: Oxford University Press,1933); Gary Greenberg, *101 Myths of the Bible: How Ancient Scribes Invented*

Biblical History (Naperville, IL: Sourcebooks, 2000); Alexander Heidel, *The Babylonian Genesis: The Story of the Creation*, 2nd ed. (Chicago: University of Chicago Press, 1963); Bruce M. Metzger and Michael David Coogan, eds. *The Oxford Companion to the Bible* (New York: Oxford University Press, 1993).

9. Metzger and Coogan, *Oxford Companion to the Bible.*

10. Greenberg, *101 Myths of the Bible*, p. 53.

11. Ibid.

12. Mike Kruger, "What about the Snake in the Garden of Eden?" Answers in Genesis, January 21, 1998, http://www.answers ingenesis.org/docs/268.asp (accessed January 12, 2015).

13. "Understanding Abuse," Abuse Hurts, University of Michigan, 2009, http://stopabuse.umich.edu/about/understanding .html (accessed January 14, 2015).

14. Todd Charles Wood, "Two of Every Kind: The Animals on Noah's Ark," Answers in Genesis, March 19, 2007, available online at https://narrowgatejournal.wordpress.com/2009/12/27/noahs-ark -how-many-animals/ (accessed January 14, 2015).

15. See, for example, Darren Curnoe, A. Thorne, and J. A. Coate, "Timing and Tempo of Primate Speciation," *Journal of Evolutionary Biology* 19, no. 1 (2005): 59–65.

16. Greenberg, *101 Myths of the Bible.*

17. Sandmel, Suggs, and Tkacik, *New English Bible*, p. 7.

18. Robert M. Best, *Noah's Ark and the Ziusudra Epic: Sumerian Origins of the Flood Myth* (Winona Lake, IN: Eisenbrauns, 1999).

19. Greenberg, *101 Myths of the Bible.*

20. Ralph Ellis, *Eden in Egypt: A Translation of the Book of Genesis out of the Original Egyptian Text* (Kempton, IL: Adventures Unlimited, 2005), p. 145.

21. William A Ward, "Summary and Conclusions," in *Exodus: The Egyptian Evidence*, eds. Ernest Frerichs and Leonard Lesko (Winona Lake, IN: Eisenbrauns, 1997), p. 105.

CHAPTER TWENTY-SIX: THE BIBLICAL GOD IS A LOCAL, TRIBAL GOD WHO FAVORS ONLY THE ISRAELITES

1. Robert Deffinbaugh, "The Wrath of God," in *Let Me See Thy Glory: A Study of the Attributes of God* (Richardson, TX: Biblical Studies Press, 2009), available online at Bible.org, http://bible.org/seriespage/wrath-god (accessed February 21, 2015).

2. See, for example, Gregorio del Olmo Lete, *Canaanite Religion: According to the Liturgical Texts of Ugarit* (Winona Lake, IN: Eisenbrauns, 2004), and Frank Moore Cross, ed., *Canaanite Myth and Hebrew Epic: Essays in the History of the Religion of Israel* (Cambridge, MA: Harvard University Press, 1997).

CHAPTER TWENTY-SEVEN: THE BIBLICAL GOD IS A VIOLENT KILLER

1. Steve Wells, "How Many Has God Killed?" *Dwindling in Unbelief*, August 2, 2006, http://dwindlinginunbelief.blogspot.com/2006/08/how-many-has-god-killed.html (accessed January 16, 2015).

CHAPTER TWENTY-NINE: THE BIBLE CONTAINS NUMEROUS CONTRADICTIONS, ERRORS, AND FALSEHOODS

1. The contradictions and errors noted in the text, and hundreds more as well, are catalogued on a number of different websites. Some of the contradictions and errors noted here can be found at the following websites (all accessed on August 12, 2017): Scott Bidstrup, "What the Christian Fundamentalist Doesn't Want You to Know: A Brief Survey of Biblical Errancy," *Veritas Et Ratio*, last revised October 9, 2001, http://www.bidstrup.com/bible2.htm; Donald Morgan, "Bible Inconsistencies: Bible Contradictions?" The Secular Web, http://www.infidels.org/library/modern/donald_morgan/inconsistencies.html; Bible Babble, 2002, bible babble.curbjaw.com; 1001 Errors in the Christian Babble, 2015,

http://www.1001errors.com/index.html; ThoughtCo., "The Bible," https://www.thoughtco.com/the-bible-4133208; Curt van den Heuvel, "New Testament Problems," 2think.org, http://www.2think .org/hii/matt_err; Shabir Ally, "101 Contradictions in the Bible," Answering Christianity, http://www.answering-christianity.com/ 101_bible_contradictions.htm.

2. John Dominic Crossan, *Who Killed Jesus? Exposing the Roots of Anti-Semitism in the Gospel Story of the Death of Jesus* (San Francisco: HarperCollins, 1995).

3. Christopher Hitchens, *God Is Not Great: How Religion Poisons Everything* (New York: Twelve, 2007), p. 131.

4. Denffer, Ahmad von, "Makkan and Madinan Revelations," Quran Institute of America, http://www.quran-institute.org/ articles/makkan-and-madinan-revelations (accessed August 12, 2017).

CHAPTER THIRTY: DIVINE(?) ORIGIN OF THE BIBLE

1. W. Gunther Plaut, Bernard J. Bamberger, and William W. Hallo, *The Torah: A Modern Commentary* (New York: Union of American Hebrew Congregations, 1981).

2. Richard Elliot Friedman, *Who Wrote the Bible?* (New York: HarperCollins, 1997), p. 28.

3. Bart Ehrman, *Lost Christianities: The Battle for Scripture and the Faiths We Never Knew* (New York: Oxford University Press, 2003), p. 235.

4. Ibid., p. 4.

5. Ibid.

CHAPTER THIRTY-ONE: THE PUTATIVE DIVINE LITERALITY AND INERRANCY OF THE BIBLE

1. "Position Statements: Creation," Bob Jones University, http:// www.bju.edu/about/positions.php (accessed February 7, 2015).

2. See, for example, Norman Geisler and Thomas Howe, "2

Timothy 3:16—Does This Passage Prove the Inspiration of All Scripture or Just Some?" Defending Inerrancy, 2014, http://defending inerrancy.com/bible-solutions/2_Timothy_3.16.php; and Brian Edwards, "Why Should We Believe in the Inerrancy of the Scriptures?" Answers in Genesis, July 5, 2011 https://answersingenesis .org/is-the-bible-true/why-should-we-believe-in-the-inerrancy-of -scripture/ (both accessed August 13, 2017).

3. John Barton and John Muddiman, eds., *Oxford Bible Commentary* (Oxford, UK: Oxford University Press, 2001), p. 436.

4. "Statement of Faith," Patrick Henry College, http://www .phc.edu/statement_2.php (accessed February 7, 2015).

5. "Doctrinal Statement," Liberty University, http://www.liberty .edu/index.cfm?PID=6907 (accessed February 7, 2015).

6. David Ewert, *A General Introduction to the Bible: From Ancient Tablets to Modern Translations* (Grand Rapids, MI: Zondervan, 1990); Joel B. Green, ed., *Hearing the New Testament: Strategies for Interpretation* (Grand Rapids, MI: Eerdmans, 1995).

7. Bart Ehrman, *Misquoting Jesus: The Story Behind Who Changed the Bible and Why* (New York: HarperSanFrancisco, 2005), p. 10.

CHAPTER THIRTY-TWO: EITHER FALSE OR NONFALSIFIABLE

1. James Lett, "Science, Religion, and Anthropology," in *Anthropology of Religion: A Handbook*, ed. Stephen D. Glazier (Westport, CT: Greenwood, 1997).

CHAPTER THIRTY-THREE: AGNOSTICISM

1. Thomas Henry Huxley, "Agnosticism," *Collected Essays*, vol. 5, *Science and Christian Tradition* (London, UK: Macmillan, 1889), pp. 237–38.

2. Bertrand Russell, "What Is an Agnostic? (1953)," in *The Collected Papers of Bertrand Russell*, vol. 11, *Last Philosophical Testament, 1943–68*, ed. John G. Slater and Peter Köllner (London and New York: Routledge, 1997), p. 550.

3. Søren Kierkegaard, *Concluding Unscientific Postscript to* Philosophical Fragments (Princeton, NJ: Princeton University Press, 1941).

4. C. S. Lewis, "On Obstinacy in Belief," in *They Asked for a Paper: Papers and Addresses* (London: Geoffrey Bles, 1962), p. 184.

5. Ibid.

6. Ibid., p. 194.

7. Augustine, "In Joannis Evangelium Tractatus," in *An Augustine Synthesis*, ed. Erich Pryzywara (New York: Harper and Brothers, 1958), p. 59.

CHAPTER THIRTY-FOUR: MORAL ARGUMENTS FOR THE EXISTENCE OF GOD

1. Michel Onfray, *Atheist Manifesto: The Case against Christianity, Judaism, and Islam*, trans. Jeremy Leggatt (New York: Arcade, 2007).

2. Christopher Hitchens, *God Is Not Great: How Religion Poisons Everything* (New York: Twelve, 2007).

3. "For 2016 Hopefuls, Washington Experience Could Do More Harm Than Good," Pew Research Center, Washington, DC, May 19, 2014, http://www.people-press.org/2014/05/19/for-2016-hopefuls-washington-experience-could-do-more-harm-than-good/ (accessed July 12, 2015).

4. "US Religious Knowledge Survey," Pew Research Center, Washington, DC, September 28, 2010, http://www.pewforum.org/2010/09/28/u-s-religious-knowledge-survey/ (accessed July 12, 2015).

5. Jean Paul Sartre, *Existentialism Is a Humanism*, trans. Carol Macomber (New Haven, CT: Yale University Press, 2007), pp. 28–29.

6. Immanuel Kant, *Fundamental Principles of the Metaphysic of Morals*, trans. T. K. Abbot (1785; Amherst, NY: Prometheus Books, 1988), p. 49.

7. Erik Trinkaus and Pat Shipman, *The Neandertals: Changing the Image of Mankind* (New York: Alfred A. Knopf, 1992).

8. David Lordkipanidze et al., "The Earliest Toothless Hominin

Skull," *Nature* 434, no. 7034 (April 7, 2005): 717–18; David Lordkipanidze et al., "A Fourth Hominin Skull from Dmanisi, Georgia," *The Anatomical Record, Part A* 288, no. 11 (November 2006): 1146–57.

9. Ron Grossman, "Tales of Warmth in a Frozen Land," *Chicago Tribune*, May 13, 1990, http://articles.chicagotribune.com/1990-05-13/features/9002080341_1_eskimos-hunting-overnight-guest (accessed August 14, 2017).

10. Robyn Ryle, *Questioning Gender: A Sociological Exploration*, 3rd ed. (Los Angeles: SAGE, 2017), pp. 170–71.

11. E. E. Evans-Pritchard, *Kinship and Marriage Among the Nuer* (Oxford: Oxford University Press, 1951).

12. Both in the context of fraternal polyandry. See, Nancy Levine, *The Dynamics of Polyandry: Kinship, Domesticity, and Population on the Tibetan Border* (Chicago: University of Chicago Press, 1988).

13. Albert Camus, *The Myth of Sisyphus: and Other Essays* (New York: Vintage, 1991).

CHAPTER THIRTY-FIVE: THE ARGUMENT FROM UNIVERSAL CAUSATION

1. Michio Kaku, *Hyperspace: A Scientific Odyssey through Parallel Universes, Time Warps, and the Tenth Dimension* (New York: Oxford University Press, 1994).

2. David Hume, *An Enquiry Concerning Human Understanding* (1748; Oxford, UK: Oxford University Press, 2000).

3. Pat Robertson, "Why Evangelical Christians Support Israel," Official Site of Pat Robertson, www.patrobertson.com/Speeches/IsraelLauder.asp.

4. Victor Stenger, *Physics and Psychics: The Search for a World beyond the Senses* (Amherst, NY: Prometheus Books, 1990), p. 88.

CHAPTER THIRTY-SIX: ARGUMENT FROM CONTINGENCY

1. Michiel Hazewinkel, "Hilbert Infinite Hotel," in *Encyclopaedia of Mathematics*, ed. Michiel Hazewinkel (New York: Springer-Verlag, 1997), p. 193.

2. Bruce Reichenbach, "Cosmological Argument," in *The Stanford Encyclopedia of Philosophy*, ed. Edward N. Zalta, last revised September 16, 2004, http://plato.stanford.edu/archives/fall2006/entries/cosmological-argument/ (accessed January 16, 2015).

3. Victor Stenger, "Why Is There Something Rather Than Nothing?" in *Skeptical Briefs* 16, no. 2 (June 2006), http://www.csicop.org/sb/show/why_is_there_something_rather_than_nothing (accessed October 21, 2014).

4. Stephen Hawking, *A Brief History of Time* (New York: Bantam Dell Doubleday, 1988), p. 129.

5. B. C. Johnson, *The Atheist Debater's Handbook* (Amherst, NY: Prometheus Books, 1981).

CHAPTER THIRTY-SEVEN: ARGUMENT FROM DESIGN

1. William Paley, *Natural Theology* (1802; Indianapolis, IN: Bobbs-Merrill, 1963).

2. David Hume, *Dialogues Concerning Natural Religion* (1779; New York: Penguin Classics, 1990).

3. S. Jay Olshansky, Bruce A. Carnes, and Robert N. Butler, "If Humans Were Built to Last," *Scientific American* 13, no. 2 (2003): 94–100.

4. Ibid.

5. Frank Zindler, "Does an Objective Look at the Human Eye Show Evidence of Creation?" 2think.org, http://www.2think.org/eye.shtml (accessed November 14, 2015).

6. Jeremy Narby, *Intelligence in Nature: An Inquiry into Knowledge* (New York: Jeremy P. Tarcher, 2006).

7. Martin Rees, *Just Six Numbers* (London, UK: Weidenfeld and Nicolson, 1999).

8. Steven Weinberg, "Living in the Multiverse," in *Universe or Multiverse?* ed. Bernard Carr (Cambridge, UK: Cambridge University Press, 2007), p. 31.

9. Jürgen Schmidhuber, "Algorithmic Theories of Everything," *International Journal of Foundations of Computer Science* 13, no. 4 (2002): 587–612, http://arxiv.org/abs/quant-ph/0011122 (accessed September 28, 2014).

10. Richard Dawkins, *The God Delusion* (New York: Houghton Mifflin, 2006), p. 164.

11. Robert Lawrence Kuhn, "Why This Universe? Toward a Taxonomy of Possible Explanations," *Skeptic* 13, no. 2 (2007): p. 29.

12. Erik Petigura, Andrew Howard, and Geoffrey Marcy, "Prevalence of Earth-Size Planets Orbiting Sun-Like Stars," *Proceedings of the National Academy of Sciences* 110, no. 48 (November 26, 2013).

13. Michael Rogers, "The 10 Most Bizarre Species of Sharks," SharkSider, September 5, 2016, https://www.sharksider.com/10 -bizarre-species-sharks/ (accessed August 15, 2017).

14. Royal Ontario Museum, "Oldest Horseshoe Crab Fossil Found, 445 Million Years Old," ScienceDaily, February 8, 2008, https://www.sciencedaily.com/releases/2008/02/080207135801 .htm (accessed August 15, 2017).

15. Kuhn, "Why This Universe?" p. 29.

16. Ibid., p. 30.

17. Ibid.

18. Dawkins, *God Delusion*.

19. Victor Stenger, *God: The Failed Hypothesis—How Science Shows That God Does Not Exist* (Amherst, NY: Prometheus Books, 2007), p. 145.

20. Anthony Aguirre, "The Cold Big-Bang Cosmology as a Counterexample to Several Anthropic Arguments," *Physical Review* D64 (2001): 083508, cited in Stenger, *God: The Failed Hypothesis*, pp. 148–49.

21. Richard Carrier, "The Argument from Biogenesis: Probabilities against a Natural Origin of Life," *Biology & Philosophy* 19, no. 5 (November 2004): 739–64.

22. Richard Carrier, "Addendum B: Are the Odds against the Origin of Life Too Great to Accept?" in *Bad Science, Worse Philosophy: the Quackery and Logic-Chopping of David Foster's* The Philosophical Scientists *(2000)*, The Secular Web, http://www.infidels.org/ library/modern/richard_carrier/addendaB.html#Barrow (accessed October 20, 2014).

23. Ibid.

24. Theodore M. Drange, "The Fine-Tuning Argument (1998)," The Secular Web, http://www.infidels.org/library/modern/ theodore_drange/tuning.html (accessed October 22, 2014).

CHAPTER THIRTY-EIGHT: THE PROBLEM OF EVIL

1. John Hick, "Evil and the God of Love," in *Exploring the Philosophy of Religion*, ed. David Stewart (Englewood Cliffs, NJ: Prentice Hall, 1980), p. 258.

2. Ibid., p. 259.

3. According to Robert E. Black, Saul S. Morris, and Jennifer Bryce ("Where and Why Are 10 Million Children Dying Every Year?" *Lancet* 361, no. 9376 [2003]: 2226–34.) approximately 16,000 children die of starvation every day. Dividing that number into the total number of seconds in a day results in an average of one every 5.4 seconds.

4. "Child Abuse Statistics & Facts," Childhelp, https://www.childhelp.org/child-abuse-statistics/ (accessed November 2, 2014).

5. Fyodor Dostoyevsky, *The Brothers Karamazov*, Dover Thrift Editions (Mineola, NY: Dover Publications, 2005), p. 221.

6. J. P. Moreland and William Lane Craig, *Philosophical Foundations for a Christian Worldview* (Downers Grove, IL: InterVarsity, 2003).

7. Ibid., p. 544.

8. Ibid.

9. Ibid., p. 545.

10. Ibid.

11. Steven Pinker, *The Better Angels of our Nature: Why Violence Has Declined* (New York: Viking, 2011).

12. Moreland and Craig, *Philosophical Foundations*, p. 547.

13. Ibid.

14. Ibid.

15. Ibid., pp. 547–48.

16. Ibid., p. 552.

17. Jerry Falwell, "You Helped This Happen," transcript, *700 Club*, September 13, 2001, http://www.beliefnet.com/faiths/christianity/2001/09/you-helped-this-happen.aspx (accessed August 11, 2017).

18. Ibid.

19. Iraq Body Count, http://www.iraqbodycount.org/.

20. Ryan Chiachiere and Kathleen Henehan, "Will MSNBC

Devote as Much Coverage to McCain's Embrace of Hagee's Support as It Did to Obama's Rejection of Farrakhan?" Media Matters for America, February 28, 2008, http://mediamatters.org/research/2008/02/28/will-msnbc-devote-as-much-coverage-to-mccains-e/142724 (accessed January 14, 2015).

21. Quoted in Jody Brown and Allie Martin, "New Orleans Residents: God's Mercy Evident in Katrina's Wake," Agape Press, September 2, 2005, available online at http://freerepublic.com/focus/f-news/1476026/posts (accessed October 17, 2014).

22. Walter Russell, "Remember and Repent," *Covenant News*, September 2, 2005, https://www.covenantnews.com/repent-remember-and-repent/ (accessed March 15, 2015).

23. Gottfried Wilhelm Leibniz, *Theodicy*, ed. Austin Farrer, trans. E. M. Huggard (1710; New Haven, CT: Yale University Press, 1952).

24. Alvin Plantinga, *The Nature of Necessity* (Oxford, UK: Clarendon Press, 1979).

25. Andrea Weisberger, "Depravity, Divine Responsibility and Moral Evil: A Critique of a New Free Will Defence," *Religious Studies*, vol. 31, no. 3 (September 1995): 375–90, http://www.infidels.org/library/modern/andrea_weisberger/depravity.html (accessed September 28, 2015).

26. Bart Ehrman, *God's Problem: How the Bible Fails to Answer Our Most Important Question—Why We Suffer* (New York: Harper One, 2008), p. 1.

CHAPTER THIRTY-NINE: THE BURDEN OF PROOF

1. C. Stephen Evans, "Moral Arguments," in *A Companion to Philosophy of Religion*, ed. Philip L. Quinn and Charles Taliaferro (Malden, MA: Blackwell, 1997), p. 345.

2. Peter Kreeft, *Summa of the Summa: The Essential Philosophical Passages of Saint Thomas Aquinas' Summa Theologica* (Fort Collins, CO: Ignatius, 1990).

3. Søren Kierkegaard, *Concluding Unscientific Postscript to Philosophical Fragments* (Princeton, NJ: Princeton University Press, 1941).

4. Bryan A. Garner, ed., *Black's Law Dictionary* (St. Paul, MN: Thomson/West, 2006).

CHAPTER FORTY: THIS ILLUSION HAS NO FUTURE

1. Joanne O'Brien and Martin Palmer, *The State of Religion Atlas* (New York: Simon and Schuster, 1993).

2. Henry E. Jones, *Religion: The Etiology of Mental Illness* (Mental Health Education, 2007).

3. Jean-Paul Sartre, *Existentialism Is a Humanism* (New Haven, CT: Yale University Press, 2007), p. 29.

4. Ernest Becker, *The Denial of Death* (New York: Free Press, 1973).

INDEX